Fixed Income Readings
for the
Chartered Financial Analyst® Program

Frank J. Fabozzi, Ph.D., CFA
Editor

Sponsored by

 **Association for Investment Management and Research**

Published by Frank J. Fabozzi Associates

Dedication

This book is dedicated to the countless volunteers who have made the CFA Charter the most respected professional designation in the financial world today.

ISBN: 1-883249-73-2

Printed in the United States of America

Foreword

These two volumes in fixed income analysis and portfolio management represent an effort by the Association for Investment Management and Research to produce a set of coordinated, comprehensive, and practitioner-oriented textbook readings specifically designed for the three levels of the Chartered Financial Analyst® Program.

In producing these books, AIMR was actively involved in establishing the tables of contents, drawing on inputs from CFA Charterholder volunteer reviewers, fixed income specialist consultants, and AIMR professional staff. Amy F. Lipton, CFA and Richard O. Applebach, CFA were especially helpful. The chapters were designed to include detailed learning outcome statements at the outset, illustrative in-chapter problems with solutions, and extensive end-of-chapter questions and problems with answers, all prepared with CFA candidate distance learners in mind. This treatment of fixed income materials represents a substantial improvement over the previous collections of articles and chapters by various authors. These books provide the evenness of subject matter treatment, consistency of mathematical notation, and continuity of topic coverage so critical to the learning process. Given the expected favorable reception of these fixed income books in the CFA Program, coordinated textbooks in other topic areas are planned for the future.

When considering possible authors or editors of the volumes, one name stood out among the rest: Frank J. Fabozzi, Ph.D., CFA. Because his published work has been used extensively in the CFA Program fixed income curriculum for almost 20 years and because of his widely recognized involvement in fixed income practice, Dr. Fabozzi was an obvious first choice. Given the quality of the completed project, it was an excellent choice and we are grateful he accepted the challenge.

The treatment in these volumes, intended to communicate practical fixed income knowledge, skills, and abilities for the investment generalist, is a hallmark of the CFA Program. Starting from a U.S.-based program of about 2,000 examinees each year in the 1960s and 1970s, the CFA Program has evolved into a pervasive global certification program involving over 70,000 candidates from 136 countries in 2000. Through curriculum improvements such as these two coordinated fixed income textbooks, the CFA Program should continue to appeal to potential new candidates in future years.

Finally, the strong support of Tom Bowman and the AIMR Board of Governors through their authorization of these fixed income volumes should be acknowledged. Without their encouragement and support, this project, intended to materially enhance the CFA Program, could not have been possible.

Robert R. Johnson, Ph.D., CFA
Senior Vice President
Association for Investment
   Management and Research

Donald L. Tuttle, Ph.D., CFA
Vice President
Association for Investment
   Management and Research

June 2000

Preface

Since 1993, I have authored, edited, and published numerous books on fixed income securities and portfolio management for my press, Frank J. Fabozzi Associates. Chapters from some of these books have been included in readings required of CFA Candidates. In mid-1999, the Association for Investment Management and Research approached me with a list of chapters from several books I published and asked if I would be willing to use those chapters as the basis for an edited book for the fixed income part of the Level III CFA examination. The book was not to be a mere compilation of these chapters. Rather, it was to be an integrated, comprehensive product written under the direction of AIMR.

In addition to providing me with content direction, AIMR also provided feedback from professional staff and reviewers in the practitioner and academic communities. Every topic and concept was scrutinized with great care.

The book that was desired was to be written keeping the following in mind. First, because CFA candidates come from all over the world, I was asked to avoid idiomatic expressions and jargon that would be unfamiliar to non-North American candidates. Second, I was asked to prepare meaningful end-of-chapter questions designed to test candidates' knowledge of topics covered.

Of all the books I have authored and edited, this book has been the most difficult to write. To the benefit of the reader, the reviewers made me an almost "paranoid" writer and editor. By this I mean that every word and statement was scrutinized to make sure it would be clearly understood by the CFA candidate. In particular, members of the Executive Advisory Board of the Candidate Curriculum Committee guided me through topics that, based on their experience, required special attention.

There is no doubt that this book will generate supplemental publications from vendors who seek to provide products and services for CFA candidates. I expect two types of books to appear. The first is a publication that will simply dilute the contents of this book, claiming that a candidate can review summary points without reading the full book. I think that a CFA candidate who accepts such a claim will be misled. The reason why is that there is no extraneous material in this book. All the topics are critical and were carefully selected. The end of chapter questions and problems were designed to bring out major points. Given the resources and time involved in producing this book, to believe that a vendor could put together a comparable book in a short period of time (without violating copyright laws) — especially if the author is not a specialist in fixed income and is effectively staying one step ahead of the candidate — would be a mistake. On the topic of summaries, I do believe that good summary points are helpful to the candidate in assessing what may need to be reviewed before an examination. For this reason, I have put together an extensive listing of key points at the end of each chapter.

The other type of supplemental book that I believe, and hope, will be produced is one that seeks to expand on some of the concepts in this book and provide additional problem-oriented questions. While I believe that all concepts are clearly explained in this book, there is no doubt that someone with extensive fixed income teaching experience has developed a different approach to explain some of the concepts and this approach will provide additional insights for the candidate. Assuming the author has solid qualifications, I would applaud such an effort.

Frank J. Fabozzi, Ph.D., CFA

Acknowledgments

I would like to acknowledge the assistance of the following individuals.

Dr. Robert R. Johnson, CFA, Senior Vice President of AIMR, reviewed more than a dozen of the books published by Frank J. Fabozzi Associates. Based on his review, he provided me with an extensive list of chapters that contained material that would be useful to CFA candidates for all three levels. Rather than simply put these chapters together into a book, he suggested that I use the material in them to author a book based on explicit content guidelines. His influence on the substance and organization of this book was substantial.

My day-to-day correspondence with AIMR regarding the development of the material and related issues was with Dr. Donald L. Tuttle, CFA, Vice President. It would seem fitting that he would serve as one of my mentors in this project because the book he co-edited, *Managing Investment Portfolios: A Dynamic Process* (first published in 1983), has played an important role in shaping my thoughts on the investment management process; it also has been the cornerstone for portfolio management in the CFA curriculum for almost two decades. The contribution of his books and other publications to the advancement of the CFA body of knowledge, coupled with his leadership role in several key educational projects, recently earned him AIMR's highly prestigious C. Stewart Sheppard Award.

Before any chapters were sent to Don for his review, the first few drafts were sent to Amy F. Lipton, CFA of Lipton Financial Analytics, who was a consultant to AIMR for this project. Amy is currently a member of the Executive Advisory Board of the Candidate Curriculum Committee (CCC). Prior to that she was a member of the Executive Committee of the CCC, the Level I Coordinator for the CCC, and the Chair of the Fixed Income Topic Area of the CCC. Consequently, she was familiar with the topics that should be included in a fixed income analysis book for the CFA Program. Moreover, given her experience in the money management industry (Aetna, First Boston, Greenwich, and Bankers Trust), she was familiar with the material. Amy reviewed and made detailed comments on all aspects of the material. She recommended the deletion or insertion of material, identified topics that required further explanation, and noted material that was too detailed and showed how it should be shortened. Amy not only directed me on content, but she checked every calculation, provided me with spreadsheets of all calculations, and highlighted discrepancies between the solutions in a chapter and those she obtained. On a number of occasions, Amy added material that improved the exposition; she also contributed several end-of-chapter questions. Amy has been accepted into the doctoral program in finance at both Columbia University and Lehigh University, and will begin her studies in Fall of 2000.

I engaged William McLellan to review all of the chapter drafts. Bill has completed the Level III examination and is now accumulating enough experience to be awarded the CFA designation. Because he took the examinations recently, he reviewed the material as if he were a CFA candidate. He pointed out statements that might be confusing and suggested ways to eliminate ambiguities. Bill checked all the calculations and provided me with his spreadsheet results.

Helen K. Modiri of AIMR provided valuable administrative assistance in coordinating between my office and AIMR.

Megan Orem of Frank J. Fabozzi Associates typeset the entire book and provided editorial assistance on various aspects of this project.

Frank J. Fabozzi, Ph.D., CFA
June 2000

Table of Contents

About the Contributors

Mark J. P. Anson, Ph.D., CFA, C.P.A., Esq.

Mark Anson is the Senior Principal Investment Officer for domestic equity at CalPERS, and also has the responsibility for CalPERS' hybrid vehicle investment program. Prior to joining CalPERS, he held positions as a Portfolio Manager for the Oppenheimer Real Asset Fund, a Registered Options Principal in Equity Derivatives for Salomon Brothers Inc., and a practicing attorney specializing in the derivatives and hedge fund industry. Dr. Anson earned his law degree from the Northwestern University School of Law in Chicago and his Ph.D. and Masters in Finance from the Columbia University Graduate School of Business in New York City. He has also earned the Chartered Financial Analyst, Certified Public Accountant, Certified Management Accountant, and Certified Internal Auditor designations. Dr. Anson is an author of two books on derivatives — *Credit Derivatives* (Frank J. Fabozzi Associates, 1999) and *Accounting and Tax Rules for Derivatives* (Frank J. Fabozzi Associates, 1999) — and is a frequent contributor to academic and professional publications on the topics of risk management, derivatives, and portfolio management.

Frank J. Fabozzi, Ph.D., CFA, CPA

Frank J. Fabozzi is editor of the *Journal of Portfolio Management*, an Adjunct Professor of Finance at Yale University's School of Management, and a consultant in the fixed income and derivatives area. From 1986 to 1992, he was a full-time professor of finance at MIT's Sloan School of Management. Dr. Fabozzi, who has earned the designations Chartered Financial Analyst and Certified Public Accountant, has edited and authored numerous books in finance. He has coauthored three books with Franco Modigliani, the 1985 Nobel Prize winner in economic science. In 1993 he started a publishing company, Frank J. Fabozzi Associates, specializing in finance books. Dr. Fabozzi developed *BondVal* software for fixed income valuation jointly with Andrew Kalotay Associates. He is on the board of directors of the BlackRock complex of funds and the Guardian Life family of funds. He earned a doctorate in economics from the City University of New York in 1972 and in 1994 received an honorary doctorate of Humane Letters from Nova Southeastern University. Dr. Fabozzi is a Fellow of the International Center for Finance at Yale University.

J. Hank Lynch, CFA

Hank Lynch is a Vice President and Senior Options Trader in Foreign Exchange at Fleet National Bank (formerly BankBoston). He is a market-maker in currency options for the Bank's global customer base and applies a proactive portfolio approach toward the risk-management and positioning of the bank's currency derivatives portfolio. He has been a central figure in helping build the Boston-based bank into a full service provider of currency hedging solutions, including exotic and emerging market currency options. Prior to joining Fleet, he was a vice president at Scudder, Stevens and Clark where he most recently served on the firm's global bond management team with a focus on portfolio allocation and quantitative strategy. While at Scudder, Mr. Lynch also worked in quantitative bond research where he was responsible for yield curve strategy, relative value analysis, and analysis of structured notes. He holds a B.A. from Amherst College and earned the designation of Chartered Financial Analyst.

Jack Malvey, CFA

Jack Malvey is a Managing Director and the Chief Global Fixed Income Strategist at Lehman Brothers. Prior to joining Lehman Brothers as Corporate Bond Strategist in 1992, he was director of Corporate Bond Research at Kidder Peabody and an analyst at Moody's Investors Service. Mr. Malvey earned the Chartered Financial Analyst designation and is a former President of the Fixed Income Analysts Society. He received an A.B. in economics from Georgetown University and did graduate work in economics at the New School for Social Research in New York. Mr. Malvey has lectured at the Georgetown, Wharton, Columbia, Polytechnic University, and Yale graduate business schools. In 1993, 1994, 1995, 1996, and 1997, he was elected to Institutional Investor's first team for corporate bond strategy. After moving from corporate strategist to general strategist, Mr. Malvey was elected to Institutional Investor's first team for general fixed-income strategy in 1997, 1998, and 1999.

Mark Pitts, Ph.D.

Mark Pitts is a Principal at White Oak Capital Management in New Jersey. Prior to forming White Oak Capital Management, Dr. Pitts was a Senior Vice President at Lehman Brothers. At that firm he created and traded interest rate swap products and also served as the Director of the Quantitative Strategies Group in the firm's Futures Division. He has served on the editorial board of the *Journal of Portfolio Management* and was an associate editor of *Advances in Futures and Options Research*. Papers by Dr. Pitts have been published in leading academic and practitioner journals, and he is the coauthor of *Interest Rate Futures and Options* (Probus Publishing, 1990). He has a doctorate in economics from Duke University.

Shrikant Ramamurthy

Shrikant Ramamurthy is a Senior Vice-President and Director of Fixed-Income Research at Prudential Securities Incorporated. In this role, he is responsible for taxable fixed-income strategy and quantitative research. He has published in the areas of hedging, asset/liability management, interest-rate swaps, futures and options, and OAS modeling. Mr. Ramamurthy has a B.A from Earlham College and an M.B.A. from Duke University.

Christopher B. Steward, CFA

Christopher B. Steward is a Vice President and Relationship Manager at Wellington Management Company, LLP where he works with portfolio managers across different asset classes to provide investment service to Wellington's endowment and foundation clients. Mr. Steward's prior positions include serving as a portfolio advisor to global fixed income and global asset allocation clients at Putnam Investments, and serving as a research analyst and portfolio manager within the global bond group at Scudder, Stevens and Clark. Mr. Steward also spent five years at the Federal Reserve Bank of New York as a senior market analyst. He holds an M.A. in economics from Cambridge University and a B.A. from Vassar College. Mr. Steward earned the designation of Chartered Financial Analyst, and is an adjunct professor at the Graduate School of International Economics and Finance at Brandeis University. He has also published other pieces on international bond investing including two chapters in *Perspectives on International Fixed Income Investing* published by Frank J. Fabozzi Associates.

Jonathan J. Stokes, J.D.

Jonathan J. Stokes is Vice President, Associate General Counsel of the Association for Investment Management and Research where he is responsible for overseeing the AIMR-PPS™ program, the investigation of professional conduct cases, and AIMR ethics education efforts. Mr. Stokes is staff liaison to several professional conduct and standard setting committees. Prior to joining AIMR, he was an Associate in the law firm of McGuire, Woods, Battle & Boothe. Mr. Stokes received his B.A. (1988) and J.D. (1991) from the University of Virginia.

Kenneth E. Volpert, CFA

Kenneth E. Volpert is Principal and Senior Portfolio Manager at The Vanguard Group, in Valley Forge, PA, where he oversees Vanguard's bond indexing group which manages over $18 billion in mutual fund assets. He currently manages over $14 billion in three bond index mutual fund portfolios. The investments in his portfolios cover the full range of domestic markets (Treasury, mortgage-backed, and corporate securities with maturities out to 100 years). Prior to joining Vanguard in 1992, Mr. Volpert was Vice President and Senior Portfolio Manager with Mellon Bond Associates where he was responsible for managing over $5 billion in bond index portfolios. He is a member of the Lehman Index Advisory Council and the Philadelphia Analysts' Society. In 1998, Mr. Volpert testified before a U.S. House of Representatives subcommittee on "Improving Price Competition for Mutual Funds and Bonds." Mr. Volpert has over 19 years of fixed income management experience (over 14 years of bond indexing experience), earned the Chartered Financial Analyst designation, and holds a B.S. in Finance from the University of Illinois-Urbana and an M.B.A. from the University of Chicago.

Note on Rounding Differences

It is important to recognize in working through the numerical examples and illustrations in this book that because of rounding differences you may not be able to reproduce some of the results precisely. The two individuals who verified solutions and I used a spreadsheet to compute the solution to all numerical illustrations and examples. For some of the more involved illustrations and examples, there were slight differences in our results.

Moreover, numerical values produced in interim calculations may have been rounded off when produced in a table and as a result when an operation is performed on the values shown in a table, the result may appear to be off. Just be aware of this. Here is an example of a common situation that you may encounter when attempting to replicate results.

Suppose that a portfolio has four securities and that the market value of these four securities are as shown below:

Security	Market value
1	8,890,100
2	15,215,063
3	18,219,404
4	12,173,200
	54,497,767

Assume further that we want to calculate the duration of this portfolio. (At Levels I and II we discussed this measure of interest rate risk.) This value is found by computing the weighted average of the duration of the four securities. This involves three steps. First, compute the percentage of each security in the portfolio. Second, multiply the percentage of each security in the portfolio by its duration. Third, sum up the products computed in the second step.

Let's do this with our hypothetical portfolio. We will assume that the duration for each of the securities in the portfolio is as shown below:

Security	Duration
1	9
2	5
3	8
4	2

Using an Excel spreadsheet the following would be computed specifying that the percentage shown in Column (3) below be shown to seven decimal places:

(1)	(2)	(3)	(4)	(5)
Security	Market value	Percent of portfolio	Duration	Percent × duration
1	8,890,100	0.1631278	9	1.46815
2	15,215,063	0.2791869	5	1.395935
3	18,219,404	0.3343147	8	2.674518
4	12,173,200	0.2233706	2	0.446741
Total	54,497,767	1.0000000		5.985343

I simply cut and paste the spreadsheet from Excel to reproduce the table above. The portfolio duration is shown in the last row of Column (5). Rounding this value (5.985343) to two decimal places gives a portfolio duration of 5.99.

There are instances in the book where it was necessary to save space when I cut and paste a large spreadsheet. For example, suppose that in the spreadsheet I specified that Column (3) be shown to only two decimal places rather than seven decimal places. The following table would then be shown:

(1)	(2)	(3)	(4)	(5)
Security	Market value	Percent of portfolio	Duration	Percent × duration
1	8,890,100	0.16	9	1.46815
2	15,215,063	0.28	5	1.395935
3	18,219,404	0.33	8	2.674518
4	12,173,200	0.22	2	0.446741
	54,497,767	1.00		5.985343

Excel would do the computations based on the precise percent of the portfolio and would report the results as shown in Column (5) above. Of course, this is the same value of 5.985343 as before. However, if you calculated for any of the securities the percent of the portfolio in Column (3) multiplied by the duration in Column (4), you do not get the values in Column (5). For example, for Security 1, 0.16 multiplied by 9 gives a value of 1.44, not 1.46815 as shown in the table above.

Suppose instead that the computations were done with a hand-held calculator rather than on a spreadsheet and that the percentage of each security in the portfolio, Column (3), and the product of the percent and duration, Column (5), are computed to two decimal places. The following table would then be computed:

(1)	(2)	(3)	(4)	(5)
Security	Market value	Percent of portfolio	Duration	Percent × duration
1	8,890,100	0.16	9	1.44
2	15,215,063	0.28	5	1.40
3	18,219,404	0.33	8	2.64
4	12,173,200	0.22	2	0.44
Total	54,497,767	1.00		5.92

Note the following. First, the total in Column (3) is really 0.99 (99%) if one adds the value in the columns but is rounded to 1 in the table. Second, the portfolio duration shown in Column (5) is 5.92. This differs from the spreadsheet result earlier of 5.99.

Suppose that you decided to make sure that the total in Column (3) actually totals to 100%. Which security's percent would you round up to do so? If security 3 is rounded up to 34%, then the results would be reported as follows:

(1)	(2)	(3)	(4)	(5)
Security	Market value	Percent of portfolio	Duration	Percent × duration
1	8,890,100	0.16	9	1.44
2	15,215,063	0.28	5	1.40
3	18,219,404	0.34	8	2.72
4	12,173,200	0.22	2	0.44
	54,497,767	1.000		6.00

In this case, the result of the calculation from a hand-held calculator when rounding security 3 to 34% would produce a portfolio duration of 6.

Another reason why the result shown in the book may differ from your calculations is that you may use certain built-in features of spreadsheets that we did not use. For example, you will see in this book how the price of a bond is computed. In some of the illustrations in this book, the price of one or more bonds must be computed as an interim calculation to obtain a solution. If you use a spreadsheet's built-in feature for computing a bond's price (if the feature is available to you), you might observe slightly different results.

Please keep these rounding issues in mind. You are not making computations for sending a rocket to the moon wherein slight differences could cause you to miss your target. Rather, what is important is that you understand the procedure or methodology for computing the values requested.

Web Site Updates

While I made every effort to produce an error-free book, it is highly likely that there will be errors in this book. If you find an error, please send me an email identifying the error. The email should be sent to: info@frankfabozzi.com.

All errors will be posted on my web site: http://www.frankfabozzi.com/cfa/readings. In addition to any corrections, I may make some comments to clarify the explanation of a topic. Please note that the web site is *not* a vehicle for asking questions about topics or for assistance in explaining topics.

You should check the web site periodically. Alternatively, you can register on line (www.frankfabozzi.com) so that when any change is made to the web site, you will be notified.

Frank J. Fabozzi, Ph.D., CFA

Chapter 1

INTRODUCTION TO BOND PORTFOLIO MANAGEMENT

Frank J. Fabozzi, Ph.D., CFA
Adjunct Professor of Finance
School of Management
Yale University

LEARNING OUTCOME STATEMENTS

After reading this chapter you should be able to:

- identify the activities in the investment management process (setting investment objectives, developing and implementing a portfolio strategy, monitoring the portfolio, and adjusting the portfolio).
- explain the two types of benchmarks (liability structure and bond index) used to measure an investment objective.
- describe the nature of liabilities.
- identify the major broad-based bond market indexes.
- classify different types of liabilities.
- explain what a funded investor is and the investment objective of a funded investor.
- explain what tracking error and tracking error risk are.
- identify the various risks associated with liabilities.
- explain what the duration of a liability is.
- explain what the economic surplus of an entity is and how its exposure to changes in interest rates is assessed.
- identify the types of constraints imposed on investors.
- identify the elements in developing and implementing a portfolio strategy (writing an investment policy, selecting the type of investment strategy, formulating the inputs for portfolio construction, and constructing the portfolio).
- distinguish between active and passive strategies.
- explain what bond indexing is.
- explain how the degree of departure of a managed portfolio from the benchmark index determines the degree of active management.
- explain the degree of tracking error risk associated with bond indexing.
- explain the role of forward rates in formulating the inputs for constructing a portfolio.
- explain what relative value means and its use in portfolio construction.
- explain what is involved in the monitoring activity phase of the investment management process.
- distinguish between performance measurement and performance evaluation.
- explain the issues associated with performance evaluation.

SECTION I
INTRODUCTION

At Level I the products of the fixed income market, the risks associated with investing in fixed-income securities, and the fundamentals of valuation and interest rate risk measurement were covered. At Level II, in depth coverage of the valuation of fixed income securities and interest rate derivatives, a framework for the assessment of trading strategies with embedded options, and the principles of credit analysis were covered. At Level III, we will put all these tools together to demonstrate how to construct portfolios to increase the likelihood of meeting an investment objective and for measuring and evaluating investment performance.

In this chapter we set forth the framework for the investment management process. Regardless of the asset class that is being managed (i.e., stocks, bonds, or real estate) the investment management process follows the same integrated activities. John Maginn and Donald Tuttle define these activities as follows:

"1. An investor's objectives, preferences, and constraints are identified and specified to develop explicit investment policies;
2. Strategies are developed and implemented through the choice of optimal combinations of financial and real assets in the marketplace;
3. Market conditions, relative asset values, and the investor's circumstances are monitored; and
4. Portfolio adjustments are made as appropriate to reflect significant change in any or all of the relevant variables."[1]

We will use the Maginn-Tuttle framework for describing the investment management process for fixed-income portfolios in this chapter. We shall refer to these four activities in the investment management process as:

1. setting the investment objectives
2. developing and implementing a portfolio strategy
3. monitoring the portfolio
4. adjusting the portfolio

A discussion of the investment management process will provide a context in which to appreciate the significance of the chapters to follow in this book. Our focus, of course, is on the management of fixed-income portfolios.

SECTION II
SETTING
INVESTMENT
OBJECTIVES
FOR
FIXED-INCOME
INVESTORS

The investment objectives of a fixed-income investor is often specified in terms of return and risk, as well as constraints. The investment objectives should be expressed quantitatively in terms of some benchmark. The benchmark will vary by the type of investor.

In general, we can divide fixed-income investors into two categories based on the characteristic of the benchmark. The first category of investor specifies the benchmark in terms of its liability structure. The investment objective is to generate sufficient cash flow from the fixed-income portfolio that, at a minimum, satisfies the liability structure. The second category of fixed-income investor specifies the benchmark as some bond index. The investment objective may be to match the bond index after management fees or outperform the index after management fees by at least a predetermined number of basis points. Below we will discuss each category of investor further in terms of their investment objectives.

---

[1] John L. Maginn and Donald L. Tuttle, "The Portfolio Management Process and Its Dynamics," Chapter 1 in John L. Maginn and Donald L. Tuttle (editors), *Managing Investment Portfolios: A Dynamic Process* (New York, NY: Warren, Gorham & Lamont, sponsored by the Institute of Chartered Financial Analysts, Second Edition)., pp. 1-3 and 1-5.

A. Return Objectives The investor will identify the benchmark to its managers. The manager may be employed by the investor or may be an external manager. Once the investment objective is specified in terms of a benchmark, it is relative to that benchmark that the performance of a manager will be evaluated. It is important to note that a manager may be successful in terms of outperforming the benchmark but the client may not realize its investment objective. This occurs because the client did not specify a benchmark which properly reflected its investment needs from a risk, return, and cash flow perspective. A good example is a defined benefit pension fund that specifies the investment objective in terms of some bond index when in fact a more appropriate benchmark would have been the liability structure of the fund. If the manager outperformed the benchmark the manager was successful. However, if sufficient cash flow was not generated to satisfy the pension liabilities, then the failure was not with the manager but with the client's failure to properly specify an appropriate benchmark.

1. Liabilities as the Investment Objective

In general, investors who specify the benchmark in terms of a liability structure that must be satisfied fall into two categories. The first category consists of investors that borrow funds and then invest those funds. The objective is to earn a higher return on the funds borrowed than the cost of borrowing. The difference between the return on the funds invested and the cost of borrowing is called the **spread**. These managers are referred to as **funded investors**.

Institutional investors that are clearly funded investors are depository institutions (banks, savings and loan associations, and credit unions). Insurance companies have a wide range of products. For some products, the insurance company is a funded investor. For example, an insurance company that issues a guaranteed investment contract (i.e., a policy where the insurance company guarantees an interest rate to policyholders for a specific time period) has basically borrowed money from policyholders and created a liability. Another example of a funded investor is a hedge fund. A hedge fund is a highly leveraged entity that borrows on a short-term basis, typically using a term repo agreement. (At Level II we discussed how the repo market can be used to borrow funds using the securities purchased as collateral.) The objective is to earn a return on the funds obtained through the repo agreement that is higher than the repo rate.

The second category consists of institutional investors who have a liability structure that must be satisfied but where the investor did not borrow the funds that created the liability structure. One example is a pension sponsor that has a liability structure based on defined benefits. A second example is a state that is investing proceeds from a lottery so as to meet the state's obligation to make payments to a lottery winner.

At Levels I and II, the focus was on fixed-income products. Since at Level III we will be concerned with bond portfolio management, we must understand how the liability structure affects the selection of a portfolio strategy. In this section we will take a closer look at the nature of liabilities.

a. Liabilities Defined

A liability is a potential cash outlay that must be made at a future date to satisfy the contractual terms of an obligation. An institutional investor is concerned with both the **amount of the liability** and the **timing of the liability**, because its assets must produce sufficient cash flow to meet any payments it has promised to make.

Exhibit 1: Classification of Liabilities of Institutional Investors

Liability Type	Amount of Outlay	Timing of Cash Outlay	Example
Type I	known	known	Fixed rate CD issued by a depository institution
Type II	known	uncertain	Standard life insurance policy
Type III	uncertain	known	Floating rate CD issued by a depository institution
Type IV	uncertain	uncertain	Insurance policy by a property and casualty insurance company

b. Classification of Liabilities

Liabilities are classified according to the degree of certainty of their amount and timing, as shown in Exhibit 1. This exhibit assumes that the holder of the obligation will not elect to cancel the obligation prior to any actual or projected payout date.

The classification of cash outlays as either "known" or "uncertain" is undoubtedly broad. When we refer to a cash outlay as being uncertain, we do not mean that it cannot be predicted. There are some liabilities where the "law of large numbers" makes it easier to predict the timing and/or the amount of the cash outlays. This work is typically done by actuaries, but even actuaries have difficulty predicting natural catastrophes such as floods and earthquakes. Below we illustrate each type of liability.

A Type-I liability is one for which both the amount and timing of the liabilities are known with certainty. An example would be a liability where an institution knows that it must pay $8 million six months from now. Depository institutions know the amount that they are committed to pay (principal plus interest) on the maturity date of a fixed-rate deposit, assuming that the depositor does not withdraw funds prior to the maturity date. Type-l liabilities are not limited to depository institutions. A guaranteed investment contract is an example of this type of liability created by a life insurance company.

A Type-II liability is one for which the amount of the cash outlay is known, but the timing of the cash outlay is uncertain. The most obvious example of a Type-II liability is a typical life insurance policy. There are many types of life insurance policies, but the most basic type provides that, for an annual premium, a life insurance company agrees to make a specified dollar payment to policy beneficiaries upon the death of the insured. Naturally, the timing of the insured's death is uncertain.

A Type-III liability is one for which the timing of the cash outlay is known, but the amount is uncertain. A 2-year floating-rate certificate of deposit issued by a depository institution where the interest rate resets quarterly based on some market interest rate is an example.

A Type-IV liability is one where there is uncertainty as to both the amount and the timing of the cash outlay. There are numerous insurance products and pension obligations in this category. Probably the most obvious examples are automobile and home insurance policies issued by property and casualty insurance companies. When, and if, a payment will have to be made to the policyholder is uncertain. Whenever damage is done to an insured asset, the amount of the payment that must be made is uncertain.

The liabilities of pension plans can also be Type-IV liabilities. In defined benefit plans, retirement benefits depend on the participant's income for a specified number of years before retirement and the total number of years the participant worked. This will affect the amount of the cash outlay. The timing of the cash outlay depends on when the employee elects to retire, and whether the employee remains with the sponsoring plan until retirement. Moreover, both the amount and the timing will depend on how the employee elects to have payments made — over only the employee's life or those of the employee and spouse.

2. Bond Index as the Investment Objective

When there are no liabilities that must be met, the investment objective is often to either match or outperform a designated bond index. It is important to note that there are clients that have a liability structure but they specify that the manager retained manage against a bond market index. This is particularly true of pension sponsors. The expectation of the plan sponsor is that the performance of the bond index selected will generate sufficient cash flow to satisfy the liability structure.

The wide range of bond market indexes available can be classified as broad-based market indexes and specialized market indexes. The three broad-based bond market indexes are the Lehman Brothers Aggregate Index, the Salomon Brothers Broad Investment-Grade Bond Index (BIG), and the Merrill Lynch Domestic Market Index. The bond market sectors covered by these indexes are the Treasury, agency, investment-grade corporate, residential mortgage-backed, asset-backed securities, commercial mortgage-backed securities, and Yankee markets.

All three indexes exclude issues that are non-investment grade (i.e., below BBB) and issues that have a maturity of one year or less. The mortgage sector consists of only agency passthrough securities: Ginnie Mae, Fannie Mae, and Freddie Mac passthrough securities. (The securities were covered at Level II (Chapter 3).)Thus, agency collateralized mortgage obligations and agency stripped mortgage-backed securities are not included. Nor are nonagency mortgage-backed securities (residential and commercial) included in the mortgage sector.

The specialized market indexes focus on one sector of the bond market or a subsector of the bond market. Indexes on sectors of the market are published by the three firms that produce the broad-based market indexes. For example, Lehman Brothers produces a Government Bond Index, a Government/Corporate Bond Index, a Corporate Bond Index, and a Mortgage Index based on the component sectors of the Lehman Brothers Aggregate Index.

Non-brokerage firms have created specialized indexes for sectors. For example, Ryan Labs produces a Treasury index. Since none of the broad-based bond market indexes include non-investment grade or high-yield issues, the three firms that have created the broad-based indexes and CS First Boston and Donaldson Lufkin and Jenrette have created indexes for this sector. There are also specialized indexes that have been created that better reflect the liability structure of defined benefit pension plans.

B. Risks

The inability to satisfy an investment objective is called **performance risk**. Let's look at the risks associated with strategies for institutional investors managing funds against a bond market index and those managing funds against a liability structure. A more detailed discussion for quantifying performance risk is covered in Chapter 2.

1. Risks Associated with Managing Relative to a Bond Market Index

We will refer to the specific bond market index that the manager's performance is compared against as the benchmark index. The difference between the performance of the managed portfolio and the performance of the benchmark index is called **tracking error**. That is,

tracking error =
    performance of managed portfolio − performance of benchmark index

What do we mean by performance? By performance we mean the actual return on the portfolio over the period of time that the evaluation is made. It could be a quarter, a 6-month period, a year, or a longer time period. In Chapter 9 we will see the proper method for computing the return on a portfolio over some time period.

What is the risk that the manager faces? In active portfolio strategies (described later), the risk is that the tracking error will be negative; that is, the return on the managed portfolio will be less than the return on the benchmark index. This risk is called **tracking error risk**.

Why does tracking error risk occur? Suppose that a manager purchases all the bonds in the index in the precise proportion of their market value in the benchmark index. So, if the benchmark index has 0.03% of issue X, then the manager's portfolio will have exactly 0.03% of issue X. That is, the portfolio is a mini-version of the benchmark index. (We will see in Chapter 4 that this is not a simple thing to do.) So, if we could reproduce the benchmark exactly at very little cost, there would be virtually no tracking error and therefore tracking error risk would be close to zero.

But, if a manager constructs a portfolio that is not a mini-version of the benchmark index, tracking error risk will be greater. The reason is that the managed portfolio will have risks associated with it that are different from the risks associated with the benchmark. The magnitude of these risks will differ for the managed portfolio and the benchmark index. Here are three examples.

1. If the benchmark index includes only investment grade bonds but the managed portfolio has investment grade and non-investment grade bonds, then the managed portfolio has greater credit risk than the benchmark index.

2. If the benchmark index includes mortgage-backed securities but the managed portfolio does not include mortgage-backed securities, then the managed portfolio is not exposed to prepayment risk.

3. If the duration (a measure of interest rate risk) for the benchmark index is 4 but the duration for the managed portfolio is 5, then the managed portfolio has greater interest rate risk than the benchmark index.

Whether or not the tracking error is positive or negative depends on whether accepting or reducing the particular risk pays off.

2. Risks Associated with Managing Against a Liability Structure

There are institutional investors who want their managers to construct portfolios to meet a liability structure. A liability structure can be as simple as a single future liability, or multiple liabilities. The risk associated with managing portfolios versus liabilities is that the managed portfolio will not generate sufficient cash flow to satisfy the liability structure. Managing relative to a liability structure is popularly referred to as **asset-liability management**. (Our focus at Level III is on managing the assets to satisfy the liability structure, not in managing liabilities.)

Just like assets, there are risks associated with liabilities. Here are three examples that should give you a feel for some of these risks. We will see more examples — and more details — in other chapters.

a. Call Risk for Liabilities

Consider a liability where the holder of the liability can terminate the liability at his or her option. The simplest case is a certificate of deposit where the depositor can withdraw funds prior to the maturity date but must pay a penalty to do so. If one or more depositors terminate the CD prior to the maturity date due to a rise in interest rates, then consider the impact on the depository institution. It will have to fund itself with new deposits (or borrow in the market) at a higher rate. But, if the depository institution previously invested in a fixed-rate asset that pays less than the new borrowing rate, the depository institution realizes a negative spread. This risk is very much like call risk but in this case, the depository institution is concerned with the premature withdrawal of funds when interest rates rise, not fall.

b. Cap Risk

Funded investors may invest in a floating-rate bond. Typically, the floater will have a cap (i.e., a maximum interest rate). To fund the investment in the floater, the investor may borrow funds on a short-term basis. There is no cap on the borrowing cost. Thus, if rates rise above the cap specified for the floater but there is no cap on the liabilities, at some point the funding cost will exceed the rate paid on the floater. This risk is called cap risk.

c. Interest Rate Risk

Let's look at the interest rate risk for an institution as a whole. The **economic surplus** of any entity is the difference between the market value of all its assets and the market value of its liabilities. That is,

$$\text{economic surplus} = \text{market value of assets} - \text{market value of liabilities}$$

While the concept of a market value of assets may not seem unusual, one might ask: What is the market value of liabilities? This value is simply the present value of the liabilities, where the liabilities are discounted at an appropriate interest rate. A rise in interest rates will therefore decrease the present value or market value of the liabilities; a decrease in interest rates will increase the present value or market value of liabilities. Thus, the economic surplus can be expressed as:

$$\text{economic surplus} = \text{market value of assets} - \text{present value of liabilities}$$

For example, consider an institution that has a portfolio of only bonds and liabilities. Let's look at what happens to the economic surplus if interest rates rise. This will cause the bonds to decline in value; but it will also cause the liabilities to decline in value. Since both the assets and liabilities decline, the economic surplus can either increase, decrease, or not change. The net effect depends on the relative interest-rate sensitivity of the assets compared to the liabilities.

What we can do for assets, we can do for liabilities. We can define the duration of liabilities as their responsiveness to a 100 basis point change in interest rates. If the duration of the assets is greater than the duration of the liabilities, the economic surplus will increase if interest rates fall. For example, suppose that the current market value of a portfolio of assets is equal to $100 million and the present value of liabilities is $90 million. Then the economic surplus is $10 million. Suppose that the duration of the assets is 3 and the duration of the liabilities is 5.

Consider the following two scenarios. In the first scenario, interest rates decline by 100 basis points. Because the duration of the assets is 3, the market value of the assets will increase by approximately 3% or $3 million (3% × $100 million) to $103 million. The liabilities will also increase. Since the duration of the liabilities is assumed to be 5, the present value of the liabilities will increase by $4.5 million (5% × $90 million) to $94.5 million. Thus, the economic surplus decreased from $10 million to $5.5 million as a result of a decline in interest rates.

In the second scenario, assume that interest rates rise by 100 basis points. Because the duration of the assets is 3, the market value of the assets will decrease by approximately 3% to $97 million. The liabilities will also decrease. Since the duration of the liabilities is 5, the present value of the liabilities will decrease by $4.5 million to $85.5 million. The economic surplus therefore increases to $11.5 million from $10 million as a result of the rise in interest rates.

Notice that if we just looked at the interest rate risk of the portfolio of bonds for this institution, the assets would increase if interest rates fall. The interest rate risk for the assets alone is that interest rates increase. However, when we consider both assets and liabilities and analyze the change in interest rates, we see that a decline in interest rates is the interest rate risk to this institution because it reduces the economic surplus.

This example is particularly important for corporate pension sponsors since financial accounting rules specify that assets and liabilities must be marked-to-market (FASB 87). Moreover, the accounting rules require that if the surplus becomes negative, the deficit must be reported as a liability in the corporate sponsor's balance sheet.

While our focus has been on the duration of assets, recall that duration is only a first approximation of the sensitivity of an asset or a liability to a change in rates. In analyzing the interest rate sensitivity of assets relative to liabilities, the convexity of both most be considered. Recall from Level I (Chapter 7) that assets can have negative convexity. This means that even if the duration of the assets and liabilities is matched, the performance of assets that are negatively convex will not be as good as the performance of the liabilities. This would result in a decline in the economic surplus in a declining interest rate environment if the convexity of the assets and liabilities is ignored.

C. Constraints

Clients will impose constraints on managers. Examples of constraints that a client might impose are a maximum allocation of funds to one particular issuer or industry, a minimum acceptable credit rating for an issue to be eligible for purchase, the minimum and maximum duration for the portfolio, whether or not leverage is permitted, whether or not shorting is permitted, and limitations on the use of derivative instruments (i.e., futures, options, swaps, caps, and floors).

The constraints imposed should be realistic and consistent with the investment objective. For example, suppose an insurance company issues a 5-year guaranteed investment contract (GIC) in which the rate guaranteed is 200 basis points over the on-the-run 5-year Treasury issue and the 5-year Treasury issue is 6%. The investment objective is then to earn 8% plus a spread for the risk that the insurance company incurs. However, if the constraint that is imposed on the manager is to invest in only AAA rated securities and to restrict issues to maturities that do not exceed five years, then it will be extremely difficult for the manager to meet the investment objective without excessively trading the portfolio to try to generate short-run returns.

In addition to client-imposed constraints, regulators of state-regulated institutions such as insurance companies (both life and property and casualty companies) may restrict the amount of funds allocated to certain major asset classes. Even the amount allocated within a major asset class may be restricted, depending on the characteristics of the particular asset. Managers of pension fund monies must comply with ERISA requirements. In the case of investment companies, restrictions on asset allocation are set forth in the prospectus when the fund is launched and may be changed only with approval of the fund's board of directors.

Tax implications must also be considered. For example, life insurance companies enjoy certain tax advantages that make investing in tax-exempt municipal securities generally unappealing. Because pension funds too are exempt from taxes, they also are not particularly interested in tax-exempt municipal securities.

SECTION III
DEVELOPING AND IMPLEMENTING A PORTFOLIO STRATEGY

The second activity in the investment management process is developing and implementing a portfolio strategy. The strategy must be consistent with the investment objective and all constraints. This activity can be divided into the following activities:

- writing an investment policy
- selecting the type of investment strategy
- formulating the inputs for portfolio construction
- constructing the portfolio

We discuss each of these activities below.

A. Writing an Investment Policy

The investment policy is a document that links together the investor's investment objectives and the types of strategies that the manager (internal and external) may employ in seeking to reach those objectives. The investment policy should specify the permissable risks and how performance risk is measured.

Typically, the investment policy may be developed by the investor in the conjunction with a consultant. Given the investment policy, investment guidelines are established for individual managers hired by the investor. For example, if the investment objective is to outperform an aggregate bond index, there may be a separate manager hired to manage each sector of the index. While at the investor level the investment objective may be to outperform the bond index, the investment objective of each manager hired would be to outperform a specific sector of the index.

The investment guidelines established for each manager are developed in conjunction with the investor, the investor's consultant, and the individual manager. The investment guidelines must be consistent with the investment policy and must be consistent with the investment philosophy of the manager being retained. The investment guidelines should also define how managers that are engaged will be evaluated.

B. Selecting the Type of Investment Strategy

Portfolio strategies can be classified as either **active strategies** or **passive strategies**. Essential to all active bond portfolio strategies is specification of expectations about the factors that influence the performance of an asset class. The factors that have historically driven the return on bond portfolios were reviewed at Level II (Chapter 1). In the case of active bond management, this may involve forecasts of interest rates, interest rate volatility, or yield spreads. Active portfolio strategies involving foreign bonds will require forecasts of exchange rates as well as local market interest rates.

Passive strategies involve minimal expectational input. One popular type of passive strategy is indexing, whose objective is to replicate the performance of a designated bond market index. While indexing has been employed extensively in the management of equity portfolios, the use of indexing for managing bond portfolios is a relatively new practice. Indexing is covered in Chapter 4.

Several bond portfolio strategies classified as **structured portfolio strategies** have been commonly used. A structured portfolio strategy involves designing a portfolio so as to achieve the performance of some designated benchmark. Such strategies are frequently followed when seeking to satisfy liabilities. When the designated benchmark is generating sufficient funds to satisfy a single liability regardless of the course of future interest rates, a strategy known as immunization is often used. When the designated benchmark involves satisfying multiple future liabilities regardless of how interest rates change, strategies such as immunization, cash flow matching (or dedication), or horizon matching can be employed. Indexing is also considered a structured portfolio strategy, since the benchmark is to achieve the performance of a designated bond market index. Structured portfolio strategies will be covered in Chapter 3.

1. Strategy Selection and Risk

By understanding the risk characteristics contained in a benchmark index, we can differentiate between the two major types of investing — passive versus active management.

In a bond indexing strategy, a portfolio is created to mirror image the benchmark index. The risk characteristics of the portfolio are constructed to be identical to the risk characteristics of the benchmark index. Typically, it is difficult to replicate the benchmark index precisely and at minimal cost for the reasons explained in Chapter 4. So, there will be tracking error risk, but this risk will be minimal.

Unlike tracking error risk for active managers discussed in Section II, tracking error risk for a manager whose goal is to match the performance of the benchmark index occurs when the managed portfolio's return is materially greater than or less than the return on the benchmark index. This may seem surprising as to why outperforming the benchmark index (i.e., positive tracking error) is a risk. The reason is that it is an indication that the manager does not have the demonstrated ability to do what he or she is mandated to do: match the benchmark index.

In active management the manager deliberately creates a portfolio that departs from the characteristics of the benchmark index. The types of departure determines the differences in the risk characteristics of the actively managed portfolio and the benchmark index. Just what greater or lesser risks than inherent in the benchmark index the active manager wants to accept is based on the manager's expectations. Here tracking error risk is clearly the risk of underperforming the benchmark index.

Active management can be differentiated in terms of the "degree" of departure from the benchmark index. Some managers create portfolios that differ in just a small way from the benchmark index. Such a management strategy is referred to as enhanced indexing. The problem is that "in a small way" is difficult to quantify, so knowing where enhanced indexing ends and active management begins is subjective. (Enhanced indexing is covered in Chapter 4.)

2. Role of Derivatives in Investment Strategies

Regardless of whether an active or a passive strategy is selected, a manager must decide whether or not to employ derivatives in implementing a strategy. Derivatives include futures, forwards, swaps, options, caps, and floors. The fundamental characteristics of these instruments and how they are valued was covered at Level II (Chapters 7 and 8). Of course, the use of derivatives and any restrictions on how they are used is established by the client.

Derivative instruments can be used to control the interest rate risk of a portfolio. The advantages of using derivative instruments rather than cash market instruments are explained in Chapter 7. Bond portfolio strategies employing derivatives to control interest rate risk is also explained in Chapter 7. In recent years derivative instruments for controlling credit risk have been developed. These instruments and strategies for using them are covered in Chapter 8.

C. Formulating the Inputs for Portfolio Construction

Formulating the inputs for portfolio construction in an active portfolio strategy requires two tasks. The first is a forecast by the manager of the inputs that are expected to impact the performance of a security and a portfolio. For many strategies this involves forecasting changes in interest rates, changes in interest rate volatility, changes in credit spreads, and, for international bond portfolios, changes in exchange rates. A discussion of forecasting models is beyond the scope of this book.

The second task is to extrapolate from market data the market's "expectations." Recall from Level I that a manager's view is always relative to what is "priced" into the market. We illustrated this at Level I (Chapter 6) where we introduced forward rates. To illustrate the essential point, we can use a simple example of a manager who has a 1-year investment horizon and is deciding between the following two alternatives:

- buy a 1-year Treasury bill
- buy a 6-month Treasury bill, and when it matures in six months buy another 6-month Treasury bill

The alternative selected by the manager will not be made based solely on the manager's forecast of the 6-month Treasury bill rate six months from now. Rather, it will be based on that forecast relative to the 6-month rate that is "priced" into the 1-year Treasury bill rate. For example, suppose that the 6-month Treasury bill rate is 3.0% (on a bond-equivalent basis) and the 1-year Treasury bill rate is 3.3% (on a bond-equivalent basis).[2] At Level I, it was shown that the 6-month interest rate six months from now that would make the manager indifferent to investing in either alternative is 3.6%.[3] This 3.6% interest rate is sometimes referred to as "breakeven rate," or more commonly a "forward rate." The manager would be indifferent between the two alternatives if her forecast is that the 6-month rate six months from now is 3.6%. The manager would prefer the 1-year Treasury bill if her forecast is that the 6-month rate six months from now will be less than 3.6%. The manager would prefer the 6-month Treasury bill if her forecast is that the 6-month rate six months from is greater than 3.6%.

---

[2] This is the same example used at Level I (Chapter 6). By a bond-equivalent basis it is meant the doubling of a semiannual yield.

[3] To see this, suppose $100,000 is invested in both alternatives. For the 1-year Treasury bill alternative, the manager earns 1.65% (one half the 1-year rate of 3.3%) each 6-month period for two periods (i.e., one year). The total dollars at the end of one year will be:

$$100,000 (1.0165)^2 = \$103,327$$

For the 6-month Treasury bill alternative, the manager invests $100,000 for six months at 1.5% (one half the annual rate) and then reinvests the proceeds received for another six months at 1.8% (one half the 3.6% rate). The total dollars at the end of one year will be

$$100,000 (1.015) (1.018) = \$103,327.$$

Thus, both alternatives provide the same amount.

As explained at Level II (Chapter 1) in discussing forward rates, while it is common in the market to refer to them as the market's consensus of future rates, it is irrelevant from the perspective of the manager whether or not the rate is truly a "consensus" value. The manager is only concerned with her view on future rates relative to what rates are built into today's prices. Consequently, forward rates can be viewed as "hedgeable rates." That is, if a manager purchases the 1-year Treasury bill, she is hedging the 6-month Treasury bill rate six months from now. By doing so, the manager in our illustration has locked in a 6-month Treasury bill rate six months from now of 3.6%.

Forward rates are just one example of using market information. Another example is when a manager wants to express a view of an issue's credit rating versus the spread at which it is trading in the market. We will see other examples in some of the chapters that follow.

D. Constructing the Portfolio

Given the manager's forecasts and market-derived information, the manager must assemble the portfolio with specific issues. In active bond portfolio management, asset selection involves identifying opportunities to enhance return relative to the benchmark. In doing so, the manager will determine the **relative value** of the securities that are candidates for purchase in the portfolio and candidates for sale from the portfolio.

According to Jack Malvey, in the bond market the term "relative value" refers to "the ranking of fixed-income investments by sectors, structures, issuers, and issues in terms of their expected performance during some future interval."[4] The various methodologies for performing relative value analysis are explained in Chapters 5 and 6.

SECTION IV MONITORING THE PORTFOLIO

Once the portfolio has been constructed, it must be monitored. Monitoring involves two activities. The first is to assess whether or not there have been changes in the market that might suggest that any of the key inputs used in constructing the portfolio may not be realized. The second task is to monitor the performance of the portfolio.

Monitoring the performance of a portfolio involves two phases. The first is **performance measurement**. This involves the calculation of the return realized by a manager over some time interval. In Chapter 9, the various measures for calculating a portfolio's return and their limitations are explained. The Association for Investment Management and Research Performance Presentation Standards for computing returns are also explained in that chapter.

Given a performance measurement over some evaluation period, the second task is **performance evaluation**. This task is concerned with two issues. The first issue is to determine whether or not the manager added value by outperforming the established benchmark. The second issue is to determine how the manager achieved the calculated return. The decomposition of the performance results to explain the reasons why those results were achieved is called return attribution analysis. Performance evaluation is described in Chapter 9.

SECTION V ADJUSTING THE PORTFOLIO

Investment management is an ongoing process. The activities involved in monitoring the portfolio will indicate whether or not adjustments need be made to the portfolio. By monitoring developments in the capital market, a manager will be able to determine whether or not to revise the inputs used in the portfolio construction process. Based on the new inputs, a manager will then construct a new portfolio. In constructing the new

---

[4] Chapter 5 in this book.

portfolio, the cost of trading issues currently in the portfolio will be evaluated. These costs include transaction costs and any adverse tax or regulatory consequences.

Performance measurement will indicate how well the manager is performing relative to the investment objectives. Performance will be used by the client in deciding whether or not to retain a manager. However, a client must understand that the time horizon must be adequate for assessing the performance of the manager and the strategy selected by the manager. For example, if an analysis of the first quarter of a newly hired active manager indicates that he has underperformed the benchmark by 20 basis points, this may not be sufficient time for a fair evaluation. Instead, suppose that a new manager is hired and given cash to invest using a bond indexing strategy. If the same 20 basis point underperformance for this manager is found, a quarter may be adequate time for assessing the manager's ability to index a portfolio. In fact, even if there is outperformance of the benchmark of 20 basis points of a bond indexed portfolio, this may be sufficient evidence to question the ability of a manager.

SECTION VI
KEY POINTS

❏ *The investment management process involves the following four activities: setting investment objectives, developing and implementing a portfolio strategy, monitoring the portfolio, and adjusting the portfolio.*

❏ *The investment objectives depend on the characteristics of the investor.*

❏ *The investment objectives are typically expressed in terms of risk and return, both of which are subject to constraints.*

❏ *The benchmark may be either a liability structure or a bond market index.*

❏ *A manager will be evaluated relative to the benchmark.*

❏ *Investors that have a liability structure are either (1) funded investors where the borrowed funds created the liability structure or (2) investors who did not borrow funds that created the liability structure.*

❏ *For funded investors, the spread is the difference between the return on the funds invested and the cost of borrowing.*

❏ *A liability can be characterized in terms of both the amount of the liability and the timing of the liability.*

❏ *Liabilities can be classified according to the degree of certainty of their amount and timing.*

❏ *When there are no liabilities that must be met, the investment objective is to either match or outperform a designated bond index.*

❏ *Bond indexes can be classified as broad-based market indexes or specialized market indexes.*

❏ *The three broad-based bond market indexes are the Lehman Brothers Aggregate Index, the Salomon Brothers Broad Investment-Grade Bond Index (BIG), and the Merrill Lynch Domestic Market Index.*

❏ *The specialized market indexes focus on one sector of the bond market or a subsector of the bond market.*

❏ *There are specialized indexes that have been created that better reflect the liability structure of defined benefit pension plans.*

❏ *Client-imposed constraints include maximum allocation of funds to one particular issuer or industry, a minimum acceptable credit rating for an issue to be eligible for purchase, the minimum and maximum duration for the portfolio, any restrictions on leverage and shorting, and limitations on the use of derivative instruments.*

❏ *There may be regulatory constraints and tax factors that must be considered by an investor.*

❏ *Performance risk is the risk that the investment objective will not be satisfied.*

❏ *Tracking error is the difference between the performance of the managed portfolio and the performance of the benchmark index.*

❏ *Tracking error risk is the risk that the return on the managed portfolio will be less than the return on the benchmark index.*

❏ *Developing and implementing a portfolio strategy involves writing an investment policy, selecting the type of investment strategy, formulating the inputs for portfolio construction, and constructing the portfolio.*

❏ *Portfolio strategies can be classified as either active strategies or passive strategies.*

❏ *All active bond portfolio strategies are based on expectations about the factors that influence bond performance.*

❏ *Passive strategies involve minimal expectational input.*

❏ *Structured portfolio strategies involve designing a bond portfolio to achieve the performance of some designated benchmark.*

❏ *Bond indexing, immunization, and cash flow matching are structured portfolio strategies.*

❏ *Passive and active management can be distinguished in terms of the degree to which the risk characteristics of the managed portfolio differs from that of the benchmark index.*

❏ *For bond indexing, a form of passive management, the manager attempts to construct a portfolio such that the risk characteristics of the managed portfolio are identical to the risk characteristics of the benchmark index, resulting in minimal tracking error risk.*

❏ *In active management, the manager deliberately creates a portfolio that departs from the risk characteristics of the benchmark index and tracking error risk is therefore greater the greater the departure from the risk characteristics of the benchmark index.*

❏ *When the benchmark is a liability structure, there may be a single liability or multiple liabilities.*

❏ *There are risks associated with liabilities as there are with assets.*

❏ *The economic surplus of any entity is the difference between the market value of all its assets and the present value of its liabilities.*

❏ *The sensitivity of liabilities to interest rate changes can be approximated by its duration and convexity.*

❏ *The duration of the surplus of an institution is the difference between the duration of the assets and the duration of the liabilities.*

❏ *To properly assess the interest rate sensitivity of the economic surplus of an entity it is necessary to assess the duration and convexity of both the assets and liabilities.*

❑ *In formulating the inputs to be used in portfolio construction, a manager will forecast key factors and compare those forecasts to market-derived values (i.e., forward rates).*

❑ *A manager will assess the relative value of the universe of securities that are eligible for purchase.*

❑ *A manager will monitor a portfolio in terms of the inputs used in the portfolio construction process and the performance of the portfolio.*

❑ *Performance measurement involves calculating the return achieved by a manager over some time period.*

❑ *Performance evaluation is concerned with determining if the manager added value by outperforming the established benchmark and how the manager achieved the calculated return.*

❑ *Return attribution analysis decomposes the performance results in order to explain the reasons why those results were achieved.*

❑ *After monitoring the portfolio, adjustments may be necessary based on changes in market conditions and/or the performance of the portfolio.*

END OF CHAPTER QUESTIONS

1. a. What are the two dimensions of a liability?
   b. Why is it not always simple to estimate the liability of an institution?

2. What is meant by the economic surplus of an institution?

3. a. What is meant by a funded investor?
   b. What is the investment objective of a funded investor?

4. What are the dangers of a defined benefit pension plan using as its benchmark the performance of a broad-based bond market index?

5. Some specialized bond indexes have been developed that are based on the characteristics of liabilities of typical defined benefit pension funds. Explain why such indexes have been developed?

6. The Reliable Performance Management firm was retained by a client. The investment objective specified by the client was to outperform a broad-based bond market index by at least 50 basis points. In the first year, Reliable was able to earn more than 80 basis points over the benchmark index. However, the client was dissatisfied with the performance of Reliable because the client was not able to meet its liabilities. Ms. Florez of Reliable is responsible for client accounts. How should Ms. Florez respond to the client's dissatisfaction with the performance of Reliable?

7. Why are tax considerations important in developing an investment policy?

8. a. What is the difference between an active and a passive bond portfolio strategy?
   b. What factors should a client consider in determining whether to retain a manager to follow an active or a passive bond portfolio strategy?

9. a. What is meant by tracking error risk?
   b. Explain why tracking error risk occurs?

10. A client retained the Conservative Management Company to manage funds on an indexed basis. The benchmark selected was the Lehman Brothers U.S. Aggregate index. In each of the first four quarters, the management company outperformed the benchmark by a minimum of 70 basis points. In its annual review, a representative of the management company stressed its company's superior performance. You are a consultant that has been retained by the client. Comment on the claim of the representative of the management company.

11. a. Explain why a liability may expose an institution to call risk?
    b. Why might a funded investor be exposed to cap risk?

12. Suppose that the present value of the liabilities of a British financial institution is £6 billion and the surplus is £8 billion. The duration of the liabilities is equal to 5. Suppose further that the portfolio of this financial institution includes only British government bonds and the duration for the portfolio is 6.

    a. What is the market value of the portfolio of bonds?
    b. What does a duration of 6 mean for the portfolio of assets?

c. What does a duration of 5 mean for the liabilities?

d. Suppose that interest rates increase by 50 basis points, what will be the approximate new value for the surplus?

e. Suppose that interest rates decrease by 50 basis points, what will be the approximate new value for the surplus?

13. You and a friend are discussing the savings and loan (S&L) crisis in the United States. She states that "the whole mess started in the early 1980s. When short-term rates increased dramatically, S&Ls were adversely affected — their spread income went from positive to negative. They were borrowing short and lending long."

a. What does she mean by "borrowing short and lending long"?

b. Do increasing or decreasing interest rates adversely affect an institution that borrows short and lends long?

c. How would you restate the risk exposure of S&Ls in terms of duration?

14. Why do you think a debt instrument whose interest rate is changed periodically based on some market interest rate (i.e., a floater) would be more suitable for a depository institution than a long-term debt instrument with a fixed interest rate?

15. In a publication by the ICFA Continuing Education, *Managing Asset/Liability Portfolios*, the following appeared in an article by Martin L. Leibowitz ("Setting the Stage"):

> The importance of surplus measurement differs for each type of financial intermediary.... [and] can range from being all-encompassing (as in spread banking) to almost insignificant for some highly funded corporate and public pension funds.

a. What does Leibowitz means by surplus management?

b. Why is surplus management more important for banks than for highly funded pension funds (i.e., pension funds with a large surplus)?

16. a. What is the difference between performance measurement and performance evaluation?

b. What are the two issues that performance evaluation seeks to address?

SOLUTIONS TO END OF CHAPTER QUESTIONS

1. a. The two dimensions of a liability are the timing of the cash outlay that must be made and the amount of the cash outlay that must be made to satisfy the obligation.

   b. There are some products sold by financial institutions or created by pension plans where the amount of the cash outlay and/or the timing of the cash outlay are not known with certainty. Many times the estimates of the liability will depend on actuarial assumptions.

2. The economic surplus of an institution is the difference between the market value of the assets and the market value of the liabilities. The market value of the liabilities is measured in terms of the present value of the liabilities, using an appropriate interest rate to compute the present value.

3. a. A funded investor borrows funds and uses those funds to purchase securities.
   b. The investment objective of a funded investor is to earn a return greater than the cost of the borrowed funds.

4. The investment objective of a defined benefit pension plan is to generate sufficient cash flow from its portfolio of assets to satisfy its future liabilities. By selecting a broad-based bond market index, there is no assurance that the cash flow generated from the portfolio will be sufficient to satisfy the pension fund's future obligations.

5. Broad-based bond market indexes have cash flow characteristics that may differ significantly from the cash outlays that are projected to be required for a pension plan. For example, the duration of a typical defined benefit pension plan's liabilities may exceed that of a broad-based bond market index. Thus, there would be a mismatch between the duration of the assets (as determined by the broad-based bond market index) and the duration of the pension fund's liabilities. Specialized indexes for defined benefit pension funds seek to correct this problem.

6. Ms. Florez should inform the client that Reliable did in fact outperform the benchmark as specified in the investment objective. The failure of the client to meet the liabilities was probably due to the wrong benchmark being selected by the client. Assuming that Reliable had nothing to do with setting up the benchmark, the unfortunate failure to meet the liability was due to the client's benchmark selection, not the performance of Reliable's managers. The client should reconsider the benchmark to ensure that it more accurately reflects the characteristics of the liabilities that it faces.

7. Tax considerations are important in selecting the assets classes in which a manager may invest. For example, a qualified tax-exempt pension fund may not find tax-exempt securities (such as municipal bonds) acceptable because they offer a lower yield relative to taxable securities.

8. a. In an active strategy, the manager is permitted by the investment policy to create a portfolio that deviates from the characteristics of the benchmark. The deviations are based on the manager's view as to where the performance will be better than that of the benchmark index. For example, if the manager believes that corporate bonds will outperform Treasury securities, then the manager will overweight the amount of corporate bonds relative to the index and underweight Treasury securities relative to the benchmark index.

With a passive strategy, the manager creates a portfolio that has the identical (or very similar) characteristics of the benchmark. That is, a mini-version of the index is created.

b. The selection of a passive or an active bond portfolio management strategy depends on the belief of the client as to whether or not there are inefficiencies in the bond market. If a client believes that the bond market is inefficient, then the client will seek a manager who the client believes can capitalize on any perceived inefficiency. The expectation is that the manager can outperform the index after the management fee.

9. a. Tracking error risk is the risk that the portfolio will underperform the benchmark.
   b. Tracking error risk occurs because the portfolio deviates from the benchmark in terms of the composition and weight of the securities in the portfolio relative to the benchmark.

10. When an indexing strategy is pursued, tracking error occurs when the performance deviates from the benchmark. It does not make a difference whether the tracking error is positive or negative. While the Conservative Management Company did outperform the benchmark (i.e., positive tracking error), this indicates a risk position significantly different from that of the index, and demonstrates a lack of ability to index a portfolio. The firm's claim of superior performance is incorrect given the investment objective. Thus, it is likely that you as a consultant would recommend not using Conservative Management Company as an indexer – however, you might recommend that the firm be retained as an active manager!

11. a. A holder of a liability may be able to terminate the liability prior to the stated maturity date. This will occur when interest rates rise and the holder of the liability wants to benefit from reinvesting proceeds at the then prevailing higher interest rate. The risk faced by the issuer of the liability is call risk.

    b. A funded investor will typically borrow on a floating-rate basis and seek to invest in a floating-rate asset. The latter typically has a cap (i.e., maximum interest rate). The liability does not have a cap. Thus, if rates rise, the rate paid on the floater will eventually reach the cap but the liability's rate will continue to increase. At some interest rate level the rate on the floater will be less than the cost of the borrowed funds. This risk is cap risk.

12. a. The market of the portfolio of bonds is £14 billion. (£14 billion assets minus £6 billion liabilities gives a surplus of £8 billion.)

    b. A duration of 6 for the portfolio assets means that if interest rates increase by 100 basis points, the market value of the assets will change by approximately 6%.

    c. A duration of 5 for the liabilities means that if interest rates increase by 100 basis points, the market value of the liabilities will change by approximately 5%.

    d. If interest rates increase by 50 basis points, the assets will decrease in value by approximately 3%. Since the current value of the assets is £14 billion, the assets will decrease by £420 million. The liabilities will decrease by approximately 2.5%. Since the current value of the liabilities is £6 billion, the liabilities will decrease by £150 million (2.5% × £6 billion). Thus, a 50 basis point change in rates decreases the assets by £420 million and decreases the liabilities by £150 million. The net effect on the surplus is a decline of £270 million. Since the initial surplus is £8 billion, the surplus after a 50 basis point rate increase would £7.73 billion (£8 billion minus £270 million).

e. If interest rates decrease by 50 basis points, the assets will increase by £420 million and the liabilities will increase by £150 million. Hence, the surplus will increase by £8.27 billion (£8 billion plus £270 million).

13. a. By borrowing short she means that S&Ls were borrowing on a short-term basis. Thus, when interest rates increased, S&Ls had to retain depositors by offering a higher deposit rate or if they borrowed funds in the market they had to pay a higher interest rate. S&L's lent long by investing in long maturity assets (such as mortgages loans and mortgage-backed securities) with a fixed coupon rate.

b. When any entity borrows short and lends long it is adversely affected by a rise in interest rates. This is because its cost of funds increases (since the cost of funds rise when interest rates increase) while the coupon income from the long term asset does not change.

c. In terms of duration, the duration of the assets exceeds the duration of the liabilities. That is, there is a mismatch of the duration of the assets and liabilities.

14. A depository institutions seeks to generate spread income. If its assets and liabilities are benchmarked to the same market interest rate and the spread between these two costs is positive, it will generate positive spread income (ignoring any cap risk and credit risk) regardless to changes in that market interest rate.

15. a. The surplus of an entity is the different between the market value of it assets and the present value of its liabilities. Surplus management means managing the exposure of the surplus to changes in interest rates.

b. The surplus of an entity is sensitive to changes in interest rates. A bank is a highly leveraged institution and so even small changes in interest rates can dramatically affect its surplus. In contrast, a highly funded pension fund — one with a large surplus — may not be materially affected by a change in interest rates compared to a bank.

16. a. Performance measurement involves the calculation of the return realized by a manager over some time interval. Performance evaluation involves the assessment of the calculated performance.

b. The two issues that performance evaluation addresses are: (1) assessing whether the manager added value by outperforming the established benchmark and (2) determining how the manager achieved the calculated return using return attribution analysis.

Chapter 2

ALTERNATIVE MEASURES OF PORTFOLIO RISK

Frank J. Fabozzi, Ph.D., CFA
Adjunct Professor of Finance
School of Management
Yale University

LEARNING OUTCOME STATEMENTS

After reading this chapter you should be able to:

- explain what the expected value and standard deviation of a probability distribution is.
- explain why the standard deviation of returns is used as a measure of risk.
- identify the limitations of using the standard deviation as a measure of risk.
- explain the alternative measures of risk that focus on downside risk — target semivariance, shortfall risk, and value at risk — and the difficulties of using these risk measures.
- explain how the portfolio standard deviation is computed.
- explain the role of the covariance/correlation of returns in the computation of the portfolio standard deviation.
- compute the standard deviation of a two bond portfolio.
- discuss the problems of estimating the standard deviation from historical bond returns.
- explain why a duration approach should be employed instead of a portfolio's variance as a measure of risk.
- compute the duration of a portfolio and a market index.
- compute the contribution to portfolio duration of a bond.
- explain how to compute the duration of a portfolio that includes leverage and derivatives.
- compute the duration of a market index.
- explain what spread duration is.
- identify the different types of spread duration measures.
- compare the spread duration exposures of a portfolio with its index.
- identify the difficulties of computing the duration of a portfolio that includes foreign bonds.
- determine the contribution of a foreign bond to a portfolio's risk using a yield beta.

SECTION I
INTRODUCTION

At Level I (Chapter 2), we described the risks associated with individual bonds. These risks include

- Interest rate risk
- Call and prepayment risk
- Yield curve risk
- Reinvestment risk
- Credit risk
- Liquidity risk
- Exchange-rate risk
- Volatility risk
- Inflation or purchasing power risk
- Event risk

It is assumed that the reader is familiar with these risks.

At Level III the focus will be on bond portfolio strategies. In this chapter we will describe alternative measures of portfolio risk associated with a portfolio strategy. These measures draw upon several basic concepts in probability theory and statistical analysis. Consequently, we begin this chapter with a review of two important concepts — the standard deviation and the normal distribution.

SECTION II
REVIEW OF
STANDARD
DEVIATION
AND NORMAL
DISTRIBUTION

Professor Harry Markowitz changed how the investment community thought about the notion of "risk" by quantifying the concept of risk.[1] He defined risk in terms of a well-known statistical measure known as the variance or its conceptual equivalence, standard deviation which is the square root of the variance. As a result of the acceptance of the portfolio theory put forth by Professor Markowitz, the standard deviation or variance is widely accepted as a measure of portfolio risk. We will review this measure below. After we review the normal probability distribution, we will then discuss the appropriateness of using the standard deviation as a measure of risk.

A. The Standard Deviation

A **random variable** is a variable that can take on more than one possible value in the future. A **probability distribution** or **probability function** describes all the values that the random variable can take on and the probability associated with each possible value.

Typically, probability distributions are obtained from historical observations of the random variable. For example, if the random variable is the 1-year rate of return on a 5-year Treasury strip, then observations on the 1-year rate of return for 5-year Treasury strips are used.

Various measures are used to summarize the probability distribution of a random variable. The two most often used measures are the average value and the standard deviation. The **average value** or **mean value** is simply found by adding up the observed values for the random variable and dividing the sum by the number of observations. For example, let r denote the 1-year rate of return and T denote the number of observations, then the average value, denoted by r_{avg}, is:

$$r_{avg} = \sum_{t=1}^{T} \frac{r_t}{T} \tag{1}$$

where r_t is the t-th observed rate of return.

---

[1] Harry M. Markowitz, "Portfolio Selection," *Journal of Finance* (March 1952), pp. 71- 91.

The average value is also referred to as the **expected value** of the probability distribution. We will use the term expected value in the discussion below and denote the expected value of the return as r_{EV} rather than r_{avg}.

A portfolio manager is interested not only in the expected value of a probability distribution but also in the dispersion of the random variable around the expected value. A measure of dispersion of the probability distribution is the **variance** of the distribution, denoted var(r). It is calculated as follows:

$$\text{var}(r) = \sum_{t=1}^{T} \frac{(r_t - r_{EV})^2}{T-1} \tag{2}$$

Notice that the variance is measuring the deviations of each observed value from the expected value. The greater the variance, the greater the dispersion of the observations for the random variable. The reason that the deviations from the expected value are squared in equation (2) is to avoid observations above and below the expected value from canceling each other out.

The problem with using the variance as a measure of dispersion is that it is in terms of squared units of the random variable. Consequently, the square root of the variance which is called the **standard deviation** is used as a more understandable measure of the degree of dispersion. Mathematically this can be expressed as follows:

$$\text{std}(r) = \sqrt{\text{var}(r)}$$

where std(r) denotes the standard deviation of the random variable r. At Level II (Chapter 1), we explained how to compute the standard deviation of interest rates or yields (which we referred to as interest rate volatility or yield volatility) from historical yields. The procedure is the same for computing the standard deviation of the return of a bond or a bond index. Consequently, the procedure for computing the standard deviation will not be explained in this chapter.

Exhibit 1 shows quarterly returns for the Lehman Brothers Treasury Index and the Lehman Brothers High Yield Index for the first quarter of 1984 to the third quarter of 1997. There are 55 observations. The expected value (average value), variance, and standard deviation for the quarterly returns are reported in Exhibit 2. (Note that there are other risk measures shown in Exhibit 1 and they will be described later.) We will use these indexes throughout the chapter to illustrate how portfolio risk measures are calculated and how they can be used to compare the risk and return characteristics of portfolios. Just as we use two indexes as proxies for portfolios, these measures can also be used to compare the risk of a portfolio and its benchmark.

When the random variable is the rate of return over some investment horizon, it can be used to measure the risk associated with an investment. There are some important qualifications of using the standard deviation as a risk measure, and we will address these concerns below. Before doing so, it will make it easier to understand these qualifications if we first introduce a probability distribution called the normal distribution.

B. Normal Probability Distribution

In many applications of probability theory, it is assumed that the underlying probability distribution is a **normal distribution**. As explained below, for this probability distribution, given the expected value and the standard deviation, the probability of realizing a value or values can be obtained. A diagram of a normal distribution is shown in Exhibit 3.

Exhibit 1: Quarterly Returns (%) for the Lehman Brothers Treasury Index and Lehman Brothers High Yield Index: First Quarter 1984 to Third Quarter 1997

Year	Qtr	Treasury Index	High Yield Index	Year	Qtr	Treasury Index	High Yield Index	Year	Qtr	Treasury Index	High Yield Index
1984	1	0.51	1.69	1989	1	1.07	1.19	1994	1	−3.02	−1.95
	2	−1.23	−3.57		2	8.16	3.64		2	−1.13	−0.32
	3	7.63	7.43		3	0.8	−1.47		3	0.42	1.58
	4	7.13	4.14		4	3.8	2.41		4	0.35	−0.3
1985	1	2.13	5.56	1990	1	−1.35	−1.65	1995	1	4.68	5.97
	2	7.95	7.49		2	3.48	4.22		2	6.24	6.12
	3	2.09	3.85		3	0.77	−10.22		3	1.75	2.82
	4	7.43	6.62		4	5.52	−1.75		4	4.6	2.8
1986	1	9.16	9.26	1991	1	2.12	20.7	1996	1	−2.28	1.77
	2	1.24	3.85		2	1.32	7.37		2	0.46	1.66
	3	1.88	1.73		3	5.69	7.04		3	1.67	3.77
	4	2.68	1.75		4	5.42	5.37		4	2.9	3.5
1987	1	1.16	7.08	1992	1	−1.81	7.39	1997	1	−0.86	1.05
	2	−1.81	−1.54		2	3.96	2.75		2	3.45	4.62
	3	−2.87	−2.29		3	5.05	3.89		3	3.37	4.54
	4	5.72	1.91		4	0	0.97				
1988	1	3.25	5.58	1993	1	4.54	6.07				
	2	0.95	2.38		2	2.91	4.21				
	3	1.67	1.78		3	3.23	2.08				
	4	0.96	2.29		4	−0.34	3.78				

Exhibit 2: Summary of Alternative Risk Measures for the Lehman Brothers Treasury Index and High Yield Index Based on Quarterly Returns: First Quarter 1984 to Third Quarter 1997

	Treasury Index	High Yield Index
Expected value	2.45%	3.14%
Risk Measures:		
Variance	8.9268	17.3930
Std. deviation	2.99%	4.17%
Target semivariance assuming 3% target return		
Target semivariance	9.3796	14.9415
Target semi-std deviation	3.06%	3.87%
Target semivariance assuming 0% target return		
Target semivariance	3.8417	15.1944
Target semi-std deviation	1.96%	3.90%
Semivariance below the expected value		
Semivariance	7.4809	15.7244
Semi-standard deviation	2.74%	3.97%

Exhibit 3: Normal Distribution

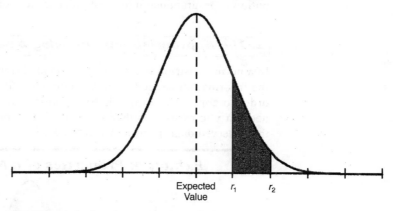

Expected
Value r_1 r_2

Probability of realizing a value between r_1 and r_2 is shaded area.

The area under the normal distribution or normal curve between any two points on the horizontal axis is the probability of obtaining a value between those two values. For example, the probability of realizing a value for the random variable r that is between r_1 and r_2 in Exhibit 3 is shown by the shaded area. The entire area under the normal curve is equal to 1, which means the sum of the probabilities is 1.

1. Properties of the Normal Distribution

The normal distribution has the following properties:

1. The point in the middle of the normal curve is the expected value for the distribution.
2. The distribution is *symmetric* around the expected value. That is, half of the distribution is to the left of the expected value and the other half is to the right. Thus, the probability of obtaining a value less than the expected value is 50%. The probability of obtaining a value greater than the expected value is also 50%.
3. The probability that the actual outcome will be within a range of one standard deviation above the expected value and one standard deviation below the expected value is 68.3%.
4. The probability that the actual outcome will be within a range of two standard deviations above the expected value and two standard deviations below the expected value is 95.5%.
5. The probability that the actual outcome will be within a range of three standard deviations above the expected value and three standard deviations below the expected value is 99.7%.

Exhibit 4 graphically presents these properties.

There are tables available that give the probability of realizing a value greater than or less than some value or a value between two values. Abridged versions of these tables are reprinted in most textbooks on statistics. The information that is needed is the expected value and the standard deviation. From this information, there is a formula that is used to obtain a *standardized value* so that the table can be used.

We'll dispense with describing how this is done. Today, the normal probability distribution is programmed into most popular electronic spreadsheets.[2]

2. The Appropriateness of Using a Normal Distribution

In a normal distribution, the expected value (mean) and the standard deviation are all the information needed to make statements about the probabilities of outcomes. In order to apply the normal distribution to make statements about probabilities, it is necessary to assess whether a historical distribution (i.e., a distribution created from the observed data) is normally distributed.

Exhibit 4: Properties of a Normal Distribution

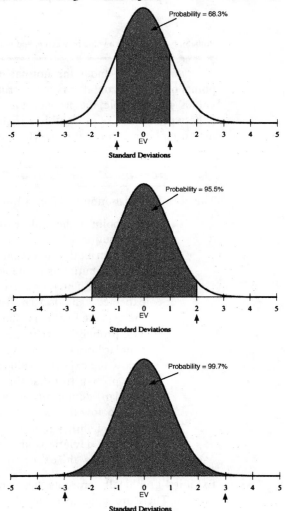

---

[2] For example, when using Excel, the normal distribution can be calculated using the function NORMDIST. The inputs required are the values for the random variable sought, the average (mean or expected) value, and the standard deviation.

Exhibit 5: Distribution Skewed to the Right (Positively Skewed)

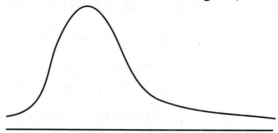

Exhibit 6: Distribution Skewed to the Left (Negatively Skewed)

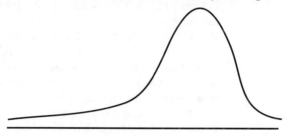

Exhibit 7: Fat Tails

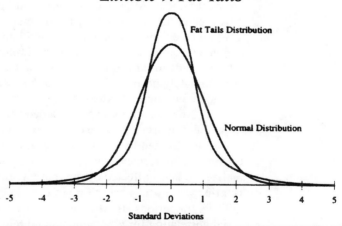

For example, as noted earlier, a property of the normal probability distribution is that the distribution is symmetric around the expected value. However, a probability distribution might be best characterized like those shown in Exhibits 5 and 6. Such distributions are referred to as **skewed distributions**. The skewed distribution shown in Exhibit 5 is one which has a long tail on the right hand side of the distribution. Such a distribution is referred to as a **positively skewed distribution**. Exhibit 6 shows a skewed distribution that has a long tail on the left hand side of the distribution and is called a **negatively skewed distribution**.

In addition to skewness, a historical distribution may have more outliers (i.e., observations in the "tails") than the normal distribution predicts. Distributions with this characteristic are said to have **fat tails**. This is depicted in Exhibit 7. Notice, that if a distribution does indeed have fat tails but it is assumed that it is normally distribution, the probability of getting a value in a tail will be assumed to be less than the actual probability.

The following two questions must be addressed to determine whether or not a historical distribution can be characterized as a normal distribution:

1. Does the data fit the values predicted by the normal distribution?
2. Are the returns today independent of the returns of the prior periods?

Most introductory courses in statistics explain how to test if the historical data for some random variable can be characterized by a normal distribution. Basically the test involves breaking the historical observations into intervals. For each interval, the number of expected or predicted observations based on the normal probability distribution are determined. Then the number predicted for the interval and the number actually observed are compared. This is done for all intervals. Statistical tests can then be used to determine if the historically observed distribution differs significantly from a normal distribution.

Let's look at the evidence on bond returns. For bonds, there is a lower limit on the loss. For Treasury securities, the limit depends on how high rates can rise. Since Treasury rates have never exceeded 15%, this places a lower bound on a negative return from holding a bond. However, there is maximum return. Assuming that negative interest rates are not possible, the maximum price for a bond is the undiscounted value of the cash flow (i.e., the sum of the interest payments and maturity value). In turn, this determines the maximum return. On balance, government bond return distributions are negatively skewed. JP Morgan reports that this occurs for government bonds.[3] Moreover, government bond returns exhibit fat tails and a peakedness greater than predicted by the normal distribution.

One way to overcome the problem of negative skewedness of bond returns is to convert returns into the logarithm of returns. The transformation to the logarithm of returns tends to pull in the outlier negative returns resulting in a distribution that is approximately normal. The resulting probability distribution of logarithmic returns is said to be **lognormally distributed**.

Now let's look at the independence of returns. For any probability distribution, it is important to assess whether or not the value of a random variable in one period is affected by the value that the random variable took on in a prior period. Casting this in terms of returns, it is important to know whether the return that can be realized today is affected by the return realized in a prior period. The terms **serial correlation** and **autocorrelation** are used to describe the correlation between the return in different periods. JP Morgan's analysis suggests that there is only a small positive serial correlation for government bond returns.[4]

SECTION III
DOWNSIDE RISK
MEASURES

Now that you understand why the standard deviation can be used as a measure of risk and the limitations of that measure if a distribution is not normally distributed or symmetric, let's look at other measures of risk that have been proposed.

Other measures of risk focus on only that portion of the return distribution for an investment that is below a specified level. These measures of risk are referred to as **downside risk measures** and they include target semivariance, shortfall probability, and value at risk. We will discuss each below.

---

[3] *RiskMetrics™ — Technical Document*, JP Morgan, May 26, 1995, New York, p. 48.
[4] *RiskMetrics™ — Technical Document*, p. 48.

For the different downside risk measures, the portfolio manager must define the **target return**. Returns less than the target return represent adverse consequences. In the case of the standard deviation, it is assumed that the target return is the expected return. However, in practice, this need not be the case. For example, in managing money against a market index, the target return may be X basis points over the market index return. Outcomes that are less than the market index return plus X basis points would represent downside risk. In managing money against liabilities, the target return may be the rate guaranteed on liabilities plus a spread of S basis points. Returns with an outcome of less than the rate guaranteed on liabilities plus S basis points would then represent downside risk.

It is important to understand that the notion of defining the risk of an investment in terms of only adverse consequences has been around a lot longer than the notion of using standard deviation as a measure of risk. In fact, when Professor Markowitz wrote his seminal work on investment risk, he argued that a downside risk measure would be more appropriate, but would be more complicated to deal with mathematically. He actually devoted an entire chapter in his classic book to one of the downside risk measures discussed below as a candidate for risk. Today, while vendors have employed downside risk measures in asset allocation models, not a great deal has been done in using some of these measures in bond portfolio management. The focus has been on the standard deviation as a measure of risk.

A. Target Semivariance

The **target semivariance** is a measure of the dispersion of the outcomes below the target return specified by the portfolio manager. Mathematically, the target semivariance can be expressed as:

$$\text{target semivariance} = \sum_{\text{for } r_t < r_\text{target}}^{T_{<\text{target}}} \frac{(r_t - r_\text{target})^2}{T_{<\text{target}} - 1} \tag{3}$$

where $T_{<\text{target}}$ is the number of observations with a value less than the target return. The summation in equation (3) means the observations used in the calculations are those with a value less than the target return.

For example, suppose that the quarterly target return is 3%. Then for all of the quarterly return observations in Exhibit 1, only the returns of less than 3% represent downside risk and are used in the target semivariance given by equation (3). The results for the target semivariance for the Treasury Index and the High Yield Index are reported in Exhibit 2. Also reported in Exhibit 2 is the target semivariance if the target return is zero.

A special case of the target semivariance is where the target return is the expected value. The resulting value is called the **semivariance**. The equation for the semivariance is:

$$\text{semivariance} = \sum_{\text{for } r_t < r_\text{EV}}^{T_{<\text{EV}}} \frac{(r_t - r_\text{EV})^2}{T_{<\text{EV}} - 1} \tag{4}$$

where $T_{<\text{EV}}$ is the number of observations with a value less than the expected value. The summation in equation (4) means that *only* values below the expected value are used. Exhibit 2 reports the semivariance and corresponding standard deviation.

When a probability distribution is symmetric around the expected value, then using the semivariance as a risk measure will give the same ranking of risk as using the variance.

While theoretically the semivariance is superior to the variance (standard deviation) as a risk measure (and, in fact, this is the measure Professor Markowitz considered), it is not used in bond portfolio management to any significant extent. Ronald Kahn gave the following reasons why semivariance (which he defines as downside risk) is not used:[5]

First, its definition is not as unambiguous as standard deviation or variance, nor are its statistical properties as well known, so it isn't an ideal choice for a universal risk definition. We need a definition which managers, plan sponsors, and beneficiaries can all use.

Second, it is computationally challenging for large portfolio construction problems. In fact, while we can aggregate individual bond standard deviations into a portfolio standard deviation, for other measures of risk we must rely much more on historical extrapolation of portfolio return patterns.

Third, to the extent that investment returns are reasonably symmetric, most definitions of downside risk are simply proportional to standard deviation or variance and so contain no additional information. To the extent that investment returns may not be symmetric, there are problems forecasting downside risk. Return asymmetries are not stable over time, and so are very difficult to forecast. Realized downside risk may not be a good forecast of future downside risk. Moreover, we estimate downside risk with only half the data, losing statistical accuracy.

Later in this chapter we look at how individual bond standard deviations of return are combined to determine a bond portfolio's standard deviation. In addition, we will address the problem of using historical return patterns for individual bonds.

B. Shortfall Risk

Shortfall risk is the probability that the outcome will have a value less than the target return. From a historical distribution of returns, shortfall risk is the ratio of the number of observations below the target return to the total number of observations.

Assuming a target return of 3%, for the quarterly returns in Exhibit 1, the number of observations with a return below 3% is 33 for the Treasury Index and 28 for the High Yield Index. Thus, the shortfall risk is 60% (33/55) for the Treasury Index and 51% (28/55) for the High Yield Index. Notice that this risk measure suggests that there is less risk for the High Yield Index than the Treasury Index. One problem with this risk measure is that the *magnitude* of the losses below the target return is ignored.

When the target return is zero, the shortfall risk measure is commonly called the **risk of loss**. Again, it is calculated from historical data by dividing the number of observations with a return less than zero by the total number of observations. The risk of loss for both the Treasury Index and the High Yield Index is 18% since 10 of the 55 observations had a return that is less than zero.

As Ronald Kahn notes, when using shortfall risk the same problems are encountered as noted for target semivariance, namely, "ambiguity, poor statistical understanding, difficulty of forecasting."[6]

---

[5] Ronald N. Kahn, "Fixed Income Risk," Chapter 1 in Frank J. Fabozzi (ed.), *Managing Fixed Income Portfolios* (New Hope, PA: Frank J. Fabozzi Associates, 1997), pp. 2-3.
[6] Kahn, "Fixed Income Risk," p.3.

Exhibit 8: Graphical Depiction of Value at Risk

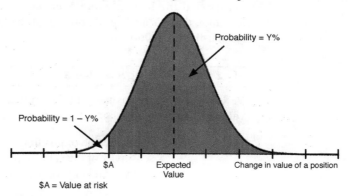

$A = Value at risk

C. Value at Risk   In shortfall risk, the portfolio manager specifies a target return and then computes the percentage of returns less than the target return. A similar approach is for the portfolio manager to specify a target probability; the return will not fall below a yet-to-be determined value the percentage of time represented by the target probability.

For example, suppose that the portfolio manager specifies a target probability of 95%. The portfolio manager then determines the return for which the area in the left hand tail would have a 5% probability. The target return computed is commonly called the **value at risk** (VaR).

While we have expressed VaR in terms of return, it is more commonly used to measure dollar exposure. For example, suppose that a manager wants to make the following statement: "There is a Y% probability that the loss in value from a position will be less than $A in the next T days." The $A in this statement is the value at risk. The VaR can be determined from probability theory assuming a normal distribution, the expected value and standard deviation of the distribution, the target probability (Y%), and the number of days (T).

The VaR can be exhibited graphically. Exhibit 8 shows a normal distribution for the change in the value of a position over the next T days. The VaR is the loss of $A where the probability to the right of that value is Y%. Or equivalently, the VaR is where the probability to the left of that value (i.e., the probability in the tail) is equal to $1 - Y$%.

Let's see how we obtain the VaR using a numerical example. Suppose that the probability distribution for the change in value of a bond over the next four days is normally distributed with an expected value of zero and a standard deviation of $20,000. Assume also that the target probability specified by the manager is 95%. From a normal distribution table, the standardized value that will give a probability in the tail of 5% can be found. (This is done by searching a normal probability distribution table for where the probability is 5%.) One would find that this is where the standardized value is about 1.65.

The standardized value indicates the number of standard deviations above or below the expected value. The VaR is the value which is 1.65 standard deviations *below* the expected value. Since the expected value of the change in value of the bond over the next four days is zero and the standard deviation is $20,000, then the VaR is $33,000. Therefore, there is a 95% probability that the loss in value from the bond will be less than $33,000 in the next four days.

Alternatively, the VaR can be expressed as follows: "There is a $1 - Y\%$ probability that the loss in value over the next T days will be greater than A." In our example, there is a 5% probability that the loss in value over the next four days will be greater than $33,000.

1. Daily Earnings at Risk

VaR begins with measuring the **daily earnings at risk** (DEaR). This is simply the value at risk for a day. For a single position in a bond, DEaR is measured as follows:

> DEaR = market value of position
> × sensitivity of the value of position to a 1 basis point adverse change in yield
> × adverse yield movement per day (in basis points)

Since the duration of a position is the approximate percentage change for a 100 basis point change in yield, dividing the duration by 100 gives the percentage change in value for a 100 basis point change in yield. That is,

> percentage change in value for a 100 basis point change in yield
> = duration/100

Dividing by 100 gives the percentage change in value for a 1 basis point change in yield. That is,

> percentage change in value for a 1 basis point change in yield
> = duration/10,000

DEaR can then be restated as follows:

> DEaR = market value of position × duration/10,000
> × adverse yield movement per day (in basis points)

The adverse yield movement per day is based on the daily yield volatility, the yield level, and the target probability specified. At Level II (Chapter 1) we saw how daily yield volatility can be estimated. It is the daily standard deviation of yield changes. The product of the yield level and the daily standard deviation of yield changes gives the change in yield. The adverse yield movement per day is the product of the daily standard deviation of yield changes, the yield level, and the standardized value from the normal distribution. That is,

> adverse yield movement per day
> = daily standard deviation × yield level
> × standardized value from normal distribution

For example, suppose that the daily standard deviation for the yield change of the 30-year Treasury zero-coupon bond is 0.63% and the yield is 8%. Assuming a normal distribution, then the standardized value is 1.65 if the target probability is 95% for the VaR. Therefore, the adverse yield movement per day is:

> adverse yield movement per day $= 0.0063 \times 0.08 \times 1.65$
> $= 0.00083$

In basis points, the adverse yield movement per day is 8.3.

If the market value of a position of Treasury bonds is \$5 million and its duration is 4, then the DEaR is:

$$\text{DEaR} = \$5,000,000 \times (4/10,000) \times 8.3 = \$16,600$$

2. Relationship Between DEaR and VaR

Given the DEaR, the VaR is calculated as follows:

$$\text{VaR} = \text{DEaR} \sqrt{\text{days expected until position can be neutralized}}$$

where "days expected until position can be neutralized" is the number of days that it is expected it will take to neutralize the risk of the position.

3. Limitations of VaR

There are several criticisms that have been levied against the VaR framework. First, VaR depends on good estimates for both the sensitivity of a position to rate changes and for daily volatility of yield changes as measured by the daily standard deviation. As explained at Levels I and II, for a complex security, estimating the effective duration is not simple. Moreover, as demonstrated at Level II (Chapter 1), there could be substantial variations in the estimated daily standard deviation. In one study, Tanya Beder found that there is a wide variation in the VaR for a given position based on different assumptions about the required inputs.[7]

A second limitation of the VaR framework is that it assumes yield changes are normally distributed. Finally, multiplying the DEaR by the square root of the number of days expected until the position can be neutralized assumes that the distribution for the daily percentage change in yield is not serially correlated.

D. Confidence Intervals

When a range for the possible values of a random variable and a probability associated with that range are calculated, the range is referred to as a *confidence interval*. In general, for a normal distribution, the confidence interval is calculated as follows:

(expected value − standardized value × standard deviation) to
(expected value + standardized value × standard deviation)

The standardized value indicates the number of standard deviations away from the expected value and corresponds to a particular probability. For example, suppose a manager wants a confidence interval of 95%. This means that there will be 2.5% in each tail. A standardized value with a 2.5% probability is 1.96. Thus, a 95% confidence interval is:

(expected value − 1.96 × standard deviation) to
(expected value + 1.96 × standard deviation)

For example, suppose that a manager wants to construct a confidence interval for the change in the value of a bond over the next four days. Assuming that the

---

[7] See Tanya Styblo Beder, "VAR: Seductive but Dangerous," *Financial Analysts Journal* (September-October 1995), pp. 12-24.

change in value is normally distributed with an expected value of zero and a standard deviation of $20,000, then a 95% confidence interval would be:

($0 − 1.96 × $20,000) to ($0 + 1.96 × $20,000)
or −$39,200 to $39,200

SECTION IV
PORTFOLIO
VARIANCE

One of the advantages of the standard deviation or variance as a measure of risk is the ability to move from the risk of an individual bond position to the risk of a bond portfolio. For a bond portfolio, the expected return for the portfolio is the weighted average of the expected return for the individual bonds. The weight assigned to each bond in the portfolio is simply the percentage of the market value of the bond to the market value of the portfolio. No surprises here. However, the variance of a portfolio is not simply a weighted average of the variances of the bonds comprising the portfolio. The basic principle of modern portfolio theory is that the variance of a portfolio of assets depends not only on the variance of the assets, but also their covariances or correlations.[8] We'll explain what is meant by the covariance and correlation below.

A. The Risk for a 2-Bond Portfolio

Let's first illustrate the calculation of the variance of a bond portfolio consisting of just two bonds, identified as bond 1 and bond 2. The variance of this portfolio is equal to

$$\text{var}(r_{\text{Port}}) = W_1^2 \text{var}(r_1) + W_2^2 \text{var}(r_2) + 2W_1 W_2 \text{cov}(r_1, r_2) \tag{5}$$

where

$\text{var}(r_{\text{Port}})$ = variance of the rate of return of a portfolio comprised of bond 1 and bond 2
$\text{var}(r_1)$ = variance of the rate of return of bond 1
$\text{var}(r_2)$ = variance of the rate of return of bond 2
$\text{cov}(r_1,r_2)$ = covariance between the rate of return on bond 1 and bond 2
W_1 = percentage of the portfolio in bond 1
W_2 = percentage of the portfolio in bond 2

In words, equation (5) says that the variance of the portfolio return is the sum of the weighted variances of the two bonds plus the weighted covariance between the two bonds.

The key to the risk of a bond portfolio as measured by the standard deviation or variance is the covariance between the two bonds. The covariance is related to a more commonly understood statistical measure called the correlation coefficient.

---

1. Correlation Coefficient

The *correlation coefficient* measures the association between two random variables. No cause and effect relationship is assumed when a correlation coefficient is computed. The correlation coefficient can have a value between −1 and 1.

For example, if the random variable is the rate of return on a bond, then a positive value for the correlation between the rates of return on two particular bonds means that the rates of return for both bonds tend to move together. In such cases, the two random variables are said to be *positively correlated*. A negative value means that the two rates of

---

[8] Markowitz, "Portfolio Selection."

return tend to move in the opposite direction. Two random variables that exhibit this characteristic are said to be *negatively correlated*. A correlation close to zero means that the rates of return for the two bonds tend not to track each other in any systematic way.

The correlation between the quarterly returns for the Lehman Brothers Treasury Index and the Lehman Brothers High Yield Index based on the first quarter of 1984 through the third quarter of 1997 is 0.46. This means that Treasury returns (as measured by the Treasury index) and high yield returns are somewhat positively correlated.

2. Covariance

The *covariance* also measures how two random variables vary together. The covariance is related to the correlation coefficient as follows:

$$cov(r_1, r_2) = std(r_1)\ std(r_2)\ cor(r_1, r_2)$$

where $cor(r_1, r_2)$ is the correlation between the return on bond 1 and bond 2.

Since the standard deviations will always be a positive value, the covariance will have the same sign as the correlation coefficient. Thus, if two random variables are positively correlated they will have a positive covariance. Similarly, the covariance will be negative if the two random variables are negatively correlated.

The covariance between the rates of return for bond 1 and bond 2 for the quarterly returns for the Treasury Index and the High Yield Index is found as follows using more precise values for the standard deviations and the correlation:

standard deviation for the Treasury index	= 2.987773266
standard deviation for the High Yield index	= 4.170496801
correlation between Treasury index and High Yield Index	= 0.456459351

Therefore, the covariance is[9]

$$cov\ (r_1,\ r_2) = (2.987773266)\ (4.170496801)\ (0.456459351) = 5.6877$$

3. Portfolio Variance for Different Allocations

Notice from Exhibit 9 that the expected return for the Treasury Index is less than for the High Yield Index. However, as expected, the risk, as measured by the standard deviation, is greater for the High Yield Index than for the Treasury Index.

Exhibit 9 shows the portfolio standard deviation for different allocations to the Treasury Index and the High Yield Index. To see the importance of the correlation/covariance on the portfolio's standard deviation, Exhibit 10 shows the portfolio standard deviation for different assumed correlations for the returns between the two indexes. Note that the expected value is unchanged from that shown in Exhibit 9 since it is unaffected by the correlation. The four correlations assumed are −1, −0.5, 0, and 1, as well as the estimated correlation of 0.46. For a given allocation between the two bond indexes in the portfolio, the more negatively correlated, the lower the portfolio standard deviation. The minimum variance (for a given allocation) occurs when the correlation is −1.

---

[9] When using a spreadsheet built-in function for covariance, the covariance may be calculated incorrectly. The reason is that the number of observations may be used in the numerator of the covariance formula rather than the number of observations minus one. So, when the covariance function was used in Excel, the covariance computed was 5.5843 rather than 5.6877.

Exhibit 9: Portfolio Risk and Expected Quarterly Return for Different Allocations between the Treasury Index and the High Yield Index (Based on Quarterly Returns from First Quarter of 1984 to the Third Quarter of 1997)

	Lehman Brothers Treasury Index	Lehman Brothers High Yield Index
Expected value	2.45%	3.14%
Variance	8.9268	17.3930
Standard dev.	2.99%	4.17%
Covariance	5.6877	
Correlation	0.46	

	Weight (Allocation) in Treasury Index						
	20%	30%	40%	50%	60%	70%	80%
Expected value (%)	3.00	2.93	2.86	2.79	2.72	2.65	2.59
Std. deviation	3.65	3.42	3.23	3.07	2.95	2.89	2.87

Exhibit 10: Portfolio Standard Deviation for Different Correlations and Weights for the Treasury Index and the High Yield Index

Assumed		Weight (Allocation) in Treasury Index						
Corr.	Covar.	20%	30%	40%	50%	60%	70%	80%
−1.00	−12.461	2.74	2.02	1.31	0.59	0.12	0.84	1.56
−0.50	−6.230	3.08	2.59	2.17	1.86	1.73	1.82	2.10
0	0	3.39	3.05	2.77	2.57	2.45	2.44	2.53
0.46	5.6877	3.65	3.42	3.23	3.07	2.95	2.89	2.87
1.00	12.461	3.93	3.82	3.70	3.58	3.46	3.34	3.22

There is another important implication of the results reported in Exhibit 10 for our discussion in Chapter 7 when we cover hedging a portfolio. Suppose that a portfolio manager wants to hedge a position in the Treasury Index. By hedging it is meant that the portfolio manager seeks to employ some hedging instrument such that the combined position in the Treasury Index and the hedging instrument will produce a portfolio standard deviation of zero. Look at the first line of Exhibit 10. If a hedging instrument, say Instrument X, can be identified that has a −1 correlation with the Treasury Index and the portfolio manager takes a position in Instrument X such that the portfolio has 60% of the Treasury Index and 40% of Instrument X, then the standard deviation of the portfolio will be close to zero.

Consequently, hedging involves identifying one or more instruments that have a correlation of close to −1 with the position that the portfolio manager seeks to protect and selecting the appropriate amount of the hedging instrument. If the position in a bond portfolio is a long position, then this typically involves shorting a position in the hedging instrument.

B. Measuring the Variance of a Portfolio with More than Two Bonds

Thus far we have looked at the variance and standard deviation for a portfolio consisting of two bonds. The extension to three bonds is as follows:

$$
\mathrm{var}(r_{\mathrm{Port}}) = W_1^2 \mathrm{var}(r_1) + W_2^2 \mathrm{var}(r_2) + W_3^2 \mathrm{var}(r_3)
$$
$$
+ 2W_1 W_2 \mathrm{cov}(r_1, r_2) + 2W_1 W_3 \mathrm{cov}(r_1, r_3) + 2W_2 W_3 \mathrm{cov}(r_2, r_3)
$$

In other words, the portfolio's variance is the sum of the weighted variances of the individual bonds plus the sum of the weighted covariances of the bonds.

The formula for the portfolio variance and standard deviation can be generalized to any number of bonds. The computation of a portfolio of J bonds requires the computation of all pairwise covariances. Typically, the formula for the portfolio's variance is presented using the mathematical notation from matrix algebra. While we will not use that notation here, the key input is the variance-covariance matrix. This is nothing more than a table that has variances of each bond in the diagonal of the table and the covariance between each pair of bonds as the off-diagonal terms. For a portfolio of J bonds, there will be J variances that must be computed plus all of the covariances. The number of covariances will be $J(J + 1)/2 - J$. Thus, for a portfolio of J bonds, the number of inputs (variances plus covariances) that must be estimated is equal to

$$\text{number of variances and covariances} = \frac{J(J + 1)}{2}$$

C. Implementation Problems

If the standard deviation is used as the measure of risk, this means that the variance and covariance for each bond must be estimated to compute the portfolio's standard deviation. Let's look at two major problems with this approach. After we discuss these problems, we will see how to handle this situation.

The first problem with this approach is that the number of estimated inputs increases dramatically as the number of bonds in the portfolio or the number of bonds being considered for inclusion in the portfolio increases. For example, consider a manager who wants to construct a portfolio in which there are 5,000 bonds that are candidates for inclusion in the portfolio. (If this number sounds large, consider that the broad-based bond market indexes have much more than this number of bonds.) Then the number of variances and covariances that must be estimated is

$$\text{Number of variances and covariances} = \frac{5,000(5,000 + 1)}{2}$$

$$= 12,502,500$$

That is a good size matrix that requires calculation and working with to estimate a portfolio's standard deviation or risk.

The second problem is that whether it is 55 variances and covariances for a 10-bond portfolio or 12,502,500 for a 5,000-bond portfolio, these values must still be estimated. Where does the portfolio manager obtain these values? They must be estimated from historical data. While equity portfolio managers have the luxury of working with a long time series of returns on stocks, bond portfolio managers do not have good sources of historical bond data. In addition, even with time series data on the return of a particular bond, a portfolio manager must question what the returns mean. The reason is that the characteristics of a bond change over time.

For example, consider a 10-year Treasury note issued 8 years ago and for which quarterly returns have been calculated. The first quarterly return is the return on a 10-year Treasury note. However, the second quarterly return is the return on a 9¾-year Treasury note. The third quarterly return is the return on a 9.5-year Treasury note, and so on. If that original 10-year Treasury note is in the current portfolio and the manager wants to estimate the standard deviation for that security, looking at its historical standard deviation will not be meaningful. This security is now a 2-year Treasury note since it was purchased 8 years ago and will not necessarily share the return volatility characteristics of the earlier maturities it had. It is not only the changing time to maturity that will affect the historical data and render it of limited use, but there are some securities whose characteristics change dramatically over time because of call provisions. For example, in Level II (Chapter 3) we discussed mortgage-backed securities. CMO support bonds have average lives that change dramatically due to prepayments and this will affect the historical return pattern.

Now, if we couple the problem of a large number of estimates required and the lack of good data, we can see another major problem. Consider a 100-bond portfolio. There are 5,050 inputs that must be estimated. Suppose that just 10% are misestimated because of a lack of good historical or meaningful data. This means that there will be 505 misestimated numbers and this could have a material impact on the estimated portfolio risk.

SECTION V DURATION MEASURES

Because of the problems with using historical data to estimate the standard deviation, bond portfolio managers have turned to factor models. **Factor models** seek to analyze historical data and identify the key risk factors that drive bond returns. The risk of a bond portfolio is then gauged in terms of the exposure of a portfolio to these risk factors.

Several studies have examined the factors that drive returns. At Level II (Chapter 1) we discussed these studies. The conclusion of these studies is that three factors tend to drive Treasury bond returns: (1) changes in the level of interest rates, (2) twists in the shape of the yield curve (i.e., flattening and steepening), and (3) changes in the curvature of the yield curve. The first factor typically explains 90% of Treasury bond returns and the second factor about 8%. The third factor's importance is minor relative to the first two factors. Consequently, a manager needs measures of a portfolio's exposure to changes in the first two factors.

As we explained at Levels I and II, a portfolio's duration is used to measure its exposure to changes in the level of interest rates assuming a parallel shift in the yield. For a portfolio, *duration is interpreted as the approximate percentage change in the market value of a portfolio for a 100 basis point change in interest rates assuming a parallel shift in the yield curve.* So, a portfolio duration of 4 means that the portfolio's market value will change by approximately 4% for a 100 basis point change in the interest rate for all maturities. At Level I (Chapter 7) we explained how to compute the duration of a portfolio given the duration of the individual securities included in the portfolio.

There are different duration measures used to quantify a securities exposure to a parallel shift in the yield curve. They are modified duration, Macaulay duration, and effective duration. As explained at Level I (Chapter 7), modified duration assumes that when interest rates change, the cash flow does not change. This is a severe limitation for measuring the exposure of a bond with an embedded option (e.g., callable bonds, mortgage-backed securities, and some asset-backed securities) to changes in interest rates. Macaulay duration is related to modified duration and suffers from the same limitation of failing to consider how the cash flow can change when interest rates change. In contrast, effective duration takes into account how changes in interest rates can affect the cash flow. Thus, it is the appropriate measure for bonds with embedded options.

The calculation of a bond's duration requires the use of a valuation model. Duration is found by shocking (i.e., changing) interest rates and determining what the new value of the security will be. Consequently, the duration measure is only as good as the valuation model. We explained how the effective duration of a bond with an embedded option is computed using the binomial model at Level II (Chapter 2) and for mortgage-backed and asset-backed securities at Level II (Chapter 5).

Exposure of a portfolio to twists in the shape of the yield curve is measured by rate durations. A rate duration is a measure of the exposure of the portfolio to a change in the yield for one specific maturity. In theory, there is a rate duration for every maturity. In practice, a rate duration is computed for certain "key" maturities and these durations are called key rate durations. Thus, a portfolio's key rate durations measure a portfolio's exposure to changes in twists in the yield curve. We discussed key rate duration at Level I (Chapter 7).

The historical evidence on the factors that drive bond returns has focused on Treasury returns. One would expect that other factors influence the return on portfolios that include non-Treasury securities as well as Treasury securities. The most obvious is a portfolio's exposure to changes in spreads. For portfolios that include bonds outside of the domestic market, a duration must also be computed. The problem is that such a portfolio's exposure is to changes not only in domestic interest rates but to interest rates in all the economies whose bonds are represented in the portfolio.

In this section we will discuss various topics pertaining to portfolio duration that are important in understanding the chapters to follow.

A. Portfolio Duration

A portfolio's duration can be obtained by calculating the weighted average of the duration of the bonds in the portfolio. The weight is the proportion of the portfolio that a security comprises. Mathematically, a portfolio's duration can be calculated as follows:

$$w_1 D_1 + w_2 D_2 + w_3 D_3 + \dots + w_K D_K$$

where

w_i = market value of bond i/market value of the portfolio
D_i = duration of bond i
K = number of bonds in the portfolio

To illustrate this calculation, consider the following 3-bond portfolio in which all three bonds are option free:

Bond	Par amount owned	Market Value
10% 5-year	$4 million	$4,000,000
8% 15-year	5 million	4,231,375
14% 30-year	1 million	1,378,586

In this illustration, it is assumed that the next coupon payment for each bond is six months from now. The market value for the portfolio is $9,609,961. The market price per $100 par value of each bond, its yield, and its duration are given below:

Bond	Price ($)	Yield (%)	Duration
10% 5-year	100.0000	10	3.861
8% 15-year	84.6275	10	8.047
14% 30-year	137.8586	10	9.168

In this illustration, K is equal to 3 and:

w_1 = $4,000,000/$9,609,961 = 0.416 D_1 = 3.861
w_2 = $4,231,375/$9,609,961 = 0.440 D_2 = 8.047
w_3 = $1,378,586/$9,609,961 = 0.144 D_3 = 9.168

The portfolio's duration is:

$$0.416 \, (3.861) + 0.440 \, (8.047) + 0.144 \, (9.168) = 6.47$$

A portfolio duration of 6.47 means that for a 100 basis point change in the yield for *all* three bonds, the market value of the portfolio will change by approximately 6.47%. But keep in mind, the yield on all three bonds must change by 100 basis points for the duration measure to be useful. This is a critical assumption and its importance cannot be overemphasized. We introduced this assumption at Levels I and II.

An alternative procedure for calculating the duration of a portfolio is to calculate the dollar price change for a given number of basis points for each security in the portfolio and then adding up all the price changes. Dividing the total of the price changes by the initial market value of the portfolio produces a percentage price change that can be adjusted to obtain the portfolio's duration.

For example, consider the 3-bond portfolio shown above. Suppose that we calculate the dollar price change for each bond in the portfolio based on its respective duration for a 50 basis point change in yield. We would then have:

Bond	Market value	Duration	Change in value for 50 bp yield change
10% 5-year	$4,000,000	3.861	$77,220
8% 15-year	4,231,375	8.047	170,249
14% 30-year	1,378,586	9.168	63,194
		Total	$310,663

Thus, a 50 basis point change in all rates changes the market value of the 3-bond portfolio by $310,663. Since the market value of the portfolio is $9,609,961, a 50 basis point change produced a change in value of 3.23% ($310,663 divided by $9,609,961). Since duration is the approximate percentage change for a 100 basis point change in rates, this means that the portfolio duration is 6.46 (found by doubling 3.23). This is the same value for the portfolio's duration as found earlier.

1. Contribution to Portfolio Duration

Some portfolio managers look at their exposure to an issue or to a sector in terms of the market value percentage of that issue or sector in the portfolio. A better measure of exposure of an individual issue or sector to changes in interest rates is in terms of its contribution to portfolio duration. This is found by multiplying the percentage that the individual issue or sector is of the portfolio by the duration of the individual issue or sector. That is,

$$\text{contribution to portfolio duration}$$
$$= \frac{\text{market value of issue or sector}}{\text{market value of portfolio}} \times \text{duration of issue or sector}$$

The exposure can also be cast in terms of dollar exposure. To do this, the dollar duration of the issue or sector is used instead of the duration of the issue or sector.

For example, the contribution to duration for the 10.5% 5-year bond in the 3-bond portfolio used to illustrate how to calculate portfolio duration is:

$$\frac{\text{market value of 10.5\% 5-year bond}}{\text{market value of portfolio}} \times 3.861$$

$$\frac{\$4,000,000}{\$9,609,964} \times 3.861 = 1.61$$

A portfolio manager who wants to determine the contribution to portfolio duration of a sector relative to the contribution of the same sector in a broad-based market index can compute the difference between the two contributions. This will be illustrated in more detail in Chapter 3.

2. Allowing for Leverage and Derivatives in Computing Duration

The question is why bother looking at dollar price changes for each position in the portfolio if the same duration is computed by just calculating a weighted average of the durations? The reason is that when a manager borrows to leverage a portfolio and/or uses derivatives, it is easier to compute the portfolio's duration using this approach. The portfolio is then composed of the assets, liabilities, and derivatives. The percentage price change of a portfolio that includes borrowed funds and derivatives is equal to:

$$\frac{\begin{array}{l}\text{dollar price change of all the bonds when rates change}\\ -\ \ \text{dollar price change of the liabilities when rates change}\\ +\ \ \text{dollar price change of the derivatives when rates change}\end{array}}{\text{total change in the portfolio value when rates change}}$$

Dividing the total change in the portfolio value by the initial value of the portfolio and adjusting based on the number of basis points used to change rates gives the duration of the portfolio.

If the liabilities are short term, then the duration value of a short-term liability like that of a short-term asset will be small. In Chapter 7, we look at how to calculate the dollar price change for derivative instruments.

To illustrate the above calculation of portfolio duration, suppose that in our previous portfolio $2 million was borrowed to buy the securities in our 3-bond portfolio and that there are no derivatives in the portfolio. Since $2 million was borrowed, the amount of the client's funds invested (i.e., the equity) is $7,609,961. The client is interested in how the rate changes will affect the equity investment of $7,609,961. Suppose further that the funds are borrowed via a 3-month reverse repurchase agreement so that the duration of the liabilities is close to zero and the dollar price change in the liabilities for a 50 basis point change in rates is close to zero. Then the change in the value of the portfolio for a 50 basis point change in rates is as follows:

$$\frac{\begin{array}{ll}\text{dollar price change of the bonds} & =\ \ \$310,663\\ -\ \ \text{dollar price change of the liability} & =\ \ \ \ \ \ \ \ \ \ 0\end{array}}{\begin{array}{ll}\text{total change in portfolio value} & =\ \ \$310,663\end{array}}$$

Thus, the percentage change in the portfolio's value for a 50 basis point change in rates is 4.08% ($310,663 divided by $7,609,961). The portfolio's duration is then 8.16. The higher duration with the $2 million short-term reverse repo borrowing (8.16 versus 6.47) is due to the leveraging of the portfolio.

3. Controlling Interest Rate Risk

The general principle in controlling interest rate risk is to combine the dollar value exposure of the current portfolio and that of another position so that it is equal to the target dollar exposure. This means that the manager must be able to accurately measure the dollar exposure of both the current portfolio and the other position employed to alter the exposure. We will refer to the other position that is used to adjust the current portfolio to achieve the target dollar exposure as the "controlling position." The controlling position could be simply the sale of cash market instruments in the portfolio, the short sale of Treasuries, the purchase of bonds, and/or positions in derivative instruments.

Dollar duration can be used to approximate the change in the dollar value of a bond or bond portfolio to changes in interest rates. Suppose that a manager has a $250 million portfolio with a duration of 5 and wants to reduce the duration to 4. Thus, the target duration for the portfolio is 4. Given the target duration, a target dollar duration for say a 50 basis point rate change can be obtained. A target duration of 4 means that for a 100 basis point change in rates (assuming a parallel shift in rates of all maturities), the target percentage change in the portfolio's value is 4%. For a 50 basis point change, the target percentage change in the portfolio's value is 2%. Multiplying the 2% by $250 million gives a target dollar duration of $5 million for a 50 basis point change in rates.

The manager must then determine the dollar duration of the current portfolio for a 50 basis point change in rates. Since the current duration for the portfolio is 5, the current dollar duration for a 50 basis point change in interest rates is $6.25 million. The target dollar duration is then compared to the current dollar duration. The difference between the two dollar durations is the dollar exposure that must be provided by the controlling position. If the target dollar duration exceeds the current dollar duration, a controlling position must be such that it increases the dollar exposure by the difference. If the target dollar duration is less than the current dollar duration, a controlling position must be created such that it decreases the dollar exposure by the difference.

Once a controlling position is taken, the portfolio's dollar duration is equal to the current dollar duration without the controlling position plus the dollar duration of the controlling position. That is,

> portfolio's dollar duration
> = current dollar duration without controlling position
> + dollar duration with controlling position

The objective is to control the portfolio's interest rate risk by establishing a controlling position such that the portfolio's dollar duration is equal to the target dollar duration. That is,

> portfolio's dollar duration = target dollar duration

or, equivalently,

> target dollar duration
> = current dollar duration without controlling position
> + dollar duration of controlling position   (6)

Over time, the portfolio's dollar duration will move away from the target dollar duration. The manager can alter the controlling position to adjust the portfolio's dollar duration to the target dollar duration.

In Chapter 7 where we discuss the price volatility characteristics and duration of derivative instruments, we will see how these instruments can be used to alter the dollar duration of a portfolio.

Exhibit 11: Data for the Salomon Brothers' BIG Index as of May 1, 1998 and a Hypothetical Portfolio

(a) Salomon Brothers' BIG Index

Sector	Sector weight (%)	Effective duration	Spread duration*
Treasury	41.38	5.19	0
Government sponsored	7.38	4.81	4.73
Mortgage	29.52	2.46	3.41
Corporate	21.72	5.99	5.89
Index	100.00	4.53	2.63

(b) Hypothetical Portfolio

Sector	Sector weight (%)	Effective duration	Spread duration*
Treasury	30.00	5.19	—
Government sponsored	5.00	4.81	4.73
Mortgage	40.00	3.09	3.41
Corporate	25.00	5.99	5.89
Portfolio	100.00	4.53	3.07

* Spread is defined in terms of OAS.

B. Duration of a Market Index

In the same way that the effective duration of a portfolio is computed, the duration of a market index can be computed since a market index is simply a portfolio. Let's look at how the duration of a broad-based bond market index is computed. Panel a in Exhibit 11 shows for the four sectors of the Salomon Brothers' Broad-Investment Grade (BIG) Index the weights for each sector and the effective duration for each sector as of May 1, 1998. The effective duration for the index as reported by Salomon Brothers for that date was 4.53, calculated by multiplying the sector weights by the effective duration for the sector and summing. The effective duration for the index is found as follows:

$$W_{Tre} D_{Tre} + W_{GS} D_{GS} + W_{Mort} D_{Mort} + W_{Corp} D_{Corp}$$

where the subscripts *Tre*, *GS*, *Mort*, and *Corp* denote the Treasury, government sponsored, mortgage, and corporate sectors, respectively. Substituting the values reported in Exhibit 5 into the above equation we obtain the index's effective duration of 4.53:

$$0.4138 (5.19) + 0.0738 (4.81) + 0.2952 (2.46) + 0.2172 (5.99) = 4.53$$

The index's effective duration of 4.53 means that if the yield for all four sectors increased by 100 basis points and the option-adjusted spread (OAS) did not change, then the index's value will change by approximately 4.53%.

C. Spread Duration for Fixed-Rate Bonds

Duration is a measure of the change in the value of a bond for a parallel shift in interest rates. The interest rate that is assumed to shift is the Treasury rate. However, for non-Treasury securities, the yield is equal to the Treasury yield plus a spread to the Treasury yield curve. We discussed the "spread sectors" of the bond market at Level I. The risk that the price of a bond changes due to changes in spreads in the marketplace is referred to as **spread risk**. A measure of how a non-Treasury issue's price will change if the spread sought by the market changes is called **spread duration**.

1. Types of Spread Duration Measures

The problem is, what spread is assumed to change? As explained at Level I (Chapter 6), there are three spread measures that are used for fixed-rate bonds: nominal spread, zero-volatility spread, and option-adjusted spread.

The **nominal spread** is the traditional spread measure. That is, it is the difference between the yield on a non-Treasury issue and the yield on a comparable maturity Treasury issue. Thus, spread duration when spread is defined as the nominal spread indicates the approximate percentage change in price for a 100 basis point change in the nominal spread holding the Treasury yield constant.

The **zero-volatility spread**, also called the **static spread**, is the spread that when added to the Treasury spot rate curve will make the present value of the cash flows (when discounted at the spot rates plus the spread) equal to the price of the bond plus accrued interest. It is a measure of the spread over the Treasury spot rate curve. When spread is defined in this way, spread duration is the approximate percentage change in price for a 100 basis point change in the zero-volatility spread holding the Treasury spot rate curve constant.

The **option-adjusted spread** is another spread measure. Spread duration based on OAS can be interpreted as the approximate percentage change in price of a non-Treasury issue for a 100 basis point change in the OAS, holding the Treasury rates constant. So, for example, if a corporate bond has a spread duration of 4, this means that if the OAS changes by 20 basis points, the price of the corporate will change by approximately 0.8% ($0.04 \times 0.002 \times 100$).[10]

How do you know whether a spread duration for a fixed-rate bond is a spread based on the nominal spread, zero-volatility spread, or the OAS? You do not know. You must ask the broker/dealer or vendor of the analytical system.[11]

2. Spread Duration for a Portfolio and an Index

The spread duration for a portfolio is found by computing a market weighted average of the spread duration for each sector. The same is true for a market index.

Let's use the data reported in panel a of Exhibit 11 for the Salomon Brothers' BIG Index on May 1, 1998 to illustrate this. The last column of the exhibit reports the spread duration for the spread sectors. Spread duration in this index is based on OAS. The spread duration for the index is found as follows:

$$0.4138\,(0) + 0.0738\,(4.73) + 0.2952\,(3.41) + 0.2172\,(5.89) = 2.63$$

The computed value of 2.63 agrees with the value reported at the bottom of Exhibit 11. This value is interpreted as follows: if the OAS of all spread sectors changes by 100 basis points while Treasury yields do not change, then the index's value will change by approximately 2.63%.

Given the effective duration and spread duration of a portfolio and a bond index, a manager can compare the exposure of his or her portfolio to that of the index. For example, suppose that an analysis of a manager's portfolio is as shown in panel b of Exhibit 11.

---

[10] The procedure for calculating a spread duration where the spread is defined as the OAS is as following. Using a valuation model such as binomial model explained at Level II (Chapter 2), the interest rate tree is kept constant but the OAS is shocked up and down by the same number of basis points. In the numerator of the effective duration formula presented at Levels I and II, the two values are then the values when the OAS is reduced and when it is increased.

[11] To add further to the confusion of spread duration, consider the term OAS duration that is referred to by some market participants. What does that mean? On the one hand, it could mean simply the spread duration that we just described. On the other hand, many market participants have used it interchangeably with the term "effective duration." Once again, the only way to know what an OAS duration is measuring is to ask the broker/dealer or vendor.

Assume that the benchmark index is the Salomon Brothers' BIG Index. The portfolio's duration of 4.53 matches that of the index (see Exhibit 11). Thus, the portfolio has the same exposure to a small parallel shift in Treasury rates as that of the index. However, the portfolio has greater exposure to spread risk. Notice that the portfolio is underweighted in Treasury securities relative to the index (30.00% versus 41.38%) and so has greater exposure to the spread sectors. The largest deviation from the index sector exposure is in the mortgage market (29.52% versus 40.00%). The portfolio's spread duration is 3.07 versus 2.63 for the index.

D. Contribution to Duration of Foreign Bonds

In describing how to compute the duration of a portfolio, it was assumed that all the bonds are U.S.-dollar-pay bonds whose coupon rate is based on a U.S. rate. When a portfolio includes non-U.S. bonds or foreign bonds, the estimation of the contribution to a portfolio's duration by including a foreign bond is not straightforward.

For example, suppose a portfolio consists of government bonds of the United States, Germany, Canada, France, the U.K., and Japan. Assume further that you are told that the duration of this portfolio comprised of both U.S. and foreign government bonds is 6. What does that mean? The quick interpretation is that if "rates" change by 100 basis points, the value of this portfolio will change by approximately 6%. But which country's rates changed by 100 basis points? Germany? Canada? France? U.S.? Japan? To interpret duration as we just did assumes that the rates of all countries change by 100 basis points. That is, it assumes that rates are perfectly correlated for all of these countries so that they move up and down in unison.

Obviously, this interpretation of duration is not meaningful. Rather, a measure of duration for a U.S. portfolio that includes foreign bonds must recognize the correlation between the movement in rates in the U.S. and each non-U.S. country. Lee Thomas and Ram Willner suggest a methodology for computing the contribution of a foreign bond's duration to the duration of a domestic portfolio.[12]

The Thomas-Willner methodology begins by expressing the change in a bond's value in terms of a change in the foreign yield as follows:

change in value of foreign bond
= duration × change in foreign yield × 100

From the perspective of a U.S. manager, the concern is the change in value of the foreign bond when domestic (U.S.) rates change. This can be determined by incorporating the relationship between changes in domestic (U.S.) rates and changes in foreign rates as follows:

change in value of foreign bond = duration
× (change in foreign yield given a change in domestic yield) × 100

The relationship between the change in foreign yield and the change in U.S. yield can be estimated empirically using monthly data for each country. The following relationship is estimated:

$$\Delta y_{f,t} = \alpha + \beta \, \Delta y_{US,t}$$

---

[12] Lee R. Thomas and Ram Willner, "Measuring the Duration of an Internationally Diversified Portfolio," *Journal of Portfolio Management* (Fall 1997), pp. 93-100.

Exhibit 12: Country Betas

Country	β	(t-stats)	R^2
Australia	1.04	(8.68)	0.49
Austria	0.23	(3.61)	0.13
Belgium	0.29	(3.00)	0.09
Canada	0.89	(8.67)	0.49
Denmark	0.48	(3.68)	0.14
France	0.51	(4.95)	0.23
Germany	0.42	(5.32)	0.26
Holland	0.45	(5.51)	0.27
Ireland	0.55	(4.65)	0.21
Italy	0.43	(2.53)	0.06
Japan	0.30	(2.75)	0.08
Spain	0.47	(2.82)	0.08
Sweden	0.49	(2.95)	0.09
Switzerland	0.25	(2.59)	0.07
UK	0.51	(4.30)	0.18

Source: Exhibit 1 in Ram Willner, "Improved Measurement of Duration Contributions of Foreign Bonds in Domestic Portfolios," Chapter 8 in Frank J. Fabozzi (ed.), *Perspectives on International Fixed Income Investing* (New Hope, PA: Frank J. Fabozzi Associates, 1998), p. 169.

where

$$\Delta y_{f,t} = \text{change in a foreign bond's yield in month } t$$
$$\Delta y_{\text{US},t} = \text{change in U.S. yield in month time } t$$

and α and β are the parameters to be estimated for the countries whose bonds are candidates for inclusion in the portfolio. The parameter β_i is called the **country beta**. The duration that is attributed to a foreign bond in a U.S. portfolio is found by multiplying the country beta by the duration.

Exhibit 12 shows the estimated country betas for the period July 1992 to July 1997 of a number of countries versus the United States. For example, consider the U.K. This country's beta is 0.51. This means that if the duration for a U.K. bond is calculated to be 4, the duration contribution to a U.S. portfolio is not 4 but 4 times 0.51 or 2.04. Therefore, a change of 50 basis points in U.S. rates would result in an approximate change in value of 1.02% for a U.K. bond.

SECTION VI
KEY POINTS

❏ *The variance of a probability distribution is a measure of the dispersion of the outcomes of a random variable around its expected value.*

❏ *The standard deviation is the square root of the variance.*

❏ *The standard deviation of the return of a bond is used as a measure of the bond's risk.*

❏ *The standard deviation is a misleading measure of risk if the probability distribution for bond returns is not symmetric (i.e, if the distribution is skewed).*

❏ *In many applications of probability theory, it is assumed that the underlying probability distribution is a normal distribution.*

❏ *A normal probability distribution is a symmetric distribution around the expected value and the only information needed to make probability statements about outcomes is the expected value and the standard deviation.*

❑ *Two issues that must be addressed to determine whether a historical distribution can be characterized as a normal distribution are whether or not the data fit the values predicted by the normal distribution and whether or not there is serial correlation of returns.*

❑ *One way to overcome the problem of negative skewedness observed for bond returns is to convert returns into the logarithm of returns.*

❑ *Downside risk measures focus on only that portion of the return from an investment that is below a specified level.*

❑ *Downside risk measures include target semivariance and shortfall probability.*

❑ *For the different downside risk measures, the portfolio manager must define the target return so that returns less than the target return represent adverse consequences.*

❑ *The target semivariance is a measure of the dispersion of the outcomes below the target return specified by the portfolio manager.*

❑ *The semivariance is a special case of the target semivariance where the target return is the expected value.*

❑ *When a probability distribution is symmetric around the expected value, using the semivariance as a risk measure will give the same ranking of risk as using the variance or standard deviation.*

❑ *Shortfall risk is the probability that the outcome will have a value less than the target return.*

❑ *A special case of shortfall risk is the risk of loss which is based on a target return of zero.*

❑ *While theoretically the target semivariance is superior to the variance (standard deviation) as a risk measure it is not used in bond portfolio management to any significant extent because of the ambiguity in its use, the poor statistical understanding of these measures, and the difficulty of forecasting the necessary required data.*

❑ *In a value at risk measure the portfolio manager specifies a target probability and then computes the return that the outcomes will not fall below that return that percentage of times.*

❑ *Computing the value at risk begins with the computation of daily earnings at risk (DEaR).*

❑ *Value at risk relies good estimates of the variance of the returns and the effective durations, and assumes that the probability distribution of returns is normal.*

❑ *A portfolio's variance is not simply the weighted average of the variance of the return of the component bonds.*

❑ *A portfolio's variance depends not only on the variance of the return of the component bonds but also the covariances (correlations) between each pair of bonds.*

❑ *The lower the covariance (correlation) between the returns of bonds in the portfolio, the greater the reduction in the portfolio's variance.*

❑ *The two problems in computing a portfolio's variance are (1) the number of estimated inputs increases dramatically as the number of bonds in the portfolio or the number of bonds being considered for inclusion in the portfolio increases and (2) the difficulty of obtaining meaningful historical return data for bonds.*

❑ *Duration can be used to overcome the problems associated with using historical standard deviations to compute the risk of a bond portfolio.*

❑ *Studies of the returns on Treasury bonds found that the two dominant factors that drive returns are (1) changes in the level of interest rates, and (2) twists in the shape of the yield curve (i.e., flattening and steepening).*

❑ *A portfolio's duration is used to measure its exposure to changes in the level of interest rates assuming a parallel shift in the yield.*

❑ *The appropriate measure of duration for the individual bonds in the portfolio that is used to compute a portfolio's duration is effective duration.*

❑ *Effective duration measures the sensitivity of a bond to changes in interest rates allowing for the cash flow to change when interest rates change.*

❑ *The calculation of a bond's duration requires the use of a valuation model and the duration estimate is only as good as the valuation model.*

❑ *The effect of exposure of a portfolio to twists in the shape of the yield curve is measured by a portfolio's key rate durations.*

❑ *A portfolio duration can be computed from the effective duration for the individual bonds in the portfolio.*

❑ *A portfolio's duration is found by computing the weighted average of the effective duration of the bonds in the portfolio where the weight assigned to each bond is the percentage of the market value of the bond relative to the market value of the portfolio.*

❑ *Contribution to portfolio duration is a better measure of exposure of an individual issue or sector to changes in interest rates than the weight of an individual issue or sector in a portfolio.*

❑ *The contribution to portfolio duration is found by multiplying the percentage that the individual issue or sector is of the portfolio by the duration of the individual issue or sector*

❑ *Leverage and derivatives affect a portfolio's duration.*

❑ *The interest rate risk of a portfolio can be controlled by first computing the difference between the current dollar duration of the portfolio and the target dollar duration, and then taking a position to attain the target duration.*

❑ *Since a bond market index is simply a portfolio of all the issues in the index, the duration of a bond market index is computed in the same manner as the duration of a portfolio.*

❑ *A portfolio's spread duration is a measure of the exposure of a portfolio to changes in spreads.*

❑ *When a portfolio includes foreign bonds, the change in the value of the portfolio depends on the change in yields in the countries in which the foreign bonds originated that are held.*

❑ *When a portfolio includes foreign bonds, the portfolio's duration is complicated by the fact that the interest rates in all countries whose bonds are represented in the portfolio do not change by the same number of basis points.*

❑ *The contribution of a foreign bond to a portfolio's duration must take into account the correlation between the movement in interest rates in the domestic market of the manager and each foreign market. This is captured using yield beta.*

END OF CHAPTER QUESTIONS

1. Mr. Felder is a consultant to the Hole Punchers pension fund. Suppose that the bond market index selected by the trustees is a customized index, which the trustees refer to as the "HP Index." On January 1 the trustees asked Mr. Felder to assess the likelihood that if its bond portfolio is indexed to the HP Index the return for the year will exceed 14%. The trustees also asked Mr. Felder to determine the likelihood that the return for the year will be at least 0.5%.

    To comply with the trustees' request, Mr. Felder undertook a statistical analysis of the HP Index. He found that the 15-year historical *annual* average return was 5% with a standard deviation of 4.5%. He also found that the distribution of the annual returns was approximately normal.

    a. What would Mr. Felder report to the trustees as to the probability that the return this year will exceed 14%?
    b. What would Mr. Felder report to the trustees as to the probability that the return this year will be at least 0.5%.

2. A trustee of a pension fund is discussing with one of the fund's portfolio managers a consultant's report regarding the probability that the fund will realize various returns for its bond portfolio. The trustee questioned the portfolio manager as to the continual emphasis in the consultant's report that the results assume that the "return distribution is normal" and that the results "depended on the standard deviation." The trustee also asked the portfolio manager what would be the implications for the results given in the consultant's report if the standard deviation is greater than that assumed. How should the portfolio manager respond?

3. A consultant is discussing with the trustees of a pension plan the likelihood of realizing returns less than the amount necessary to meet the estimated liabilities of the fund. In her discussion, the consultant stated that it is assumed that the distribution for future returns is normal rather than being characterized by "fat tails." If there are fat tails, the consultant noted, the risk of not meeting the estimated liabilities is underestimated." One of the trustees asked you to explain what the consultant meant by this statement. How would you respond?

4. The board of directors of a bank has retained you to advise the board regarding the risk of the strategies pursued by its portfolio managers. At the current time, the board is using the standard deviation of the future return on the portfolio as a measure of risk. Several board members do not feel that this measure is appropriate because it does not recognize the funding costs associated with a strategy and the need to obtain a minimum spread over that funding cost. The board wants to know if there are any other measures similar to the standard deviation that can be used as a measure of risk that take into consideration the bank's funding cost and spread requirement. What would you recommend to the board?

5. a. When the return distribution is not a normally distributed, why is the semivariance a better measure of risk?
   b. Why is the semivariance not commonly used in bond portfolio management even when a return distribution is not normally distributed?

6. a. What is the relationship between "shortfall risk" and "risk of loss"?
   b. What is the limitation of the shortfall risk measure?

7. Suppose that the probability for the change in the value of a U.S. government bond portfolio over the next five days is normally distributed with an expected value of zero and a standard deviation of $1 million. The manager specifies a target probability of 95% and this is equivalent to a standardized value of 1.65.

   a. What does the standardized value of 1.65 mean?
   b. What is the value at risk for this position?
   c. What is the interpretation for the value at risk found in part b?

8. If a position can be neutralized in one day, why is the daily earnings at risk equal to the value at risk?

9. The following information has been computed for two bond indexes:

	Bond index 1	Bond index 2
Expected value (annual)	6.00%	9.50%
Variance (annual)	10.00	15.00

   Correlation between bond index 1 and bond index 2 = 0.65

   a. What is the standard deviation for the two bond indexes?
   b. What is the covariance between the two bond indexes?
   c. Compute the expected value and the standard deviation for the portfolio given the allocations to bond index 1 shown below with the remainder in bond index 2:

	Allocation to bond index 1				
	20%	30%	60%	70%	80%
Expected value (%)					
Standard deviation					

10. a. What are the computational difficulties of using the standard deviation of a portfolio as a measure of risk?
    b. How does a factor model attempt to overcome the computational difficulties discussed in part a.

11. a. What is the duration for the following portfolio?

Bond	Market value	Duration
1	$10 million	7.2
2	8 million	6.1
3	4 million	1.1
4	12 million	4.8

    b. What is the contribution to portfolio duration of bond 1?

12. a. What is meant by spread duration?
    b. Why are there different types of spread duration measures?
    c. Suppose that using an analytical system of a commercial vendor a portfolio manager finds that the spread duration of bond K is 2. However, suppose that when the portfolio manager asks a dealer for the spread duration of bond K the dealer reports a value of 3. Explain why this can occur.

13. Suppose that a bond index consists of five sectors and that the effective duration and spread duration (based on OAS) for each sector are as shown below:

Sector	Weight (%)	Effective duration	Spread duration
Treasury	38.00	4.60	—
Agencies	7.00	4.10	3.90
Mortgages	31.00	3.20	6.10
Corporates	20.00	5.10	5.40
ABS	4.00	2.70	5.80

a. What is the (effective) duration for the bond index?

b. What is the spread duration for the bond index?

14. Suppose that a portfolio manager uses as his benchmark the bond index whose characteristics were described in the previous question. Assume further that the characteristics of the portfolio are as follows:

Sector	Weight (%)	Effective duration	Spread duration
Treasury	15.00	4.60	—
Agencies	7.00	4.10	3.90
Mortgages	35.00	3.20	6.10
Corporates	38.00	5.10	5.40
ABS	5.00	2.70	5.80

a. What is the portfolio's (effective) duration?

b. What is the portfolio's spread duration?

c. Compare the portfolio's risk exposure to changes in the level of Treasury rates and to changes in spread relative to the exposure of the bond index.

d. Suppose that the manager altered the portfolio as follows:

Sector	Weight (%)	Effective duration	Spread duration
Treasury	16.00	4.60	—
Agencies	7.00	4.10	3.90
Mortgages	35.00	3.20	6.10
Corporates	20.00	5.10	5.40
ABS	22.00	2.70	5.80
	100.00%	3.76	4.75

How does this portfolio's risk exposure compare to that of the bond index?

15. Tom Reed is a portfolio manager for the MMM Investment Management Company. Recently he received $200 million from a new client to invest. The investment guidelines established by the client allow the manager to leverage the portfolio up to 25% of the $200 million, or $50 million. The investment guidelines impose a restriction on the portfolio's duration. Specifically, the investment guidelines state that the portfolio's duration may not exceed 5.

Mr. Reed invested the $200 million in bonds with a duration of 4. He then used the maximum permissible leverage and purchased $50 million of bonds via a 1-month reverse repo transaction. The $50 million of bonds purchased have a duration of 5.

a. What is the duration of the client's portfolio?

b. Has Mr. Reed violated the duration restriction?

16. A junior portfolio manager reported to a client that the duration of a global bond portfolio that included non-dollar denominated securities is 5. The client asked whether or not he should interpret that value to mean that if interest rates changed by 100 basis points, then the market value of the portfolio would change by approximately 5%. What should be the junior portfolio manager's response?

17. Suppose that a British portfolio manager has invested in several government bonds throughout the world. The portfolio manager has estimated yield betas from the following relationship:

> change in non-British bond's yield in month $t =$
> $\alpha + \beta \times$ (change in 10-year British government rates)

The β in the above relationship is referred to as the yield beta.

a. Suppose that the duration of the 10-year Italian government bond is 6 and that the yield beta is 1.5. What is the estimated change in the value of the Italian government bonds if the 10-year British government bond rate changes by 50 basis points?

b. Suppose that the duration of the 10-year French government bond is 5 and that the yield beta is 0.7. What is the estimated change in the value of the French government bonds if the 10-year British government bond rate changes by 25 basis points?

SOLUTIONS TO END OF CHAPTER QUESTIONS

1. a. Based on the assumption that the distribution of the annual returns for the HP Index is normal, a return greater than 14% would be 9% above the annual average return of 5%. In terms of the number of standard deviations above the average value, it is two standard deviations (9% divided by the standard deviation of 4.5%). From the normal probability distribution Mr. Felder knows that approximately 96% of the time the return will fall within two standard deviations of the average value. This means that there is a 4% probability (100% minus 96%) that the probability will be outside of this range. Since a normal probability distribution is symmetric, this means that half, or 2%, is the probability that the return for the year will be above 14%. So, Mr. Felder would tell the trustees that there is a 2% probability of realizing a return above 14% based on his assumptions.

   b. A return of 0.5% is −4.5% below the average value. In terms of standard deviations, it is one standard deviation below the average value (−4.5% divided by the standard deviation of 4.5%). From the normal probability distribution Mr. Felder knows that within one standard deviation below and above the average value the probability is 68%. Outside of this range, the probability is 32%. Since a normal probability distribution is symmetric, this means that half of 32%, or 16%, is the probability that the return for the year will be less than 0.5%. Consequently, the probability that the return will be greater than 0.5% is 84% (100% minus 16%). So, Mr. Felder would tell the trustees that there is an 84% probability of realizing a return greater than 0.5% based on his assumptions.

2. Statements about the probability of an outcome, such as the return on a bond portfolio, depend on the probability distribution assumed and the standard deviation assumed. The assumption that the return distribution is normal means that given the expected value for the return (i.e., the average value) and the standard deviation, the consultant was able to determine the probability of realizing various returns cited in the consultant's report. The results depend on the standard deviation also. With a higher standard deviation, the probability of realizing a given return increases.

3. The tails of a probability distribution indicate the likelihood of getting extreme values. The lower tail of a return distribution indicates the risk of getting values in the lower range — that is, the lower tail indicates the risk of not realizing a specified return. When a probability distribution has "fat tails," this means that the probability in the lower tail is greater than the probability in the lower tail of a normal probability distribution. Consequently, if the return distribution has fat tails but is assumed to be a normal distribution, there is an underestimate the probability of not realizing a specified return.

4. Rather than using the traditional standard deviation, a target semivariance can be used. The target in the case of the bank would be the target return as identified by the bank's funding cost plus a spread. Thus, the target semivariance would indicate the risk in terms of realizing a return less than the bank's funding cost plus a spread.

5. a. When a return distribution is normally distributed, the variance and the semivariance are equivalent in terms of the ranking of risk. When a return distribution is not normal, the more appropriate measure of risk is the deviation below the expected value. The semivariance measures that exposure.

b. There are three reasons (cited by Kahn in the chapter) of why semivariance is not commonly used. First, its statistical properties are not as well known as the standard deviation (variance) and so is not an ideal choice for risk that can be understand by all market participants. Second, computing it for a large bond portfolio is challenging. Third, if a return distribution is reasonably normal, then the relative rankings of risk based on the standard deviation (variance) will not differ from that for the semivariance.

6. a. Shortfall risk is the ratio of the number of observations below the target return to the total number of observations. When the target return is zero, shortfall risk is referred to as the risk of loss.

b. One problem with shortfall risk is that the magnitude of the losses below the target return is ignored. Also, shortfall risk suffers from the same problems as a semivariance measure: "ambiguity, poor statistical understanding, difficulty of forecasting" (as discussed by Ron Kahn).

7. a. The standardized value indicates the number of standard deviations above or below the mean.

b. The value at risk is the product of the standard deviation of $1 million and the standardized value based on a 95% probability, 1.65. Therefore, the value at risk is $1.65 million.

c. A value at risk of $1.65 million means that there is a 95% probability that the loss in value for this government bond portfolio will be less than $1.65 million in the next five days. Alternatively, a value of risk of $1.65 million means that there is a 5% probability of losing more than $1.65 million in the next five days.

8. Value at risk is derived from daily earnings at risk. Specifically,

$$\text{VaR} = \text{DEaR}\sqrt{\text{days expected until position can be neutralized}}$$

If the number of days until a position can be neutralized is 1, the above relationship indicates the equality of VaR and DEaR.

9. a. The standard deviation for each bond index is simply the square root of the variance. Thus,

	Bond index 1	Bond index
Standard deviation	3.1623	3.8730

b. The covariance is found as follows:

covariance = std dev (bond index 1) × std dev (bond index 2) × correlation

Therefore,

$$3.1623 \times 3.8730 \times 0.65 = 7.96089$$

c.

	Allocation to bond index 1				
	20%	30%	60%	70%	80%
Expected value (%)	8.80	8.45	7.40	7.05	6.70
Standard deviation	3.54	3.40	3.13	3.10	3.09

10. a. To compute the portfolio's standard deviation, the variance and covariance for each bond must be estimated. There are two major problems in obtaining these estimates. First, as the number of bonds in the portfolio or the number of bonds being considered for inclusion in the portfolio increases, the number of estimated inputs (variances and covariances) increases dramatically.

　　　The second problem is obtaining good estimates for the variances and covariances for each bond issue. Typically, historical data must be used to obtain these values. Time series return data in the bond market, particularly for certain types of bonds such as collateralized mortgage obligations, may not be readily available. In addition, even with time series data on the return of a particular bond, the observed returns over time may have little meaning because the characteristic of the observed bond changes over time.

　b. Because of the problems with using historical data to estimate the standard deviation, bond portfolio managers have turned to factor models. Factor models seek to analyze historical return data and identify the key factors that drive bond returns. The risk of a bond portfolio is then measured in terms of its exposure to these risk factors.

11. a.

Bond	Market value	Percent	Duration	Percent × duration
1	10,000,000	29.41176%	7.2	2.1176
2	8,000,000	23.52941%	6.1	1.4353
3	4,000,000	11.76471%	1.1	0.1294
4	12,000,000	35.29412%	4.8	1.6941
Total	34,000,000	100.00000%		5.3765

　b. The contribution to portfolio duration of bond 1 is:

$$\frac{\text{market value of bond 1}}{\text{market value of portfolio}} \times \text{duration of bond 1}$$

therefore,

$$\frac{\$10 \text{ million}}{\$34 \text{ million}} \times 7.2 = 2.1176$$

12. a. Spread duration is the risk exposure of a bond or a bond portfolio to changes in the spread between non-Treasury and Treasury rates.

　b. There are different spread duration measures depending on the measure of spread used. Specifically, one can measure a nominal spread, zero volatility spread, or option-adjusted spread.

　c. The reason this can occur is that the vendor of the analytical system and the dealer may use a different definition for what the spread is. Without qualifying what spread measure it is used, the spread duration measure will be ambiguous and the reported values can be different.

13. a. The portfolio effective duration is 4.16.
　b. The portfolio spread duration is 3.48.

14. a. The portfolio effective duration is 4.17.
    b. The portfolio spread duration is 4.75.
    c. A comparison of the risk exposure of the portfolio and the bond index is provided below:

	Portfolio	Bond index
effective duration	4.17	4.16
spread duration	4.75	3.48

    Both the portfolio and the bond index have the same exposure to a small parallel shift in interest rates. The portfolio has a greater exposure to changes in the spread as evidenced by the higher spread duration for the portfolio. The difference in the spread durations is 1.27. So, if spreads on average change by 50 basis points, for example, the portfolio's value will change by approximately 0.64% more than the bond index.

    d. A comparison of the risk exposure of the portfolio and the bond index is provided below:

	Portfolio	Bond index
effective duration	3.76	4.16
spread duration	4.75	3.48

    This portfolio has a lower duration, and hence less exposure to a small parallel shift in Treasury rates than the bond index. However, the portfolio still has greater exposure to changes in spread than the bond index.

15. a. Since the duration of the $200 million invested is 4, the portfolio's value will change by approximately $8 million for a 100 basis point change in rates. The duration of 5 for the $50 of bonds purchased via a reverse repurchase agreement means that their value will change by approximately $2.5 million for a 100 basis point change in rates. Consequently, the portfolio's value will change by approximately $10.5 million ($8 million plus $2.5 million) for a 100 basis point change in rates. The change in value of the 1-month liability (i.e., the reverse repo) for a 100 basis point change in rates is zero. Therefore, we have

$$
\begin{array}{lll}
\text{dollar duration of the bonds} & = & \$10.5 \text{ million} \\
- \quad \text{dollar duration of the liabilities} & = & \$0 \\
\hline
\text{total change in portfolio value} & = & \$10.5 \text{ million}
\end{array}
$$

    Relating the $10.5 million to the client's $200 million investment (not the amount of funds invested by Mr. Reed of $250 million) means that the portfolio's value changed by 5.25% for a 100 basis point change in rates. Hence, the duration is 5.25.

    b. Since the computed duration for the portfolio is 5.25, Mr. Reed has exceeded the maximum duration of 5 set forth in the investment guidelines.

16. For a portfolio of domestic bonds that are dollar denominated, the client can interpret the duration as suggested. However, the meaning of duration becomes ambiguous in the context of a portfolio with bonds outside the domestic market when interpreted the way suggested The reason is that one must question what

country's interest rates are changing. Basically, the interpretation must be as follows: if the interest rates of every country whose bonds are represented in the portfolio change by 100 basis points, then the portfolio's market value will change by approximately 5%.

17. a. The approximate change in the value of the Italian government bond holdings is found as follows. The duration of the Italian 10-year government bond is 6 and the yield beta is estimated to be 1.5, so the duration is adjusted by multiplying the duration of 6 by 1.5, giving a duration contribution to a British portfolio of 9. For a 100 basis point change in British 10-year rates, the Italian bonds will change by approximately 9% in value. For a 50 basis point change in British 10-year rates the change would be approximately 4.5%.

   b. The approximate change in the value of the French government bond holdings is found as follows. The duration of the French 10-year government bond is 5 and the yield beta is estimated to be 0.7, so the duration is adjusted by multiplying the duration of 5 by 0.7, giving a duration contribution to a British portfolio of 3.5. For a 100 basis point change in British 10-year rates, the French bonds will change by approximately 3.5% in value. For a 25 basis point change in British 10-year rates the change would be approximately 0.875%.

Chapter 3

MANAGING FUNDS AGAINST LIABILITIES

Frank J. Fabozzi, Ph.D., CFA
Adjunct Professor of Finance
School of Management
Yale University

LEARNING OUTCOME STATEMENTS

After reading this chapter you should be able to:

- describe what an immunization strategy is and why it is used.
- identify the interest rate risk exposure for a portfolio whose duration is not equal to the duration of a liability.
- explain why the key to immunization is in constructing a portfolio to match the duration of the investment horizon.
- identify the risks associated with immunizing a portfolio.
- explain the ways in which classical immunization has been extended.
- identify the factors to consider in creating an immunized portfolio.
- describe what a contingent immunization strategy is.
- identify the key considerations in implementing a contingent immunization strategy.
- describe for a contingent immunization strategy the following concepts: safety net level return, excess achievable return, return achievable with an immunization strategy, and trigger point.
- discuss the three conditions for creating an immunized portfolio to satisfy multiple liabilities.
- explain how the appropriate discount rate is selected for determining the present value of liabilities and why this is important.
- illustrate how a cash flow matching strategy can be used to construct a portfolio to satisfy multiple liabilities.
- explain the advantages and disadvantages of a cash flow matching strategy relative to multiple liability immunization.
- explain a combination matching strategy.

SECTION I
INTRODUCTION

In this chapter we will explain strategies for managing bond portfolios to satisfy predetermined liabilities. The two strategies we will discuss are immunization and cash flow matching. **Immunization** is a hybrid strategy having elements of both active and passive strategies. It is used to minimize reinvestment risk over a specified investment horizon. Immunization can be employed to structure a portfolio designed to fund a single liability or multiple liabilities. **Cash flow matching** is used to construct a portfolio designed to fund a schedule of liabilities from portfolio return and asset value, with the portfolio's value diminishing to zero after payment of the last liability.

SECTION II
IMMUNIZATION
STRATEGY FOR
A SINGLE
LIABILITY

Classical immunization can be defined as the process by which a bond portfolio is created having an assured return for a specific time horizon irrespective of interest rate changes.[1] The fundamental principle underlying immunization is to structure a portfolio that balances the change in the value of the portfolio at the end of the investment horizon with the return from the reinvestment of portfolio cash flows (coupon payments and maturing bonds). That is, immunization requires offsetting interest rate risk and reinvestment risk. The general principle of immunization is summarized in Exhibit 1.

Exhibit 1: General Principle of Classical Immunization

Objective: Lock in a minimum target rate and target accumulated value regardless of how interest rates change over the investment horizon.

Risk when interest rates change:
    Reinvestment risk
    Interest rate or price risk

Assumption: Parallel shift in the yield curve (i.e., all yields rise and fall uniformly)

Principle:

    Scenario 1: Interest rates increase

    Implications:

        1. Reinvestment income increases
        2. Value of portfolio of bonds with maturities greater than the investment horizon declines in value

    Goal: Gain in reinvestment income ≥ loss in portfolio value

    Scenario 2: Interest rates decline

    Implications:

        1. Reinvestment income decreases
        2. Value of portfolio of bonds with maturities greater than the investment horizon increases in value

    Goal: Loss in reinvestment income ≤ gain in portfolio value

---

[1] The classical theory of immunization is set forth in F. M. Reddington, "Review of the Principles of Life Insurance Valuations," *Journal of the Institute of Actuaries*, 1952; and Lawrence Fisher and Roman Weil, "Coping with Risk of Interest Rate Fluctuations: Returns to Bondholders from Naive and Optimal Strategies," *Journal of Business* (October 1971), pp. 408-31.

A. Illustration

To accomplish this balancing requires the controlling of duration. By setting the duration of the portfolio equal to the desired portfolio time horizon, the offsetting of positive and negative incremental return sources is highly likely to be achieved. This is a necessary condition for effectively immunized portfolios.

To demonstrate the principle of immunization, consider the situation faced by a life insurance company that sells a guaranteed investment contract (GIC). This policy specifies that for a lump sum payment a life insurance company guarantees that specified dollars will be paid to the policyholder at a specified future date. Or, equivalently, the life insurance company guarantees a specified rate of return on the payment.

For example, suppose that a life insurance company sells a 5-year GIC that guarantees an interest rate of 7.5% per year on a bond-equivalent yield basis (or, equivalently, 3.75% every six months for the next ten 6-month periods). Also suppose that the payment made by the policyholder is $9,642,899. Then the value that the life insurance company has guaranteed the policyholder five years from now is $13,934,413. When investing the $9,642,899, the target accumulated value for the manager of the portfolio of supporting assets is $13,934,413 after five years, which is the same as a target yield of 7.5% on a bond-equivalent basis.

Suppose the manager buys $9,642,899 par value of a bond selling at par with a 7.5% yield to maturity that matures in five years. The portfolio manager will not be assured of realizing a total return at least equal to the target return of 7.5% because to realize 7.5% the coupon interest payments must be reinvested at a minimum rate of 3.75% every six months. That is, the accumulated value will depend on the reinvestment rate.

To demonstrate this, we will suppose that immediately after investing the $9,642,899 in the 7.5% 5-year bond, yields in the market change and stay at the new level for the remainder of the five years. Exhibit 2 illustrates what happens at the end of five years. The first column shows the new yield level. The second column shows the total coupon payments. The third column gives the reinvestment earned over the five years if the coupon payments are reinvested at the new yield level shown in the first column. The price of the bond at the end of five years shown in the fourth column is the par value. The fifth column is the accumulated value from all three sources: coupon interest, reinvestment income, and bond price. The total return is shown in the last column.[2]

If yields do not change so that the coupon payments can be reinvested at 7.5% (3.75% every six months), the portfolio manager will achieve the target accumulated value. If market yields rise, an accumulated value (total return) higher than the target accumulated value (target yield) will be achieved. This is because the coupon payments can be reinvested at a higher rate than the initial yield to maturity. Contrast this with what happens when the yield declines. The accumulated value (total return) will be less than the target accumulated value (target yield). Therefore investing in a coupon bond with a yield to maturity equal to the target yield and a maturity equal to the investment horizon does not assure that the target accumulated value will be achieved.

Suppose that instead of investing in a bond maturing in five years the portfolio manager invests in a 12-year bond with a coupon rate of 7.5% that is selling at par to yield 7.5%. Exhibit 3 presents the accumulated value and total return if the market yield changes immediately after the bond is purchased and remains at the new yield level. The fourth column of the exhibit is the market price of a 7.5% 7-year bond (since five years have passed at the horizon date), assuming the market yields shown

---

[2] The value in this column is found as follows: $2\left(\dfrac{\text{Accumulated value}}{\$9,642,899}\right)^{1/10} - 1$

in the first column. If the market yield increases, the portfolio will fail to achieve the target accumulated value; if the market yield decreases, the accumulated value (total return) will exceed the target accumulated value (target yield).

Exhibit 2: Accumulated Value and Total Return After Five Years for a 5-Year 7.5% Bond Selling to Yield 7.5%

Investment horizon:	5 years	Price:	100.00
Coupon rate:	7.50%	Par value purchased:	$9,642,899
Maturity:	5 years	Purchase price:	$9,642,899
Yield to maturity:	7.50%	Target accumulated value:	$13,934,413

New Yield (%)	Coupon ($)	Reinvestment Income ($)	Price of Bond ($)	Accumulated Value ($)	Total Return (%)
11.00	3,616,087	1,039,753	9,642,899	14,298,739	8.04
10.50	3,616,087	985,615	9,642,899	14,244,601	7.96
10.00	3,616,087	932,188	9,642,899	14,191,175	7.88
9.50	3,616,087	879,465	9,642,899	14,138,451	7.80
9.00	3,616,087	827,436	9,642,899	14,086,423	7.73
8.50	3,616,087	776,093	9,642,899	14,035,079	7.65
8.00	3,616,087	725,426	9,642,899	13,984,412	7.57
7.50	3,616,087	675,427	9,642,899	13,934,413	7.50
7.00	3,616,087	626,087	9,642,899	13,885,073	7.43
6.50	3,616,087	577,398	9,642,899	13,836,384	7.35
6.00	3,616,087	529,352	9,642,899	13,788,338	7.28
5.50	3,616,087	481,939	9,642,899	13,740,925	7.21
5.00	3,616,087	435,153	9,642,899	13,694,139	7.14
4.50	3,616,087	388,985	9,642,899	13,647,971	7.07
4.00	3,616,087	343,427	9,642,899	13,602,414	7.00

Exhibit 3: Accumulated Value and Total Return After Five Years for a 12-Year 7.5% Bond Selling to Yield 7.5%

Investment horizon:	5 years	Price:	100.00
Coupon rate:	7.50%	Par value purchased:	$9,642,899
Maturity:	12 years	Purchase price:	$9,642,899
Yield to maturity:	7.50%	Target accumulated value:	$13,934,413

New Yield (%)	Coupon ($)	Reinvestment Income ($)	Price of Bond ($)	Accumulated Value ($)	Total Return (%)
11.00	3,616,087	1,039,753	8,024,639	12,680,479	5.55
10.50	3,616,087	985,615	8,233,739	12,835,440	5.80
10.00	3,616,087	932,188	8,449,754	12,998,030	6.06
9.50	3,616,087	879,465	8,672,941	13,168,494	6.33
9.00	3,616,087	827,436	8,903,566	13,347,090	6.61
8.50	3,616,087	776,093	9,141,907	13,534,087	6.90
8.00	3,616,087	725,426	9,388,251	13,729,764	7.19
7.50	3,616,087	675,427	9,642,899	13,934,413	7.50
7.00	3,616,087	626,087	9,906,163	14,148,337	7.82
6.50	3,616,087	577,398	10,178,367	14,371,852	8.14
6.00	3,616,087	529,352	10,459,851	14,605,289	8.48
5.50	3,616,087	481,939	10,750,965	14,848,992	8.82
5.00	3,616,087	435,153	11,052,078	15,103,318	9.18
4.50	3,616,087	388,985	11,363,569	15,368,642	9.54
4.00	3,616,087	343,427	11,685,837	15,645,352	9.92

**Exhibit 4: Change in Reinvestment Income and
Price Due to Interest Rate Change After Five Years for a
12-Year 7.5% Bond Selling to Yield 7.5%**

New Yield (%)	Change in Reinvestment Income ($)	Change in Price ($)	Total Change in Accumulated Value ($)
11.0	364,326	(1,618,260)	(1,253,934)
10.5	310,188	(1,409,160)	(1,098,972)
10.0	256,762	(1,193,145)	(936,383)
9.5	204,039	(969,958)	(765,919)
9.0	152,010	(739,333)	(587,323)
8.5	100,666	(500,992)	(400,326)
8.0	49,999	(254,648)	(204,649)
7.5	—	—	—
7.0	(49,340)	263,264	213,924
6.5	(98,029)	535,468	437,439
6.0	(146,075)	816,952	670,877
5.5	(193,487)	1,108,066	914,579
5.0	(240,273)	1,409,179	1,168,905
4.5	(286,441)	1,720,670	1,434,229
4.0	(331,999)	2,042,938	1,710,939

The reason for this result can be seen in Exhibit 4, which summarizes the change in reinvestment income and the change in price resulting from a change in the market yield. For example, if the market yield rises instantaneously by 200 basis points, from 7.5% to 9.5%, reinvestment income will be $204,039 greater; however, the market price of the bond will decrease by $969,958. The net effect is that the accumulated value will be $765,919 less than the target accumulated value. The reverse will be true if the market yield decreases. The change in the price of the bond will more than offset the decline in reinvestment income, resulting in an accumulated value that exceeds the target accumulated value. Now we can see what is happening to the accumulated value. There is a trade-off between interest rate (or price) risk and reinvestment risk. For this 12-year bond, the target accumulated value will be realized only if the market yield does not increase.

Because neither a coupon bond with the same maturity nor a bond with a longer maturity ensures realization of the target accumulated value, maybe a bond with a maturity shorter than five years will. Consider a 7.5% bond with six months remaining to maturity selling at par. Exhibit 5 shows the accumulated value and total return over the 5-year investment horizon. The second column shows the accumulated value after six months. The third column shows the value that is accumulated after five years by reinvesting the value accumulated after six months at the yield shown in the first column.[3]

By investing in this 6-month bond, the manager incurs no price risk, although there is reinvestment risk. The target accumulated value will be achieved only if the market yield remains at 7.5% or rises. Once again, the manager is not assured of achieving the target accumulated value.

If we assume there is a one-time instantaneous change in the market yield, is there a coupon bond that the manager can purchase to assure the target accumulated value whether the market yield rises or falls? The manager should look for a coupon bond so that regardless of how the market yield changes, the change in reinvestment income will be offset by the change in price.

---

[3] This value is found as follows: $10,004,508 $(1 + \text{new yield}/2)^9$

Exhibit 5: Accumulated Value and Total Return After Five Years for a 6-Month 7.5% Bond Selling to Yield 7.5%

Investment horizon:	5 years	Price:	100.00
Coupon rate:	7.50%	Par value purchased:	$9,642,899
Maturity:	0.50 years	Purchase price:	$9,642,899
Yield to maturity:	7.50%	Target accumulated value:	$13,934,413

New Yield (%)	After One Period ($)	Accumulated Value ($)	Total Return (%)
11.00	10,004,508	16,198,241	10.65
10.50	10,004,508	15,856,037	10.20
10.00	10,004,508	15,520,275	9.75
9.50	10,004,508	15,190,848	9.30
9.00	10,004,508	14,867,650	8.85
8.50	10,004,508	14,550,580	8.40
8.00	10,004,508	14,239,534	7.95
7.50	10,004,508	13,934,415	7.50
7.00	10,004,508	13,635,117	7.05
6.50	10,004,508	13,341,549	6.60
6.00	10,004,508	13,053,613	6.15
5.50	10,004,508	12,771,214	5.70
5.00	10,004,508	12,494,259	5.25
4.50	10,004,508	12,222,656	4.80
4.00	10,004,508	11,956,313	4.35

Exhibit 6: Accumulated Value and Total Return After Five Years for a 6-Year 6.75% Bond Selling to Yield 7.5%

Investment horizon:	5 years	Price:	100.00
Coupon rate:	6.75%	Par value purchased:	$10,000,000
Maturity:	6 years	Purchase price:	$9,642,899
Yield to maturity:	7.5%	Target accumulated value:	$13,934,413

New Yield (%)	Coupon ($)	Reinvestment Income ($)	Price of Bond ($)	Accumulated Value ($)	Total Return (%)
11.00	3,375,000	970,432	9,607,657	13,953,089	7.53
10.50	3,375,000	919,903	9,652,592	13,947,495	7.52
10.00	3,375,000	870,039	9,697,846	13,942,885	7.51
9.50	3,375,000	820,831	9,743,423	13,939,253	7.51
9.00	3,375,000	772,271	9,789,325	13,936,596	7.50
8.50	3,375,000	724,350	9,835,556	13,934,906	7.50
8.00	3,375,000	677,061	9,882,119	13,934,180	7.50
7.50	3,375,000	630,395	9,929,017	13,934,413	7.50
7.00	3,375,000	584,345	9,976,254	13,935,599	7.50
6.50	3,375,000	538,902	10,023,832	13,937,734	7.50
6.00	3,375,000	494,059	10,071,755	13,940,814	7.51
5.50	3,375,000	449,808	10,120,027	13,944,835	7.52
5.00	3,375,000	406,141	10,168,650	13,949,791	7.52
4.50	3,375,000	363,051	10,217,628	13,955,679	7.53
4.00	3,375,000	320,531	10,266,965	13,962,495	7.54

Consider a 6-year 6.75% bond selling at $96.42899 to yield 7.5%. Suppose $10 million of par value of this bond is purchased for $9,642,899. Exhibit 6 provides the same information for this bond as Exhibits 2, 3, and 5 do for the previous bonds considered for purchase. Looking at the last two columns, we see that the accumulated value and the total return are never less than the target accumulated value and target yield. Thus the target accumulated value is assured regardless of what happens to the market yield.

Exhibit 7 shows why. When the market yield rises, the change in the reinvestment income more than offsets the decline in price. When the market yield declines, the increase in price exceeds the decline in reinvestment income. What characteristic of this bond assures that the target accumulated value will be realized regardless of how the market yield changes? The duration for each of the four bonds is shown in Exhibit 8.

The duration of the liability is equal to 4.82.[4] Notice that the 6-year 6.75% bond which assures that the target accumulated value will be achieved regardless of what happens to the market yield, has a duration equal to the duration of the liability, 4.82. This is the key. To immunize a portfolio's target accumulated value (target yield) against a change in the market yield, a manager must invest in a bond (or a bond portfolio) such that (1) the portfolio's duration is equal to the liability's duration, and (2) the initial present value of the cash flows from the bond (or bond portfolio) equals the present value of the future liability.

Exhibit 7: Change in Reinvestment Income and Price Due to Interest Rate Change after Five Years for a 6-Year 6.75% Bond Selling to Yield 7.5%

New Yield (%)	Change in Reinvestment Income ($)	Change in Price ($)	Total Change in Accumulated Value ($)
11.0	340,036	(321,360)	18,676
10.5	289,507	(276,426)	13,081
10.0	239,643	(231,171)	8,472
9.5	190,435	(185,595)	4,840
9.0	141,875	(139,692)	2,183
8.5	93,955	(93,461)	494
8.0	46,666	(46,898)	(232)
7.5	—	—	—
7.0	(46,050)	47,237	1,187
6.5	(91,493)	94,815	3,322
6.0	(136,336)	142,738	6,402
5.5	(180,587)	191,009	10,422
5.0	(224,254)	239,632	15,378
4.5	(267,344)	288,611	21,267
4.0	(309,865)	337,947	28,082

Exhibit 8: Duration for the Four Bonds Analyzed as Potential Candidates for Immunization

Bond	Duration	Risk
5-year, 7.5% coupon at par	4.11	Reinvestment
12-year, 7.5% coupon at par	7.83	Price
6-month, 7.5% coupon at par	0.48	Reinvestment
6-year, 6.75% coupon at 96.42899	4.82	Immunization

---

[4] The duration of a zero-coupon liability is equal to the number of years to maturity of the liability divided by 1 plus one-half the yield. In our illustration, it is 5 divided by $(1 + 0.075/2)$.

The two bonds with a duration shorter than the duration of the liability expose the portfolio to reinvestment risk. The one bond with a duration greater than the investment horizon exposes the portfolio to price risk.

When bonds with embedded options are included in an immunized portfolio, it is the effective duration that is the appropriate duration measure. The effective duration of the liability is the same as the modified duration of the liability. Thus, the requirements for immunization can be restated in more general terms as: (1) the effective duration must equal the effective duration of the liability and (2) the initial present value of the projected cash flows from the bond (or bond portfolio) must equal the present value of the future liability.

B. Rebalancing an Immunized Portfolio

Our illustration of the principles underlying immunization assumes a one-time instantaneous change in the market yield. In practice, the market yield will fluctuate over the investment horizon. As a result, the duration of the portfolio will change as the market yield changes. In addition, the duration will change simply because of the passage of time. In any interest rate environment different from a flat term structure, the duration of a portfolio will change at a different rate than time.

Even in the face of changing market yields, a portfolio can be immunized if it is rebalanced periodically so that its duration is readjusted to the shorter duration of the liability. For example, if the investment horizon is initially five years and the yield is 7.5%, the initial portfolio should have a duration of 4.82. After six months the investment horizon will be 4.5 years and the liability's duration will be 4.34 (= 4.5/ 1.0375). However, the duration of the portfolio will probably be different from 4.34. Thus the portfolio must be rebalanced so that its duration is equal to 4.34. Six months later the portfolio must be rebalanced again so that its duration will equal the duration of a liability due in four years.

How often should the portfolio be rebalanced to adjust its duration? On the one hand, more frequent rebalancing increases transaction costs, thereby reducing the likelihood of achieving the target return. On the other hand, less frequent rebalancing will result in the portfolio's duration wandering from the target duration (i.e., the duration of the liability), which will also reduce the likelihood of achieving the target return. Thus the manager faces a trade-off: some transaction costs must be accepted to prevent the portfolio duration from wandering too far from its target; but some maladjustment in the portfolio duration must be lived with, or transaction costs will become prohibitively high.

C. Application Considerations

In the actual process leading to the construction of an immunized portfolio, the selection of the universe is extremely important. The lower the credit quality of the securities considered, the higher the potential risk and return. Immunization theory assumes there will be no defaults and that securities will be responsive only to overall changes in interest rates. The lower the credit quality, the greater the possibility that these assumptions will not be met. Further, securities with embedded options such as call features or mortgage-backed prepayments complicate and may even prevent the accurate measure of cash flows and hence duration, frustrating the basic requirements of immunization. Finally, liquidity is a consideration for an immunized portfolio because, as noted above, the portfolio must be rebalanced over time.

Optimization procedures can be used for the construction of an immunized portfolio. Typically, immunization takes the form of minimizing the initial portfolio cost subject to the constraint of having sufficient cash to satisfy the liability at the horizon date. Further considerations such as average credit quality, minimum and maximum concentration constraints, and, perhaps, issuer constraints may be included. Throughout this process the need to establish realistic guidelines and objectives is critical. In addition, because the optimization is very sensitive to the pricing of the universe being considered, accurate pricing and the interface of an experienced trader are valuable. Because of the many inputs and variations that are typically available, the optimization process should be approached in an iterative manner where the final solution is the result of a number of trials.

Transaction costs are important in meeting the target rate for an immunized portfolio. Transaction costs must be considered not only in the initial immunization (i.e., when the immunized portfolio is first created), but also in the periodic rebalancing necessary to avoid duration wandering. The manager does not want to get into a situation where the portfolio will incur a substantial number of trades and enjoy only marginal benefits from risk minimization. Fortunately, transaction costs can be included in the optimization framework such that a trade-off between transaction costs and risk minimization can take place.

D. Extensions of Classical Immunization Theory

The sufficient condition for classical immunization is that the duration of the portfolio match the duration of the liability. Classical theory is based on the following assumptions:

Assumption 1. Any changes in the yield curve are parallel changes, i.e., interest rates move either up or down by the same amount for all maturities.

Assumption 2. The portfolio is valued at a fixed horizon date and there are no cash inflows or outflows during the horizon.

Assumption 3. The target value of the investment is defined as the portfolio value at the horizon date if the interest rate structure does not change (i.e., no change in forward rates).

Perhaps the most critical assumption of classical immunization techniques concerns Assumption 1 — the type of interest rate change anticipated. A property of a classically immunized portfolio is that the target value of the investment is the lower limit of the value of the portfolio at the horizon date if there are parallel interest rate changes.[5] This would appear to be an unrealistic assumption, since such interest rate behavior is rarely, if ever, experienced in reality. According to the theory, if there is a change in interest rates that does not correspond to this shape preserving shift, matching the duration of the portfolio to the duration of the liability no longer assures immunization.[6]

A natural extension of classical immunization theory is a technique for modifying the assumption of parallel shifts in interest rates. One approach is a strategy that can handle any arbitrary interest rate change so that it is not necessary to specify an alternative duration measure. The approach, developed by Gifford Fong and Oldrich Vasicek, establishes a measure of **immunization risk** against any arbitrary interest rate change.[7] The immunization risk measure can then be minimized subject to the constraint that the duration of the portfolio be equal to the investment horizon resulting in a portfolio with minimum exposure to any interest rate movements.

---

[5] Fisher and Weil, "Coping with Risk of Interest Rate Fluctuations: Returns to Bondholders from Naive and Optimal Strategies."

[6] For a more complete discussion of these issues, see John C. Cox, Jonathan E. Ingersoll Jr., and Stephen A. Ross, "Duration and the Measurement of Basis Risk," *Journal of Business* (January 1979), pp. 51-61.

[7] H. Gifford Fong and Oldrich A Vasicek, "A Risk Minimizing Strategy for Portfolio Immunization," *Journal of Finance* (December 1984), pp. 1541-1546.

Exhibit 9: Illustration of Immunization Risk Measure

Portfolio A: High-risk immunized portfolio:

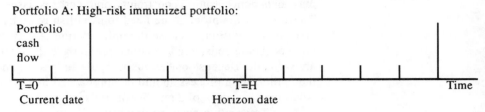

Note: Portfolio duration matches horizon length. Portfolio's cash flow dispersed.

Portfolio B: Low-risk immunized portfolio:

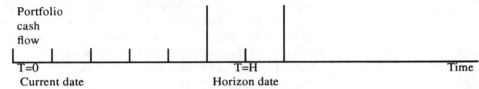

Note: Portfolio duration matches horizon length. Portfolio's cash flow concentrated around horizon dates.

One way of minimizing immunization risk is shown in Exhibit 9. The spikes in the two panels of Exhibit 9 represent actual portfolio cash flows. The taller spikes depict the actual cash flows generated by matured securities while the smaller spikes represent coupon payments. Both portfolio A and portfolio B are composed of two bonds whose weighted durations equal the investment horizon. Portfolio A is, in effect, a "barbell" portfolio — a portfolio comprised of short and long maturities and interim coupon payments. For portfolio B, the two bonds mature very close to the investment horizon and the coupon payments are nominal over the investment horizon. When a portfolio has the characteristics of portfolio B it is called a "bullet" portfolio.

It is not difficult to see why the barbell portfolio should have greater immunization risk than the bullet portfolio. Assume that both portfolios have durations equal to the liability's duration, so that both portfolios are immune to parallel rate changes. This immunity is attained as a consequence of balancing the effect of changes in reinvestment rates on payments received during the investment horizon against the effect of changes in capital value of the portion of the portfolio still outstanding at the end of the investment horizon. When interest rates change in an arbitrary nonparallel way, however, the effect on the two portfolios is very different. Suppose, for instance, that short rates decline while long rates go up. Both portfolios would realize a decline of the portfolio's value at the end of the investment horizon below the target accumulated value, since they experience a capital loss in addition to lower reinvestment rates. The decline, however, would be substantially higher for the barbell portfolio for two reasons. First, the lower reinvestment rates are experienced for the bonds in the barbell portfolio for longer time intervals than on the bullet portfolio, so that the reinvestment risk is much greater. Second, the maturities of the bonds in the barbell portfolio at the end of the investment horizon is much longer than the maturities of the bonds in the bullet portfolio, which means that the same rate increase would result in a much greater capital loss. Thus the bullet portfolio has less exposure to whatever the change in the interest rate structure may be than the barbell portfolio.

It should be clear from the foregoing discussion that immunization risk is reinvestment risk. The portfolio that has the least reinvestment risk will have the least immunization risk. When there is a high dispersion of cash flows around the horizon date, as in the barbell portfolio, the portfolio is exposed to higher reinvestment risk. In contrast, when the cash flows are concentrated around the horizon date, as in the bullet portfolio, the portfolio is subject to minimum reinvestment risk.

An example of a zero immunization risk portfolio is a portfolio consisting of zero-coupon bonds maturing at the investment horizon. This is because there is no reinvestment risk. Moving from these bonds to coupon-paying bonds, the portfolio manager encounters the problem of how to select coupon-paying bonds that provide the best protection against immunization risk. The foregoing discussion indicates that the manager should select bonds which have most of their cash flow payments around the horizon date. Therefore, if the manager can construct a portfolio that replicates zero-coupon bonds that mature at the investment horizon, that portfolio will be the lowest immunization risk portfolio.

Now let us formalize the measure of immunization risk. As explained earlier, the target accumulated value of an immunized portfolio is a lower bound on the terminal value of the portfolio at the investment horizon if yields on all maturities change by the same amount. If yields of different maturities change by different amounts, then the target accumulated value is not necessarily the lower bound on the investment value. Fong and Vasicek demonstrate that if the yield curve changes in any arbitrary way, the relative change in the portfolio value depends on the product of two terms.[8] The first term depends solely on the structure of the investment portfolio while the second term is a function of interest rate movement only. The second term characterizes the nature of the yield curve shift. Since this shift can be arbitrary, this term is an uncertain quantity and therefore outside of the control of the manager. However, the first term is under the control of the manager since it depends solely on the composition of the portfolio. This first term is thus a measure of risk for immunized portfolios and defined as follows:

Immunization risk measure =

$$\frac{PVCF_1(1-H)^2 + PVCF_2(2-H)^2 + \ldots + PVCF_n(n-H)^2}{\text{Initial investment value}}$$

where

$PVCF_t$ = present value of the cash flow in period t discounted at the prevailing yield

H = length of the investment horizon

n = time to receipt of the last portfolio cash flow

The immunization risk measure agrees with the intuitive interpretation of risk discussed earlier. For portfolio A in Exhibit 9, the barbell portfolio, the portfolio payments are widely dispersed in time and the immunization risk measure would be high. The portfolio payments occur close to the investment horizon for portfolio B in Exhibit 9, the bullet portfolio, so that the immunization risk measure is low.

Given the measure of immunization risk that is to be minimized and the constraint that the duration of the portfolio equals the duration of the liability as well as any other applicable investment constraints, the optimal immunized portfolio can be found using optimization models.[9]

---

[8] Fong and Vasicek, "A Risk Minimizing Strategy for Portfolio Immunization."

[9] More specifically, linear programming can be employed because the risk measure is linear in the portfolio payments.

SECTION III CONTINGENT IMMUNIZATION

Contingent immunization consists of the identification of both the available immunization target rate and a lower **safety net level return** with which the client would be minimally satisfied.[10] The manager can continue to pursue an active strategy until an adverse investment experience drives the then available potential return — combined active return (from actual past experience) and immunized return (from expected future experience) — down to the safety net level; at such time the manager would be obligated to completely immunize the portfolio and lock in the safety net level return. As long as this safety net return is not violated, the manager can continue to actively manage the portfolio. Once the immunization mode is activated because the safety net return is violated, the manager can no longer return to the active mode unless the contingent immunization plan is abandoned.

A. Key Considerations

The key considerations in implementing a contingent immunization strategy are:

1. establishing well defined immunized initial and ongoing available target returns
2. identifying a suitable and immunizable safety net
3. implementing an effective monitoring procedure to ensure that the safety net return is not violated

B. An Illustration

To illustrate the basic principles of the contingent immunization strategy suppose that a plan sponsor is willing to accept a 6% return over a 5-year investment horizon at a time when a possible immunized rate of return is 7.5%. The 6% rate of return is called the safety net (or minimum target or floor) return. The difference between the possible immunized rate of 7.5% and the safety net return is called the **cushion spread** or **excess achievable return**. It is this cushion spread of 150 basis points in our example that offers the manager latitude in pursuing an active strategy. The greater the cushion spread the more scope the manager has for an active management policy.

Assuming an initial portfolio of $100 million, the required terminal asset value when the safety net return is 6% is $134.39 million. The general formula for the required terminal value assuming semiannual compounding is:

$$\text{Required terminal value} = I(1 + s/2)^{2H}$$

where

I = initial portfolio value
s = safety net rate
H = number of years in the investment horizon

In our example, the initial portfolio value is $100 million, s is 6%, and H is five years. Therefore, the required terminal value is:

$$\$100 \text{ million} (1.03)^{10} = \$134.39 \text{ million}$$

Since the current available return is assumed to be 7.5%, the assets required at the inception of the plan in order to generate the required terminal value of $134.39 million are $93 million. This is found as follows assuming semiannual compounding.

---

[10] Martin L. Leibowitz and Alfred Weinberger, "Contingent Immunization — Part I: Risk Control Procedures," *Financial Analysts Journal* (November-December 1982), pp. 17-31.

The required assets at any given point in time, t, necessary to achieve the required terminal value are:

$$\text{Required assets at time } t = \frac{\text{Required terminal value}}{(1 + i_t)^{2(H - t)}}$$

where

$$i_t = \text{the immunized semiannual yield available at time } t$$

The other variables were defined earlier.

Since in our example the required terminal value is $134.39 million and the market yield that can be realized if the immunization mode is activated is 7.5%, the required assets are:

$$\frac{\$134.39 \text{ million}}{(1.0375)^{10}} = \$93 \text{ million}$$

Consequently, the safety cushion of 150 basis points translates into an initial dollar safety margin of $7 million (= $100 million – $93 million).

Now suppose that the portfolio manager invested the initial $100 million in a portfolio of 30-year par bonds with a coupon of 7.5%. Let's look at what happens if there is a change in the yield level immediately following the purchase of these bonds.

First assume the yield level decreases to 5.6% from 7.5%. The value of the portfolio of 30-year bonds would increase to $127.46 million. However, the asset value required to achieve the required terminal value if the portfolio is immunized at a 5.6% rate is $102 million. This is found by using the previous formula. The required terminal value is $134.39 million and the market yield for immunizing (following the yield change) is 5.6%, therefore:

$$\frac{\$134.39 \text{ million}}{(1.028)^{10}} = \$102 \text{ million}$$

The amount by which the $102 million exceeds the required asset value (i.e., the dollar safety margin) in this case is $25.49 million. This amount is $18.49 million greater than the initial dollar safety margin and therefore allows the manager more freedom to pursue active management.

Suppose instead of a decline in the yield level the immediate change is an increase in the yield level to 8.6%. At that yield level the portfolio of 30-year bonds would decline in value to $88.23 million. The required asset value to achieve the terminal value of $134.39 million is $88.23 million. Consequently, an immediate rise in the yield by 110 basis points to 8.6% will decrease the dollar safety margin to zero. At this yield level the immunization mode would be triggered with an immunization target rate of 8.6% to ensure that the required terminal value will be realized. If this were not followed, further adverse movements of interest rates would not ensure the required terminal value for the portfolio of $134.39 million. The yield level at which the immunization mode becomes operational is called the **trigger point**.

C. Controlling and Monitoring the Strategy

For purposes of monitoring a contingent immunization plan, it is useful to recast the dollar safety margin in terms of the potential return. This return, also called the **return achievable with an immunization strategy**, measures the yield that would be realized if, at any given point in time, the current value of the portfolio is immunized at the prevailing market yield.

Since duration approximates the price sensitivity of a portfolio to changes in market yields, trigger yields can be computed for portfolios of different durations so that the manager would know how much leeway there is for a given risk position with respect to an adverse movement in the market yield; that is, how much of an adverse movement in the market yield can be tolerated before the immunization mode must be activated.

The key to a contingent immunization plan is the ability to control and monitor the performance of the portfolio over time so that the manager knows how much leeway he has to actively manage the portfolio, and when the portfolio should be immunized in order to achieve the minimum target return.

An accurate immunization target is critical in determining not only the basis for the initial problem set-up (e.g., the safety net return will usually be a certain basis point difference from the target over a specified time period), but also in determining what immunization levels are available over the investment horizon. A safety net return too close to the initial target return makes triggering the immunization process highly likely, while too low a safety net defeats the purpose of the process since the very low satisfactory minimum return would probably never trigger immunization. Finally, without an adequate monitoring procedure, the benefits of the strategy may be lost because of the inability to know when action is appropriate.

In spite of good control and monitoring procedures, attainment of the minimum target return may not be realized due to factors beyond the control of the manager. There are two reasons for this.[11] The first is that there is the possibility of a rapid adverse movement in market yields that is of sufficient magnitude that the manager may not have enough time to shift from the active to immunization mode at a rate needed to achieve the minimum target. Frequent jumps of market yields of several hundred basis points would hinder the effective implementation of a contingent immunization strategy. The second reason why the minimum target return may not be attained is that, if the immunization mode becomes operational, there is no guarantee that the immunized rate will be achieved even if the portfolio is reconstructed at the required rate.

SECTION IV
IMMUNIZATION
FOR MULTIPLE
LIABILITIES

Immunization with respect to a single investment horizon is applicable to situations where the objective of the investment is to preserve the value of the investment at the horizon date. This may be the case when a single given liability is payable at the horizon date or a target investment value is to be attained at that date. More often, however, there would be a number of liabilities to be paid from the investment funds and no single horizon would correspond to the schedule of liabilities (i.e., multiple liabilities). Examples of a schedule of liabilities are projected payouts for a pension fund, annuity payments for an insurance policy, contractual payments to parties in a structured settlement of a legal case, and payments to winners of state lotteries.

There are two strategies that can be employed in seeking to satisfy the liabilities. The first is an extension of the single-period immunization strategy discussed earlier. The second is a cash flow matching strategy. We discuss the immunization strategy first.

A portfolio is said to be immunized with respect to a given liability stream if there are enough funds to pay all of the liabilities when due even if interest rates change by a parallel shift. It has been demonstrated that matching the duration of the portfolio to the duration of the liabilities is not a sufficient condition for immunization

---

[11] Martin L. Leibowitz and Alfred Weinberger, "Contingent Immunization — Part II: Problem Areas," *Financial Analysts Journal* (January-February 1983).

in the presence of multiple liabilities.[12] It is necessary that the portfolio payment stream be decomposed in such a way that each liability is separately immunized by one of the component streams. The key notion here is that it is the payment stream on the portfolio, not the portfolio itself, that can be decomposed in this manner. There may be no actual securities that would give the component payment streams.

A. Conditions for Immunization

It can be demonstrated that the necessary and sufficient conditions that must be satisfied to assure multiple liability immunization in the case of parallel rate shifts are as follows.[13]

The *first condition* is that the present value of the liabilities must equal the present value of the assets. The *second condition* is that the (composite) duration of the portfolio must equal the (composite) duration of the liabilities. The duration of the liabilities is found as follows:

$$\frac{(1)PVL_1 + (2)PVL_2 + \ldots + (m)PVL_m}{\text{Total present value of liabilities}}$$

where

PVL_t = present value of the liability at time t

m = time of the last liability payment

The *third condition* is that the distribution of durations of individual assets in the portfolio must have a wider range than the distribution of the liabilities. More specifically, the mean absolute deviation of the portfolio payments must be greater than or equal to the mean absolute deviation of the liabilities at each payment date.

An implication of the second condition is that if there are liabilities that go beyond 30 years, it is not necessary to have a duration for the portfolio that is 30 years in order to immunize the entire liability stream. The condition requires that the manager construct a portfolio so that the portfolio duration matches the weighted average of the liability durations. This is important because in any reasonable interest rate environment it is unlikely that a portfolio of investment-grade coupon bonds can be constructed with a duration in excess of 15 years. However, in a corporate pension fund situation, the liability stream is typically a diminishing amount liability stream. That is, liabilities in the earlier years are the greatest and liabilities further out toward the 30-year end are generally lower. By taking a weighted average duration of the liabilities the manager can usually bring the portfolio duration down to something that is manageable, say, eight or nine years.

The third condition states that the portfolio payments be more dispersed in time than the liabilities. That is, there must be an asset with a duration equal to or less than the duration of the shortest duration liability in order to have funds to pay the liability when it is due. And there must be an asset with a duration equal to or greater than the longest duration liability in order to avoid the reinvestment risk that might jeopardize payment of the longest duration liability. This bracketing of shortest and longest duration liabilities with even shorter and longer duration assets ensures the balancing of changes in portfolio value with changes in reinvestment return.

To understand why the portfolio payments have to be more spread out in time than the liabilities to assure immunity, consider the single investment horizon case.

---

[12] G. O. Bierwag, George G. Kaufman, and Alden Toevs, "Immunization for Multiple Planning Periods," unpublished paper, Center for Capital Market Research, University of Oregon, October 1979.

[13] H. Gifford Fong and Oldrich A Vasicek, "A Risk Minimizing Strategy for Portfolio Immunization," *Journal of Finance* (December 1984), pp. 1541-1546.

There immunization was achieved by balancing changes in reinvestment return on portfolio payments maturing prior to the investment horizon date against changes in the value at the investment horizon date of the portfolio portion still outstanding. The same bracketing of each liability by the portfolio payments is necessary in the multiple liability case, which implies that the payments have to be more dispersed in time than the liabilities. This means that in selecting securities to be included in the portfolio, the manager not only has to keep track of the matching of duration between assets and liabilities, but also must have the specified distribution for the assets in the portfolio.

The three conditions for multiple liability immunization assure immunity against parallel rate shifts only. In a series of articles, Reitano has explored the limitations of the parallel shift assumption.[14] He has also developed models that generalize the immunization of multiple liabilities to arbitrary yield curve shifts. His research makes it clear that classical multiple-period immunization can disguise the risks associated with nonparallel yield curve shifts and that a model that protects against one type of yield curve shift may allow a great deal of exposure and vulnerability to other types of shifts.

In research predating that of Reitano, Fong and Vasicek also addressed the question of the exposure of an immunized portfolio to an arbitrary interest rate change and generalized the immunization risk measure to the multiple liability case.[15] Just as in the single investment horizon case, they find that the relative change in the portfolio value if the yield curve changes in any arbitrary way depends on the product of two terms — a term solely dependent on the structure of the portfolio and a term solely dependent on the interest rate movement. However the immunization risk measure in the multiple liability case is as follows:

$$\frac{PVCF_1(1-D)^2 + PVCF_2(2-D)^2 + ... + PVCF_n(n-D)^2}{\text{Initial investment value}}$$

$$-\frac{PVL_1(1-D)^2 + PVL_2(2-D)^2 + ... + PVL_m(m-D)^2}{\text{Initial investment value}}$$

where

PVL_t = present value of the liability at time t
m = time of the last liability payment
D = duration of the portfolio (which by the second condition is equal to the weighted average duration of the liabilities)

and PVCF and n are as defined earlier.[16]

An optimal immunization strategy is to minimize the immunization risk measure subject to the constraints imposed by the three conditions and any other applicable constraints on the investment portfolio. Constructing minimum risk immunized portfolios can be accomplished by the use of linear programming.

---

[14] Robert R. Reitano, "A Multivariate Approach to Immunization Theory," *Actuarial Research Clearing House*, Vol. 2 (1990), and "Multivariate Immunization Theory," *Transactions of the Society of Actuaries*, Vol. XLIII, 1991. For a detailed illustration of the relationship between the underlying yield curve shift and immunization, see Robert R. Reitano, "Non-Parallel Yield Curve Shifts and Immunization," *Journal of Portfolio Management* (Spring 1992), pp. 36-43.

[15] Fong and Vasicek, "A Risk Minimizing Strategy for Portfolio Immunization."

[16] Note that this risk measure attains its extreme value of zero if and only if the portfolio payments coincide exactly in amount and timing with the liabilities.

B. Selecting the Appropriate Discount Rate for Liabilities

The first condition for constructing a portfolio to immunize against multiple liabilities is that the present value of the assets be equal to the present value of the liabilities. How is the present value of the liabilities calculated? More specifically, what are the appropriate rates that should be used to calculate the present value of the liabilities. Note that it is inappropriate to employ a single discount rate for the same reasons that we demonstrated at Level I (Chapter 5) when valuing the cash flow of an asset.

The decision as to the appropriate discount rates is not trivial. Kenneth Choie has demonstrated that the discount rates selected will have a significant impact on the construction of the portfolio of supporting assets.[17] The following three approaches have been suggested for selecting the appropriate discount rate:

1. *Treasury yield curve plus spread approach:* The discount rates in this approach are the rates from the Treasury yield curve plus a suitable spread.

2. *Treasury spot rate curve plus spread approach:* The discount rates in this approach are the rates from the zero-coupon or spot rate Treasury curve plus a suitable spread.

3. *Yield curve derived from the portfolio of assets:* The discount rates in this approach are those obtained from a yield curve constructed from the securities in the asset portfolio.

At Level I (Chapter 5), we explained why asset cash flows should not be discounted using the rates from the yield curve. Consequently, the first approach has no theoretical basis. The second approach is the correct approach since it values liabilities in the same way that assets should be valued — using spot rates. The third approach, which is too often used in practice, has limited value since the resulting yield curve has no theoretical connection to the liabilities. For example, consider a portfolio of assets with corporate bonds with different credit ratings. If any of these issues are downgraded, the yield on the downgraded issues will rise. This would mean using a higher discount rate to calculate the present value of the liabilities, resulting in a lower liability than before the downgrade. It does not make any theoretical sense that the liabilities decline in value when bonds are downgraded.

The selection of the appropriate discount rates affects the value of the liabilities and therefore the surplus — the difference between the value of the assets and the value of the liabilities. In assessing the performance of a manager following an immunization strategy, plan sponsors commonly focus on the surplus. In addition, the second condition for immunization is that the duration of the portfolio of assets be equal to the duration of liabilities. But the calculation of the duration of the portfolio of liabilities depends on the discount rates used. Thus, controlling the interest rate risk of a portfolio is critically dependent on the discount rates selected. Consequently, in practice the simply stated second condition for immunization is not as simple after all.

The complication in trying to immunize multiple liabilities is that duration, even considering convexity, is not adequate in describing what will happen when the yield curve shifts in a nonparallel fashion.

Choie constructed several numerical examples to illustrate the effect of the three liability discounting methods on immunization portfolio construction and how the pattern of the liability stream must be taken into account. When discounting the liabili-

---

[17] Kenneth M. Choie, "Caveats in Immunization of Pension Liabilities," *Journal of Portfolio Management* (Winter 1992), pp. 54-69.

ties based on the Treasury yield curve plus spread approach or the yield derived from the portfolio of assets, his examples make clear how it is misleading to focus on the value of the surplus and the duration of the portfolio of assets. The implication is that plan sponsors can be misled by assessing the performance of a manager by concentrating on the value of the surplus. Instead, fund sponsors should require that managers value liabilities using Treasury spot rates plus a spread. The resulting value of the surplus is more meaningful for a plan sponsor in evaluating the performance of the strategy and manager.

SECTION V CASH FLOW MATCHING FOR MULTIPLE LIABILITIES

Cash flow matching is an alternative to immunization for creating a dedicated portfolio to match liabilities. It is an intuitively appealing strategy because the manager need only select securities to match liabilities.

Cash flow matching can be described intuitively as follows. A bond is selected with a maturity that matches the last liability. The amount invested in this bond is such that the principal plus final coupon payment is equal to the last liability. The remaining elements of the liability stream are then reduced by the coupon payments on this bond, and another bond is chosen for the next to last liability, adjusted for any coupon payments of the first bond selected. Going backward in time, this sequence is continued until all liabilities have been matched by payments on the securities selected for the portfolio. Exhibit 10 provides a simple illustration of this process for a 5-year liability stream. Linear programming techniques can be employed to construct a least-cost cash flow matching portfolio from an acceptable universe of bonds.

A. Cash Flow Matching Versus Multiple Liability Immunization

In the special case where all of the liability flows were perfectly matched by the asset flows of the portfolio, the resulting portfolio would have no reinvestment risk and, therefore, no immunization or cash flow matching risk. However, given typical liability schedules and bonds available for cash flow matching, perfect matching is unlikely. Under such conditions, a minimum immunization risk approach would, at worst, be equal to cash flow matching and would probably be better, because an immunization strategy would require less money to fund liabilities. This is due to two factors.

First, a relatively conservative rate of return assumption for short-term cash, which may occasionally be substantial, must be made throughout the life of the plan in cash flow matching, whereas an immunized portfolio is essentially fully invested at the remaining horizon duration. Second, funds from a cash flow matched portfolio must be available when each liability is due and, because of the difficulty in perfect matching, usually before. An immunized portfolio need only have sufficient value on the date of each liability because funding is achieved by a rebalancing of the portfolio. Because the reinvestment assumption for excess cash for cash flow matching is for many years into the future, a conservative assumption is appropriate.

Thus, even with the sophisticated linear programming techniques used in cash flow matching, in most cases it will be more costly to immunize. However, cash flow matching is easier to understand than multiple liability immunization, and this has occasionally led to its selection as the strategy for meeting liabilities (i.e., called "dedicated portfolio strategies).

B. Extensions of Basic Cash Flow Matching

In the basic cash flow matching technique described above, only asset cash flows occurring prior to a liability date can be used to satisfy the liability. The technique can be extended to handle situations in which cash flows occurring both before and after the liability date can be used to meet a liability.

2

Exhibit 10: Illustration of Cash Flow Matching Process

Assume: 5-year liability stream

Cash flow from bonds are annual.

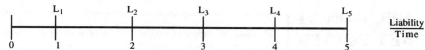

Step 1:

Cash flow from Bond A selected to satisfy L_5

Coupons = A_c; Principal = A_p and $A_c + A_p = L_5$

Unfunded liabilities remaining:

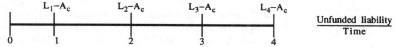

Step 2:

Cash flow from Bond B selected to satisfy L_4

Unfunded liability = $L_4 - A_c$

Coupons = B_c; Principal = B_p and $B_c + B_p = L_4 - A_c$

Unfunded liabilities remaining:

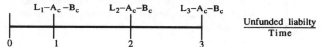

Step 3:

Cash flow from Bond C selected to satisfy L_3

Unfunded liability = $L_3 - A_c - B_c$

Coupons = C_c; Principal = C_p and $C_c + C_p = L_3 - A_c - B_c$

Unfunded liabilities remaining:

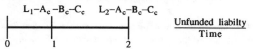

Step 4:

Cash flow from Bond D selected to satisfy L_2

Unfunded liability = $L_2 - A_c - B_c - C_c$

Coupons = D_c; Principal = D_p and $D_c + D_p = L_2 - A_c - B_c - C_c$

Unfunded liabilities remaining:

Step 5:

Select Bond E with a cash flow of $L_1 - A_c - B_c - C_c - D_c$

A popular variation of multiple liability immunization and cash flow matching to fund liabilities is one that combines the two strategies. This strategy, referred to as **combination matching** or **horizon matching**, creates a portfolio that is duration-matched with the added constraint that it be cash matched in the first few years, usually five years. The advantage of combination matching over multiple liability immunization is that liquidity needs are provided for in the initial cash flow matched period. Also, most of the positive slope or inversion of a yield curve tends to take place in the first few years. Cash flow matching the initial portion of the liability stream reduces the risk associated with nonparallel shifts of the yield curve. The disadvantage of combination matching over multiple liability immunization is that the cost is greater.

SECTION VI
KEY POINTS

❏ *Classical immunization can be defined as the process by which a bond portfolio is created having an assured return for a specific time horizon irrespective of interest rate changes.*

❏ *The fundamental mechanism underlying immunization theory is a portfolio structure that balances the change in the value of the portfolio at the end of the investment horizon with the return from the reinvestment of portfolio cash flows.*

❏ *To immunize a portfolio's target accumulated value (target yield) against a change in the market yield, a manager must construct a bond portfolio such that the portfolio's duration is equal to the liability's duration, and the initial present value of the cash flows from the portfolio equals the present value of the future liability.*

❏ *A natural extension of classical immunization theory is a technique for modifying the assumption of parallel shifts in the yield curve.*

❏ *One strategy to handle any arbitrary yield curve shift is to construct an immunization risk measure which is related to the relative dispersion of the portfolio's cash flows around the investment horizon. This measure can then be minimized over a range of yield curve changes using optimization techniques.*

❏ *Immunization risk is effectively reinvestment risk.*

❏ *In contingent immunization, the manager pursues an active strategy until an adverse investment experience drives the then available potential return down to a prespecified safety net return, at which time the manager must then immunize the portfolio.*

❏ *A contingent immunization strategy involves the identification of both the available immunization target rate and a lower safety net return with which the investor would be minimally satisfied.*

❏ *The three key considerations in implementing a contingent immunization strategy are establishing accurate immunized initial and ongoing available target returns, identifying a suitable and immunizable safety net return, and implementing an effective monitoring procedure to ensure that the safety net return is not violated.*

❏ *An immunization strategy can also be used to construct a portfolio to satisfy multiple liabilities.*

❏ *The three conditions for immunization in the case of multiple liabilities are the present value of the assets must be equal to the present value of the liabilities, the duration of the assets must be equal to the duration of the liabilities, and the distribution of durations of individual portfolio assets must have a wider range than the distribution of the liabilities.*

❏ *An immunization risk measure can be constructed for portfolios designed to immunize against multiple liabilities.*

❏ *Selection of the appropriate discount rates for calculating the present value of the liabilities has a significant impact on the construction of an immunized portfolio.*

❏ *The three approaches for selecting the appropriate discount rates are the Treasury yield curve plus spread approach, the Treasury spot rate curve plus spread approach, and the yield derived from the portfolio of assets.*

❑ *The Treasury spot rate curve plus spread is the approach that should be used and use of the other two methods can mislead sponsors as to the performance of managers since they do not accurately reflect the risks of the liabilities.*

❑ *Cash flow matching is an alternative to immunization when there are multiple liabilities.*

❑ *In cash flow matching, bonds are selected so that the portfolio's cash flow matches the liabilities as close as possible in terms of dollar amount and timing (to minimize reinvestment risk) at each liability date.*

❑ *In constructing a cash flow matched portfolio, the objective is to do so at minimum cost subject to the constraints imposed such as the credit quality of the issues that are permitted in the portfolio.*

❑ *There is a trade-off in using immunization and cash flow matching to construct a portfolio to satisfy multiple liabilities.*

❑ *An immunization strategy exposes the manager to immunization risk which is not present in a cash flow matching strategy, but the initial cost of a cash flow matched portfolio is typically higher than for an immunization portfolio.*

❑ *The basic cash flow matching strategy, in which only asset cash flows occurring prior to a liability date can be used to satisfy the liability, can be extended to handle situations in which cash flows occurring before and after the liability date can be used to meet a liability.*

❑ *Combination matching or horizon matching involves creating a portfolio that is duration matched with the added constraint that it be cash matched in the first few years.*

END OF CHAPTER QUESTIONS

1. Why will the matching of the maturity of a coupon bond to the investment horizon date not lock in a return?

2. What is the objective of a bond immunization strategy?

3. a. Why is a portfolio that has a duration of 5 not immunized against a parallel shift in the level of interest rates if the investment horizon is 3 years?
   b. How is a portfolio that has a duration of 5 impacted by a rise in interest rates over a 3-year investment horizon?
   c. Why is a portfolio that has a duration of 3 not immunized against a parallel shift in the level of interest rates if the investment horizon is 7 years?
   d. How is a portfolio that has a duration of 3 impacted by a rise in interest rates over a 7-year investment horizon?

4. What is the basic underlying principle in an immunization strategy?

5. A portfolio manager is contemplating the implication of an immunization strategy. He believes that one advantage of the strategy is that it requires no management of the portfolio once the initial portfolio is constructed. That is, it is simply a "buy-and-hold strategy." Explain whether or not you agree with the portfolio manager's assessment of the immunization strategy as a "buy-and-hold strategy."

6. A portfolio manager is considering an immunization strategy for a client. The portfolio manager is concerned that the portfolio must be rebalanced very frequently in order to match the duration of the portfolio each day to the time remaining in the investment horizon. Comment on this portfolio manager's concern.

7. A portfolio manager made the following statement: "To immunize a portfolio in order to satisfy a single liability, all that is necessary is that (1) the market value of the assets be equal to the present value of the liability and (2) the duration of the portfolio be equal to the duration of the liability. There are absolutely no risks except for the risk that any of the bonds in the portfolio will default or decline in value due to credit downgrades." Explain whether or not you agree with this statement.

8. "I can immunize a portfolio by simply investing in zero-coupon bonds." Comment on this statement.

9. Several trustees of a pension fund are discussing with the fund's consultant the possibility of structuring the fund's bond portfolio to meet future liabilities. The trustees understand that there are two possibilities for structuring such a portfolio: multiperiod immunization and cash flow matching. Which strategy has less risk of not satisfying the future liabilities and why?

10. A portfolio manager considering the use of multiperiod immunization is concerned about using the strategy for its pension fund clients. The manager's concern is that its clients have projected liabilities that are beyond 30 years and therefore it would not be possible to immunize a portfolio for 30 years since bond durations do not extend out that long. Is this portfolio manager's concern regarding this potential problem of using multiperiod immunization justified?

11. A portfolio manager is discussing with the trustees of a pension fund strategies for immunizing a portfolio dedicated to meeting liabilities. One of the strategies he discussed with the trustees is multiperiod immunization. When he mentioned that the strategy required computing the present value of the liabilities, one of the trustees asked the manager what interest rate was used to compute the present value. The portfolio manager responded that not one rate was used, but rates from a yield curve constructed from the securities that would be included in the portfolio of assets were used. Comment on the use of this approach to valuing the liabilities.

12. A client has granted permission for one of its external managers, ABC Financial Management, to employ a contingent immunization strategy. The amount invested by the client is $50 million and the client is willing to accept a 10% rate of return over a 4-year planning horizon. At the same time the client has determined that an immunized rate of return of 12% is possible.

   a. What is the safety net return for this contingent immunization strategy?
   b. What is the cushion spread?
   c. What is the minimum target value for the portfolio assuming semiannual compounding?
   d. What are the required assets at the inception of the strategy to achieve the minimum target value at the end of 4 years?
   e. What is the initial dollar safety margin?
   f. Suppose that the minimum target return that the client had set was 11% instead of 10%. What would be the cushion spread and the initial dollar safety margin?
   g. What is the relationship between the minimum target return and the initial dollar safety margin?
   h. Suppose that the manager invests the entire $50 million in a 12% coupon 20-year bond selling at par to yield 12%. The next coupon payment for this bond is six months from now. Suppose that six months later, market interest rates for this bond decline to 9%. What is the market value of the bonds plus coupon interest six months from now?
   i. Assuming that the client had specified a minimum return of 10% at inception 6 months ago, how much would be necessary to achieve the minimum target return found in part c if a portfolio can be immunized at the prevailing interest rate of 9%?
   j. Given the portfolio value found in part h and the required assets in part i, would ABC Financial Management be required to pursue an immunized strategy or allowed to continue with an active strategy? If an active strategy may be continued, what is the dollar safety margin?
   k. Suppose that instead of declining to 9% in six months, interest rates rose to 14.26%. What is the market value of the bonds plus coupon interest six months from inception?
   l. Assuming that the client specifies a minimum target return of 10%, how much would be necessary to achieve the minimum target value found in part c if a portfolio can be immunized at the prevailing interest rate of 14.26%?
   m. Given the portfolio value found in part k and the required assets in part l, would ABC Financial Management be required to pursue an immunized strategy or continue with an active strategy? If an active strategy may be continued, what is the dollar safety margin?

SOLUTIONS TO END OF CHAPTER QUESTIONS

1. For a coupon bond, the return that will be realized by holding it until the maturity date is unknown. This is because there is reinvestment risk. Therefore the return over the investment horizon (which is equal to the maturity of the bond) is unknown.

2. The objective of a bond immunization strategy is to lock in a return irrespective of how interest rates change over the investment horizon.

3. a. The duration of this portfolio is greater than the investment horizon. Consequently, at the end of the investment horizon, the investor is forced to liquidate the issues in the portfolio that have not matured. The return on the portfolio over the investment horizon will depend on the value of the issues in the portfolio at the horizon date and the portfolio is therefore not immunized.
   b. Since the return depends on the value of the issues in the portfolio at the end of the horizon date, a rise in rates will reduce the value of these issues. The increase in reinvestment income generated for the portfolio by the rise in interest rates will partially offset the capital loss.
   c. If the duration of the portfolio is less than the investment horizon, this means that any bonds maturing prior to the investment horizon must be reinvested. The return on the portfolio will depend on the reinvestment rate and therefore reinvestment income. Consequently, the portfolio is not immunized because it depends on the reinvestment income.
   d. For a portfolio whose duration is less than the investment horizon, a rise in interest rates over the investment horizon will produce higher reinvestment income for both reinvested coupon payments and principal proceeds from maturing issues. Thus, a rise in interest rates will have a favorable impact on the portfolio's return.

4. The basic principle is to lock in a rate (or target value) by offsetting changes in reinvestment income with changes in market value when interest rates change. So, a rise in interest rates will decrease the market value of the bonds in the portfolio at the end of the investment horizon but will increase reinvestment income. A decline in interest rates will increase the market value of the bonds in the portfolio at the end of the investment horizon but will decrease reinvestment income. The objective is to select bonds where the offset is such that a rate can be locked in. This may be accomplished for a parallel shift in the yield curve by matching the portfolio's duration to the investment horizon (i.e., duration of the liability).

5. The manager is incorrect in his assessment of the strategy as a buy-and-hold strategy. The portfolio must be periodically rebalanced. This occurs because the portfolio's duration will change over time due to the passage of time and the change in interest rates. The change in the portfolio's duration will not be such that the new duration is equal to the remaining time to the investment horizon. Hence, it will be necessary to rebalance the portfolio periodically to adjust the portfolio's duration to equal the remaining time to the investment horizon.

   Moreover, the proceeds from maturing bonds, called issues, and coupon income must be reinvested. The quality of the issues must be monitored.

6. While it is true that the duration of the portfolio changes every day due to the passage of time and the change in interest rates, rebalancing the portfolio each day or each week would increase transaction costs. This could easily reduce the return

over the investment horizon and discourage the use of such a strategy. In practice, however, rebalancing of the portfolio to adjust its duration is done judiciously recognizing the trade-off between being matched to the remaining investment horizon and the higher transaction costs associated with frequent rebalancing.

7. The statement is incorrect. There are in fact two other risks. First, even if the duration of the portfolio is matched to the duration of the liability, the portfolio is still exposed to a nonparallel shift in the yield curve. This risk is commonly referred to as immunization risk. Moreover, if there are callable securities in the portfolio, the portfolio is exposed to call risk.

8. While it is true that an investor can immunize a portfolio by buying zero-coupon bonds that mature on the horizon date, the problem is that the return that can be locked in may not be adequate. When a manager seeks to immunize a portfolio for a client, the manager is hoping to add value beyond what can be obtained by simply purchasing zero-coupon bonds that matures at the horizon date.

9. A cash flow matched strategy has less exposure to reinvestment risk and yield curve risk than a portfolio constructed using a multiperiod immunization strategy. Hence, a cash flow matched strategy has less risk of not satisfying the liabilities. However, typically it is initially more costly to set up a cash flow matched portfolio relative to a multiperiod immunized portfolio.

10. A condition for multiperiod immunization is not that the duration must match the longest maturity of the liability, but rather that the duration of the portfolio must match the duration of the liabilities. As long as a portfolio can be created with an average duration equal to the duration of the liabilities, then the manager can implement a multiperiod immunization strategy.

11. There are several approaches for obtaining the discount rates to use to discount the liabilities that have been suggested — Treasury yield curve plus spread approach, Treasury spot rate curve plus spread approach, and yield curve derived from the portfolio of assets. It is the last approach that the portfolio manager has indicated to the trustees that he uses. While this is a commonly used approach in practice, it has limited value since there is no relationship between the liabilities and the yield curve generated. For example, if the manager created a portfolio with high-yield bonds, then the resulting yield curve created from high-yield bonds would have high discount rates. As a result, the liabilities will have a lower present value than if the manager invested in Treasury bonds which would give a lower discount rate. However, neither of these yield curves were determined in reference to the quality of the liabilities. Allowing the manager to determine the value of the liabilities based on what the manager would invest in makes no sense.

12. a. The safety net return is the minimum target return of 10%.
    b. The cushion spread is the difference between the immunized return of 12% and the safety net return of 10%. So the cushion spread is 200 basis points.
    c. Because the initial portfolio value is $50 million, the minimum target value at the end of 4 years, based on semiannual compounding, is $73,872,772 (= $50,000,000 $(1.05)^8$). (Note that the minimum target value is found by compounding at one half of the safety net return of 10%.)

d. The rate of return at the time is 12% (the immunized rate of return), so the assets required at this time to achieve the minimum target value of $73,872,772 is the present value of $73,872,772 discounted at 12% on a semiannual basis. The required assets are therefore $46,348,691 (= $73,872,772/(1.06)^8$).

e. Since the initial value of the portfolio is $50 million and the assets required to achieve the minimum target value of $73,872,772 is $46,348,691, the initial dollar safety margin is $3,651,309 ($50,000,000 − $46,348,691).

f. The cushion spread would be 100 basis points (11% − 10%). The minimum target value is $76,734,326 (= $50,000,000 $(1.055)^8$). The required assets to achieve $76,734,326 given an immunized rate of 12% is $48,144,065 (= $76,734,326/(1.06)^8$). Therefore, the initial 100 basis points cushion spread translates into an initial dollar safety margin of $1,855,935 (= $50,000,000 − $48,144,065).

g. The higher the minimum return specified by the client, the lower the initial dollar safety margin. This can be seen by comparing the initial dollar safety margin assuming a minimum return of 10% versus 11%. In part e, the initial safety margin was found to be $3,651,309 when the minimum return is 10%. It is only $1,855,935 if the minimum return is 11% (part f).

h. Six months from now, the bond is a 12% coupon 19.5-year bond. If market rates for this issue decline to 9%, the market value of the bonds would rise from par to 127.34 per $100 of par value. Consequently, the price of $50 million of these bonds would rise to $63,672,242. Coupon interest is $3 million (0.50 × 0.12 × $50 million). Thus the portfolio value at the end of six months is $66,672,242.

i. The required assets are found by computing the present value of the minimum target value at 9% for 3.5 years. (The initial horizon is 4 years and six months later the remaining horizon is 3.5 years.) The required dollar amount is $54,283,815 (= $73,872,772/(1.045)^7$).

j. Since the portfolio value of $66.67 million is greater than the required assets of $54,283,815, the management firm can continue to manage the portfolio actively. The dollar safety margin is now $12,386,185 ($66,670,000 − $54,283,815).

k. The market value of the bond would decline to $42,615,776. The portfolio value would then equal $45,615,776 (the market value of the bonds plus $3 million of coupon interest).

l. The required assets to achieve the minimum target value of $73,872,772 at the current interest rate (14.26%) would be $45,614,893 (= $73,872,772/(1.0713)^7$).

m. The required dollar amount is approximately equal to the portfolio value (that is, the dollar safety margin is almost zero). Thus the management firm would be required to immunize the portfolio in order to try to achieve the minimum target value (safety net return) over the investment horizon.

Chapter 4

MANAGING INDEXED AND ENHANCED INDEXED BOND PORTFOLIOS

Kenneth E. Volpert, CFA
Principal and Senior Portfolio Manager
The Vanguard Group

LEARNING STATEMENT OUTCOMES

After reading this chapter you should be able to:

- describe a framework for understanding the range of portfolio management strategies — from pure indexing to full-blown active management.
- explain the motivation for pursuing an indexing strategy and an enhanced indexing strategy.
- explain why indexing a bond portfolio is more complicated than indexing an equity portfolio.
- differentiate between enhanced indexing strategies — matching primary risk factors approach and minor risk factor mismatches approach.
- differentiate between active management strategies — strategies involving larger risk factor mismatches and strategies involving full-blown active management.
- explain the factors to consider in selecting a bond index to replicate.
- describe the primary bond index risk factors.
- explain how to measure the success of an indexing and enhanced indexing strategy.

SECTION I
INTRODUCTION

As explained in Chapter 1, there are managers whose benchmark is a bond market index and managers whose benchmark is a liability structure. For the former managers, the portfolio management strategies range from pure indexing to "full-blown" active management. In this chapter we provide a framework for understanding the range of portfolio management strategies. For example, how does "pure indexing" differ from a strategy of "enhanced indexing." In providing this framework, we also explain the benefits of indexing versus active portfolio management strategies and the difficulties of replicating the benchmark index. For those familiar with equity indexing, it will become clear that indexing in the bond market is not as straightforward as in the equity market; however, the motivations for indexing in both the bond and equity markets are the same.

SECTION II
OVERVIEW OF DOMESTIC BOND MANAGEMENT

Domestic bond management is made up of many different investment styles and strategies. Exhibit 1 captures five different investment styles from pure index management to full-blown active management. Within each of these styles are varying degrees of exposure to various enhancement strategies. The goal of the enhancement strategies is to overcome the investment management fees and transaction costs of active management and hopefully outperform the index benchmark return by varying degrees based on the level of risk taken.

A. Pure Bond Index Matching

Pure bond indexing is the lowest tracking error risk (and lowest expected return) approach to bond management versus a specific benchmark. It is highly likely, if not certain, that with this approach returns will lag behind the benchmark index by the cost difference (expenses plus transaction costs). Pure bond index matching attempts to fully replicate the index by owning all the bonds in the index in the same percentage as the index. Hence, this approach is also called the **full replication approach**. In the bond market, however, such an approach is very difficult to accomplish and very costly to implement. Many bonds in the index are illiquid.

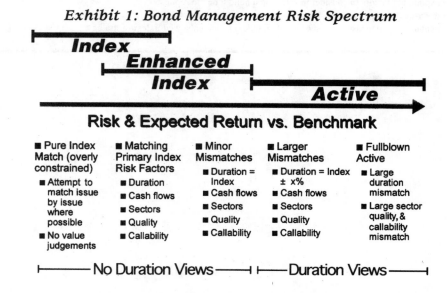

Exhibit 1: Bond Management Risk Spectrum

On June 30, 1999, the Lehman Brothers Aggregate Bond Index contained about 150 Treasury issues, 870 federal agency issues, 3,500 corporate issues, 350 asset-backed and commercial mortgage-backed issues, and 470 broadly categorized mortgage issues (essentially hundreds of thousands of mortgage pools). Full replication is feasible (although not desirable for reasons to be mentioned later) in the Treasury market, but cannot be reasonably implemented in the agency, mortgage or corporate markets. Thousands of the agency and corporate issues are held in long-term bond portfolios and could only be purchased from these investors by paying extremely high prices. For this reason, full replication of a broad bond index (including corporates and mortgages) is very inefficient, if not impossible, and is rarely, if ever, attempted.

B. Enhanced Indexing/Matching Primary Risk Factors

The **enhanced bond indexing/matching primary risk factors approach** involves investing in a large sample of bonds such that the portfolio risk factors match the index risk factors. The risk factors are duration, cash flow distribution, sector, quality, and call exposure. The result is a portfolio that, when fully implemented, will have higher average monthly tracking errors (standard deviation of tracking errors or tracking error risk)[1] than the full replication (i.e., pure index matching) approach, but it can be implemented and maintained at much lower cost resulting in net investment performance that is much closer to the index. By matching the major risk factors, the portfolio will be exposed to broad market-moving events (i.e., widening corporate spreads, changing interest rate levels, twists in the yield curve, etc.) in the same way as the index thereby tracking closely to the index. By implementing the portfolio construction in an efficient way and using under-priced securities, the portfolio return may be "enhanced" (more on this later) above the index return. This approach is considered a form of enhanced indexing because the return is enhanced (more on this later) relative to the full replication indexing approach.

C. Enhanced Indexing/Minor Risk Factor Mismatches

The **enhanced bond indexing/minor risk factor mismatches approach** allows for minor mismatches in the risk factors (except duration) to tilt the portfolio in favor of particular areas of perceived relative value (sector, quality, term structure, call risk, etc.). Because the mismatches (and impact on tracking) are very small, this is still considered enhanced indexing. These additional enhancements are essential in helping to offset the low indexing management fees and transaction costs. Since the major risk factors continue to be matched to the index the overall return of the portfolio should track closely to the return of the target index.

D. Active Management/ Larger Risk Factor Mismatches

The active management/larger risk factor mismatches approach is a conservative approach to active management. The manager will make larger mismatches in the risk factors to attempt to add greater value. This approach may also take small duration views or positions. Because in most cases the management fee and transaction costs are significantly higher than for pure or enhanced indexing, the net investment return is usually lower. These additional costs are the reason why a typical index portfolio often outperforms the average active manager in performance universes. Since this strategy has higher costs (higher management expenses and higher transaction costs), the manager will make moderate adjustments to the major risk factors with the hope that the incremental return will more than offset the higher costs. This increased risk is measured by the extent of deviation from the market's return structure (risk factors) and the market's return.

---

[1] Tracking error and tracking error risk are explained in Chapter 2.

E. Active Management/ Full-Blown Active

The **active management/full-blown active approach** is an aggressive active style where large duration and sector views are taken, and where significant value-added (or lost) relative to an index is expected. Above-average performance consistency is difficult to find in this group of managers, so investors who choose this management style need to look deeper than just at recent performance to discern the good from the bad. The active manager may significantly change the risk exposures relative to the index in the hope of adding much greater return, which may result in significant tracking error and portfolio structure variations from the index.

SECTION III WHY INDEX BOND PORTFOLIOS?

There are several reasons for indexing. First, broad bond index portfolios provide excellent diversification. The Lehman Brothers Aggregate Bond Index, which is designed to capture the entire U.S. investment-grade bond market, had over 5,300 issues and more than $5.3 trillion in market value as of June 30, 1999. A large bond index portfolio designed to replicate this Index may have 500 or more issues, resulting in significant issuer diversification benefits. Most active portfolios have much heavier specific issuer concentrations, resulting in significant exposure to issuer event (credit) risk.

In addition, an index portfolio designed to match a broad bond index will have exposure not only to Treasury and agency sectors, but also to the mortgage-backed, industrial, utility, finance, dollar-denominated foreign, and asset-backed sectors. Such a portfolio will also have broad exposure to the yield curve with holdings from one year to over 30 years to maturity. These sources of diversification result in a portfolio with lower risk for a given level of return than is available from less diversified portfolios.

The second reason is lower cost of indexed portfolios. This lower cost takes two forms: (1) lower management fees and (2) lower transaction costs associated with lower portfolio turnover rates. This lower cost advantage is durable and predictable.

Given the lower management fees and lower transaction costs of indexed portfolios, it is not surprising that they usually outperform the average active portfolios in most universes. After all, a broad index is by design a representation of the universe of investment alternatives. Therefore, the sum of all active managers should equal the index in composition. Also, the sum of the investment performance of all active managers (grossed up for the higher management fees and transaction costs) should also equal the index in performance.

Because of the low tracking error risk, a bond indexing strategy should produce consistent performance relative to an index. For the same reason, a properly managed broad bond index portfolio should be assured of performing in line with the market as a whole. Therefore, regardless of the direction the market takes, the investor can be assured of the performance of a diversified broad index (the "market").

SECTION IV WHICH INDEX SHOULD BE USED?

A bond index is comprised of a collection of bonds that satisfy a set of rules (characteristics) that are then applied to all issues in the marketplace. The rules include maturity, size, sector, and quality characteristics. The issues that fit the rules are then combined, as if in a portfolio, with each issue's weight determined by its relative market value outstanding.

One of the broadest U.S. bond indexes is the Lehman Brothers Aggregate Bond Index.[2] As of June 30, 1999, the Lehman Brothers Aggregate Bond Index had

---

[2] This index is essentially identical to the Salomon Broad Investment Grade Index and the Merrill Lynch Domestic Master Index.

more than 5,300 issues representing a market value of over $5.3 trillion. Exhibit 2 shows that the composition of the Aggregate Bond Index as of June 30, 1999 was 43% government bonds, 24% corporate, asset-backed, and commercial mortgage-backed bonds, and 33% mortgage-backed securities. The effective duration was 4.9, with an average maturity of 9 years.

Sub-indices of broad-market indexes can be created that result in different risk/return profiles. For example, a corporate-only index can be replicated for those who do not want as much exposure to Treasury and agency securities as exists in the Lehman Brothers Aggregate Bond Index; or a 1-5 year government/corporate index can be created, for those who would rather have a short duration portfolio.

A. Market Value Risk

Generally, the longer the maturity of the bond portfolio, the higher its yield, assuming a "normally" sloped yield curve.[3] The total return on a bond is made up of the coupon (or income) component and the principal (or price change) component. Since the yield curve (which impacts the principal component of total return) is likely to shift, the longer bond portfolio will not necessarily have a higher total return. As the maturity or duration of the portfolio lengthens, the market value risk increases. In addition, the lower the yield environment, the greater the market value risk, especially for the inter-mediate-term and long-term portfolios. This is the result of (1) the portfolio's duration increasing as interest rates decrease and (2) the portfolio's lower yield which provides less of a cushion to offset principal losses.[4] Therefore, for investors who are risk averse in terms of their principal, the short-term or intermediate-term index as a benchmark may be more appropriate than the long index.

B. Income Risk

Many investors invest for income, spending only the income distributed by an invest-ment without reducing the principal invested. Foundations and retirees invest for a stable and hopefully growing income stream that they can depend on for current and future consumption. If stability and durability of income are the primary concerns, then the long portfolio is the least risky and the short portfolio is the most risky.

Exhibit 2: Lehman Brothers Aggregate Bond Index Composition (As of 6/30/99)

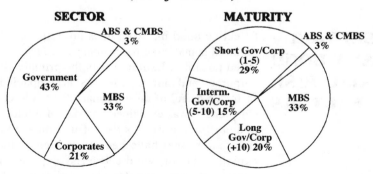

---

[3] The shape of the yield curve is covered at Level I (Chapter 6) and at Level II (Chapter 1).

[4] The current yield to maturity is the yield that is available to offset negative price moves associated with interest rate changes. A bond with a higher coupon does not provide additional protection to a bond with a lower coupon if durations and yield to maturities are equal. This is because the higher coupon rate is offset by price decline with the passage of time to generate the stated yield to maturity. These concepts flow from the characteristics of duration discussed at Level I (Chapter 7).

Exhibit 3: Bond Market Risk Summary

NAV Type	Market Value Risk	Income or Liability Risk	Average Maturity	Current Duration	Portfolios
Stable Dollar NAV	Lowest	Highest	30-90 Days	0.1	Money Market Portfolios
Variable NAV	Low	High	2-4 Years	2.5	Short-Term Portfolios
	Medium	Medium	7-10 Years	5.0	Intermediate-Term Portfolios
	High	Low	15-25 Years	10.0	Long-Term Portfolios

Exhibit 4: Primary Bond Index Matching Risk Factors

	Government	Corporate	MBS
Duration	X	X	
Present Value Distribution of Cash Flows	X	X	
Percent in Sector and Quality		X	
Duration Contribution of Sector		X	
Duration Contribution of Credit Quality		X	
Sector/Coupon/Maturity Cell Weights		X	X
Issuer Exposure Control		X	

C. Liability Framework Risk

Pension funds and financial institutions invest to finance future liabilities. Long-term liabilities (like active retired lives liabilities) require investments in long-term assets to minimize risk, resulting in both a portfolio and a liability stream that is equally sensitive to interest-rate changes. A portfolio that invests in short bonds may look less risky on an absolute return basis, but it is actually much riskier (because of its mismatch with long liabilities) when the portfolio market value is compared to the present value of the pension liability (the difference is the surplus or deficit). The "surplus" risk[5] will be minimized on a fully funded plan against small changes in market rates when the duration of the portfolio is matched (or immunized) to the duration of the liability.

Exhibit 3 contains a summary comparison showing that the investment with the lowest market value risk has the highest income or liability risk. Likewise, the investment with the highest market value risk has the lowest income or liability risk. Clearly, the risk framework chosen depends on whether the investment objective is principal preservation or income durability.

SECTION V PRIMARY BOND INDEXING RISK FACTORS

Effective bond indexing does not require full replication, nor is it desired. What is required is matching the primary risk factors of the benchmark index in a credit diversified portfolio. Exhibit 4 lists the primary risk factors that apply to the government, corporate, and mortgage sectors, accompanied by an explanation of these primary risk factors. Several of these primary factors have already been discussed. Specifically, in Chapter 2 it was explained how factor models provide information about the exposure of a portfolio to various risks. Duration and yield curve risk exposure are two primary risk factors that have been identified as major risk factors by factor models. As explained below, yield curve risk exposure for an index is commonly measured in terms of the present value distribution of cash flows. Each of the primary bond index factors is discussed below.

A. Duration

Effective duration is a measure of the exposure of an index to a parallel shift in interest rates. (Lehman Brothers refers to this measure as "modified-adjusted duration.") As has

---

[5] The economic surplus of an entity is explained in Chapter 1.

been emphasized at Levels I and II and in Chapter 2, duration is a first approximation of the exposure to changes in interest rates. However, as has been emphasized, duration does not capture the exposure to a nonparallel shift in the yield curve. So, simply matching the duration of the indexed portfolio to the duration of the bond index will not be adequate to control for the primary risks associated with a bond index.

B. Present Value Distribution of Cash Flows

Yield curve changes are composed of parallel shifts, curve twists (e.g., short rates down, intermediate rates unchanged, long rates up), and curve butterfly (e.g., short and long rates down, intermediate rates up) movements. (These types of shifts in the yield curve were explained at Level II (Chapter 1).)

There are various measures of yield curve risk exposure. One popular measure, described at Level I (Chapter 7) and Level II (Chapter 1), is key rate duration. Rather than using this measure, index managers more commonly look at the present value distribution of cash flows as a proxy for the yield curve risk of an index and seek to match that distribution.

More specifically, the indexer will first project the cash flow for each issue in the index for discrete time periods. The cash flow for each callable security needs to be allocated to the time periods in accordance with the probability of call. For example, a 10-year callable issue that is highly likely to be called in three years should have cash flows that are primarily allocated to the 3-year time period. For mortgage-backed securities, the cash flow is based on prepayment assumptions. The time period actually represents the range of cash flows attributable to that period. For example, time period 2 represents all cash flows weighted based on their proximity between period 1.5 years and 3.0 years. A cash flow occurring at 1.75 years would be distributed 50% to the 1.5 year period and 50% to the 2 year period. A cash flow occurring at 2.25 years would be distributed 75% to the 2 year period and 25% to the 3 year period. This method of distributing cash flows results in a smooth transition from one period to the next, resulting in less required rebalancing and hence lower transactions costs. These time periods are often called "cash flow vertices."

Given the cash flow for each time period, the present value of each cash flow is computed. The total present value is the market value of the index. The percentage of the present value of the cash flow attributable to each time period is computed. This is shown in the second column in Exhibit 5 for the Lehman Aggregate Index as of June 30, 1999 with the time periods shown in the first column.

Next, the time period is multiplied by the percent of the present value of the corresponding cash flow for that time period. Since the cash flow is effectively a zero-coupon payment, the time period is the duration of the cash flow. Recall from Chapter 2 that the contribution to portfolio duration of an issue or a sector is equal to

$$\frac{\text{market value of issue or sector}}{\text{market value of portfolio}} \times \text{duration for issue or sector}$$

The contribution to the duration of a bond index of a cash flow is computed in a similar manner. That is,

$$\frac{\text{present value of cash flow for period } t}{\text{market value of index}} \times \text{time period}$$

The third column of Exhibit 5 gives the duration contribution of each cash flow for the Lehman index.

Finally, the percent of each duration contribution to the duration of the index is shown in the last column of Exhibit 5. It is this column that the indexer will seek to match.

Exhibit 5: Cash Flow Distribution Analysis for
Lehman Aggregate Index (as of 6/30/99)

Time Period	Percent of PV	Duration Contribution	Percent of Duration
0	2.5	0.00	0.0
0.5	5.8	0.03	0.6
1	5.9	0.06	1.2
1.5	10.6	0.16	3.2
2	12.1	0.24	4.9
3	12.7	0.38	7.8
4	10.7	0.43	8.7
5	7.6	0.38	7.8
6	5.7	0.34	7.0
7	4.7	0.33	6.8
8	3.9	0.32	6.5
9	3.8	0.35	7.1
10	4.6	0.46	9.5
15	3.8	0.57	11.6
20	2.4	0.47	9.7
25	1.0	0.26	5.3
30	0.3	0.10	2.1
40	0.0	0.02	0.3
Total	*	4.88	100.0

* There was considerable rounding in reporting the values in this column. For this reason, the total does not add to 100%.

By matching the percent of the portfolio's present value that comes due at certain time intervals with that of the benchmark index, the portfolio will be largely protected from tracking error (versus the benchmark) associated with yield curve changes. Since all points in time are closely matched in percent, any local term structure movements (non-parallel changes) will not affect tracking (these yield change risks are essentially immunized).

C. Percent in Sector and Quality

The yield of the index is largely replicated by matching the percentage weight in the various sectors and qualities, assuming that all maturity categories are fully accounted for by the replicating portfolio. Exhibit 6 shows the Lehman Brothers Aggregate Bond Index weights in the various sectors and qualities as of 6/30/99.

D. Duration Contribution of Sector

The best way (without excessively constraining the process) to protect a portfolio from tracking errors associated with changes in sector spreads (industry risk)[6] is to match the amount of the index duration (Exhibit 6) that comes from the various sectors. If this can be accomplished, a given change in sector spreads will have an equal impact on the portfolio and the index. Note that the duration contribution of the sectors embody the exposure to spread duration (as explained in Chapter 2) of the sector.

E. Duration Contribution of Quality Spreads

Similarly, the most effective way to protect a portfolio from tracking differences related to changes in quality spreads (leverage/economic risk) is to match the amount of the index duration that comes from the various quality categories. This is particularly important in the lower-rated categories, which are characterized by larger spread changes.

[6] A sector spread is the difference between the yield on a non-Treasury security and that of a similar maturity Treasury issue. Sector spreads were explained at Level I (Chapter 4).

Exhibit 6: Sector and Quality Distribution Analysis for
Lehman Aggregate Index (as of 6/30/99)

Sector	Percent of PV	Duration	Duration Contribution	Percent of Duration
Treasury	34.7	5.35	1.85	38.0
Agency	8.4	4.67	0.39	8.1
Industrial	8.9	6.70	0.59	12.2
Electric/Gas	1.5	5.97	0.09	1.8
Finance	6.0	4.75	0.28	5.8
Canadian	1.0	6.34	0.06	1.2
Sovereign	1.0	5.19	0.05	1.1
Foreign Corporate	1.9	5.85	0.11	2.3
Supranational	0.7	5.00	0.04	0.7
GNMA	8.3	3.93	0.32	6.6
FNMA	11.6	3.86	0.45	9.2
FGLMC	13.6	3.86	0.53	10.8
Asset-Backed	1.3	2.97	0.04	0.8
Commercial MBS	1.3	5.49	0.07	1.5
Total	100.0	4.88	4.88	100.0
Quality				
Aaa	80.1	4.65	3.72	76.3
Aa	4.0	5.19	0.21	4.2
A	9.0	6.08	0.55	11.3
Baa	6.6	6.06	0.40	8.1
Total	99.6	4.88	4.88	100.0

F. Sector/ Coupon/Maturity Cell Weights

As explained at Level I (Chapter 7), duration is a first approximation as to how the market value of a portfolio will change when interest rates change. To improve upon the approximation the convexity of a portfolio should be used. Callable bonds in the index may exhibit negative convexity — the gain in market value is not as large as the loss in market value for a large change in interest rates.[7] Because of this convexity characteristic of callable bonds, the call exposure of an index is difficult for a manager to replicate. Moreover, the convexity characteristic of an index changes as interest rates change.

Managers who attempt only to match the index convexity value often find themselves having to buy or sell highly illiquid callable securities to stay matched and, in the process, generate excessive transaction costs. A better method of matching the call exposure is to match the sector, coupon, and maturity weights of the callable sectors. By matching these weights, the convexity of the index will be better matched. In addition, as rates change, the changes in call exposure (convexity) of the portfolio will be matched to the index, requiring little or no rebalancing.

In the mortgage market, prepayment risk is very significant. As explained at Level II (Chapter 5), the effective duration is dependent on the assumed prepayment rates for *generic* mortgage passthrough groups in the index. Every index provider has its own prepayment model. A manager seeking to match the mortgage sector of a given bond index must carefully examine the prepayment model in obtaining the effective duration of the index replicating portfolio relative to that used by the index provider.

---

[7] For a further discussion of negative convexity, see Level I (Chapter 2).

Exhibit 7: Issuer Exposure Comparison —
Percent of Market Value versus Duration Contribution

	Portfolio			Index		
	Market value (%)	Duration	Dur Contribution	Market value (%)	Duration	Dur Contribution
XXX Corp	5	8	0.40	5	4	0.20
ZZZ Corp	4	7	0.28	4	7	0.28
XYZ Corp	3	2	0.06	3	6	0.18

	Portfolio vs Index				
				Diff due to	Diff due to
	MV % Diff	Contr Diff	Spd Chg	MV %	Dur Contr
XXX	0	0.20	100	0	(0.20)
ZZZ	0	—	100	0	—
XYZ	0	(0.12)	100	0	0.12

The greater the refinancing activity, the shorter the index duration due to the greater likelihood that the higher coupons (issues priced above par) will be refinanced with lower coupon securities. For this reason, matching the coupon distribution of the mortgage index is critical. The best risk management is accomplished by matching the index weights in a multi-dimensional matrix of the maturity (balloon, 15-year, 30-year), sector (FNMA, FHLMC, GNMA), coupon (50 basis point increments), and seasoning (new, moderate, and seasoned).[8] This level of detail is easily accomplished in a large portfolio (more than $1 billion in assets), but more difficult to accomplish in smaller portfolios.

G. Issuer Exposure

If the major risk factors described above are matched, but with too few issues, there remains significant risk that can still be diversified away. Event risk is the final primary risk factor that needs to be measured and controlled.[9] Issuer exposure, like sector and quality, needs to be measured in more than percentage terms only, versus the index benchmark.

Setting percent of market value limits without regard to the issuer's duration and the issuer's index weights is not adequate. Immediately after a negative credit event, the spread widens. Therefore, the best measure of the issuer's event risk impact on a portfolio is the impact on portfolio market value of that spread widening. This can be measured by calculating how much of the portfolio duration (contribution to portfolio duration as explained in Chapter 2) comes from the holdings in each issuer. This calculation should also be computed for the index. The basis point impact on tracking error of a spread-widening event will be the spread change (of the issuer) multiplied by the difference in duration contribution (portfolio − index) multiplied by (−1).

Exhibit 7 contains an example of this analysis. Issuer XXX Corp has an equal market value percentage weight to the index, but its duration contribution is 0.20 greater. This could be accomplished by the portfolio manager purchasing its market value percentage of XXX's bonds in longer maturities. If an event occurred that would widen XXX Corp spreads by 100 basis points, the portfolio would suffer an unfavorable tracking error of 20 basis points versus the index (100 basis point spread change × 0.20 duration contribution overweight × −1).

---

[8] Mortgage-backed securities were covered at Level II (Chapter 3).
[9] Event risk is explained at Level I (Chapter 2).

Issuer XYZ Corp. also has the same market value percentage as the Index, but its duration contribution is 0.12 less than the index. This could be accomplished by the portfolio manager purchasing its market value percentage of XYZ's bonds in shorter maturities. If the same 100 basis points widening were to occur to XYZ Corp bonds, the tracking error would be a favorable 12 basis points (100 basis point spread change × −0.12 duration contribution underweight × −1), even though the percent market value weight is matched to the index. Because ZZZ Corp.'s duration contribution to the portfolio is equal to that of the index, any spread widening will have the same effect on both the portfolio and the Index. For effective index fund management, duration contribution exposure limits (versus the index) need to be set at the issuer level.

SECTION VI
BOND INDEX
ENHANCEMENTS

Successful bond indexing and enhanced indexing is the result of paying close attention to the details of risk management and trading execution. Various enhancement strategies are available to the index manager to help offset the portion of tracking error that would come from expenses and transaction costs. These enhancement strategies include (1) lower costs, (2) issue selection, (3) yield curve positioning, (4) sector and quality positioning, and (5) call exposure positioning.

A. Lower Cost Enhancements

One of the simplest but most overlooked forms of enhancements is to keep costs down. Costs that impact portfolio performance are expenses/management fees and transaction costs.

Enhanced indexers work hard to add an incremental 10 to 30 basis points per year to portfolio returns, yet in the mutual fund arena, the average actively managed bond fund expense ratio is 80 basis points greater than the lowest index portfolio expense ratio. As a result, returns of such funds are significantly lower. Even in the indexing arena, expenses vary by large margins. Simply shopping around for the index fund with the lowest expenses, provided the net return is competitive with other index funds, is a simple way to enhance returns. For a plan sponsor with outside index managers, having the existing manager and one or two other reputable indexers re-bid their management fees every few years will make sure the expenses are as low as possible.

The other major cost factor is transaction costs. Since bond index funds have low annual turnover (about 40%) versus active portfolios (generally over 100%), transaction costs are significantly lower for index portfolios. In addition, the development of a competitive trading process will further reduce the transaction cost impact. Including many brokers in the bidding process when seeking bids on issues is one way to do this. For rapidly growing portfolios, where most of the transactions are purchases, an effective competitive trading process is essential. Since there is no central exchange for corporate bonds, evaluating real-time offerings of target issuers from many different brokers to compare relative value will yield significant transaction cost savings, hence further enhancing the returns.

B. Issue Selection Enhancements

At Levels I and II, models for valuing bonds were explained. These models can be used to identify issues that are undervalued relative to the model's theoretical value. Undervalued or "cheap" issues identified by a valuation model offer the potential for return enhancement.

Corporate issue selection enhancements come primarily from identifying and avoiding deteriorating credits, and identifying and owning (generally overweighted versus the index) improving credits.[10] The greater the manager's confidence in the

---

[10] At Level II (Chapter 9) credit analysis was explained.

ability of the credit analyst of the firm to add value via issuer selection, the larger can be the maximum exposure of the portfolio to a specific issuer. If the manager does not believe that the firm's credit analyst can add value via issuer selection, the greater will be the diversification among issuers. (This is discussed later in Section VII.)

C. Yield Curve Enhancements

Various maturities along the term structure are consistently overvalued or undervalued. For example, the 30-year Treasury region tends to be consistently overvalued, resulting in an inverted yield curve from 25 to 30 years. Likewise, the high-coupon callable bonds maturing in 2009-2012 tend to be consistently undervalued. Strategies that overweight the undervalued maturities and underweight the overvalued maturities, while keeping the same general term structure exposure, will tend to outperform the index. This analysis is similar to looking for the maturities that have the more favorable "roll down" characteristics — meaning that the near-term passage of time may result in the bond rolling down the yield curve and, therefore, trading at a lower yield, resulting in potential price appreciation. Cheap parts of the curve tend to have favorable "roll down," while rich parts of the curve (e.g., 30-year area) tend to have little or no "roll down" opportunities. Yield curve strategies and the framework for analyzing their potential impact on total return were covered at Level II (Chapter 6).

D. Sector/Quality Enhancements

Return enhancement by overweighting bond sectors and credit sectors takes two primary forms: (1) ongoing yield tilt toward short duration corporates and (2) periodic minor over or underweighting of sectors or qualities.

The ongoing yield tilt enhancement (also called "corporate substitution") strategy recognizes that the best yield spread per unit of duration risk is available in short-term corporates (under 5 years). A strategy that underweights 1-5 year government bonds and overweights 1-5 year corporates will increase the yield of the portfolio with a less than commensurate increase in risk. Exhibit 8 shows the rolling 12-month return differential of the Lehman Brothers 1-5 Year Corporate Index versus the Lehman Brothers 1-5 Year Treasury Index.

The persistent return enhancement is obvious for all periods except the brief spread widening periods of 1990-1991 and 1998. The primary reason the strategy is effective is that the yield advantage of short corporates requires a significant corporate spread widening move over a 1-year period for short corporates to perform as poorly as short Treasuries. Exhibit 9 shows the spread increases that would be required to break-even with equal duration Treasury securities over a 1-year holding period for corporates of varying maturities and spread environments. With the passage of time, the duration of corporate bonds shorten, and the yield spread over comparable Treasury securities generally narrows (positive credit curve spread). These two risk reducing and return enhancing forces, when combined with the initial yield spread advantage of corporates, provide compelling reasons to overweight short corporates. Even at narrow spreads, significant protection is available in maturities under five years. A 2-year corporate with an initial yield spread of 20 basis points, can widen by 32 basis points versus a comparable Treasury security over the next year before it performs as poorly as the comparable Treasury security. Clearly, as the maturities increase, the spread widening protection decreases.

The risks involved in the strategy are recessionary spread widening risk and issuer default risk. The recessionary spread widening risk tends to be short lived and quickly overcome by the increased yield advantage of the strategy. The issuer default risk can be minimized by broad issuer diversification and by credit analyst oversight.

Exhibit 8: Lehman 1-5 Year Corporate Index versus Lehman 1-5 Year Treasury Index

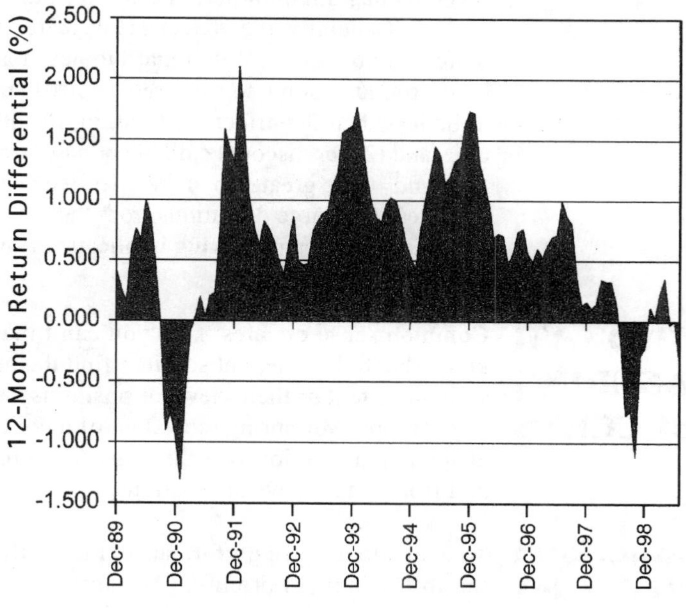

Exhibit 9: Breakeven Spread Widening Analysis — Corporates versus Treasuries

Maturity	Wide Spreads	Breakeven additional Widening	Moderate Spreads	Breakeven additional Widening	Narrow Spreads	Breakeven additional Widening
2 year	60	75	40	53	20	32
3 year	70	48	50	37	30	26
5 year	80	29	60	23	40	17
10 year	100	19	75	14	55	11
30 year	130	12	100	9	75	7

The periodic over- or underweighting of sectors and qualities is a scaled back version of active "sector rotation." The primary way this can be implemented on a cost effective basis is to allow new cash flow (net new portfolio growth) to facilitate the mismatching. For example, if spreads are narrow going into the fourth quarter and the manager expects some widening, new money may be invested primarily in Treasury securities, resulting in a gradual reduction in the corporate exposure versus the index. Once the corporate spread widening materializes, Treasury securities (with low transaction costs) can be sold and corporates overweighted. Expected first quarter asset growth will eventually bring the corporate weighting back in line with the Index. A strategy of outright selling of corporates to buy Treasury securities is always difficult to justify because of the higher transaction costs in the corporate sector, in addition to the yield "penalty" associated with Treasury securities.

E. Call Exposure Enhancements

The effective duration of a callable bond is the average of what the model duration is, if rates rise and fall marginally. These durations (under rising and falling rates) can be quite different for bonds that are trading at a price where the bond changes from trading to maturity, to trading to call (or visa versa). The result is a situation where the actual performance of a bond could be significantly different than would be expected given its beginning of period effective duration.

Generally, the greater the expected yield change, the greater the desire to have more call protection. With regard to near-term yield changes: (1) for premium callable bonds (bonds trading to call), the empirical duration (observed price sensitivity)[11] tends to be less than the effective duration, resulting in underperformance during declining rates and (2) for discount callable bonds (bonds trading to maturity), the empirical duration tends to be greater than the effective duration, resulting in underperformance in rising rates. Any large deviations from the index exposure to call risk should recognize the potential significant tracking implications and the market directionality of the bet.

SECTION VII MEASURING SUCCESS

Common sense dictates that "you can't manage what you can't measure." Managers know this to be true, yet so often find themselves without the tools necessary to measure the extent of their views or positions and the value added or lost from those views or positions. Measuring the extent of the views or positions was covered earlier in this chapter. This section will discuss how to measure whether any value has been added and from what views or positions.

A. Outperform Adjusted Index Returns

To evaluate relative performance, the portfolio returns need to be adjusted for each of the following: (1) pricing, (2) transaction costs of growth and rebalancing, and (3) expenses. Pricing is a critical factor that needs to be considered, especially in enhanced indexing where deviations versus the index are small and pricing errors can hide valuable information. To the extent possible, the portfolio needs to be valued using the same prices as the index. For example, if a Lehman Brothers Index is the benchmark, then the portfolio needs to be re-priced with Lehman Brothers prices. Small differences in either the time of pricing or the pricing matrix,[12] may result in large differences (among pricing services) in periodic returns over short measurement periods. Over longer periods, these pricing differences will average zero, but for value-added measurement purposes, periodic pricing accuracy is critical.

Since the index does not have transaction costs associated with asset growth, principal reinvestment, or income reinvestment, accurate adjustments need to be made to portfolio returns to account for these differences. A simple way to account for this is to maintain a trading log with implied transaction costs as a percent of total portfolio assets. The periodic summation of these implied costs will provide a good estimate of tracking error drag associated with growth and income reinvestment.

Finally, an adjustment for expenses is required. As was discussed earlier, keeping expenses low is a simple way to enhance returns. Nevertheless, portfolio returns should be measured before deduction of these expenses to put the portfolio on equal footing with the index for measurement purposes.

---

[11] Empirical duration was explained at Level II (Chapter 5).

[12] For matrix pricing, a pricing service develops a database of bond characteristics, beginning with basic items like security type, rating and maturity, and extending to more complex parameters including relative coupon, industry, cash flow structure, and credit enhancement. The initial yield spread for the bond is based on the basic characteristics, and is adjusted (widened or narrowed) depending on the complexity of the issue. The advantage of matrix pricing is that it is an efficient way for a portfolio manager to price a large portfolio of diverse issues, or to get an approximate idea of where a bond might be trading. The disadvantage of matrix pricing is that because each issue is unique, the actual market bid may differ from the matrix price. Furthermore, the matrix may not be updated frequently enough to keep up with changes in the market's pricing of various bond characteristics.

B. Low and Stable Monthly Tracking Differences

The other measure of success, from an indexing standpoint, is how closely the portfolio is exposed to the same risk factors of the index. This can be measured by evaluating the rolling 12-month standard deviation of *adjusted* tracking differences of the portfolio versus the index. If a portfolio is properly exposed to the index risk factors, the standard deviation will be low and stable.

C. Detailed Performance Attribution

To accurately measure the success of risk factor management and the enhancement strategies, the manager needs excellent performance attribution tools. The performance attribution analysis should be able to attribute tracking error to term structure factors, sector views, quality views, and issue selection across sectors and qualities. Return attribution analysis is covered in Chapter 9.

The term structure attribution should be analyzed at the portfolio level versus the index. The sector and quality attribution (allocation and issue selection) should be analyzed at the sector and sub-sector levels (detailed sector and maturity categories) with the ability to investigate issue level detail. Issue performance should be risk adjusted (versus Treasury equivalent returns) with sub-sector, sector, and portfolio returns rolled up from the security level. This level of attribution will provide the manager with the tools to measure with precision the risk matching and return enhancing strategies.

SECTION VIII KEY POINTS

❑ *Pure bond indexing (also called full replication indexing) is the lowest risk (and lowest expected return) approach to bond management versus a specific benchmark and attempts to fully replicate the index by owning all the bonds in the index in the same percentage as the index.*

❑ *In the bond market, a pure indexing approach is very difficult to accomplish and very costly to implement.*

❑ *The matching primary risk factors approach to enhanced indexing involves investing in a large sample of bonds such that the portfolio risk factors match the index risk factors.*

❑ *Relative to pure bond indexing, the matching primary risk factors approach to enhanced indexing has higher average monthly tracking differences (standard deviation of tracking differences).*

❑ *The minor risk factor mismatches approach to enhanced indexing allows for minor mismatches in the index risk factors (except duration) to tilt the portfolio in favor of particular areas of relative value (sector, quality, term structure, call risk, etc.).*

❑ *The larger risk factor mismatches approach to active management involves the manager making larger mismatches in the risk factors to attempt to add greater value and also allows the manager to make small duration bets.*

❑ *The full-blown approach to active management is an aggressive active style where large duration and sector bets are made, and where significant value added (or lost) relative to an index can be experienced.*

❑ *The reasons for indexing are broad diversification, competitive performance, low cost, consistent relative performance, market performance predictability, time-tested, and redirection of focus on asset allocation.*

❑ *A bond index is defined by a set of rules (characteristics such as maturity, size, sector, and quality) that are then applied to all issues in the bond market with each issue's weight determined by its relative market value outstanding.*

❑ *For indexing, the broader the index (for a given level of risk) the better the benchmark.*

❑ *The broadest U.S. bond index is the Lehman Brothers Aggregate Bond Index (essentially identical to the Salomon Broad Investment Grade Index and the Merrill Lynch Domestic Master Index).*

❑ *For investors who are risk averse in terms of their principal, the short-term or intermediate-term index may be a more appropriate benchmark than a long duration index.*

❑ *For investors where stability and durability of income are the primary concerns, a long duration index is the least risky and the short duration index is the most risky.*

❑ *For pension funds and financial institutions investing to satisfy future liabilities, surplus risk will be minimized on a fully funded plan against small changes in market rates when the duration of the portfolio is matched (or immunized) to the duration of the liability and therefore an index should be selected accordingly.*

❑ *Effective bond indexing does not require full replication, but rather the matching of the primary risk factors of the benchmark index in a credit diversified portfolio.*

❑ *The primary risk factors of an index include duration, present value of cash flows, percent in sector and quality, duration contribution of sector, duration contribution of credit quality, sector/coupon/maturity cell weights, and issuer exposure control.*

❑ *The call exposure of an index is a difficult factor to replicate.*

❑ *Index enhancement strategies include: (1) lower costs, (2) issue selection, (3) yield curve positioning, (4) sector and quality positioning, and (5) call exposure positioning.*

❑ *In measuring relative performance of an indexer, the portfolio returns need to be adjusted for: (1) pricing, (2) transaction costs of growth and rebalancing, and (3) expenses.*

❑ *Another measure of success (from an indexing standpoint) is how closely the portfolio is exposed to the same risk factors of the index, as measured in terms of a rolling 12-month standard deviation of adjusted tracking differences of the portfolio versus the index.*

❑ *To accurately measure the success of risk factor management and enhancement strategies, performance attribution analysis should be able to attribute tracking error to term structure factors, sector bets, quality bets, and issue selection across sectors and qualities.*

END OF CHAPTER QUESTIONS

1. What distinguishes bond index management (pure and enhanced) from active bond management?

2. Why is the minor risk factor mismatches approach to portfolio management considered an enhanced indexing strategy?

3. Dealer firms have worked with institutional clients to develop customized indexes that are "liability driven." Why don't clients simply use one of the broad-based bond market indexes?

4. The Car Washer National Labor Union has assets of $300 million. Currently, $200 million is allocated to bonds and $100 million to equities. The funds allocated to equities are indexed to the S&P 500 but the funds allocated to bonds are actively managed. You have been retained as a consultant to the fund. A trustee of the fund has discussed with you the possibility of indexing $100 million of the bond allocation. The trustee has asked you the following questions that you are asked to respond to:

   a. "Our equity managers index by buying all 500 stocks in the S&P 500. If we decide to index, shouldn't we require any managers that we retain to index part of our bond portfolio to follow the same strategy of buying all the bonds in the index?"

   b. "Our active managers are given the Lehman Brothers Aggregate Index as their benchmark. If we decide to index, shouldn't we use the same index to be consistent?"

   c. "Some of the managers who do bond indexing have suggested that an enhanced indexing strategy should be pursued. Isn't enhanced indexing nothing more than another form of active management and, if not, why is enhanced indexing necessary?"

5. a. Why isn't the modified duration of an index the appropriate measure for a bond indexer to use?

   b. How can the yield curve risk of an index be captured in an indexing strategy?

6. Suppose that the present value distribution for the cash flow of a bond index is as follows:

Time period	Percent of PV
0	3.4
0.5	6.2
1	6.6
1.5	11.2
2	12.5
3	12.6
4	9.1
5	7.8
6	6.1
7	4.2
8	3.3
9	3.1
10	3.8
15	3.2
20	4.2
25	2.1
30	0.5
40	0.1
	100

a. What will an indexer seek to match and why?

b. What is the duration for the index?

7. Suppose that for three issuers in the corporate bond sector of a bond index, Corporations R, S, and T, the following is determined:

Issuer	Market Value (%)	Index Duration
R Corp	2	6
S Corp	4	2
T Corp	5	9

Suppose that a manager includes these three issuers into the portfolio in the following way:

Issuer	Market Value (%)	Portfolio Duration
R Corp	2	6
S Corp	4	3
T Corp	5	7

Explain the implications of structuring the portfolio with the three issuers as shown above if a manager is seeking to match the performance of the bond index.

8. Why is event risk a significant risk for an indexer and how can this potential risk be measured?

9. Why is pricing of issues in the index critical in assessing the performance of an enhanced indexer?

SOLUTIONS TO END OF CHAPTER QUESTIONS

1. The major difference is the degree to which the manager mismatches the risk factors in the portfolio relative to the index. As the mismatch increases, we move from indexing to active management. As can be seen in Exhibit 1, in indexing and enhanced indexing there is no duration mismatch whereas in active management there may be an intended mismatch.

2. In an indexing and enhanced indexing strategy tracking error is very small. When a manager pursues a strategy of minor risk factor mismatches versus the index, there will be small tracking error risk and therefore this strategy is viewed as an enhanced indexing strategy.

3. The broad-based bond market indexes may not have the same characteristics in terms of duration and cash flow distribution as the client's liability structure. For example, the liability of a typical pension fund has a duration that is greater than that of the broad-based bond market indexes.

4. a. Unlike equities, it is difficult to purchase all of the bonds in an index. The number of issues in a bond index far exceeds the number in the S&P 500. This adds to the transaction costs associated with constructing an index. Moreover, there are issues that are difficult to obtain and trade infrequently.

   b. The index selected should reflect the liability structure of the fund. In particular, as discussed in Chapter 1, a starting point is a duration for the index that matches the duration of the liabilities so as to minimize the impact of changes in interest rates on the fund's economic surplus. The Lehman Brothers Aggregate Index may not have the duration that matches that of the duration of the liabilities and therefore should not be used just because that index was selected as the benchmark for the active bond managers.

   c. Enhanced indexing differs from active management to the extent of the divergence between the major risk factors of the index and the constructed portfolio. Enhancement strategies are necessary to provide a net return just equal to the index because the index does not incur expenses or transaction costs so it is necessary just to provide a net return equal to the index. A primary source of return shortfalls besides expenses is the transaction costs associated with portfolio growth.

5. a. As explained in earlier chapters, modified duration does not properly measure the interest rate risk of a bond with an embedded option. Instead, effective duration or option-adjusted duration is the more appropriate measure for such bonds.

   b. Duration only measures the interest rate risk of an index for a parallel shift in the yield curve. To try to match the yield curve risk of an index, the manager will seek to replicate the cash flow distribution of the index.

6. a. The indexer will seek to match the percent duration for each time period as shown below:

Time period	Percent of PV	Dur Contr	Percent Duration
0	3.4	—	0.0
0.5	6.2	0.03	0.6
1	6.6	0.07	1.3
1.5	11.2	0.17	3.2
2	12.5	0.25	4.7
3	12.6	0.38	7.2
4	9.1	0.36	6.9
5	7.8	0.39	7.4
6	6.1	0.37	7.0
7	4.2	0.29	5.6
8	3.3	0.26	5.0
9	3.1	0.28	5.3
10	3.8	0.38	7.2
15	3.2	0.48	9.1
20	4.2	0.84	16.0
25	2.1	0.53	10.0
30	0.5	0.15	2.8
40	0.1	0.04	0.8
	100	5.27	100.0

The purpose of matching the percent duration is to reduce the yield curve risk exposure of a portfolio seeking to replicate the performance of the bond index.

b. The duration for the bond index is equal to the total of the duration contributions (i.e., sum of the third column). The duration of the bond index is therefore 4.9.

7. While the market value weighting of each of the issuers is the same as in the index, because the duration of two of the three issuers (R Corp. and T Corp.) is not the same as the corresponding index duration, there is a mismatch for the duration contribution of these two issuers. A summary of the positions is given below:

	Portfolio			Index		
	Market Value (%)	Duration	Dur Contribution	Market Value (%)	Duration	Dur Contribution
R Corp	2	6	0.12	2	6	0.12
S Corp	4	3	0.12	4	2	0.08
T Corp	5	7	0.35	5	9	0.45

	Portfolio vs Index				
	MV % Diff	Contr Diff	Spd Chg	Diff due to MV %	Diff due to Dur Contr
R Corp	0	—	100	0	—
S Corp	0	0.04	100	0	(0.04)
T Corp	0	(0.10)	100	0	0.10

The portfolio's duration contribution for S Corp. relative to the bond index is 4 basis points more. For the T Corp. there is a 10 basis point less duration contribution relative to the bond index. Hence, changes in spreads for these two issuers will result in tracking error of the portfolio relative to the bond index.

8. If the major risk factors of an index are matched, but with too few issues, there remains significant risk that can still be diversified away. One such risk is event risk which is described in detail in Chapter 2. With only a few issues representing

a sector, event risk that results in a downgrading of an issue used to represent a sector can have a significant impact on tracking error.

Since after a negative credit event, the spread widens, the best measure of the issuer event risk impact on a portfolio is the impact on portfolio market value of that spread widening. This can be measured by calculating how much of the portfolio duration ("duration contribution") comes from the holdings in each issuer. This calculation should also be figured for the index. The basis point impact on tracking of a spread-widening event will be the spread change (of the issuer) multiplied by the difference in duration contribution (portfolio − index) multiplied by (−1).

9. Pricing is a critical factor especially in enhanced indexing because deviations versus the index are small. Small differences in either the time of pricing or the pricing matrix by services may result in large differences (among pricing services) in periodic returns over short measurement periods. (Over longer periods, timing differences will average zero, but for value-added measurement purposes, periodic pricing accuracy is critical.)

Chapter 5

RELATIVE-VALUE METHODOLOGIES FOR GLOBAL CORPORATE BOND PORTFOLIO MANAGEMENT

Jack Malvey, CFA
Managing Director
Lehman Brothers

LEARNING OUTCOME STATEMENTS

After reading this chapter you should be able to:

- identify the types of securities that fall into the "corporate asset class."
- explain what is meant by relative value.
- describe primary market analysis.
- describe the corporate structures that dominate the bond market.
- explain the strategic portfolio implications of the structures that have come to dominate the corporate bond market.
- explain how short-term and long-term liquidity for a bond influence portfolio management decisions.
- explain the popular reasons for executing trades in the secondary market (yield/spread pickup trades, credit-upside trades, credit-defense trades, new issue swaps, sector-rotation trades, yield curve-adjustment trades, structure trades, and cash flow reinvestment).
- identify the main rationales for not trading.
- explain the reason for the acceptance of the swap spread as a relative-value measure.
- explain the commonly used spread tools for decision making (mean-reversion analysis, quality-spread analysis, and percent yield analysis) and their limitations.
- explain structure analysis.
- describe the typical shape of a corporate spread curve and the difference in the slope of the curve for issuers of different quality.
- explain sector-rotation strategies.

SECTION I
INTRODUCTION

Corporate bonds constitute a fascinating subset of the global debt capital markets. The label, "corporate," understates the scope of this burgeoning asset class. As commonly traded and administered within the context of an overall debt portfolio, the "corporate asset class" actually encompasses more than pure corporate entities. Instead of the title, "corporate asset class," this segment of the global bond market really should be classified as the "credit asset class," including any nonagency mortgage-backed securities, commercial mortgage-backed securities, and asset-backed securities issuers (i.e., sovereigns and government-controlled entities with taxable issues) thought to have more credit risk than the U.S. government.

Thousands of organizations with different credit "stories" have sold debt to sustain their operations and to finance their expansion. These borrowers use dozens of different types of debt instruments (first mortgage bonds, debentures, equipment trust certificates, subordinated debentures, medium-term notes, floating rate notes, private placements, preferred stock) that were described at Level I (Chapter 3) and in multiple currencies (dollars, yen, euros, Swiss francs, pounds) at any maturity ranging from one year to even a thousand years. Sometimes, these debt structures carry embedded options, which may allow for full or partial redemption prior to maturity at the option of either the borrower or the investor. Sometimes, the coupon payment floats with short-term interest rates or resets to a higher rate after a fixed interval or a rating change.

Investors buy corporate bonds because of the greater long-term performance despite the assumption of credit risk. Except near and during recessions, corporate bonds usually outperform U.S. Treasury securities and other higher-quality "spread sectors" like U.S. agencies, mortgage-backed securities, and asset-backed securities. Since the inception of the Lehman indices in 1973, investment-grade corporates have outperformed U.S. Treasuries by 40 basis points (bp) per year on average through the end of 1999 (9.34% versus 8.94%).[1] During the 1990s, this advantage leaped to 84 bp per year over U.S. Treasuries. And U.S. high-yield corporate debt generated an additional 311 bp per year over U.S. investment-grade corporate debt in the 1990s. On a relative basis (standardized for the duration differences among asset classes), investment-grade corporates and high-yield corporates had a compelling average annual advantage over U.S. Treasuries, 45 bp and 350 bp, respectively, during the 1990s. In contrast, the mortgage-backed securities asset class realized an average annual total return of only 16 bp over Treasuries during the 1990s.

Clearly, global corporate bond portfolio management presents a complex challenge. Each day, hundreds of corporate bond portfolio managers face thousands of choices in the primary (new issue) and secondary markets. In addition to tracking primary and secondary flows, investors have to keep tabs on ever-varying issuer fundamentals (acquisitions, earnings, ratings, etc.). The task of global corporate bond portfolio management is to process all of this rapidly changing information about the corporate bond market (issuers, issues, dealers, and competing managers) and to construct the portfolio with the best return for a given risk tolerance. This discipline combines the qualitative tools of equity analysis with the quantitative precision of fixed-income analysis. This chapter provides a brief guide to methodologies that may help portfolio managers meet this formidable challenge.

---

[1] Based on absolute returns of key Lehman indices from 1973.

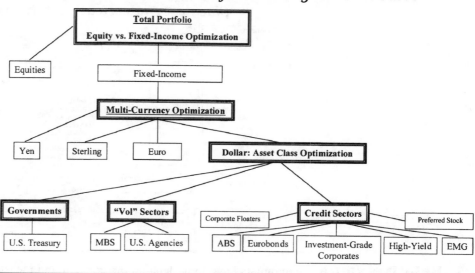

Exhibit 1: Global Portfolio Management Process

SECTION II CORPORATE RELATIVE-VALUE ANALYSIS

Corporate bond portfolio management represents a major subset of the multi-asset global portfolio management process illustrated in Exhibit 1. After setting the equity/fixed-income allocation, currency allocation (in this case, dollars were selected for illustration convenience), and distribution among fixed-income asset classes, bond managers are still left with a lengthy list of questions pertinent to the construction of the optimal corporate portfolio. Some examples are:

• Should U.S. investors add dollar-denominated Eurobonds of non-U.S. issuers?

• Should LIBOR-funded London portfolio managers buy fixed-rate U.S. industrial paper and swap into floating-rate notes?

• Should Japanese mutual funds own euro-denominated telecommunications debt, swapped back into dollars or yen using currency swaps?

• Should U.S. insurers buy perpetual floaters (i.e., floaters without a maturity date) issued by British banks and swap back into fixed-rate coupons in dollars using a currency/interest rate swap?

• When should investors reduce their allocation to the corporate sector and increase allocation to governments, pursue the "strategic upgrade trade" (sell Baa/BBBs and buy higher-rated A corporate debt), rotate from industrials into utilities, switch from consumer cyclicals to non-cyclicals, overweight airlines and underweight telephones, or deploy a credit derivative[2] (i.e., short the high-yield index) to hedge their portfolios?

To respond to such questions, managers need to begin with an analytical framework, relative-value analysis, and to develop a strategic outlook for the global corporate market.

---

[2] Credit derivatives are discussed in Chapter 8.

Exhibit 2: Credit Sector Portfolio Management Process: "Classic," Dialectical Relative Value Analysis

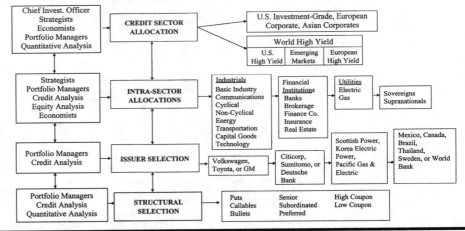

A. Relative Value

Economists have long debated the concept and measurement of "value." But fixed-income practitioners, perhaps because of the daily pragmatism enforced by the markets, have developed a consensus about the definition of value. In the bond market, **relative value** refers *to the ranking of fixed-income investments by sectors, structures, issuers, and issues in terms of their expected performance during some future interval.*

For the day trader, relative value may carry a maximum horizon of a few minutes. For the dealer, relative value may extend from a few days to a few months. For a large insurer and most investors operating in the global corporate market, relative value usually spans a multi-year horizon. Accordingly, **relative-value analysis** refers to the methodologies used to generate such rankings of expected returns.

The analytical tools and techniques presented at Level II provide the building blocks for portfolio managers to perform relative-value analysis.

B. Classic Relative-Value Analysis

There are two basic approaches to global corporate bond portfolio management — **top-down approach** and **bottom-up approach**. The top-down approach emphasizes high-level allocations to broadly defined corporate asset classes. The goal of top-down research is to form views on large-scale economic developments. These views then become the basis for asset allocation decisions. The bottom-up approach to global corporate bond portfolio management emphasizes individual issues that will outperform their peer groups. A manager who follows this approach hopes to outperform his or her benchmark due to superior security selection while maintaining a neutral stance in terms of allocation to the sectors in the benchmark.

Classic relative-value analysis is a dialectical process combining the best of top-down and bottom-up approaches as exhibited in Exhibit 2. This process blends the macro input of chief investment officers, strategists, economists, and portfolio managers with the micro input of credit analysts, quantitative analysts, and portfolio managers. The goal of this methodology is to pick the sectors with the most potential upside, populate these favored sectors with the best representative issuers, and select the structures of the designated issuers at the yield curve points that match the investor's outlook for the benchmark yield curve.[3]

---

[3] The concept of a benchmark yield curve is discussed at Level I.

For many corporate investors, the use of classic relative-value analysis has been sufficient to ensure a measure of portfolio success. Although sector, issuer, and structural analyses remain the core of superior relative-value analysis, the increased availability of information and technology have transformed the analytical process into a complex discipline. To assist their endeavors, corporate portfolio managers have far more data on the total returns of sectors, issuers, and structures, quantity and composition of new-issue flows, distribution of product demand by investor classes, aggregate credit-quality movements, multiple sources of credit analyses on individual issuers, and spreads.

C. Relative-Value Methodologies

The main methodologies for corporate relative-value maximization are:

- total return analysis
- primary market analysis
- liquidity and trading analysis
- secondary trading rationales and trading constraints
- spread analysis
- structure analysis
- corporate curve analysis
- credit analysis
- asset allocation/sector analysis

In the sections that follow, we discuss each of these methodologies.

SECTION III TOTAL RETURN ANALYSIS

Corporate relative-value analysis begins with a detailed dissection of past returns and a projection of expected returns. Capital markets have regular patterns. For instance, the economic cycle is the major determinant of overall corporate spreads. During recessions, the escalation of default risk widens spreads (which are risk premiums over underlying, presumably default-free government securities) and reduces corporate returns relative to Treasuries. Conversely, economic prosperity reduces bankruptcies and enhances overall credit fundamentals of most issuers.[4] Economic prosperity usually leads to tighter corporate spreads and boosts corporate returns relative to Treasuries. For brief intervals, noncylical technical factors can offset fundamentals. For example, the inversion of the U.S. Treasury yield curve during the first quarter of 2000 actually led to wider corporate spreads and corporate underperformance despite rising global economic growth and corporate profitability.

Thanks to the development of corporate indices (effectively databases of prices, spreads, issuer, and structure composition), analyses of monthly, annual, and multi-year total returns have uncovered numerous patterns (i.e., large issue versus small issue performance variation, seasonality, election-cycle effects, and government benchmark auction effects) in the global corporate market. Admittedly, these patterns do not always re-occur. But an awareness and understanding of these total-return patterns are essential to optimizing portfolio performance.

---

[4] This was explained at Level I (Chapter 4).

SECTION IV PRIMARY MARKET ANALYSIS

The primary market is the market for new issues. Primary market analysis involves an analysis of the supply and demand for new issues. Supply is often a misunderstood factor in the tactical relative-value analysis. Prospective new supply induces many traders, analysts, and investors to advocate a defensive stance toward the overall corporate market as well as toward individual sectors and issuers. Yet the premise, "supply will hurt spreads," that may apply to an individual issuer, does not generally hold up for the entire corporate market. During the 1990s, increases in new issuance (most notably during the first quarter of each year) were associated with market-spread contraction and strong relative returns for corporates. In contrast, sharp supply declines were accompanied frequently by spread expansion and a major decline in both relative and absolute returns for corporates. This was most noticeable during the August-October 1998 interval when new issuance nearly disappeared in the face of the substantial increase in credit spreads. (This period is referred to as the "Great Spread-Sector Crash.")

In the investment-grade corporate market, heavy supply often helps spreads and returns as new primary valuations validate and enhance secondary valuations. When primary origination declines sharply, secondary traders lose reinforcement from the primary market and tend to raise their bid spreads. Counter to intuition and cliche, relative corporate returns often perform best during periods of heavy supply. For example, November 1998 marked both the then all-time record for new corporate origination as well as the single best month ever for corporate spread contraction.

A. The Effect of Market-Structure Dynamics

Given their immediate focus on the deals of the day and week, portfolio managers often overlook short-term and long-term market-structure dynamics in making portfolio decisions. Because the pace of change in market structure is often gradual, market dynamics have less effect on short-term tactical investment decision-making than on long-term strategy.

The composition of the global corporate bond market has shifted markedly during the 1980s and 1990s. Medium-term note (MTN) origination has come to dominate the front end of the corporate yield curve.[5] Structured notes[6] and swaps products have heralded the introduction of derivative instruments into the mainstream of the corporate market. The high-yield corporate sector has become an accepted asset class. Global origination has become a more popular technique for agencies, supranationals (e.g., The World Bank), sovereigns, Canadians, and large corporate borrowers.

Although the growth of derivatives and high-yield instruments stands out during the 1990s, the globalization of the corporate market has been the most important development. The rapid growth of the Eurobond market since 1975, the introduction of many non-U.S. issuers into the dollar markets during the 1990s, and the birth of the euro on January 1, 1999 have led to the proliferation of truly transnational corporate portfolios.

These long-term structural changes in the composition of the global corporate asset class arise due to the desire of issuers to minimize funding costs under different yield curve and spread regimes, as well as the needs of both active and asset/liability bond managers to satisfy their risk and return objectives. Portfolio managers will adapt their portfolios either in anticipation of or in reaction to these structural changes.

---

[5] Medium-term notes were explained at Level I (Chapter 3).
[6] Structured notes were explained at Level I (Chapter 3).

B. The Effect of Product Structure

Partially offsetting this proliferation of issuers over the past two decades, the global corporate market has become structurally more homogeneous. Specifically, bullet and intermediate structures have come to dominate the market. A **bullet maturity** means that the issue is not callable, putable, or sinkable. The trend toward bullet securities does not pertain to the high-yield market, where callables remain the structure of choice. With the hope of credit-quality improvement, many high-yield issuers expect to refinance prior to maturity at lower rates.

There are three strategic portfolio implications for this structural evolution. First, the dominance of bullet structures translates into scarcity value for structures with embedded call and put features. That is, securities structured with embedded options are scarce and therefore demand a premium price. Typically, this premium price is not captured by option-valuation models described at Level II (Chapter 2). Yet, this "scarcity value" should be considered by managers in relative-value analysis of corporate bonds.

Second, long-dated maturities will decline as a percentage of outstanding corporate debt. This shift will lower the effective duration of the corporate asset class and reduce aggregate sensitivity to interest-rate risk. For asset/liability managers with long horizons, this shift of the maturity distribution suggests a rise in the value of long corporates and helps to explain the warm reception afforded initially to most new offerings of issues with 100-year maturities in the early and mid-1990s.

Third, the use of credit derivatives will escalate rapidly. The maturation of the credit derivative market will lead investors and issuers to develop new strategies to match desired exposures to credit sectors, issuers, and structures.

SECTION V
LIQUIDITY AND TRADING ANALYSIS

Short-term and long-term liquidity influence portfolio management decisions. Citing lower expected liquidity, some investors are reluctant to purchase certain types of issues such as smaller-sized issues (less than $1.0 billion), private placements, MTNs, and non-local corporate issuers. Other investors gladly exchange a potential liquidity disadvantage for incremental yield. For investment-grade issuers, these liquidity concerns often are exaggerated.

As explained at Level I (Chapter 2), corporate debt liquidity changes over time. More specifically, liquidity varies with the economic cycle, credit cycle, shape of the yield curve, supply, and the season. As in all markets, stark shocks, like a surprise wave of defaults, can dry up corporate debt liquidity as investors become unwilling to purchase new issues at any spread level, and dealers become reluctant to position secondary issues except at very wide spreads. In reality, these transitory bouts of liquidity volatility mask an underlying trend toward heightened liquidity across the global corporate asset class. With a gentle push from regulators, the global corporate asset class is well along in converting from its historic "over-the-counter" domain to a fully transparent, equity/Treasury-style marketplace. New technology has fostered the late 1990s' formation of ECNs (electronic communication networks), essentially electronic trading exchanges. In turn, corporate bid/ask differentials generally have trended lower for very large, brand-name corporate issues. This powerful twin combination of technological innovation and competition promise the rapid development of an even more liquid and efficient global corporate market during the early 21st Century.

SECTION VI SECONDARY TRADE RATIONALES

Capital market and issuer expectations constantly change. Recession may arrive sooner rather than later. The yield curve may steepen rather than flatten. The auto and paper cycles may be moving down from their peaks. Higher oil and natural gas prices may benefit the credit quality of the energy sector. An industrial may have announced a large debt-financed acquisition, earning an immediate ratings rebuke from the agencies. A major bank may plan to repurchase 15% of its outstanding common stock (great for shareholders but leading to higher financial leverage for debtholders). In response to such daily information flows, portfolio managers amend their portfolios. To understand trading flows and the real dynamics of the corporate market, investors should consider the most common rationales to trade and not to trade.

A. Popular Reasons for Trading

There are dozens of rationales to execute secondary trades in the pursuit of portfolio optimization. Several of the most popular are discussed below. The framework for assessing the potential outcome of any secondary trade is the total return framework explained at Level II (Chapter 6).

1. Yield/Spread Pickup Trades

Yield/spread pickup trades account for the most common secondary transactions across all sectors of the global corporate market. Based on our observations, more than half of all secondary swaps reflect investor intentions to add additional yield within the duration and credit-quality constraints of a portfolio. If 5-year, A2/A GMAC paper trades at 99 bp, 5 bp more than 5-year, A1/A+ Ford Motor Credit at 94 bp, then some investors will deem the rating differential irrelevant and swap into GMAC for a spread gain of 5 bp per annum.

This "yield-first psychology" mirrors the institutional yield needs of long-term asset/liability managers. Despite the passage of more than two decades, this investor bias toward yield maximization also may be a methodological relic left over from the era prior to the introduction and market acceptance of total-return indices in the mid-1970s. At Level I (Chapter 6) the limitations of yield measures as an indicator of potential performance were explained. At Level II (Chapter 6), the total return framework was demonstrated to be a superior framework for assessing potential performance for a trade.

2. Credit-Upside Trades

Credit-upside trades are trades where the manager expects an upgrade in an issuer's credit quality that is not already reflected in the current spread required by the market. In the illustration of the GMAC and Ford Motor Credit trade described above, some investors may swap based on their view of potential credit-quality improvement for GMAC. Obviously, such trades rely on the credit analysis skills of the investment management team. Moreover, the manager must be able to identify a potential upgrade before the market, otherwise the spread for the upgrade candidate will already embody the benefits of a credit upgrade.

Credit-upside trades are particularly popular in the crossover sector — securities with ratings between Ba2/BB and Baa3/BBB− by either major rating agency. In this case, the portfolio manager is expressing his or her expectation that an issue of the highest speculative grade rating (Ba2/BB) has sufficiently positive credit fundamentals that it will soon be upgraded to investment grade (i.e., Baa3/BBB−). If this were to occur, not only would the issue's spread narrow based on the credit improvement (with an accompanying increase in total return, all else equal), but the issue also would benefit from improved liquidity, as managers prohibited from buying high-yield bonds could then purchase that credit. Further, the manager would be expecting an improvement in the portfolio's overall risk profile.

3. Credit-Defense Trades

Credit-defense trades become more popular as economic uncertainty increases. Secular sector transformations often generate uncertainties and induce defensive repositioning by investors. In anticipation of greater competition, some investors reduced their portfolio exposures in the mid-1990s to sectors like electric utilities and telecommunications. And as some Asian currencies and equities swooned in mid-1997, some portfolio managers cut their allocation to the Asian debt market. Unfortunately because of yield-maximization needs and a general reluctance to realize losses by some institutions (i.e., insurers), many investors tend to react more slowly to credit-defense propositions. Ironically once a credit is downgraded by the rating agencies, internal portfolio guidelines often dictate security liquidation immediately after the loss of single-A or investment-grade status. This is usually the worst possible time to sell a security and maximizes the harm incurred by the portfolio.

4. New Issue Swaps

New-issue swaps contribute to secondary turnover. Because of perceived superior liquidity, many portfolio managers prefer to rotate their portfolios gradually into more current and usually larger sized on-the-run issues. This disposition, reinforced by the usually superior market behavior of newer issues in the U.S. Treasury market (i.e., the on-the-run issues), has become a self-fulfilling prophecy for many corporate issues. In addition, some managers use new issue swaps to add exposure to a new issuer or a new structure.

5. Sector-Rotation Trades

Sector-rotation trades, within corporates and among fixed-income asset classes, have become more popular during the 1990s but do not rival similar activity in the equity market. In this strategy, the manager shifts the portfolio out of a sector or industry that she expects to underperform and into an industry which she believes will outperform on a total return basis. With the likely development of enhanced liquidity and lower trading transaction costs across the global bond market in the early 21st Century, sector-rotation trades should become more prevalent in the corporate bond asset class.

Such intra-asset class trading already has played a major role in differentiating performance among corporate bond portfolio managers. For example, as soon as the Fed launched its preemptive strike against inflation in February 1994, some investors correctly exchanged fixed-rate corporates for floating-rate corporates. In 1995, the specter of U.S. economic weakness prompted some investors in high-yield corporates to rotate from consumer-cyclical sectors like autos and retailing into consumer non-cyclical sectors like food, beverage, and healthcare. The anticipation of slower

U.S. economic growth in 1998 induced a defensive tilt by some portfolio managers away from other cyclical groups like paper and energy. The resurrection of Asian and European economic growth in 1999 stimulated increased portfolio interest in cyclicals, financial institutions, and energy debt.

6. Curve Adjustment Trades

Yield curve-adjustment trades, or simply, **curve-adjustment trades** are undertaken to reposition a portfolio's duration. For most corporate investors, their portfolio duration is typically within a range from 20% below to 20% above the duration of the benchmark index. If corporate investors could have predicted yield curve movements perfectly in 1994 and 1995, then they would have lowered their portfolio duration at the beginning of 1994 in anticipation of an increase in interest rates and extended their duration in late 1994 in anticipation of a decrease in interest rates. The reverse pattern prevailed in 1998 (extend duration) and 1999 (reduce duration). Although most fixed-income investors prefer to alter the duration of their aggregate portfolios in the more-liquid Treasury market, strategic portfolio duration tilts also can be implemented in the corporate market.

This is also done with respect to anticipated changes in the corporate curve. For example, if a portfolio manager believes that corporate bond spreads will tighten (either overall or in a particular sector), with rates in general remaining relatively stable, he or she might shift the portfolio's exposure to longer duration issues in that sector.

7. Structure Trades

Structure trades involve swaps into structures (e.g., callable structures, bullet structures, and put structures) that are expected to have better performance given expected movements in volatility and the shape of the yield curve. Here are some examples of how different structures performed in certain periods in the 1990s. (These results follow from the price/yield properties of the different structures that were explained at both Levels I and II.) Structural analysis is discussed in Section VIII of this chapter.

1. During the second quarter of 1995, the rapid descent of the yield curve contributed to underperformance of high-coupon callable structures because of their negative convexity property. (This characteristic of a callable bond, explained at Level I (Chapter 7) and Level II (Chapter 2) means that when interest rates decline, callable structures will not realize the same price appreciation as an otherwise comparable bullet (i.e., option-free) bonds.)

2. When the yield curve stabilized during the third quarter of 1995, investors were more willing to trade into an extra 35 bp of spread for high-quality callables compared to bullets of high quality.

3. The sharp downward rotation of the U.S. yield curve during the second half of 1997 also contributed to poor relative performance by put structures. The yield investors had sacrificed for protection against higher interest rates instead constrained total return as rates fell.

4. The plunge in U.S. interest rates and escalation of yield-curve volatility during the second half of 1998 again restrained the performance of callable struc-

tures compared to bullet structures. Recall from Level I (Chapter 5) and Level II (Chapter 2) that yield volatility adversely impacts that performance of a callable structure because an increase in volatility increases the value of the embedded call option.

5. The upward rebound in U.S. interest rates and the fall in interest-rate volatility during 1999 contributed to relative outperformance of callable structures.

8. Cash Flow Reinvestment

Cash flow reinvestment needs force investors into the secondary market on a regular basis. During 1999, the sum of all coupon, maturity, and partial redemptions (via tenders, sinking funds, and other issuer prepayments) equaled approximately 99% of all new gross origination across the dollar bond market. Before the allocation of any net new savings to the bond market, investors had sufficient incoming portfolio cash to absorb nearly all new bond supply. Some portfolio cash flows arrive during interludes in the primary market. And sometimes, the composition of recent primary supply may not be compatible with portfolio objectives. In these periods, corporate portfolio managers must shop the secondary market to remain fully invested. Portfolio managers who incorporate analysis of cash flow reinvestment into their evaluation of the corporate market can position their portfolios to take advantage of the potential effect on spreads.

B. Trading Constraints

Portfolio managers also should review their main rationales for not trading. Some of the best investment decisions are not to trade. Conversely, some of the worst investment decisions emanate from stale views based on dated and anachronistic constraints (e.g., avoid investing in bonds rated below Aa/AA). The best portfolio managers retain very open minds, constantly self-critiquing both their successful and unsuccessful methodologies.

1. Portfolio Constraints

Collectively, portfolio constraints are the single biggest contributor to the persistence of market inefficiency across the global corporate market. Here are some examples:

- Some U.S. state employee pension funds cannot purchase corporate securities with ratings below A3/A− under administrative and legislative guidelines.

- Some U.S. pension funds also have limitations on their ownership of MTNs and non-U.S. corporations.

- Regulators have limited the exposure of U.S. insurance companies to high-yield corporates.

- Many European investors are restricted to issues rated at least single-A and sometimes Aa3/AA− and above, created originally in annual-pay Eurobond form.

- Globally, many commercial banks must operate exclusively in the floating-rate realm: all fixed-rate securities, unless converted into floating-rate cash flows via an interest rate swap, are prohibited.

2. "Story" Disagreement

Traders, salespersons, sell-side analysts and strategists, and buy-side colleagues have dozens of potential trade rationales that supposedly will benefit portfolio performance. The proponents of a secondary trade may make a persuasive argument, but the portfolio manager may be unwilling to accept the "shortfall risk"[7] if the investment recommendation does not pan out. For example in early 1998, analysts and investors alike were divided equally on short-term prospects for better valuations of Asian sovereign debt. After a very disappointing 1997 for Asian debt performance, Asia enthusiasts had little chance to persuade pessimists to buy Asian debt at the outset of 1998. Technically, such lack of market consensus in the corporate market usually signals an investment with great outperformance potential. Indeed, most Asian debt issues recorded exceptional outperformance over the full course of 1998 and 1999.

3. Buy-and Hold

Although many long-term asset/liability managers claim to have become more total-return focused in the 1990s, accounting constraints (cannot sell positions at a loss compared to book cost or take too extravagant a gain compared to book cost) often limit the ability of these investors to transact. Effectively, these investors (mainly insurers) remain traditional "buy-and-hold" investors. And some active bond managers have converged to quasi-"buy-and-hold" investment programs at the behest of consultant recommendations to curb portfolio turnover. In the aftermath of the "Asian Contagion" in 1997-1998, this disposition toward lower trading has been reinforced by the reduction in market liquidity provided by more wary bond dealers.

4. Seasonality

Secondary trading slows at month ends, more so at quarter ends, and the most at the conclusion of calendar years. Dealers often prefer to reduce their balance sheets at fiscal year-end (November 30, December 31, or March 31 (Japan)). And portfolio managers take time to mark their portfolios, prepare reports for their clients, and chart strategy for the next investment period. During these intervals, even the most compelling secondary offerings can languish.

SECTION VII SPREAD ANALYSIS

By custom, some segments of the high-yield, emerging (EMG), and Eurobond markets still prefer to measure value by bond price or bond yield rather than spread. But for the rest of the global corporate market, nominal spread (the yield difference between corporate and government bonds of similar maturities) has been the basic unit of both price and relative-value analysis for more than two centuries.

A. Alternative Spread Measures

For comparability with the volatility ("vol") sectors (mortgage-backed securities and U.S. agencies),[8] many U.S. practitioners also prefer to cast the valuations of investment-grade corporate securities in terms of option-adjusted spreads (OAS). But given

---

[7] Shortfall risk is explained in Chapter 2.

[8] These sectors are referred to as "vol" sectors because the value of the securities issued in these sectors depends on expected interest rate volatility. These "vol" securities have embedded call options and the value of the options, and hence the value of the securities, depends on expected interest rate volatility. This was discussed extensively at Levels I and II.

the rapid reduction of corporate structures with embedded options during the 1990s (see structural discussion above), the use of OAS in primary and secondary pricing has diminished within the investment-grade corporate asset class. Moreover, the standard one-factor binomial models[9] of the 1990s do not account for credit spread volatility. Especially given the exclusion of default risk in OAS option-valuation models, OAS valuation has seen only limited extension into the higher-risk realms of the quasi-equity, high-yield corporate, and EMG-debt asset classes.

Starting in Europe during the early 1990s and gaining momentum during the late 1990s, interest rate swap spreads have emerged as the common denominator to measure relative value across fixed- and floating-rate note structures. During the next decade, the U.S. investment-grade and high-yield markets eventually may switch to swap spreads to be consistent with Europe and Asia.[10]

Other U.S. corporate spread calculations have been proposed, most notably off the U.S. agency benchmark curve. These proposals emanate from the assumption of persistent U.S. budgetary surplus and significant liquidation of outstanding U.S. Treasury securities during the first decade of the 21st Century. History teaches that these assumptions unfortunately may prove to be faulty. The inevitability of economic cycles and the potential for U.S. tax cuts will probably temper the realized reduction in U.S. Treasury debt by 2010. Moreover, the U.S. Treasury appreciates the benefits of a well-defined yield curve for the global capital markets. Although some practitioners may choose to derive corporate-agency spreads for analytical purposes, this practice will be unlikely to become standard market convention.

The market, therefore, has an ability to price any corporate debt instrument in multiple spread guises. These include the spread measures discussed at Level I (Chapter 6) — nominal spread, static or zero-volatility spread, and OAS — and credit-swap spreads (or simply swap spreads). The spread measures discussed at Level I (Chapter 6) used the Treasury yield curve or Treasury spot rate curve as the benchmark. Given the potential that swap spreads will become the new benchmark, these same measures can be performed relative to swaps rather than the U.S. Treasury sector.

B. Closer Look at Swap Spreads

Swap spreads were discussed at Level II (Chapter 7). They became a popular valuation yardstick for corporate bonds in Europe during the 1990s. This practice was enhanced by the unique nature of the European corporate asset class. Unlike its American counterpart, the European corporate market has been consistently homogeneous. Most issuance was of high quality (rated Aa3/AA– and above) and intermediate maturity. Consequently, swap spreads are a good proxy for credit spreads. Most issuers were financial institutions, natural swappers between fixed-rate and floating-rate obligations. And European corporate investors, often residing in financial institutions like commercial banks, have been much more willing to use swap methodology to capture value discrepancies between the fixed- and floating-rate markets.

Structurally, the Asian corporate market more closely resembles the European than the U.S. corporate market. As a result, the use of swap spreads as a valuation benchmark also has become common in Asia.

The investment-grade segment of the U.S. corporate bond market may well be headed toward an embrace of swap spreads. The U.S. MBS, agency, and ABS sectors made the transition to swap spreads as a valuation benchmark during the second half

---

[9] The binomial model was described at Level I (Chapter 2). The model is referred to as a one-factor model because only the short-term rate is the factor used to construct the tree.

[10] Swap spread were discussed at Level II (Chapters 7 and 8).

of the 1990s. And classical, nominal corporate spreads derived directly from the U.S. Treasury yield curve have been distorted by the special effects of U.S. fiscal surpluses and buybacks of U.S. Treasury securities. Accordingly, many market practitioners envision a convergence to a single global spread standard derived from swap spreads.

Here is an illustration of how a bond manager can use the swap spread framework. On March 21, 2000, Ford Motor Credit 7½'s of 2005 traded at a bid side price (i.e., the price at which a dealer is willing to buy the issue) of 113 bp over the 5-year U.S. Treasury yield of 6.43%. This equates to a yield-to-maturity of 7.56% (6.43% + 113 bp). On that date, 5-year swap spreads were at 83 bp (to the 5-year U.S. Treasury). Recall that swaps are quoted such that the fixed-rate payer pays the yield on a Treasury with a maturity equal to the initial term of the swap plus the swap spread. The fixed-rate payer receives LIBOR flat — that is, no increment over LIBOR. So, if the bond manager invests in the Ford Motor Credit issue and simultaneously enters into this 5-year swap, the following would result:

Receive from Ford Motor Credit (6.43% + 113 bp)	7.56%
− Pay on swap (6.43% + 83 bp)	7.26%
+ Receive from swap	LIBOR
Net	LIBOR + 30 bp

Thus, a bond manager could exchange this Ford Motor Credit bond's fixed coupon flow for LIBOR + 30 bp. On March 21, 2000, LIBOR was 6.24%, so that the asset swapper would earn 6.54% (= 6.24% + 30 bp) until the first reset date of the swap. A total return manager would want to take advantage of this swap by paying fixed and receiving floating if he expects that interest rates would increase in the future.

The swaps framework allows managers (as well as issuers) to more easily compare securities across fixed-rate and floating-rate markets. The extension of the swap spread framework may be less relevant for speculative-grade securities, where default risk becomes more important. In contrast to professional money managers, individual investors do not understand bond valuation couched in terms of swap spreads. The traditional nominal spread framework is well understood by individual investors, has the advantages of long-term market convention, and works well across the entire credit-quality spectrum from Aaas to Bs. However, this nominal spread framework does not work very well for investors and issuers in comparing the relative attractiveness between the fixed-rate and floating-rate markets.

C. Spread Tools

Investors should also understand how best to use spread tools for valuation decision-making. Spread tools include mean-reversion analysis, quality-spread analysis, and percent yield spread analysis.

1. Mean-Reversion Analysis

The most common technique for analyzing spreads among individual securities and across industry sectors is **mean-reversion analysis**. By "mean" it is meant the average value of some variable over a defined interval (usually one economic cycle for the corporate bond market). The term "mean reversion" means the tendency for some variable's value to revert (i.e., move towards) its average value. Mean-reversion analysis is a form of relative-value analysis based on the assumption that the spread between two sectors or two issuers will revert back to its historical average value. This would lead investors to buy a sector or issuer identified as "cheap" because the spread used to be much tighter and will eventually revert back to that tighter spread. Also, this would lead investors to sell a sector or issuer identified as "rich" because the spread used to be much wider and is expected to widen in the future.

Mean-reversion analysis involves the use of statistical analysis to assess whether the current deviation from the mean spread is significant. For example, suppose the mean spread for an issuer is 80 basis points over the past six months and the standard deviation is 12 basis points. Suppose that the current spread of the issuer is 98 basis points. The spread is 18 basis points over the mean spread or equivalently 1.5 standard deviations above the mean spread. The manager can use that information to determine whether or not the spread deviates enough to purchase the issue. The same type of analysis can be used to rank on a relative basis a group of issuers in a sector.

Mean-reversion analysis can be instructive as well as misleading. The mean is highly dependent on the interval selected. And there is no market consensus on the appropriate interval. And "persistence" frequents the corporate bond market. Cheap securities, mainly a function of credit uncertainty, often tend to become cheaper. Rich securities, usually high-quality issues, tend to remain on the rich side.

2. Quality-Spread Analysis

Quality-spread analysis examines the spread differentials between low and high-quality credits. For example, portfolio managers would be well advised to consider the "credit upgrade trade" discussed in Section VI when quality-spreads collapse to cyclical troughs. The incremental yield advantage of lower-quality products may not compensate for the potential of lower-quality spread expansion under less robust economic conditions. Alternatively, corporate bond portfolio managers have long profited from the over-weighting of lower-quality debt at the outset of an upward turn in the economic cycle.

3. Percent Yield Spread Analysis

Dating from the early 20th Century, **percent yield spread analysis** (the ratio of corporate yields to government yields for securities of similar duration[11]) is another popular technical tool with some investors. This methodology has serious drawbacks that undermine its usefulness. Percent yield spread is more a derivative than an explanatory or predictive variable. The usual expansion of corporate percent yield spreads during low-rate periods like 1997 and 1998 overstates the risk as well as the comparative attractiveness of corporate debt. And the typical contraction of corporate percent yield spreads during upward shifts of the benchmark yield curve does not necessarily signal an imminent bout of underperformance for the corporate asset class. Effectively, the absolute level of the underlying benchmark is merely a single factor among many factors (demand, supply, profitability, defaults, etc.) that determine the relative value of the corporate asset class. These other factors can offset or reinforce any insights derived from percent yield spread analysis.

SECTION VIII STRUCTURAL ANALYSIS

As explained earlier in this chapter, there are bullet, callable, putable, and sinking fund structures. **Structural analysis** is simply an analysis of the performance of the different structures as illustrated earlier in this chapter. While structural decision-making was extremely important in the 1980s, it became less influential in corporate

---

[11] This ratio was explained at Level I (Chapter 4).

bond portfolio management during the 1990s for several reasons. The European corporate bond market almost exclusively features intermediate bullets. The U.S. corporate and the global dollar-bond markets have moved to embrace this structurally homogeneous European bullet standard. Plenty of structural diversity still resides within the U.S. high yield and EMG debt markets. But portfolio decisions in these speculative-grade sectors understandably hinge much more on pure credit differentiation than the structural diversity of the issue-choice set.

Still, structural analysis can enhance risk-adjusted returns of corporate portfolios. As we discussed at Level II, leaving credit aside, issue structure analysis and structural allocation decisions usually hinge on yield curve and volatility forecasts as well as interpretation of option-valuation model outputs (see the discussion below). This is also a key input in making relative value decisions among structured corporate issues, mortgage-backed securities, and asset-backed securities. In the short run and assuming no change in the perceived creditworthiness of the issuer, yield curve and volatility movements will largely influence structural performance. But investors should also take into account long-run market dynamics that affect the composition of the market and, in turn, corporate index benchmarks.

Specifically, callable structures have become a rarer species in the U.S. investment-grade corporate bond market. This is due to an almost continuously positively-sloped U.S. term structure during the 1990s and the yield curve's intermittent declines to approximately three-decade lows in 1993, 1997, and 1998. As a result, the composition of the public U.S. corporate bond market converged toward the intermediate-bullet Eurobond and euro-denominated bond market. To see this, we need only look at the structure composition of Lehman's investment-grade corporate bond index. Bullets increased from 24% of this index at the start of 1990 to 68% on December 31, 1999 (principal value basis). Over this decade-long interval, callables declined at a remarkable rate from 72% to just a 25% index share. Sinking-fund structures, once the structural mainstay of natural-gas pipelines and many industrial sectors, are on the "structural endangered species list" with a drop from 32% of the public bond market in 1990 to only 2% at the end of 1999. Despite several brief flurries of origination in the mid-1990s and the late-1990s introduction of callable/putable structures, putable structure market share fell from 5% in 1990 to 4% by late 1999. Pure corporate zeros are in danger of extinction with a fall from 4% market share in 1990 to negligible by 1999.

A. Bullets

Here is a review of how different types of investors are using bullet structures with different maturities.

Front-end bullets (i.e., bullet structures with 1- to 5-year maturities) have great appeal to the growing number of investors who pursue a "barbell strategy." A barbell strategy was described at Level II (Chapter 6) in which both the short and long end of the barbell are U.S. Treasury securities. Today, there are "barbellers" who use corporates at the front or short-end of the curve and Treasuries at the long-end of the yield curve. There are non-U.S. institutions who convert short bullets into floating-rate products by using interest rate swaps. The transactions are referred to as "asset swaps" and the investors who employ this transaction are referred to as "asset swappers." The mechanism for doing an asset swap using interest rate swaps was described at Level II (Chapter 8).

Intermediate corporate bullets (5- to 12-year maturities), especially in the 10-year maturity sector, have become the most popular segment of the U.S. and European investment-grade and high-yield corporate markets. Fifteen-year maturities are comparatively rare and have been favored by banks that occasionally use them for certain types of swaps. Because 15-year structures take five years to roll down a positively-sloped yield curve, these structures hold less appeal for many investors. In contrast, 20-year structures are favored by many investors. Spreads for these structures are benched off the 30-year Treasury. With a positively-sloped yield curve, the 20-year structure provides higher yield than a 10-year or 15-year security and less vulnerability (lower duration) than a 30-year security.

The **30-year maturity** is the most popular form of long-dated security in the global corporate market. In 1992, 1993, late 1995, and 1997, there was a minor rush to issue 50-year (half-Centuries) and 100-year (Centuries) securities in the U.S. corporate bond market. These longer-dated securities provide investors with extra positive convexity for only a modest increase in effective (or modified-adjusted) duration.[12] In the wake of the "Asian Contagion" and especially the "Great Spread-Sector Crash" of August 1998, the cyclical increases in risk aversion and liquidity premiums greatly reduced both issuer and investor interest in these ultra-long maturities.

B. Callables

Typically after a 5-year or 10-year wait (longer for some rare issues), corporate structures are callable at the option of the issuer at any time. Call prices usually are set at a premium above par (par + the initial coupon) and decline linearly on an annual basis to par by 5-10 years prior to final scheduled maturity. The ability to refinance debt in a potentially lower-interest rate environment is extremely valuable to issuers. Conversely, the risk of earlier-than-expected retirement of an above-current market coupon is bothersome to investors.

In issuing callables, issuers pay investors an annual spread premium (about 30 bp to 40 bp for high-quality issuers) for being short the call option. Like all security valuations, this call premium varies through time with capital market conditions. Given the higher chance of exercise, this call option becomes much more expensive during low rate and high volatility periods. During the 1990s, this call premium ranged from approximately 20 bp to 50 bp for investment-grade issuers. Callables significantly underperform bullets when interest rates decline because of their negative convexity feature. When the bond market rallies, callable structures often do not fully participate given the upper boundary imposed by call prices. Conversely, callable structures outperform bullets in bear bond markets as the probability of early calls diminishes.

C. Sinking Funds

The various types of sinking fund structures were explained at Level I. A sinking fund structure allows an issuer to execute a series of partial calls (annually or semiannually) prior to maturity. There is also usually a provision to retire an additional portion of the issue on the sinking fund date, typically ranging from 1 to 2 times the mandatory sinking fund obligation. Historically, especially during the early 1980s, keen total return investors favored the collection of sinking fund structures at sub-par prices. These discounted sinking funds retained price upside during interest rate rallies (provided the indicated bond price remained below par). And given the issuers' requirement to retire at least annually some portion of the issue at par, the price of these sinking fund structures did not fall as much compared to callables and bullets when interest rates rose.

---

[12] Recall from the explanation at Level I (Chapter 7) that the longer the maturity, the greater the convexity.

D. Putables

Conceptually, put structures are simpler than callables. Yet in trading circles, put bond valuations often are the subject of much debate. American-option callables grant issuers the right to call an issue at any time at the designated call price after expiration of the non-callable or non-redemption period. Put bonds typically provide investors with a one-time, one-date put option (European option) to demand full repayment at par. Less frequently, put bonds include a second or third put option date. A very limited number of put issues afford investors the privilege to put such structures back to the issuers at par in the case of rating downgrades (typically to below investment-grade status).

Thanks to falling interest rates, issuers shied away from new put structures as the 1990s progressed. Rather than incur the risk of refunding the put bond in 5 or 10 years at a higher cost, many issuers would prefer to pay an extra 10 bp to 20 bp in order to issue a longer-term liability.

Put structures provide investors with a partial defense against sharp increases in interest rates. Assuming that the issuer still has the capability to meet its sudden obligation, put structures triggered by a credit event enable investors to escape from a deteriorating credit. Perhaps because of its comparative scarcity, the performance and valuation of put structures have been a challenge for many portfolio managers. Unlike callable structures, put prices have not conformed to expectations formed in a general volatility-valuation framework. Specifically, as explained at Level II (Chapter 1), the implied yield volatility of an option can be computed from the option's price and a valuation model. In the case of a putable bond, the implied volatility can be obtained using a valuation model such as the binomial model covered at Level II (Chapter 2). The implied volatility should be the same for both puts and calls, all factors constant. Yet, for putable structures, implied volatility has ranged between 4%-9% during the 1990s, well below the 10%-20% volatility range associated with callable structures for the same time period.

Unless put origination increases sharply, allowing for greater liquidity and the creation of more standardized trading conventions for this rarer structural specimen, this asymmetry in implied volatility between putable and corporate structures will persist. Meanwhile, this structure should be favored as an outperformance vehicle only by those investors with a decidedly bearish outlook for interest rates.

SECTION IX CORPORATE CURVE ANALYSIS

The rapid growth of credit derivatives[13] since the mid-1990s has inspired a ground-swell of academic and practitioner interest in the development of more rigorous techniques to analyze the term structure (1-100 years) and credit structure (Aaa/AAA through B2/Bs; defaulted high-yield securities trade on a price rather than a spread basis) of corporate spread curves.

Credit curves, both term structure and credit structure, are almost always positively sloped. In an effort to moderate portfolio risk, many portfolio managers choose to assume credit risk in short and intermediate maturities and to substitute less-risky government securities in long-duration portfolio buckets. This strategy is called a **credit barbell strategy**. Accordingly, the application of this strategy diminishes demand for longer-dated credit risk debt instruments by many total return, mutual fund, and bank portfolio bond managers. Fortunately for corporate issuers who desire to issue long maturities, insurers and pension plan sponsors often meet long-term liability needs through the purchase of corporate debt with maturities that range beyond 20 years.

---

[13] Credit derivatives are covered in Chapter 8.

Exhibit 3: Illustration of Corporate Curves as of March 15, 2000

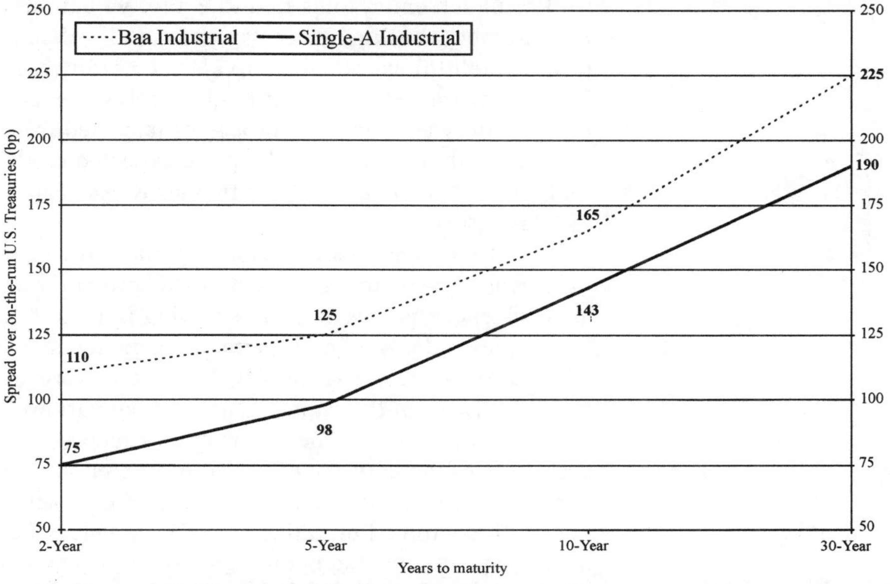

Default risk increases non-linearly as creditworthiness declines. The absolute risk of issuer default in any one year remains quite low through the investment-grade rating categories (Aaa/AAA to Baa3/BBB−). But investors constrained to high-quality investments often treat downgrades like quasi-defaults. In some cases like a downgrade from single-A to the Baa/BBB category, investors may be forced to sell securities under rigid portfolio guidelines. In turn, investors justifiably demand a spread premium for the increased likelihood of potential credit difficulty as rating quality descends through the investment-grade categories.

Credit spreads increase sharply in the high-yield rating categories (Ba1/BB+ through D). Default risk, especially for weak single Bs and CCCs, becomes a major possibility. The corporate market naturally assigns higher and higher risk premia (spreads) as credit and rating risk escalate. Exhibit 3 shows the corporate curve for two credit sectors (Baa and single A industrials) and illustrates the higher spread as maturity increases the lower the credit rating.

In particular, the investment-grade corporate market has a fascination with the slope of issuer credit curves between 10-year and 30-year maturities. Like the underlying Treasury benchmark curve, corporate spread curves change shape over the course of economic cycles. Typically, spread curves steepen when the bond market becomes more wary of interest rate and general credit risk. Spread curves also have displayed a minor propensity to steepen when the underlying benchmark curve flattens or inverts. This loose spread curve/yield curve linkage reflects the diminished appetite for investors to assume both curve and credit risk at the long end of the yield curve when higher total yields may be available in short and intermediate credit products.

**SECTION X
CREDIT
ANALYSIS**

In the continuous quest to seek credit upgrades and contraction in issuer/issue spread resulting from upgrades and, more importantly, to avoid credit downgrades resulting in an increase in issuer/issue spread, superior credit analysis has been and will remain the most important determinant of the relative performance of corporate bond portfolios. Fundamental credit analysis of corporate issues was covered at Level II (Chapter 9). Credit screening tools tied to equity valuations, relative spread movements, and the Internet (intelligent agents tracking all related news on portfolio holdings) can provide helpful supplements to classic credit research and rating agency opinions. But self-characterized credit models, relying exclusively on variables like interest-rate volatility and binomial processes imported from option-valuation techniques, are not especially helpful in ranking the expected credit performance of individual credits like IBM, British Gas, Pacific Gas & Electric, Pohang Iron & Steel, Sumitomo, and Argentina.

Credit analysis is both non-glamorous and arduous for many top-down portfolio managers and strategists, who focus primarily on macro variables. Genuine credit analysis encompasses actually studying issuers' financial statements and accounting techniques, interviewing issuers' managements, evaluating industry issues, reading indentures and charters, and developing an awareness of (not necessarily concurrence with) the views of the rating agencies about various industries and issuers.

Unfortunately, the advantages of such analytical rigor may clash with the rapid expansion of the universe of global bond credits. At the beginning of 2000, there were approximately 5,000 different credits scattered across the global corporate bond market. With continued privatization of state enterprises, new entrants to the high-yield market, and expected long-term growth of the emerging-debt markets, the global roster of issuers could swell to 7,500 or more by 2010. The sorting of this expanding roster of global corporate issues into outperformers, market performers, and underperformers demands the establishment and maintenance of a formidable credit-evaluation function by asset managers. Anything less would be a prescription for portfolio credit casualties.

SECTION XI ASSET ALLOCATION/ SECTOR ROTATION

Sector rotation strategies have long played a key role in equity portfolio management. In the corporate bond market, "macro" sector rotations among industrials, utilities, financial institutions, sovereigns, and supranationals also have a long history. During the last quarter of the 20th Century, there have been major variations in investor sentiment toward these major corporate bond sectors. Utilities endured market wariness about heavy supply and nuclear exposure in the early-to-mid 1980s. U.S. and European financial institutions coped with investor concern about asset quality in the late 1980s and early 1990s. Similar investor skittishness affected demand for Asian financial institution debt in the late 1990s. Industrials embodied severe "event risk"[14] in the mid-to-late 1980s, recession vulnerability during 1990-1992, and a return of event risk in the late 1990s amid a general boom in corporate mergers and acquisitions. And sovereigns were exposed to periodic market reservations about the implications of independence for Quebec, political risk for various countries (i.e., Russia), and the effects of the "Asian Contagion" during 1997-1998.

In contrast, "micro" sector rotation strategies have a briefer history in the corporate bond market. A detailed risk/return breakdown (i.e., average return and standard deviation) of the main corporate sectors (industrial, utility, finance, sovereigns, and supranationals) was not available from corporate index providers until 1993 in the United States and until 1999 in Europe. Beginning in the mid-1990s, these "micro" sector rotation strategies in the corporate asset class have become much more influential as portfolio managers gain a greater understanding of the relationships among intra-corporate sectors from these statistics.

---

[14] Event risk was covered at Level I (Chapter 2).

Exhibit 4: Some Outperformance Methodologies

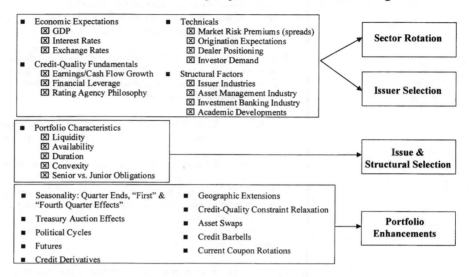

Exhibit 4 illustrates the main factors bearing on sector rotation and issuer selection strategies. For example, an actual or perceived change in rating agency philosophy toward a sector and revision in profitability expectations for a particular industry represent just two of many factors that can influence relative sectoral performance.

Common tactics to enhance, hopefully, corporate portfolio performance are also highlighted in Exhibit 4. In particular, seasonality deserves comment. The annual rotation toward risk aversion in the bond market during the second half of most years contributes to a "fourth-quarter effect" — that is, there is underperformance of lower-rated corporates, Bs in high-yield and Baas in investment-grade, compared to higher-rated corporates. A fresh spurt of market optimism greets nearly every New Year. Lower-rated corporates outperform higher-quality corporates — this is referred to as the "first-quarter effect." This pattern suggests a very simple and popular portfolio strategy: underweight low quality and possibly even corporate product until the mid-third quarter of each year and then overweight lower-quality and corporate product through the fourth quarter of each year.

SECTION XII
KEY POINTS

❑ *The "corporate asset class" includes more than pure corporate entities; this segment of the global bond market is more properly called the "credit asset class," including any nonagency mortgage-backed securities, commercial mortgage-backed securities, and asset-backed securities.*

❑ *Relative value refers to the ranking of fixed-income investments by sectors, structures, issuers, and issues in terms of their expected performance during some future interval.*

❑ *Relative-value analysis refers to the methodologies used to generate rankings of expected returns.*

❑ *Within the global corporate market, classic relative-value analysis combines top-down and bottom-up approaches, blending the macro input of chief investment officers, strategists, economists, and portfolio managers with the micro input of credit analysts, quantitative analysts, and portfolio managers.*

❑ *The objective of relative value analysis is to identify the sectors with the most potential upside, populate these favored sectors with the best representative issuers, and select the structures of the designated issuers at the yield curve points that match the investor's outlook for the benchmark yield curve.*

❑ *The main methodologies for corporate relative-value maximization are total return analysis, primary market analysis, liquidity and trading analysis, secondary trading rationales and trading constraints, spread analysis, structure analysis, corporate curve analysis, credit analysis, and asset allocation/sector analysis.*

❑ *Corporate relative-value analysis starts with a detailed decomposition of past returns and a projection of expected returns.*

❑ *Primary market analysis involves an analysis of the supply and demand for new issues.*

❑ *The global corporate market has become structurally more homogeneous, with the bullet structure (noncallable issues) with an intermediate maturity coming to dominate the high-grade market.*

❑ *The trend toward bullet securities does not pertain to the high-yield market, where callable structures dominate the market.*

❑ *Short-term and long-term liquidity influence portfolio management decisions.*

❑ *Corporate liquidity changes over time, varying with the economic cycle, credit cycle, shape of the yield curve, supply, and the season.*

❑ *Despite the limitations of yield measures, yield/spread pickup trades account for the most common secondary market trades across all sectors of the global corporate market.*

❑ *Credit-upside trades seek to capitalize on expectations of issues that will be upgraded in credit quality with such trades particularly popular in the crossover sector (securities with ratings between Ba2/BB and Baa3/BBB– by either rating agency).*

❑ *Credit-defense trades involve trading up in credit quality as economic uncertainty increases.*

❑ *Sector-rotation trades involve altering allocations among sectors based on relative-value analysis; such strategies can be used within the corporate bond market (intra-asset class sector rotation) and among fixed-income asset classes.*

❑ *Sector-rotation trades are not as popular in the bond market as in the equity market because of less liquidity and higher costs of trading; however, with the expected development of enhanced liquidity and lower trading transaction costs in the future, sector-rotation trades should become more prevalent in the corporate asset class.*

❑ *Trades undertaken to reposition a portfolio's duration are called yield curve-adjustment trades, or simply, curve-adjustment trades.*

❑ *Structure trades involve swaps into structures (e.g., callable structures, bullet structures, and put structures) that are expected to have better performance given anticipated movements in volatility and the shape of the yield curve.*

❑ *Portfolio managers should review their main rationales for not trading.*

❑ *Portfolio constraints are the single biggest contributor to the persistence of market inefficiency across the global corporate bond market*

❑ *Many U.S. practitioners prefer to cast the valuations of investment-grade corporate securities in terms of option-adjusted spreads (OAS), but given the rapid reduction of corporate structures with embedded options during the 1990s, the use of OAS in primary and secondary pricing has diminished within the investment-grade corporate asset class.*

❑ *Swap spreads have become a popular valuation yardstick for European corporates, Asian corporates, and U.S. MBS, agency, and ABS sectors.*

❑ *The popularity of swap spreads has taken root in the U.S. corporate market because the U.S. Treasury yield curve has been distorted by the special effects of U.S. fiscal surplus and the buyback of U.S. Treasuries.*

❑ *In the global corporate bond market, nominal spread (the yield difference between corporate and government bonds of similar maturities) has been the basic unit of both price and relative-value analysis.*

❑ *Mean-reversion analysis is the most common technique for analyzing spreads among individual securities and across industry sectors.*

❑ *Mean-reversion analysis can be misleading because the mean or average value is highly dependent on the time period analyzed.*

❑ *In quality-spread analysis, a manager examines the spread differentials between low- and high-quality credits.*

❑ *Structural analysis involves an analysis of the performance of different structures on a relative-value basis.*

❑ *Put structures provide investors with a partial defense against sharp increases in interest rates; this structure should be favored as an outperformance vehicle only by those investors with a decidedly bearish outlook for interest rates.*

❑ *Credit curves, both term structure and credit structure, are almost always positively sloped.*

❑ *In credit barbell strategies many portfolio managers choose to assume credit risk in short and intermediate maturities and to substitute less risky government securities in long-duration portfolio buckets.*

❑ *Like the underlying Treasury benchmark curve, corporate spread curves change shape over the course of economic cycles; typically, spread curves steepen when the bond market becomes more wary of interest rate and general credit risk.*

❑ *Superior credit analysis has been and will remain the most important determinant of the relative performance of corporate bond portfolios, allowing managers to identify potential credit upgrades and to avoid potential downgrades.*

END OF CHAPTER QUESTIONS

1. What is meant by relative value in the corporate bond market?

2. a. What is the dominant type of structure in the high-grade corporate bond market?
   b. What are the strategic portfolio implications of the dominance of the structure discussed in part (a)?
   c. What is the dominant structure in the high-yield corporate bond market and why is it not the same structure as discussed in part (a)?

3. The following quote is from Lev Dynkin, Peter Ferket, Jay Hyman, Erik van Leeuwen, and Wei Wu, "Value of Security Selection versus Asset Allocation in Credit Markets," Fixed Income Research, Lehman Brothers, March 1999, p. 3:

   > Most fixed income investors in the United States have historically remained in a single-currency world. Their efforts to outperform their benchmarks have focused on yield curve placement, sector and quality allocations, and security selection. The style of market participants is expressed in the amount of risk assumed along each of these dimensions (as measured by the deviation from their benchmarks), and their research efforts are directed accordingly.

   a. What is meant by "yield curve placement, sector and quality allocations, and security selection"?
   b. What is meant by the statement: "The style of market participants is expressed in the amount of risk assumed along each of these dimensions (as measured by the deviation from their benchmarks)"?

4. The following two passages are from Peter J. Carril, "Relative Value Concepts within the Eurobond Market," Chapter 29 in Frank J. Fabozzi (ed.), *The Handbook of Corporate Debt Instruments* (New Hope, PA: Frank J. Fabozzi Associates, 1998), p. 552.

   a. In discussing Eurobond issuers, Carril wrote: "Many first time issuers produce tighter spreads than one may anticipate because of their so called scarcity value." What is meant by scarcity value?
   b. In describing putable bonds Carril wrote: "Much analytical work has been devoted to the valuation of the put's option value, especially in the more mature U.S. investment grade market." However, he states that in the high-yield market the overriding concern for a putable issue is one of credit concern. Specifically, he wrote: "traditional analysis used to quantify the option value which the issuer has granted the investor is overridden by the investor's specific view of the creditworthiness of the issuer at the time of first put." Explain why.

5. In describing the approaches to investing in corporate bonds in emerging markets, Christopher Taylor wrote the following in "Challenges in the Credit Analysis of Emerging Market Corporate Bonds," Chapter 16 in Frank J. Fabozzi (ed.), *The Handbook of Corporate Debt Instruments* (New Hope, PA: Frank J. Fabozzi Associates, 1998), p. 311:

   > There traditionally have been two approaches to investing in emerging market corporate bonds: top-down and bottom-up. ... The *top-down approach* essentially treats investing in corporates as "sover-

eign-plus." The *bottom-up approach* sometimes has a tendency to treat emerging market corporates as "U.S. credits-plus."

What do you think Mr. Taylor means by "sovereign-plus" and "U.S. credits-plus"?

6. Chris Dialynas in "The Active Decisions in the Selection of Passive Management and Performance Bogeys," (in Frank J. Fabozzi (ed.), *Perspectives on Fixed Income Portfolio Management*, Volume 2) wrote:

> Active bond managers each employ their own methods for relative value analysis. Common elements among most managers are historical relations, liquidity considerations, and market segmentation. Market segmentation allegedly creates opportunities, and historical analysis provides the timing cure.

a. What is meant by "historical relations, liquidity considerations, and market segmentation" that Chris Dialynas refers to in this passage?
b. What do you think he means by: "Market segmentation allegedly creates opportunities, and historical analysis provides the timing cure."?

7. The following passages are from Leland Crabbe "Corporate Spread Curve Strategies," Chapter 28 in Frank J. Fabozzi (ed.), *The Handbook of Corporate Debt Instruments* (New Hope, PA: Frank J. Fabozzi Associates, 1998).

> In the corporate bond market, spread curves often differ considerably across issuers...
>
> Most fixed income investors understand the relation between the term structure of interest rates and implied forward rates. But some investors overlook the fact that a similar relation holds between the term structure of corporate spreads and forward corporate spreads. Specifically, when the spread curve is steep, the forward spreads imply that spreads will widen over time. By contrast, a flat spread curve gives rise to forwards that imply stability in corporate spreads. Essentially the forward spread can be viewed as a breakeven spread...
>
> Sometimes, investors may disagree with the expectations implied by forward rates, and consequently they may want to implement trading strategies to profit from reshapings of the spread curve.

a. What is meant by "spread curves" and in what ways do they differ across issuers?
b. At Level I (Chapter 6) and Level II (Chapter 1), the relationship between the term structure of interest rates and implied forward rates (or simply forward rates) was explained. What is a "forward spread" that Mr. Crabbe refers to and why can it be viewed as a breakeven spread?
c. How can implied forward spreads be used in relative-value analysis?

8. What is the limitation of a yield-pickup trade?

9. In the 1990s, increases in new issuance of investment-grade corporate bonds were observed to be accompanied by a contracting of spreads and strong relative bond returns. In contrast, spread expansion and a major decline in both relative and

absolute returns accompanied a sharp decline in the supply of new corporate issues. These outcomes are in stark contrast to the conventional wisdom held by many portfolio managers that supply hurts spreads on corporate bonds. What reason can be offered for the observed relationship between new supply and changes in spread for corporate bonds?

10. a. What is meant by the "crossover sector of the bond market"?
    b. How do portfolio managers take advantage of potential credit upgrades in the crossover sector?

11. When would a portfolio manager consider implementing a credit-defense trade?

12. What is the motivation for portfolio managers to trade into more current and larger sized on-the-run issues?

13. a. Why has the swap spread framework become a popular valuation yardstick in Europe for corporate bonds?
    b. Why might U.S. managers embrace the swap spread framework for the corporate asset class?
    c. Compare the advantages/disadvantage of the nominal spread framework to the swap spread framework.

14. The ABC Corporate issue traded at a bid side price of 120 bp over the 5-year U.S. Treasury yield of 6.00% at a time when LIBOR was 5.7%. At the same time, 5-year LIBOR-based swap spreads were at 100 bp (to the 5-year U.S. Treasury).

    a. If a manager purchased the ABC Corporate issue and entered into a swap to pay fixed and receive floating, what is the spread over LIBOR that will be realized until the first swap reset date?
    b. Why would a total return manager buy the issue and then enter into a swap to pay fixed and receive floating?

15. The following was reported in the "Strategies" section of the January 3, 2000 issue of *BondWeek* ("Chicago Trust to Move Up in Credit Quality," p. 10):

> The Chicago Trust Co. plans to buy single A corporate bonds with intermediate maturities starting this quarter, as the firm swaps out of lower-rated, triple B rated paper to take advantage of attractive spreads from an anticipated flood of single A supply. ...

The portfolio manager gave the following reasoning for the trade:

> ... he says a lack of single A corporate offerings during the fourth quarter has made the paper rich, and he expects it will result in a surge of issuance by single A rated companies this quarter, blowing out spreads and creating buying opportunities. Once the issuance subsides by the end of the quarter, he expects spreads on the single A paper will tighten.

    a. What type of relative value analysis is the portfolio manager relying on in making this swap decision and what are the underlying assumptions? (Note: When answering this question, keep the following in mind. The manager made the statement at either the last few days of December 1999 or the first two days in January 2000. So, reference to the fourth quarter means the last quarter in 1999. When the statement refers to the end of the quarter or to "this quarter" it is meant the first quarter of 2000.)

b. Further in the article it was stated that the portfolio manager felt that on an historical basis the corporate market as a whole was cheap. The portfolio manager used new cash to finance purchases of healthcare credits, doubling the portfolio's allocation to the healthcare sector. The portfolio manager felt that the issuers in the healthcare sector he purchased for the portfolio had fallen out of favor with investors as a result of concerns with healthcare reform. He thought that the cash flows for the issuers purchased were strong and the concerns regarding reform were "overblown." Discuss the key elements to this strategy.

16. The following was reported in the "Strategies" section of the January 3, 2000 issue of *BondWeek* ("... Even as Wright Moves Down." p. 10):

> Wright Investors Services plans to buy triple B rated corporate paper in the industrial sector and sell higher rated corporate paper on the view that stronger-than-anticipated economic growth will allay corporate bond investor fears.

In the article, the following was noted about the portfolio manager's view:

> spreads on higher rated investment grade paper already have come in some from last summer's wides, but he believes concerns over year-end and rising rates have kept investors from buying lower rated rated corporate paper, keeping spreads relatively wide.

Discuss the motivation for this strategy and the underlying assumptions.

17. The following appeared in the "Strategies" section of the September 27, 1999 issue of *BondWeek* ("Firm Sticks to Corps, Agencies," p.6):

> The firm, which is already overweight in corporates, expects to invest cash in single A corporate paper in non-cyclical consumer non-durable sectors, which should outperform lower-quality, cyclicals as the economy begins to slow.

Discuss this strategy and its assumptions.

18. a. Suppose that a manager believes that corporate spreads are mean reverting. Below are three issues along with the current spread, the mean (average) spread over the past six months, and the standard deviation of the spread. Assuming that the spreads are normally distributed, which issue is the most likely to be purchased based on mean-reversion analysis.

Issue	Current spread	Mean spread for past 6 months	Standard deviation of spread
A	110 bp	85 bp	25 bp
B	124	100	10
C	130	110	15

b. What are the underlying assumptions in using mean-reversion analysis?

19. Ms. Xu is the senior portfolio manager for the Solid Income Mutual Fund. The fund invests primarily in investment-grade corporate bonds and agency mortgage-backed securities. For each quarterly meeting of the board of directors of the mutual fund, Ms. Xu provides information on the characteristics of the portfolio and changes in the composition of the portfolio since the previous board meeting. One of the board members notices two changes in the composition of the portfolio. First, he notices that while the percentage of the portfolio invested in corporate bonds was unchanged, there was a sizeable reduction in callable corporate bonds relative to noncallable corporate bonds. Second, while the portfolio had the same percentage of mortgage passthrough securities, there was a greater percentage of low-coupon securities relative to high-coupon securities.

When Ms. Xu was asked why she changed the structural characteristics of the securities in the portfolio, she responded that it was because the management team for the fund expected a significant drop in interest rates in the next quarter and the structures included would benefit more than the structures held in the previous quarter. One of the directors asked why. How should Ms. Xu respond?

20. Ms. Smith is the portfolio manager of the Good Corporate Bond Fund, which invests primarily in investment-grade corporate bonds. The fund currently has an overweighting within the industrial sector in bonds of retailers. Ms. Smith is concerned that increased competition from internet retailers will negatively impact the earnings and cash flow of the traditional retailers. The fund is also currently underweighted in the U.S. dollar-denominated bonds of European issuers placed in the United States, which she believes should benefit from increased opportunities afforded by European Union. She believes that many of these companies may come to market with new U.S. dollar issues to fund some of their expansion throughout Europe.

Formulate and support a strategy for Ms. Smith that will capitalize on her views about the retail and European corporate sectors of her portfolio. What factors might negatively impact this strategy?

SOLUTIONS TO END OF CHAPTER QUESTIONS

1. Relative value refers to the ranking of corporate bond sectors, structures, issuers, and issues in terms of their expected performance over some future time period.

2. a. The dominant structure in the high-grade corporate bond market is the bullet structure with an intermediate maturity.

   b. There are three strategic portfolio implications of the bullet structure with an intermediate maturity:

      1. The dominance of bullet structures creates a scarcity value for structures with embedded call and put features, resulting in premium price for bonds with embedded call options. This "scarcity value" should be considered by managers in relative-value analysis of corporate bonds.

      2. Because long-dated maturities will decline as a percentage of outstanding corporate debt, there will be a lower effective duration of all outstanding corporate debt and, as a result, a reduction in the aggregate sensitivity to interest-rate risk.

      3. There will be increased use of corporate derivatives in strategies, whether on a stand-alone basis or embedded in structured notes, so that investors and issuers can gain exposure to the structures that they desire.

   c. High-yield issuers will continue to issue callable bond structures in order to have the opportunity to refinance at a lower credit spread should credit quality improve.

3. a. Yield curve placement is simply the positioning of a portfolio with respect to duration and yield curve risk. Trades involving yield curve placement are referred to as curve adjustment trades in the chapter. Sector and quality allocations refer to allocations based on relative value analysis of the different bond market sectors and quality sectors. Security selection involves the purchase or avoidance of individual issues based on some relative value basis.

   b. For a manager who is evaluated relative to some bond index, the deviation of the portfolio from the benchmark in terms of yield curve exposure, sector exposure, quality exposure, and exposure to individual issues is the appropriate way to measure risk. The methodology for this is illustrated in Chapter 4, Section IV of this book.

4. a. Scarcity value means that an issue will trade at a premium price due to a lack of supply (relative to demand) for that issue. This is the same as saying that the issue will trade at a narrower spread. If investors want exposure to a particular issue that is first coming to market, the spread can be narrower than otherwise comparable issuers.

   b. Analytical models for valuing bonds with embedded put options ignore the ability of the issuer to fulfill the obligation to repurchase an issue if the bondholder exercises the put option. For high-yield issuers there is the credit risk associated with this inability to satisfy the put obligation. Thus, for high-yield issuers the credit risk may override the value for a putable issue derived from a valuation model.

5. In general, the top-down approach involves beginning with a macro-economic outlook and making allocation decisions to sectors based on that outlook. With respect to corporate bonds in emerging markets, the top-down approach begins with the assessment of the economic outlook for emerging market countries and then basing the allocation of funds across emerging market corporate issuers in different coun-

tries on that macroeconomic outlook. This is what Mr. Taylor means by "sovereign plus." The bottom-up approach focuses on the selection of corporate issuers in emerging market countries that are expected to outperform U.S. corporate issuers. This is what Mr. Taylor means by "U.S. credits-plus."

6. a. Historical relations help a portfolio manager identify opportunities when current spreads are out of line and relative-value opportunities may be available. Liquidity considerations affect spreads and the ability to trade. Market segmentation means factors affecting supply and demand within sectors of the bond market due to impediments or restrictions on investors from reallocating funds across bond sectors.

   b. Market segmentation may create relative value opportunities when spreads get out of line due to impediments that prevent or impede investors from allocating funds to certain sectors due to regulatory constraints and asset/liability constraints. Market segmentation may affect the supply of bonds in a sector for the same reasons. Historical analysis of spreads, based on mean-reversion analysis, for example, identifies those opportunities which, in turn, drives spreads to some "normal" equilibrium level.

7. a. Spread curves show the relationship between spreads and maturity. They differ by issuer or sector in terms of the amount of the spread and the slope of the spread curve.

   b. At Levels I and II, forward rates were discussed and how they are derived was demonstrated. It was shown that forward rates are derived from spot rates using arbitrage arguments. A forward spread, or an implied forward spread, can be derived in the same way. Also, it was explained that forward rates are basically hedgeable or breakeven rates — rates that will make an investor indifferent between two alternatives. For example, for default-free instruments a 2-year forward rate 3 years from now is a rate that will make an investor indifferent between investing in a 5-year zero-coupon default-free instrument or investing in a 3-year zero-coupon default-free instrument and reinvesting the proceeds for two more years after the 3-year instrument matures.

   A forward spread can be interpreted in the same way. For example, a 2-year forward spread 3 years from now is the credit spread that will make an investor indifferent to investing in a 5-year zero-coupon instrument of an issuer or investing in a 3-year zero-coupon instrument of the same issuer and reinvesting the proceeds from the maturing instrument in a 2-year zero-coupon instrument of the same issuer.

   The forward spread is a breakeven spread because it is the spread that would make the investor indifferent between two alternative investments with different maturities over a given investment horizon.

   c. Because a forward spread is one that will make an investor indifferent between two alternatives, a manager must compare his or her expectations relative to the forward spread. Relative-value analysis involves making this comparison of expectation for the spread versus what is built into market prices (i.e., forward spreads).

8. At Level I, it was emphasized that yield measures are poor indicators of the total return that will be realized by holding a security to maturity or over some investment horizon that a manager will be evaluated. Thus, an asset manager does not

know what a yield pick-up of, say, 20 basis point means for subsequent total return. A bond manager can pickup yield on a trade (holding credit quality constant), but on a relative value basis underperform an alternative issue with a lower yield over the manager's investment horizon.

An example of this would be if at the beginning of the month, a portfolio manager sold the 5-year Ford issue at a spread of 94 basis points, and purchased the 5-year GMAC issue at a spread of 99 basis points, for a yield pickup of 5 basis points. If the spread on the Ford issue continued to tighten throughout the month, while the GMAC issue's spread remained constant, the Ford issue would outperform the GMAC issue on a total return basis.

9. The reason suggested as to why heavy supply of new investment-grade corporate issues will help spreads contract and enhance returns is that new primary bond valuations validate and enhance secondary valuations. In contrast, when new issuance declines sharply, secondary traders lose reinforcement from the primary market and tend to require higher spreads.

10. a. The crossover sector refers to the sector with issuers whose ratings are between Ba2/BB and Baa3/BBB– by either rating agency. These issuers are on the border between investment grade and high yield.
 b. A manager can purchase a below-investment grade issue which his credit analysis projects will be upgraded to investment grade. If the manager's assessment is correct, then the issue will outperform due to spread narrowing resulting from the upgrade, and also from increased liquidity of the issue as it becomes available to a broader class of investors.

11. A portfolio manager would consider implementing a credit-defense trade when there is increased concern about the outlook for the economy and there is a concern with a widening of credit spreads.

12. The motivation is to increase the liquidity.

13. a. The European corporate market has been consistently homogeneous with most issues of high quality (rated Aa3/AA– and above) and intermediate maturity. So swap spreads were a good proxy for credit spreads. Because of the homogeneous character of the corporate market in Europe, the swaps framework allows managers as well as issuers to more easily compare securities across fixed- and floating-rate markets. Moreover, in Europe, financial institutions such as commercial banks have been much more willing to use swap methodology to capture value discrepancies between the fixed- and floating-rate markets.
 b. U.S. managers have started to embrace swap spreads for the MBS, agency, and ABS sectors because nominal spreads derived directly from the U.S. Treasury curve have been distorted by the special effects of U.S. fiscal surplus and buybacks of U.S. Treasury securities.
 c. Individual investors understand the traditional nominal spread framework as a market convention. Moreover, despite its limitations this framework can be used across the entire credit-quality spectrum from Aaas to Bs. The disadvantage is that the nominal spread framework does not work very well for investors and issuers in comparing the relative attractiveness between the fixed- and floating-rate markets. This is the advantage of using the swap framework.

14. a. By buying ABC Corporation issue and entering into a 5-year swap to pay fixed and receive floating, the spread over LIBOR until the first reset date for the swap is:

Receive from ABC Corp. (6.00% + 120 bp)	7.20%
− Pay on swap (6.00% + 100 bp)	7.00%
+ Receive from swap	LIBOR
Net	LIBOR + 20 bp

Since LIBOR is 5.7%, the manager is locking in a rate of 5.9% (= 5.7% + 20 basis points) until the first reset date.

b. If the manager expects that interest rates will increase, total return performance will be better using the swap.

15. a. The manager is relying on primary market analysis. The manager believes that one of the reasons why the spread on single A rated issues may be out of line in the fourth quarter of 1999 is due to the lack of single A rated issues coming to market in that quarter. The lack of supply increased the spread and this lack of supply is the main cause of the attractive spread level. The manager expects that in the first quarter of 2000, there will be a surge of single A rated issues that will come to market, resulting in a widening of the spread and thereby providing an opportunity to purchase single A rated issues relatively cheaply versus BBB issues.

The assumption is that the attractive level of the corporate spread for single A rated issuers is driven principally by new issuance and not any structural issue or other factor that determines corporate spreads. Furthermore, it is assumed that once the market is cleared of the increase in supply of single A rated issuers will narrow the spread and provide better performance relative to BBB rated issuers. (See the question based on another article in *BondWeek* that appeared in the same issue.)

b. The keys to this strategy are (1) that the cash flows will in fact remain strong, (2) that the spread for these health care issuers are not justified by the strong cash flow due to concerns with healthcare reform, and (3) that investors in the bond market will recognize this (by some time period), resulting in a decline in the credit spread for these issuers.

16. The motivation for this strategy is that while investment grade issues may decline due to stronger-than-anticipated economic growth, a good amount of spread reduction has already occurred in the above BBB rated sectors. Thus, on a relative basis, the decline in corporate spreads on investment grade bonds due to stronger-than-anticipated growth will be primarily in the BBB rated sectors. The assumption is that spreads will contract more in the BBB rated sector.

17. This relative value strategy has two elements to it. First, there appears to be an allocation to single A rated corporates versus lower quality corporates. Hence, it appears to be a credit-defense trade because of a concern with the economy slowing down. Moreover, there is an allocation within the single A rated corporates to a sector — non-cyclical consumer non-durables — that is expected to outperform an alternative sector — cyclicals — should the economy slow down.

18. One can use mean-reversion analysis in this question as follows. For each issue, the number of standard deviations that the current spread is above the historical average (the mean spread for the past six months) is computed as shown below:

Issue	Number of standard deviations above mean
A	$(110 - 85)/25 = 1.0$
B	$(124 - 100)/10 = 2.4$
C	$(130 - 110)/15 = 1.3$

Issue B has the largest deviation above the mean and it therefore the one more likely to contract. Actually, based on a normal probability the probability associated with realizing a specified number of standard deviation above the mean can be determined.

b. The assumptions are that (1) the spreads will revert back to their historic means, (2) the spreads are normally distributed, and (3) there have been no structural changes in the market that would render the historical mean and standard deviation useless for purposes of the analysis.

19. Ms. Xu should first explain that callable bonds exhibit negative convexity when interest rate decline while noncallable bonds exhibits positive convexity. This means that when rates decline, the price appreciation for a callable bond will not be as great as an otherwise noncallable bond. Since the management team for the fund expected a significant drop in interest rates in the next quarter, to better participate in the rise in bond prices, there was a shift to noncallable corporate bonds.

All mortgage passthrough securities exhibit negative convexity. However, low-coupon issues exhibit less negative convexity than high-coupon issues. That is, there will be greater price appreciation for low-coupon issues when rates decline. Given the anticipated decline in interest rates, the low-coupon issues will appreciate more and hence the reason for the shift to such issues.

20. Ms. Smith could sell retail issues and use the proceeds to purchase U.S. dollar-denominated corporate bonds of European issuers. This would be consistent with her expectation of underperformance of the retail microsector and outperformance of the European corporate sector. She could make her purchases in the new issue market, if she believes that the new issuance will be attractively priced.

Ms. Smith should use credit analysis to select which issues to buy or sell within each sector. She must consider the possibility of a risk premium in the European corporate sector, as some managers cannot purchase bonds in that sector. Seasonality may also be a factor, depending on the timing of her purchases/sales.

Chapter 6

INTERNATIONAL BOND PORTFOLIO MANAGEMENT

Christopher B. Steward, CFA
Vice President
Wellington Management Company, LLP

J. Hank Lynch, CFA
Vice President
BankBoston

Frank J. Fabozzi, Ph.D., CFA
Adjunct Professor of Finance
School of Management
Yale University

LEARNING OUTCOME STATEMENTS

After reading this chapter you should be able to:

- explain how the investment objectives of investors are related to the management of an international bond portfolio.
- explain how the investment guidelines for an international bond portfolio should incorporate the investor's investment objectives.
- identify the benchmarks available to international bond investors.
- explain the difference between the active and passive approach to currency management.
- identify the key trading blocs.
- discuss the styles of international bond portfolio management (the experienced trader, the fundamentalist, the black box, and the chartist).
- explain the broad strategies (bond market selection, currency selection, duration management/yield curve plays, sector/credit/security selection, and investing in markets outside the benchmark) that can potentially generate excess returns relative to an international bond index.
- identify the fundamental economic factors used by a portfolio manager to create an economic outlook for a country.
- explain the objective measures of value and technical indicators used by international bond portfolio managers (real yields, technical analysis, and market sentiment surveys).
- explain the three components of excess returns (excess returns on bonds, excess returns on currencies, and short-term risk interest rate) from international bond portfolio management.
- explain what a currency forward contract is.
- compute the fair value of a currency forward contract.
- explain what interest rate parity is.
- explain what covered interest arbitrage is.
- explain the following strategies for managing currency risk exposure: hedge, cross currency hedge, and proxy hedge.
- compute the components of excess returns for an unhedged strategy, a hedged strategy, a cross currency hedged strategy, and a proxy hedged strategy.
- determine whether an unhedged or some hedged strategy should be employed by a manager to handle currency risk exposure.
- explain what bond and currency breakeven rates are.
- explain the role of forward interest rates and currency forward rates in identifying investment opportunities in countries.

SECTION I
INTRODUCTION

Management of an international bond portfolio poses more varied challenges than management of a domestic bond portfolio. Differing time zones, local market structures, settlement and custodial issues, and currency management all complicate the fundamental decisions facing every fixed income manager in determining how the portfolio should be positioned with respect to duration, sector, and yield curve.

In Chapter 1 the fundamental steps in the investment management process were explained. These steps include:

1. setting investment objectives
2. developing and implementing a portfolio strategy
3. monitoring the portfolio
4. adjusting the portfolio

The added complexities of cross-border investing magnify the importance of a well defined, disciplined, investment process. The chapter is organized to address these challenges for steps 1, 2, and 4.

To provide a broad overview of the many aspects of international fixed income investing within the scope of one chapter implies that many topics do not receive the depth of discussion that they deserve. The topic of currency management is extensive and we provide only the fundamental principals here. However, the same principles involved with currency management apply equally to international equity portfolio management.

While many of the examples and illustrations in this chapter apply to international investing from the perspective of a U.S. manager investing in bond markets outside of the United States, it is important to keep in mind that the principles apply to any cross-border manager investing outside of his or her domestic bond market. The same issues faced by U.S. managers regarding currency management apply to managers throughout the world when they invest in bonds in which the cash flows are not denominated in their local currency.

SECTION II
INVESTMENT
OBJECTIVES
AND
POLICY
STATEMENTS

Most investors are attracted to global bonds as an asset class because of their historically higher returns than U.S. bonds. Others are drawn to global bonds because of their diversification value in reducing overall portfolio risk.[1] *The investor's rationale for investing in international bonds is central to developing appropriate return objectives and risk tolerances for a portfolio.*

Broadly speaking, investor objectives include:

1. return objectives
2. risk tolerances

Each of these investment objectives has implications for the management of an international bond portfolio and should be reflected in the investment policy statement.

---

[1] Some investors were concerned that the diversification benefits of global bond investing would be substantially diminished by the commencement of European Monetary Union (EMU) in 1999. But, in fact, the economies of continental Europe were already very closely tied together before EMU with most European central banks following the interest rate policies of the German Bundesbank for several years before the move to a single currency. Thus, the impact on diversification of a global bond portfolio caused by EMU has been a small one. EMU, however, has created a much more robust credit market in Europe as issuers and investors, no longer confined to their home markets, have access to a larger, more liquid pan-European bond market. Corporate bond issuance has increased sharply in Europe, and seems likely to continue, building toward a broader range of credits and instruments similar to those available in the U.S. bond market. This was discussed in Chapter 5.

Return objectives are often expressed in terms of the benchmark return, e.g., benchmark return plus 100 basis points after management fees. The return objectives and risk tolerances will indicate not only the most appropriate benchmark, but also the most suitable management style. Investors who are primarily concerned with diversification may wish to place tight limits on the size of positions taken away from the benchmark to ensure that the diversification benefit is not weakened. A total-return oriented investor might be far less concerned with how the portfolio composition differs from the benchmark, but may be more critical of shortfalls in performance.

Investment policy statements should be flexible enough to allow the portfolio manager sufficient latitude for active management while keeping the portfolio close enough to the benchmark to ensure that the portfolio remains diversified. The policy statements should address allowable investments including:

1. the countries in the investment universe
2. minimum credit ratings
3. the use of derivatives such as futures, options, and structured notes

The time horizon over which investment performance is to be measured is also important. A short-term time horizon, such as a calendar quarter, may encourage more short-term trading which could diminish the natural diversification benefit from international bonds as an asset class. Investors who emphasize the risk reduction, or diversification aspect of international bond investing, should have a longer time horizon of perhaps two to three years. As differences between economic cycles can be prolonged, this would provide enough time for a full economic cycle to play out and the diversification benefit to be realized.

A. Benchmark Selection

Benchmark selection for an international bond portfolio has many ramifications and should therefore be done carefully. As is the case when choosing an international equity benchmark index, the choice of a pure capitalization (market value) weighted index may create a benchmark that exposes the investor to a disproportionate share in the Japanese market relative to the investor's liabilities or diversification preferences. While international equity indices chosen for benchmarks are most often quoted in the investor's local currency (i.e., unhedged), international bond benchmarks may be hedged, unhedged, or partially hedged depending on the investor's objectives. The choice of a hedged, unhedged, or hybrid benchmark will likely alter the risk and return profile of the resulting investment portfolio and should thus be done with careful consideration of the primary rationale for investing in international bonds.

B. Available Benchmarks

Benchmarks can be selected from one, or a combination, of the many existing bond indices:

- global
- international (ex-U.S.)
- currency-hedged
- G7 only
- maturity constrained, e.g., 1-3 year, 3-5 year, 7-10 year
- emerging markets

Alternatively, a customized index or "normal" portfolio can be created.[2]

---

[2] A normal portfolio is explained in Chapter 9.

The most frequently used fixed-income benchmarks are the **J.P. Morgan Global Government Bond Index**, and the **Salomon Smith Barney World Government Bond Index (WGBI)**, although many other investment houses such as Merrill Lynch, Lehman Brothers, and Goldman Sachs offer full index services as well. Since the launch of European Monetary Union, corporate bond issuance in Europe has risen sharply. New indices such as the **Lehman Euro Aggregate** that include corporate bonds may provide a better representation of the investible universe. The benchmark often provides both the return objective and the measure of portfolio risk.

C. Benchmark Currency Position

Currency management is a matter of much debate in the academic literature.[3] The natural currency exposures incurred through international investing require portfolio managers to adopt either an **active** or **passive approach to currency management**.

Many managers are attracted to active currency management because of the large gains that can be attained through correctly anticipating currency movements. Some international fixed income portfolio managers, however, prefer not to actively manage currency exposures. This may reflect doubts about their own ability to add value through active currency management, or a belief that no one can forecast currency movements with any degree of reliability. The former often hire outside currency overlay managers to manage the residual currency risk determined by the bond allocation, the latter often run fully hedged or unhedged portfolios as a matter of policy.

Both approaches are likely to be sub-optimal as compared to an integrated approach that determines bond and currency allocations simultaneously.[4] Although many international fixed income portfolio managers place greater emphasis on bond market allocations while managing currency exposure as a residual, the same fundamental economic factors (identified later in this chapter) which influence bond prices also impact currency levels.

Most of the academic research on currency hedging for U.S. dollar-based investors suggests that a partially hedged benchmark offers superior risk-adjusted returns as compared with either a fully hedged or unhedged benchmark.[5] This research has led some to recommend a 50% hedged benchmark for either a passively managed currency strategy, or as a good initial hedged position for an active currency manager. In addition to selecting an appropriate benchmark, a suitable currency hedge position needs to be determined. For example, a U.S. dollar-based fixed income manager whose primary goal is risk reduction might adopt a hedged or mostly hedged benchmark as the diversification benefit has historically been greater from hedged international bonds. Despite a higher correlation with the U.S. bond market than unhedged international bonds, hedged international bonds offer better risk reduction due to a lower standard deviation of return than even the U.S. market.[6] In addition, this lesser volatility of hedged international bonds results in more predictable returns.

[3] For an excellent overview of currency management practices, including a detailed review of historical data, see Roger G. Clarke and Mark P. Kritzman *Currency Management: Concepts and Practices* (Charlottesville, VA: The Research Foundation of the Institute of Chartered Financial Analysts, 1996).

[4] See Philippe Jorion, "Mean/Variance Analysis of Currency Overlays," *Financial Analysts Journal* (May/June 1994), pp. 48-56. Jorion argues that currency overlays, although they can add value, are inferior to an integrated approach to currency management.

[5] See Gary L. Gastineau, "The Currency Hedging Decision: A Search for Synthesis in Asset Allocation," *Financial Analysts Journal* (May-June 1995), pp. 8-17 for a broad overview of the currency hedging debate. For a full discussion of the benefits of utilizing a partially hedged benchmark, see the currency discussion in Steve Gorman, *The International Equity Commitment* (Charlottesville, VA: AIMR 1998).

[6] Recall from Chapter 2 the important role of correlation in determining the benefits from diversification.

Conversely, an investor who has a total return objective, and a greater risk tolerance, would be more likely to adopt an unhedged, or mostly unhedged benchmark and allow more latitude for active currency management.

From the perspective of a U.S. investor, Exhibit 1 shows that for the 15-year period 1985-1999 the currency component of investing in unhedged international bonds accounted for much of the volatility in total return. The international bond index used is the WGBI excluding the United States (denoted by "non-US WGBI"). Investing in international bonds on a hedged basis reduced the return in most periods, but also substantially reduced the return volatility. As can be seen in Exhibit 1, over the 15-year history of the WGBI, hedged international bonds returned far less than unhedged international bonds and even lagged the U.S. component of the WGBI slightly. However, the volatility of the hedged non-US WGBI was one third that of the unhedged index, and three quarters that of the U.S. component.

To compare returns on a risk-adjusted basis we can use the Sharpe ratio.[7] Despite the higher return of the unhedged non-US WGBI, its risk-adjusted return was lower than the hedged index and the U.S. bond component alone for the 1985 through 1999 period.

As noted above, using a 50% hedged portfolio offers a compromise in that its return is virtually midway between the return of the unhedged non-US WGBI and the U.S. bond component with substantially lower volatility than the unhedged index, giving it a higher Sharpe ratio than either the unhedged index or U.S. component.

The advantage of using a partially hedged benchmark versus a fully hedged or fully unhedged benchmark is illustrated in a mean-variance framework in Exhibit 2. The 50% hedged portfolio offers better diversification with some small reduction in return when a modest allocation to international bonds is added to U.S. bond portfolios.

D. Risk Limits

Many investment guidelines will include explicit risk limits on bond and currency positions as well as duration and credit risk. Exposure limits can be either expressed as absolute percentages, or portfolio weights relative to the benchmark.

Exhibit 1: Hedged and Unhedged Returns: 1985-1999

	Non-US WGBI	US	Non-US WGBI Hedged	50% Hedged
1985-1999				
Return	11.91%	8.89%	8.68%	10.40%
Volatility	10.7%	4.9%	3.6%	6.4%
Sharpe	0.55	0.58	0.74	0.68
1985-1989				
Return	18.83%	11.81%	8.98%	13.98%
Volatility	13.6%	6.0%	4.0%	8.3%
Sharpe	0.83	0.71	0.35	0.77
1990-1995				
Return	11.36%	7.51%	6.18%	8.84%
Volatility	8.9%	4.4%	3.7%	5.4%
Sharpe	0.69	0.53	0.27	0.67
1996-1999				
Return	5.90%	7.41%	10.94%	8.48%
Volatility	8.3%	4.1%	2.9%	4.8%
Sharpe	0.07	0.50	1.94	0.65

[7] The Sharpe ratio measures returns in excess of the risk-free rate, per unit of standard deviation.

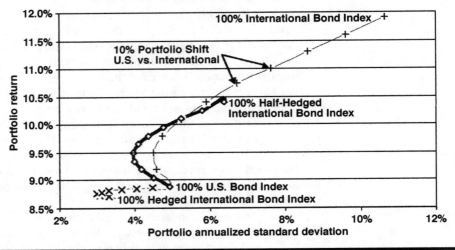

Exhibit 2: Risk-Return for Unhedged and Hedged International Bond Portfolios (U.S. Investor Perspective) Using 1985-1999 Historical Returns

Bond markets can be divided into four trading blocs:

1. dollar bloc (the U.S., Canada, Australia, and New Zealand)
2. European bloc
3. Japan
4. emerging markets

The European bloc is subdivided into two groups:

1. euro zone market bloc which has a common currency (Germany, France, Holland, Belgium, Luxembourg, Austria, Italy, Spain, Finland, and Portugal)
2. non-euro zone market bloc

The United Kingdom often trades more on its own, influenced by both the euro zone and the U.S., as well as its own economic fundamentals.

The trading bloc construct is useful because each bloc has a benchmark market that greatly influences price movements in the other markets. Investors are often focused more on the spread level of, say, Denmark to Germany, than the absolute level of yields in Denmark. (Since the beginning of the European Monetary Union in 1999, the euro zone has traded in a much tighter range.) Generally speaking, when bond markets are rallying, spreads within each bloc tend to narrow, much as corporate bond spreads tend to tighten in the United States when yields on Treasuries are falling.

Limits on investment in countries outside the benchmark should also be specified at the outset. Despite the pitfalls of using duration to measure interest rate risk across countries, risk limits on duration are nonetheless useful and should be established.[8] Typically, the range of allowable exposures is wider for bond exposures than currency exposures.

Credit risk limits, usually a minimum average credit weighting from the major credit rating agencies, and limits on the absolute amount of low or non-invest-

---

[8] For an explanation of this limitation on the use of duration, see Chapter 2.

ment grade credits, should also be included. (At Level II (Chapter 9) we discussed sovereign credit risk and the factors considered by the credit rating agencies in assigning ratings.) Apart from default risk, the illiquidity of lower rated securities poses another type of credit risk as international fixed income portfolio managers tend to shift funds in and out of markets frequently. Due to the lack of a liquid corporate bond market in most countries, and the relative illiquidity of Eurobonds compared to domestic government bond markets, most credit risk in international bond portfolios is concentrated in U.S. and emerging market bonds. The corporate bond market, however, has been growing strongly in Europe since EMU offering a greater range of credits in the international bond markets.

SECTION III DEVELOPING A PORTFOLIO STRATEGY

Once the investment policy statement has been established, the portfolio manager needs to develop a portfolio strategy appropriate to the investor's objectives and risk tolerances. Just as in many other areas of investment management, portfolio managers often subscribe to different management styles, or investment disciplines.

Since the performance of most portfolio managers is judged against the benchmark return, managers are constantly seeking opportunities to outperform the benchmark. There are a number of means by which portfolio managers can add to returns; however, the bulk of excess returns relative to the benchmark comes from broad bond market and currency allocation decisions. A disciplined investment approach, based upon fundamental economic factors and market indicators of value, can facilitate the market and currency selection process. Because of the historically high volatility of currency returns, the approach to currency management should be of primary concern.

A. Styles of International Bond Portfolio Management

The complexity of the international fixed income markets is more akin to the complexity of the U.S. equity market than the U.S. bond market. There are two reasons for this. First, the global fixed income portfolio manager must operate in the U.S. bond market plus 10 to 20 other markets, each with their own market dynamics. Second, changes in interest rates generally affect all sectors of the U.S. bond market in the same way (with the exception of mortgage-backed securities), although the magnitude of the changes may vary. Like the equity market, where it is not unusual to have some industries or market sectors move in opposite directions, international bond markets may also move in different directions depending upon economic conditions and investor risk tolerances.

Equity managers use a variety of investment disciplines, such as value, growth, or small capitalization, to try to create some sense of order out of the chaos of the market. Equity investors also use a variety of indicators, such as price-to-earnings ratios, earnings momentum, and technical analysis, to help identify attractive opportunities. As different as each of these approaches are, they are all designed to provide superior market returns. International bond managers also utilize one or more different management styles. These can be divided into four general categories:

1. the experienced trader
2. the fundamentalist
3. the black box
4. the chartist

We discuss each management style below.

1. The Experienced Trader

The **experienced trader** uses his or her experience and intuition to identify market opportunities. The experienced trader tends to be an active trader, trying to anticipate the next market shift by international fixed income and hedge fund managers. The basis for these trades is derived from estimates of competitors' positions and risk tolerances bolstered by observation of market price movements and flow information obtained from brokerage houses. The experienced trader is often a contrarian, looking to profit from situations where many investors may be forced to stop themselves out of losing positions.

2. The Fundamentalist

The **fundamental style** rests upon a belief that bonds and currencies trade according to the economic cycle, and that the cycle is forecastable. These managers rely mostly upon economic analysis and forecasts in selecting bond markets and currencies. These managers tend to have less portfolio turnover as the economic fundamentals have little impact on short-term price movements.

3. The Black Box

The **black box approach** is used by quantitative managers who believe that computer models can identify market relationships that human beings cannot. These models can rely exclusively on economic data, price data, or some combination of the two. Quantitative managers believe that use of computer models can create a more disciplined investment approach which, either because of other managers' emotional attachment to positions, their lack of trading disciplines, or their inability to process more than a few variables simultaneously, will provide superior investment results.

4. The Chartist

Some investors called **chartists** or technicians may rely primarily on technical analysis to determine which assets to buy or sell.[9] Chartists will look at daily, weekly, and monthly charts to try to ascertain the strength of market trends, or to identify potential turning points in markets. Trend following approaches, such as moving averages, aim to allow the portfolio manager to exploit market momentum. Counter-trend approaches, such as relative strength indices and oscillators try to identify when recent price trends are likely to reverse.

5. Combining Styles

Very few international bond portfolio managers rely on only one of these management styles, but instead use some combination of each. Investment managers that rely on forecasts of the economic cycle to drive their investment process will from time to time take positions contrary to their medium-term strategy to take advantage of temporary under or overvaluation of markets identified by technical analysis, or estimates of market positions. Even "quant shops" that rely heavily on computer models for driving investment decisions will sometimes look to other management styles to add incremental returns.

---

[9] Technical analysis is covered in equity management textbooks.

Regardless of the manager's investment style, investment decisions must be consistent with the investor's return objectives and risk tolerances, and within the investment guidelines.

International bond portfolio managers would do well to emulate equity investors in maintaining a disciplined approach to buy and sell decisions. This would require each allocation away from the benchmark to have a specified price target (or more often yield spread or exchange rate level), and stated underlying rationale. As long as the investment rationale that supported the initial decision remained unchanged, the position would be held, or potentially increased if the market moves in the opposite direction. Each trade should be designed with consideration for the relevant bond yield or exchange rate's behavior through time. For example, an exchange rate that exhibits a tendency to trend (i.e., tend to establish intermediate trend patterns) will require a different buy and sell discipline than one that tends to consistently revert back to an average exchange rate.

B. Sources of Excess Return

The baseline for any international bond portfolio is the benchmark. However, in order to earn returns in excess of the benchmark, after management fees, the portfolio manager must find ways to augment returns. These excess returns can be generated through a combination of five broad strategies:

1. bond market selection
2. currency selection
3. duration management/yield curve plays
4. sector/credit/security selection
5. investing in markets outside the benchmark (if permitted)

Each of these strategies can add to returns; however, currency and bond market selections generally provide the lion's share of returns. We discuss each of these sources of excess return below.

1. Bond Market Selection

Excess returns over the benchmark index from overweighting the best performing bond markets can be extremely large. Historically, annual local currency return differentials between the best and worst performing developed bond markets have ranged from 7% to 39%. The process for making the bond market selection decision is discussed further in Section III.C.

2. Currency Selection

Most investment guidelines will allow for some active management of currency exposures. The attraction of active currency management is strong because the potential gains are so large. When currency movements are added to the above local currency bond market returns, the return differentials nearly double. Thus, international bond portfolio managers can significantly enhance returns by overweighting the better performing bond markets, and currencies, in the index.

However, as the volatility of currency returns is generally higher than that of bond market returns, the incremental returns gained from currency exposures must be evaluated relative to the additional risk incurred.[10] For an active currency manage-

---

[10] Recall from Chapter 2 and Level II (Chapter 1) that volatility is measured in terms of the standard deviation.

ment strategy to consistently provide superior risk-adjusted performance, a currency forecasting method is required that can predict future spot rates (i.e., future exchange rates) better than forward foreign exchange rates (i.e., rates that can be locked in today using the market for forward contracts). As shown later, forward foreign exchange rates are not forecasts of future spot foreign exchange rates, but are determined by short-term interest rate differentials.

Academic studies have shown that several strategies have been successful in generating consistent profits through active currency management. The fact that forward foreign exchange rates are poor predictors of future spot exchange rates is well known. Historically, discount currencies (i.e., those with higher interest rates than the investor's local currency) have depreciated less than the amount implied by the forward rates, providing superior returns from holding unhedged positions in currencies with higher interest rates. Overweighting of currencies with high real interest rates versus those with lower real interest rates has also been shown to provide incremental returns.[11]

In addition, currency movements are not a random walk, but exhibit serial correlation (i.e., currency movements have a tendency to trend).[12] In a market that tends to trend, simple technical trading rules may provide opportunities for incremental currency returns.[13] These findings in several academic studies that demonstrate that excess currency returns can be generated consistently, provide a powerful incentive for active currency management.

3. Duration Management

Although closely aligned with the bond market selection decision, duration management can also enhance returns. Bullet versus barbell strategies in a curve steepening or flattening environment within a particular country's bond market can enhance yield and total return.[14] In addition to these strategies that are also available to managers investing in their domestic bond market, the international fixed income portfolio manager has the option of shifting duration between markets while leaving the portfolio's overall duration unchanged.

Duration management, however, is more difficult in international bond investing as very few foreign bond markets have liquid bond issues with an original maturity longer than 10 years. Most foreign bond markets also lack the broad range of instruments — such as stripped government securities — and a well developed market for collateralized borrowing — such as the U.S. repo market[15] — making it difficult to manage duration on a cost effective basis. Recent progress on these fronts is being made in many countries. Interest rate futures, available in most markets, offer a very liquid and low cost vehicle for changing duration or market exposure quickly. The interest rate swaps market is generally very liquid across international bond markets;[16] however, counterparty credit, technical, and operational barriers limit effective participation in this market to large institutional investors.

---

[11] See Gastineau, "The Currency Hedging Decision," pp 13-14.

[12] One suggestion as to why currency markets trend is that central banks attempt to smooth foreign exchange rate movements through intervention. Thus, because central bank participation in the foreign exchange market is not motivated by profit, their actions keep the market from being truly efficient. See Robert D. Arnott and Tan K. Pham, "Tactical Currency Allocation," *Financial Analysts Journal*, (May/June 1993) pp. 47-52.

[13] See Richard M. Levich and Lee R. Thomas, "The Merits of Active Currency Risk Management: Evidence from International Bond Portfolios," *Financial Analysts Journal*, (September/October 1993) pp. 63-70.

[14] See Level II (Chapter 6) for a discussion of this strategy and how it is analyzed.

[15] The repo market is covered at Level II (Chapter 6).

4. Sector Selection

Investing in non-government bonds can also enhance returns as most indices include only government bonds. However, choices are more limited as government and government-guaranteed issues account for more than 60% of all bond issues outstanding compared with about 13% for corporate bonds. If the U.S. bond market is excluded, where corporate bonds account for one third of all U.S. dollar-denominated bonds outstanding, the figure drops to only about 5%. Corporate bonds account for less than 15% of the market capitalization in all other bond markets with a few exceptions. In several developed countries non-financial corporate bonds are virtually nonexistent. As mentioned earlier, this picture may be changing as corporate bond issuance outside the United States has been rising strongly spurred in part by EMU. This scarcity of corporate bond markets outside the U.S. is due to a policy of discouraging the raising of capital through bond issuance in favor of bank financing and equity issuance in many countries.[17] Other instruments are also available in selected markets including Eurobonds, mortgage bonds, and inflation indexed bonds.

5. Investing in Markets Outside the Index

If allowed by investment guidelines, allocating assets to markets outside the index can significantly enhance returns without dramatically altering the risk profile of the portfolio. Here are two examples. First, Finland was one of the best performing bond markets during 1995, but, because of its small size, was not included in the Salomon Brothers World Government Bond Index (WGBI) until June 1996. Second, New Zealand's very attractive U.S. dollar return of 18% during 1996 would have ranked it as the fourth best performing market in the WGBI had it been included in the index.

The process for selecting an out-of-index market is similar to that followed by an active manager for a domestic bond portfolio manager when deciding whether or not to construct a portfolio with allocations different from the benchmark index and whether or not to invest outside the index. The manager will assess the potential performance on a total return basis of the markets outside of the index relative to that of the markets that will be underweighted in order to allocate funds to out-of-index markets. Unlike a domestic bond portfolio manager, an international bond portfolio manager must also recognize the impact of currency movements on the potential performance.

For those investors with a higher risk tolerance, exposure to emerging markets can significantly add to returns. For example, a portfolio composed of 80% exposure to the Salomon Non-U.S. Government Bond Index and 20% exposure to the J.P. Morgan EMBI (Brady Narrow) Index from 1991 through 1999 would have added 190 basis points to the return of the international index and reduced the standard deviation of returns by 15%. A 20% allocation to emerging markets in an international bond portfolio that was half-hedged against foreign exchange rate changes would have increased returns by 170 basis points while increasing the standard deviation of returns by a marginal 5%.

C. A Fundamental-Based Approach to Investing

The portfolio strategy is often composed of

1. a medium-term strategic allocation and
2. a shorter-term tactical allocation

---

[16] For an explanation of how interest rate futures and swaps can be used to manage the duration of a portfolio, see Chapter 7.

[17] Some of the issues associated with investing in non-U.S. corporate bonds are discussed in Chapter 4.

The **strategic allocation** is composed of positions designed to take advantage of longer-term economic trends designed to be held for one to three months, or longer. The fundamental-based approach is used to develop the strategic position of a portfolio. The investment style used in the fundamental-based approach is, of course, the fundamental style, but can also be combined with the quantitative or black box style for forecasting the relevant factors in making strategic decisions. The **tactical allocation** generally relies on technical analysis or flow information to identify shifts in market prices that are likely to occur within a few days to several weeks. Tactical allocations are often contrarian in nature, driven by expectations of a reversal in a recent price trend.[18] Of course, the investment styles of the experienced trader, the black box, and the chartist are used individually or in combination in tactical allocation decisions.

The strategic decision of which bond markets and currencies to overweight usually begins with an outlook for the economic cycle and bond and currency forecasts in each of the markets to be considered for investment. The long-run economic cycle is closely correlated with changes in bond yields, and trends in both the economic cycle and bond yields tend to persist for a year or longer. The millions of dollars spent each year by money management firms, banks, and brokerage houses in forecasting economic trends is testimony to the potential returns that can be achieved by correctly forecasting economic growth, especially turning points in the economic cycle.

Forecasting interest rates, however, is extremely difficult and the academic literature generally holds that interest rate forecasts are unable to generate consistent risk-adjusted excess returns. This is partly because market prices can deviate substantially over the short term from the level consistent with the economic fundamentals which only impact bond and currency prices over the medium to long term. Also, the volatile nature of certain economic data series may result in an exaggerated market reaction to an individual data release that may be at odds with the actual trend in the economy. These deviations may persist for several months until either the initial figure is revised, or several subsequent data releases reveal the error in the initial interpretation.

The creation of an independent economic outlook can be useful in several ways. First, it can help identify when market interpretations of the economic data are too extreme, or add value through correctly anticipating economic shifts not reflected in the market consensus. Second, as it is often not absolute changes in interest rates, but changes in interest rates relative to other markets that determine the margin of performance in international fixed income investing, an independent economic outlook does not require accurate growth forecasts for each individual market, but only economic growth differentials to be able to add value. Whether the portfolio will invest in U.S. bonds or not, the large influence of the U.S. dollar and the Treasury market on foreign markets underlines the importance of an independent outlook on the U.S. economy.

Thus, the economic outlook forms the foundation for the *strategic* allocation for bonds and currencies. The economic outlook should also include an indication of the relative conviction regarding the economic view for each country to assist in ranking the relative attractiveness of markets. However, even though economic fundamentals in a particular country may be extremely bond supportive, bond prices may be too high to make it an attractive investment. Likewise, bonds are sometimes excessively cheap in countries with poor economic fundamentals thereby providing an attractive

---

[18] However, tactical allocations can also be momentum following, especially if a breakout of a technical range appears likely. Again, such technical strategies are commonly discussed in investment management textbooks.

investment opportunity. Thus, the economic outlook must be compared with either consensus economic forecasts, or some measure of market value to identify attractive investment opportunities.

The strategic allocation decision regarding which markets to overweight or underweight relative to the benchmark is thus a complex interaction of expected returns derived from assessments of economic trends, and technical and value factors. Each set of variables is defined and explored below, beginning with the fundamental factors used to create the economic outlook.

1. Fundamental Economic Factors

The seven main categories of fundamental economic influences are:

1. cyclicals
2. inflation
3. monetary policy
4. fiscal policy
5. debt
6. balance of payments
7. politics

Each factor needs to be evaluated against market expectations to determine its likely impact on bond prices and currency rates. Each of these factors is covered in considerable detail in books on macroeconomics and international economics. Some of these factors were also discussed at Level II (Chapter 9) in the context of the factors considered by rating agencies in assigning ratings to sovereigns.

2. Value and Technical Indicators

Identification of trends in economic fundamentals can help identify attractive investment opportunities in markets, but some yardstick with which to measure relative value is needed. The determination of relative value is highly subjective. Three relatively objective measures of value, including real yields, technical analysis, and market sentiment surveys are discussed below.

a. Real Yields

A **real yield** is the inflation-adjusted rate of return demanded by the market for holding long-term fixed income securities whose value can be quickly eroded by sustained increases in inflation. Real yields are impacted by supply and demand for capital as well as inflation expectations. Real yields are nominal bond yields minus expected inflation; however, expected inflation is often difficult to quantify. A few countries have inflation-indexed bonds that pay a real rate of interest above the inflation rate.[19] These bonds not only provide investors with protection against a surge in inflation but also offer a means of gauging investor inflation expectations.[20]

---

[19] Inflation-indexed bonds are explained at Level I (Chapter 3).

[20] Nominal yield to maturity is composed of a real yield and an inflation expectations component (Yield to Maturity = Real Yield to Maturity + Expected Inflation to Maturity). In these markets the nominal government bond yield and the real yield offered by inflation-indexed debt of the same maturity can be used to calculate the expected inflation rate to the maturity, sometimes called the breakeven inflation rate.

Nominal bond yields deflated by current inflation, although not a precise measure of the market's real interest rate premium, are easily measurable and can still provide some useful insight into bond valuation. Real yields can be compared across markets or against their long-run averages, such as 5 or 10 years, in each market. A strong correlation exists between nominal 10-year bond yields and the 10-year average inflation rate. This relationship tends to be stable over time despite changes in the absolute level of yields. This suggests that the market has a long memory and will need to be convinced of a fundamental change in a country's inflation prospects before reducing the inflation risk premium on its debt. Thus the early recognition of such a change creates the potential for substantial profit. As global inflation rates have converged at very low levels, however, the usefulness of real yields as a measure of relative value has diminished.

b. Technicals

Technical analysis can be as simple as drawing a trend line on a chart or as complicated as calculating the target of the third impulse wave of an Elliott wave analysis. In addition to bonds and currencies, technical analysis is applied to everything from stocks, to gold, to pork bellies. What all technical analysis has in common is that it tries to predict future prices solely from examining past price movements. Most technical analysis models fall into one of two camps: trend following and counter trend. The former try to identify trends that should persist for some period of time, and the latter attempt to predict when a recent trend is likely to change. We will not discuss these models here. They are typically described in investment management textbooks.

c. Market Sentiment

Market sentiment can be used as a contra-indicator of value in the following way. A heavy overweight of a particular country's bond market implies that fewer managers are likely to add to that market, and more managers, at least eventually, are likely to sell. Several surveys of investor sentiment are available including a quarterly Merrill Lynch survey of money managers, and a monthly Lehman Brothers survey, among others.

Historic trends, as well as the overall levels, should be taken into account when assessing market sentiment. For example, an indication that managers are underweighting Japanese bonds might lead some to conclude that Japanese bonds are due for a rally, when historically, international fixed income managers have consistently underweighted the Japanese market, in part due to its low nominal yields. Sentiment surveys, however, do not tell the whole story as buying and selling by domestic investors, who are often not included in sentiment surveys, can also move markets.

SECTION IV PORTFOLIO CONSTRUCTION

Translating the strategic outlook into a portfolio allocation requires a framework for assessing expected returns against incremental portfolio risk. The following discussion on sources of return illustrates how returns can be separated into three components: **excess returns on bonds**, **excess returns on currencies**, and the **short-term risk-free interest rate**. This methodology can assist in identifying where market prices are most out of line with the strategic outlook and whether bond market exposures should be hedged or left unhedged. The trade-off is that the potential for higher returns is often associated with greater risk.

A. Components of Return

To explain the components of the total return of an international bond portfolio,[21] we will use the following notation. We will let "home currency" mean the currency of the manager. So, for a U.S. manager it is U.S. dollars. For a Japanese portfolio manager it is yen. In the notation, the subscript "H" will denote home currency.

We will let "local currency" be the currency of where the manager has invested and use the subscript "L" to denote the local currency. So, to a U.S. portfolio manager, yen would be the local currency for bonds purchased in the Japanese bond market and denominated in yen, while for a Japanese portfolio manager, U.S. dollars would be the local currency for bonds purchased in the U.S. and denominated in U.S. dollars.

The expected total return of an unhedged international bond portfolio in terms of the home currency depends on three factors:

1. the weight of the bonds for each country in the overall portfolio
2. the expected bond market return for each country in local currency
3. the expected percentage change of the exchange rate between the home currency and the local currency

Mathematically, the expected total return of an *unhedged* bond portfolio in terms of the home currency can be expressed as follows:[22]

total expected portfolio return in investor's home currency
$$= W_1 \times (r_1 + e_{H,1}) + W_2 \times (r_2 + e_{H,2}) + ... + W_N \times (r_N + e_{H,N}) \tag{1}$$

where

N = number of countries whose bonds are in the portfolio
W_i = weight of the bonds in country i in the overall portfolio
r_i = expected bond return for country i in local currency
$e_{H,i}$ = expected *percentage* change of the home currency with country i's local currency

We will refer to $e_{H,i}$ as the **currency return**.

The expected portfolio return as given by equation (1) is changed to the extent that the manager alters exposure to the exchange rate of each country. A common instrument that can be used to alter exposure to exchange rates is a **currency forward contract**. So, let's look at these contracts and how they are priced. This will lead us to an important relationship that we will use in the balance of this chapter, **interest rate parity**.

1. Currency Forward Contracts and Their Pricing

As explained at Level II (Chapter 7), a forward contract is one in which one party agrees to buy "something," and another party agrees to sell that same "something" at a designated date in the future. Forward contracts are used extensively for currency hedging.

Most currency forward contracts have a maturity of less than two years. For longer-dated forward contracts, the bid-ask spread increases;[23] that is, the size of the

---

[21] The structure of this discussion is taken from Brian D. Singer and Denis S. Karnosky, *The General Framework for Global Investment Management and Performance Attribution* (Charlottesville, VA: The Research Foundation of the Institute of Chartered Financial Analysts, 1994). The notation used is that of the authors of this chapter.
[22] The relationship in equation (1) is approximate because bond market and currency returns of a foreign investment is more accurately expressed as the compounded gain of the two components: $(1 + r_i) \times (1 + \varepsilon_{\$,i}) - 1$.
[23] Bid-ask spreads and the factors that affect them were explained at Level I (Chapter 4).

bid-ask spread for a given currency increases with the length of the time to settlement of the contract. Consequently, currency forward contracts become less attractive for hedging long-dated foreign exchange exposure.

Currency forward contracts can be used by a manager to lock in an exchange rate at the delivery date. In exchange for locking in a foreign exchange rate, the manager forgoes the opportunity to benefit from any advantageous foreign exchange rate movement but eliminates downside risk.

At Level II (Chapter 7), the relationship between spot prices and forward prices was demonstrated. Arbitrage arguments can also be used to derive the relationship for currency forward contracts. Consider a U.S. manager with a 1-year investment horizon who has two choices:

> *Alternative 1:* Deposit $100,000 in a U.S. bank that pays 6% compounded annually for one year.

> *Alternative 2:* Deposit the U.S. dollar equivalent of $100,000 in some country outside the U.S. where the bank pays 5% compounded annually for one year. We will refer to this country as country *i*.

Which is the best alternative? It will be the alternative that produces the largest number of U.S. dollars one year from now. Ignoring U.S. and country *i*'s taxes on interest income or any other taxes, we need to know two things in order to determine the best alternative:

> • the spot exchange rate between U.S. dollars and country *i*'s local currency

and

> • the spot exchange rate one year from now between U.S. dollars and country *i*'s local currency

The first is known; the second is not. However, we can determine the spot rate one year from now between U.S. dollars and country *i*'s local currency that will make the U.S. manager indifferent between the two investment alternatives.

> *For alternative 1:* The amount of U.S. dollars available one year from now would be $106,000 ($100,000 times 1.06).

> *For alternative 2:* Assume that the spot rate is $0.6757 for one unit of the local currency. Denoting the local currency units by "LC," then ignoring commissions, $100,000 can be exchanged for LC 147,995 ($100,000 divided by 0.6757). The amount of local currency units available at the end of one year would be LC 155,395 (LC 147,995 times 1.05).

The number of U.S. dollars that the LC 155,395 can be exchanged for depends on the exchange rate one year from now. Let F denote the exchange rate between these two currencies one year from now. Specifically, F will denote the number of U.S. dollars that can be exchanged for one unit of the local currency one year from now and is called the **forward exchange rate**. Thus, the number of U.S. dollars at the end of one year from the second alternative is:

amount of U.S. dollars one year from now = LC $155,395 \times F$

The investor will be indifferent between the two alternatives if the number of U.S. dollars is $106,000 — the dollars that will result from alternative 1. That is,

$$\$106,000 = LC \ 155,395 \times F, \text{ or } F = 106,000/155,395$$

Solving, we find that F is equal to $0.6821. Since the spot rate is $0.6757 and the forward exchange rate (F) is $0.6821, then the implied appreciation for the local currency versus the U.S. dollar is 0.95% [($0.6821/$0.6757) − 1]. When there is an implied appreciation, it is called a **forward exchange rate premium** (or simply **forward premium**). If, instead, there had been an implied depreciation, it would be referred to as a **forward exchange rate discount** (or simply **forward discount**).

Thus, if one year from now the spot exchange rate is $0.6821 for one unit of the local currency, then the two alternatives will produce the same number of U.S. dollars.[24] If the local currency has appreciated by more than 0.95%, i.e., one unit of the local currency can be exchanged for more than $0.6821, then there will be more than $106,000 at the end of one year. An exchange rate of $0.6910 for one unit of the local currency, for example, would produce $107,378 (LC 155,395 times $0.6910). The opposite is also true if one unit of the local currency can be exchanged for less than $0.6821. For example, if the future exchange rate is $0.6790, there will be $105,513 (LC 155,395 times $0.6790).

Now suppose that a dealer quotes a 1-year forward exchange rate between the two currencies. The 1-year forward exchange rate fixes today the exchange rate one year from now. Thus, if the 1-year forward exchange rate quoted is $0.6821 for one unit of the local currency, investing in the bank in country i will provide no arbitrage opportunity for the U.S. investor. If the 1-year forward rate quoted is more than $0.6821 for one unit of the local currency, the U.S. manager can arbitrage the situation by selling the local currency forward (and buying U.S. dollars forward for the local currency). In this example, we assume the interest rate is the same for borrowers and lenders within each country.

To understand this arbitrage opportunity, consider how a U.S. investor could take advantage of a mispricing in the market. Under the conditions in the above example, assume that the bid for a 1-year forward in local currency is quoted at a rate of $0.6910 per unit of local currency. The investor could generate an arbitrage profit by using the following strategy:

> *Strategy:* Borrow $100,000 for one year at the U.S. rate of 6% compounded annually and enter into a forward contract agreeing to deliver LC 155,395 one year from now at $0.6910 per local currency.

That is, one year from now the manager is agreeing to deliver LC 155,395 in exchange for $107,378 (LC 155,395 multiplied by $0.6910). To generate the LC 155,395, the $100,000 that was borrowed can be exchanged for LC 147,995 at today's spot rate of $0.6757 to one local currency unit, which can be invested in country i at 5% to yield LC 155,395 in one year.

Let's look at the outcome of this strategy at the end of one year:

From investment in country i:
LC from investment in country i LC 155,395

From forward contract:
U.S. $ from delivery of LC 155,395 at forward rate $107,378

---

[24] The forward rate can also be derived by looking at the alternatives from the perspective of a portfolio manager in country i.

Profit after loan repayment:

U.S. $ available to repay loan	$107,378
Loan repayment (principal plus interest)	$106,000
Profit	$1,378

Assuming that the counterparty to the forward contract does not default, this is a riskless arbitrage situation because a $1,378 profit is generated with no initial investment.[25] This will result in the U.S. dollar rising relative to the local currency in the forward exchange rate market, or possibly some other adjustment.[26]

Now consider the case where the 1-year forward exchange rate quoted is less than $0.6821 and see how a portfolio manager in country i can exploit the situation by buying the local currency forward (or, equivalently, selling U.S. dollars forward). Suppose that the 1-year forward exchange rate is $0.6790 and assume that the borrowing and lending rates within each country are equal. The strategy implemented by the portfolio manager in country i is:

> *Strategy:* Borrow LC 100,000 for one year at the local rate of 5% compounded annually and enter into a forward contract agreeing to deliver US $71,624 one year from now at $0.6790 per local currency.

When the local portfolio manager receives the LC 100,000 borrowed, she can exchange it for US $67,570. Recall that the spot foreign exchange rate in one local currency unit is equal to US $0.6757. So, LC 100,000 multiplied by the spot rate of 0.6757 gives US $67,570. This amount of U.S. dollars is then invested in the United States at an interest rate of 6% compounded annually and will generate US $71,624 at the end of one year (US $67,570 × 1.06).

Let's look at the outcome of this strategy at the end of one year:

From investment in the United States:

US $ from investment in U.S.	US $71,624

From forward contract:

LC from delivery of US $71,624 at forward rate	LC 105,485

Profit after loan repayment:

LC available to repay loan	LC 105,485
Loan repayment (principal plus interest)	LC 105,000
Profit	LC 485

Once again, assuming that the counterparty to the forward contract does not default, this is a riskless arbitrage situation because a LC 485 profit is generated with no initial investment. This will result in the U.S. dollar rising relative to the local currency in the forward exchange rate market, or possibly some other adjustment.

---

[25] A portfolio manager in country i could also arbitrage this situation.

[26] As investors move to exploit this arbitrage opportunity, their very actions will serve to eliminate it. This can occur through the combination of a number of factors: (1) the U.S. dollar will depreciate relative to the local currency (i.e., the spot exchange rate expressed in U.S. dollars per unit of local currency will rise) as investors sell dollars and buy the local currency; (2) interest rates will rise in the U.S. as investors borrow in the U.S. and invest in country i; (3) interest rates in country i will fall as more is invested in country i; and (4) the 1-year forward rate for U.S. dollars will show an appreciation relative to the local currency (i.e., the forward exchange rate expressed in U.S. dollars per unit of local currency will fall) to eliminate the arbitrage opportunity as investors sell U.S. dollars forward. In practice, the last factor will dominate.

The conclusion is that the 1-year forward exchange rate must be $0.6821 because any other forward exchange rate would result in an arbitrage opportunity for either the U.S. or the local portfolio manager.

2. Interest Rate Parity and Covered Interest Arbitrage

Our illustration indicates that the spot exchange rate and the short-term interest rates in two countries will determine the forward exchange rate. The relationship among the spot exchange rate, the interest rates in two countries, and the forward rate is called **interest rate parity**. It says that a manager, after hedging in the forward exchange rate market, will realize the same sure domestic return whether investing domestically or in a foreign country. The arbitrage process that forces interest rate parity is called **covered interest arbitrage**.

It can be demonstrated that the forward exchange rate between an investor's home currency, denoted "H" and the currency of country i, is equal to

$$F_{H,i} = S_{H,i} \left(\frac{1 + c_H}{1 + c_i} \right) \tag{2}$$

where

$F_{H,i}$ = forward exchange rate between investor's home currency and the currency of country i

$S_{H,i}$ = spot (or cash) exchange rate between investor's home currency and the currency of country i

c_H = short-term interest rate in the home country which matches the maturity of the forward contract

c_i = short-term interest rate in country i which matches the maturity of the forward contract

c_H and c_i are called the **cash rate**. The cash rate is generally the eurodeposit rate (i.e. offshore deposit rate) for funds deposited in the currency and for a maturity that matches the maturity of the forward contract. The London Interbank Offered Rate, LIBOR, is the most quoted offshore (eurodeposit) rate. LIBOR deposit rates are available for U.S. dollars and most other major currencies, including EURIBOR for euro-denominated deposits.

In our earlier illustration involving the U.S. dollar and the exchange rate of country i, we know that

$$S_{H,i} = 0.6757 \quad c_H = 6\% = 0.06 \quad c_i = 5\% = 0.05$$

$$F_{H,i} = 0.6757 \left(\frac{1.06}{1.05} \right) = 0.6821$$

This value for the 1-year forward exchange rate agrees with the value derived earlier.

By rearranging the above terms, the forward exchange rate discount or premium (or the percentage change of the forward rate from the spot exchange rate), denoted by $f_{H,i}$, becomes *approximately* the differential between the short-term interest rates of the two countries. That is,[27]

---

[27] Equation (2) assumes that exchange rates are quoted in "direct terms," i.e., the value of the home currency for one unit of the local currency, though quote conventions vary by market. Over-the-counter forward contracts use market convention, most of which for the U.S. dollar are in indirect terms (local currency units per one dollar). Using indirect terms, the forward discount *or* premium in equation (3) becomes $f_{H,i} = c_i - c_H$. To avoid the complexities of compounding, the time period is assumed to be one year.

$$f_{H,i} = \frac{F_{H,i} - S_{H,i}}{S_{H,i}} \approx c_H - c_i \tag{3}$$

The forward rate can also be expressed in "points" or the difference between the forward and spot rate, $F_{H,i} - S_{H,i}$. When interest rates are lower in the foreign country (i.e., the forward points are positive), the forward foreign exchange rate trades at a premium. That is, for the return on cash deposits to be equal in both currencies, the lower interest rate currency must appreciate to the forward foreign exchange rate.

B. The Currency Hedge Decision

If the possibility of hedging using currency forwards is allowed, the portfolio return of equation (1) changes. Specifically, if the manager hedged the exposure to the exchange rate of all countries, the total return for a hedged portfolio into the home currency can be expressed as follows:

total expected portfolio return fully hedged into investor's home currency
$$= W_1 \times (r_1 + f_{H,1}) + W_2 \times (r_2 + f_{H,2}) + \ldots + W_N \times (r_N + f_{H,N}) \tag{4}$$

where

$f_{H,i}$ = the forward exchange rate discount or premium between the home currency with country i's local currency

That is, instead of being exposed to some expected percentage change of the home currency to country i's currency, the manager will have locked in the percentage change of the forward exchange rate from the spot exchange rate (the forward discount/premium) at the time of the hedge.

Now, what will determine whether or not the manager will hedge the exposure to a given country's exchange rate using a currency forward contract? The decision is based on the following:

1. If the manager expects that the percentage return from exposure to a currency is greater than the forward discount or premium, then the manager will not use a forward contract to hedge the exposure to that currency.

2. If the manager expects the currency return to be less than the forward discount or premium, the manager will use a forward contract to hedge the exposure to a currency.

In the first case above, the unhedged return for country i can be expressed as:

unhedged expected return for country i, $R_{H,i} = r_i + e_{H,i}$ \hfill (5)

In the second case above, we can express the hedged return for a country in terms of the forward exchange rate between the home and local currencies using the interest rate parity relationship. As equation (3) showed, the forward premium or discount is effectively equal to the short-term interest rate differential; thus,

$$f_{H,i} = c_H - c_i$$

By substituting the above relationship for the forward hedge, the equation for an individual country's hedged return is:

hedged expected return for country i, $HR_{H,i} = r_i + c_H - c_i$ \hfill (6)

There remain, however, two further hedging choices for the manager: **cross hedging** and **proxy hedging**. We explain each of these below.

1. Cross Hedging

Cross hedging is a bit of a misnomer as it does not reduce foreign currency exposure but only replaces the currency exposure to country i's currency with currency exposure to country j's currency. (We explain what cross hedging is in Chapter 7.) For example, suppose a U.S. manager has an unwanted currency exposure in country i that arose from an attractive bond investment in country i. Rather than hedging with a forward contract between U.S. dollars and the currency of country i and eliminating the foreign currency exposure, the manager elects to swap exposure in country i's currency for exposure to country j's currency. This is accomplished by entering into a forward contract that delivers the currency of country j in exchange for the currency of country i where the manager has an unwanted currency exposure.

Why would a manager want to undertake a cross hedge? A manager would do so if she expects her home currency to weaken, so she does not want to hedge the currency exposure to country i, but at the same time she expects that country j's currency will perform better than country i's currency.

When there is a cross hedge, the hedged return for country i as given by equation (6) can be rewritten as follows:

$$\text{cross hedged expected return for country } i, \ CR_{H,i} = r_i + f_{j,i} + e_{H,j}$$

where $f_{j,i}$ is the forward discount or premium between country j and country i. The above expression says that the cross hedged return for country i depends on (1) the expected bond return for country i, (2) the currency return locked in by the cross hedge between country j and country i, and (3) the currency return between the home currency and country j.

We can rewrite the above equation in terms of short-term interest rates as given by interest rate parity. That is, for $f_{j,i}$ we substitute $c_j - c_i$. Doing so and rearranging terms gives:

$$\text{cross hedged expected return for country } i, \ CR_{H,i} = (r_i - c_i) + (c_j + e_{H,j}) \qquad (7)$$

Equation (7) says that the cross hedged expected return for country i depends on (1) the differential between country i's bond return and country i's short-term interest rate plus (2) the short-term interest rate in country j, and (3) the currency return between the home currency and currency j.

2. Proxy Hedging

Proxy hedging keeps the currency exposure in country i, but creates a hedge by establishing a short position in country j's currency. Why would a manager want to undertake a proxy hedge? This strategy would normally be considered only where the currencies of country i and country j are highly correlated, and the hedge costs in country j are lower than in country i. A proxy hedge can also represent a bullish view on the home currency, with a more negative view on country j's currency than country i's currency.

When there is a proxy hedge, the hedged return for country i as given by equation (6) can be rewritten as follows:

proxy hedged expected return for country i, $PR_{H,i} = r_i + e_{H,i} + f_{H,j} - e_{H,j}$

where $f_{H,j}$ is the forward discount or premium between the home country and country j.

Notice that in the above equation, there is still the exposure to the exchange rate between the home currency and currency i. The proxy hedge comes into play by the shorting of the currency return between the home currency and currency j.

Based on interest rate parity we can replace $f_{H,j}$ with the difference in short-term interest rates, $c_H - c_j$, to get

proxy hedged expected return for country i, $PR_{H,i} = r_i + e_{H,i} + c_H - c_j - e_{H,j}$

But this is equivalent to

proxy hedged expected return for country i, $PR_{H,i}$
$$= (r_i - c_i) + (c_i + e_{H,i}) + [(c_H - c_j) - e_{H,j}] \qquad (8)$$

Equation (8) states the expected return for country i using proxy hedging depends on

1. the differential between the bond return for country i and the short-term interest rate for country i
2. the short-term interest rate for country i adjusted for the currency return for country i relative to the home currency
3. the differential in the short-term interest rates between the home currency and country j adjusted for the short currency position in country j.

3. Recasting Relationships in Terms of Short-Term Interest Rates

When we substituted short-term interest rate differentials for the forward returns above, it becomes apparent from equations (6), (7), and (8) that the *difference* in return between hedging, cross hedging, and proxy hedging is entirely due to short-term interest rates and currency exposure.[28] This is also true for the unhedged return for a country as given by equation (5). This can be seen by simply rewriting equation (5) as follows:

unhedged expected return for country i, $R_{H,i} = (r_i - c_i) + (c_i + e_{H,i})$

As can be seen, the unhedged expected return is equal to (1) the differential between the bond return in country i and the short-term interest rate in country i and (2) the short-term interest rate in country i adjusted for the currency return.

These equations show how integral the short-term interest rate differential is to the currency hedge decision. This means that (1) the short-rate differential should be attributed to the currency decision and (2) bond market returns should be calculated minus the local short-term interest rate. This can be made explicit by adding and subtracting the home currency short-term interest rate to the four return relationships — unhedged, hedged, cross hedged, and proxy hedged. (The derivations are provided in the appendix to this chapter.) By doing so, this allows the forward premium ($f_{H,i} = c_H - c_i$) to be inserted into the currency term giving:

unhedged expected return for country i, $R_{H,i} = c_H + (r_i - c_i) + (e_{H,i} - f_{H,i})$ (9)

---

[28] The derivation of the relationships presented in this section are provided in the appendix to this chapter.

hedged expected return for country i, $HR_{H,i} = c_H + (r_i - c_i)$ (10)

cross hedged expected return for country i, $CR_{H,i} = c_H + (r_i - c_i) + (e_{H,j} - f_{H,j})$ (11)

proxy hedged expected return for country i, $PR_{H,i}$
$$= c_H + (r_i - c_i) + [(e_{H,i} - e_{H,j}) - f_{j,i}]$$ (12)

From equations (9) through (12), we see that the return for each strategy can be divided into three distinct components of return:

Component 1: the short-term interest rate for the home currency (c_H)

Component 2: the excess bond return of country i over the short-term interest rate of country i ($r_i - c_i$)

Component 3: the excess currency return, either unhedged, cross-hedged, or proxy hedged

The first two components, c_H and $(r_i - c_i)$, are the same for each strategy. Thus, the excess currency return (the third component) becomes the currency return in excess of the forward premium (or discount) and becomes the basis for the decision of currency hedging. (We will illustrate this next.) It can be seen that the bond decision is purely a matter of selecting the markets which offer the best expected excess return ($r_i - c_i$) and that the bond and currency allocation decisions are entirely independent. In a sense, the hedged expected return can be considered the base expected return as it is a component of the unhedged, cross hedged, and proxy hedged expected returns. Thus, the excess currency returns in the third component are assessed to see if they can add any value over the baseline hedged expected return. This method of analyzing sources of return in effect treats bond and currency returns as if they were synthetic futures or forward positions.

4. Illustration

Let's illustrate the above relationships using a U.S. portfolio manager given a specific market outlook. Since this illustration uses a U.S. portfolio manager, the home currency is U.S. dollars and therefore "H" in the notation is the U.S. dollar, denoted by "US\$." The outlook is for country i's bond market to outperform country j's bond market, but for country i's currency to provide a higher return than country j's currency. The bond and currency return forecasts may have been generated by a fundamental economic approach or from one of the other management styles discussed above.

An example comparing explicit return forecasts for government bonds with a duration of 5 in both countries is provided in Exhibit 3. Total returns are expressed as the sum of the excess bond market return plus the excess return due to currency, consistent with the approach explained in equations (9) through (12). These equations are restated below using US\$ for the home currency, H, and using currency j for the cross hedge and proxy hedge:

unhedged expected return for country i, $R_{US\$,i} = c_{US\$} + (r_i - c_i) + (e_{US\$,i} - f_{US\$,i})$

hedged expected return for country i, $HR_{US\$,i} = c_{US\$} + (r_i - c_i)$

cross hedged expected return for country i,
$$CR_{US\$,i} = c_{US\$} + (r_i - c_i) + (e_{US\$,j} - f_{US\$,j})$$

Exhibit 3: Illustration 1

	Hedged	Unhedged	Cross Hedged	Proxy Hedged
Expected Returns				
Cash	$c_{US\$}$ = 5.5%	$c_{US\$}$ = 5.5%	$c_{US\$}$ = 5.5%	$c_{US\$}$ = 5.5%
Excess Bond	$(r_i - c_i)$ = (3.5% − 3.0%) = 0.5%	$(r_i - c_i)$ = (3.5% − 3.0%) = 0.5%	$(r_i - c_i)$ = (3.5% − 3.0%) = 0.5%	$(r_i - c_i)$ = (3.5% − 3.0%) = 0.5%
Excess Currency	 = 0.0%	$e_{US\$,i} - (c_{US\$} - c_i)$ = 2.3% − (5.5% − 3.0%) = 2.3% − 2.5% = −0.2%	$e_{US\$,j} - (c_{US\$} - c_j)$ = 2.0% − (5.5% − 2.9%) = 2.0% − 2.6% = −0.6%	$(e_{US\$,i} - e_{US\$,j}) - (c_j - c_i)$ = (2.3% − 2.0%) − (2.9% − 3.0%) = 0.3% − (−0.1%) = 0.4%
Total Return	= 6.0%	= 5.8%	= 5.4%	= 6.4%

proxy hedged expected return for country i,

$$PR_{US\$,i} = c_{US\$} + (r_i - c_i) + [(e_{US\$,i} - e_{US\$,j}) - f_{j,i}]$$

The interest rates and expected returns are as follows:

$$
\begin{aligned}
r_i &= 3.5\% \\
c_i &= 3.0\% \\
e_{US\$,i} &= 2.3\% \\
c_j &= 2.9\% \\
e_{US\$,j} &= 2.0\% \\
c_{US\$} &= 5.5\%
\end{aligned}
$$

As mentioned earlier, the first two components of the above equations, the U.S. cash rate and the expected excess bond return in country i, are identical, and equal to the expected hedged bond return. Thus we can begin with the hedged bond return and compare the excess currency returns (the third component of the equations) of the unhedged, cross hedged, and proxy hedged strategies. The hedged bond return is

$$c_{US\$} + (r_i - c_i) \text{ or } 5.5\% + (3.5\% - 3.0\%) = 6.0\%.$$

Let's look at this component for the unhedged strategy. From the first equation:

excess currency return for unhedged strategy for country $i = (e_{US\$,i} - f_{US\$,i})$

or equivalently, since from interest rate parity $f_{US\$,i} = c_{US\$} - c_i$, we can rewrite the expression as

excess currency return for unhedged strategy for country $i = e_{US\$,i} - (c_{US\$} - c_i)$

Thus, the performance relative to the hedged currency strategy depends on whether the expected currency appreciation is greater than the short-term interest rate differential [i.e., $e_{US\$,i} > (c_{US\$} - c_i)$] or less than the interest rate differential [i.e., $e_{US\$,i} < (c_{US\$} - c_i)$]. In the former case, the unhedged strategy is expected to outperform the hedged strategy.

Turning to our illustration, the expected return on currency i of 2.3% is less than the short-term interest rate differential of 2.5% over the 1-year horizon (5.5% in the U.S. versus 3.0% in country i). Stated another way, the expected excess currency return component to a U.S. dollar-based investor from an unhedged holding of bonds in currency i is -0.2%. Consequently, the position would offer a higher return when hedged back into U.S. dollars.

Now consider a cross hedging strategy. Cross hedging allows the portfolio manager to create a currency exposure which can vary substantially from the underlying bond market exposure. A cross hedge replaces one foreign currency exposure with another that usually has a higher expected return. The excess currency component from the cross hedge strategy is:

excess currency return for cross hedged strategy for country $i = (e_{US\$,j} - f_{US\$,j})$

or equivalently, since from interest rate parity $f_{US\$,j} = c_{US\$} - c_j$, we can rewrite the expression as

excess currency return for cross hedged strategy for country $i = e_{US\$,j} - (c_{US\$} - c_j)$

Compared to a hedged strategy, a cross hedge is attractive if the short-term interest rate of the country used for the cross hedge plus the expected return in the cross currency is greater than the U.S. dollar short-term interest rate. If the U.S. dollar short-term interest rate is greater than the sum of these two terms, a cross hedged strategy is less attractive than a hedged strategy.

In the illustration, the short-term interest rate differential of 2.6% between the U.S. and country j ($c_{US\$} - c_j$) is greater than the 2.0% expected appreciation of the currency of country j versus the U.S. ($e_{US\$,j}$). In this case, the expected excess currency return for the cross hedge strategy for country i using country j (i.e., $e_{US\$,j} - (c_{US\$} - c_j)$) is -0.6%. The expected return from cross hedging is 5.4%, so a cross hedge with country j will not be used because the expected return is less than the unhedged position and a straight hedge of currency i.

Finally, let's look at the proxy hedging strategy. From the return of the proxy hedged strategy we know that

excess currency return for proxy hedged strategy for country i
$$= [(e_{US\$,i} - e_{US\$,j}) - f_{j,i}]$$

or equivalently, since from interest rate parity $f_{j,i} = c_j - c_i$, we can rewrite the expression as

excess currency return for proxy hedged strategy for country i
$$= [(e_{US\$,i} - e_{US\$,j}) - (c_j - c_i)]$$

To interpret the above equation, let's understand the currency position of the U.S. investor. The investor is long currency i. Consequently, the investor benefits if currency i appreciates but is hurt if currency i depreciates. In a proxy hedge, the investor is still long currency i but the investor is also short currency j. Since the investor is short currency j, the investor is adversely affected if currency j appreciates, but benefits if currency j depreciates relative to currency i.

In our illustration, both currency i and currency j are expected to appreciate relative to the U.S. dollar. The relative currency appreciation between currency i and currency j is what is important according to the equation. If the appreciation for currency i — which the investor is long — is greater than the appreciation for currency j — which the investor is short — an investor will benefit from a proxy hedge. In our illustration, country i's expected appreciation is 2.3% while country j's is only 2.0%. Thus, there will be an expected currency return from this proxy hedging strategy of 30 basis points. This is what the first bracketed term in the above equation says.

Exhibit 4: Illustration 2

Expected Returns	Hedged	Unhedged	Cross Hedged	Proxy Hedged
Cash	$c_{US\$}$ $= 5.5\%$	$c_{US\$}$ $= 5.5\%$	$c_{US\$}$ $= 5.5\%$	$c_{US\$}$ $= 5.5\%$
Excess Bond	$(r_i - c_i)$ $= (3.5\% - 3.0\%)$ $= 0.5\%$	$(r_i - c_i)$ $= (3.5\% - 3.0\%)$ $= 0.5\%$	$(r_i - c_i)$ $= (3.5\% - 3.0\%)$ $= 0.5\%$	$(r_i - c_i)$ $= (3.5\% - 3.0\%)$ $= 0.5\%$
Excess Currency	 $= 0.0\%$	$e_{US\$,i} - (c_{US\$} - c_i)$ $= 2.3\% - (5.5\% - 3.0\%)$ $= 2.3\% - 2.5\%$ $= -0.2\%$	$e_{US\$,j} - (c_{US\$} - c_j)$ $= 3.2\% - (5.5\% - 2.9\%)$ $= 3.2\% - 2.6\%$ $= 0.6\%$	$(e_{US\$,i} - e_{US\$,j}) - (c_j - c_i)$ $= (2.3\% - 3.2\%) - (2.9\% - 3.0\%)$ $= -0.9\% - (-0.1\%)$ $= -0.8\%$
Total Return	$= 6.0\%$	$= 5.8\%$	$= 6.6\%$	$= 5.2\%$

Just looking at the expected currency return from a proxy hedging strategy is not sufficient. The above equation says that the expected currency return for the proxy hedging strategy must be adjusted to get the excess currency return for the proxy hedging strategy. The adjustment is obtained by subtracting the short-term interest rate differential in countries j and i from the expected currency return from proxy hedging. If that differential is less than the expected currency return from proxy hedging, then proxy hedging is attractive. If it is greater than the expected currency return from proxy hedging, then proxy hedging is unattractive.

In our illustration, the proxy hedging strategy is attractive because the short-term interest rate differential between country j and country i is −10 basis points, which is less than the 30 basis point currency return for the proxy hedging strategy. The excess return from the proxy hedging strategy is then 30 basis points minus the −10 basis point short-term interest rate differential. So, the excess return from the proxy hedging strategy in our illustration is 40 basis points. The proxy hedged expected return is 6.4%, which is greater than the three other alternatives — unhedged, hedge with currency i, and cross hedge with currency j.

In Exhibit 4 we have changed the example in Exhibit 3 by altering one number. In this illustration, the expected appreciation for currency j is now 3.2% rather than 2.0%. Thus, the expected appreciation for currency j is greater than for currency i. The expected currency return for the proxy hedging strategy is then −90 basis points (2.3% − 3.2%). After adjusting for the short-term interest differential of −10 basis points, the excess currency return using country j in a proxy hedge is −80 basis points. Consequently, the proxy hedge return of 5.2% is unattractive, as it is less than the three other alternatives analyzed. In this illustration, the cross hedge presents the best choice based on the expected returns.

C. Adjusting Bond Yields for Coupon Payment Frequency

In the United States and most other dollar bloc countries, coupon payments are made semiannually. There are other markets that follow this practice. At Level I (Chapter 6), it was explained that in computing the yield for a semiannual-pay bond, two steps are involved. First, the semiannual interest rate that will make the present value of the semiannual cash flows equal to the price plus accrued interest is determined. Second, since the interest rate is semiannual, it is annualized by multiplying by 2. The resulting annualized yield is referred to as a **bond-equivalent yield**.

Exhibit 5: 10-Year Benchmark Bond Spreads

JP MORGAN		BENCHMARKS		JP MORGAN MEUR		
Country	Coupon	ISSUE	PRICE	CNV YLD	O/US T	O/GER
US	6.50	15/02/10	101.28	6.32		108
JAPAN	1.80	22/03/10	100.51	1.74	−467	−359
GERMANY	5.38	04/01/10	100.07	5.35	−107	
FRANCE	4.00	25/10/09	89.35	5.45	−97	10
UK	5.75	07/12/09	103.69	5.26	−109	−2
ITALY	4.25	01/11/09	90.35	5.63	−79	28
SPAIN	4.00	31/01/10	88.31	5.56	−86	21
BELGIUM	5.75	28/09/10	100.86	5.64	−78	29
HOLLAND	5.50	15/07/10	99.79	5.51	−91	16
SWEDEN	9.00	20/04/09	124.21	5.53	−89	18
DENMARK	6.00	15/11/09	102.65	5.62	−79	28

Authors' notes to exhibit: "CNV YLD" means conventional yield, or how the yield is quoted in the home market. For example, both the U.S. and U.K. bond markets are semiannual pay, whereas most of Europe is annual pay. However, in Italy, even though bonds are semiannual pay, they are quoted on an annual basis. The spreads ("O/UST" = spread over U.S. Treasuries and "O/GER" = spread over German government bonds) first convert the semiannual-pay markets (the U.S., and the U.K.) to an annual-pay basis before calculating the spread between markets.

Source: MEUR page of Reuters' market information service

In European markets (except for the United Kingdom) and Japan, the coupon payments are made annually rather than semiannually. Thus, the yield is simply the interest rate that makes the present value of the cash flows equal to the price plus accrued interest. No annualization is necessary.

The yield quoted in terms of the convention for payments in the home market is called the **conventional yield**. For example, Exhibit 5 displays data from the J.P. Morgan Europe (MEUR) page from Reuters' market information service. The column "CNV. YLD" is the conventional yield. So, the U.S. and U.K. yields of 6.32% and 5.26%, respectively, shown in Exhibit 5 are based on the bond-equivalent yield convention of doubling a semiannual yield since coupon payments are made semiannually. In countries where coupon payments are made annually, in Germany and Japan, for example, the conventional yield is simply the annual yield.

Despite the limitations of yield measures discussed at Level I (Chapter 6), managers compare yields within markets of a country and between countries. (We will give one example in the next section.) Holding aside the problem of potential changes in exchange rates, comparisons of yield begin with an adjustment of the conventional yield (i.e., the yield as quoted in the home market) to be consistent with the way that the yield is computed for another country for which the yield is being compared. For example, a French government bond pays interest annually while a U.S. government bond pays interest semiannually. If the U.S. government bond yield is being compared to a French government bond yield either (1) the U.S. government bond yield must be adjusted to the yield on an annual-pay basis or (2) the French government bond yield must be adjusted to a yield on a bond-equivalent yield basis.

The adjustment is done as follows. Given the yield on an annual-pay basis, its bond-equivalent yield (i.e., a yield computed for a semiannual-pay bond) is computed as follows:

$$\text{bond-equivalent yield of an annual-pay bond} = 2[(1 + \text{yield on annual-pay bond})^{0.5} - 1]$$

For example, the conventional yield on a French government bond shown in Exhibit 5 is 5.45%. The bond-equivalent yield is 5.38% as shown below:

$$2[(1 + 0.0545)^{0.5} - 1] = 0.0538 = 5.38\%$$

Notice that the bond-equivalent yield of an annual-pay bond is less than that of the conventional yield.

To adjust the bond-equivalent yield of a semiannual-pay bond to that of an annual-pay basis so that it can be compared to the yield on an annual-pay bond, the following formula can be used:

yield on an annual-pay basis = $(1 + $ yield on a bond-equivalent yield$/2)^2 - 1$

For example, the conventional yield of a U.S. government bond as shown in Exhibit 5 is 6.32%. The yield on an annual-pay basis is:

$$(1 + 0.0632/2)^2 - 1 = 0.0642 = 6.42\%$$

Notice that the yield on an annual-pay basis will be greater than the conventional yield.

Yield spreads are typically computed between a country's yield and that of a benchmark. As explained at Level I (Chapter 4), the U.S. government bond market and the German government bond market are the two most common benchmarks used. The next-to-the-last column in Exhibit 5, labeled "O/US T," shows the spread between a country's yield and the U.S. Treasury yield. Notice that for the French government bond, the spread is shown as −97 basis points. This spread is obtained by subtracting the French government bond of 5.45% (the conventional yield reported in Exhibit 5) from the adjusted U.S. government bond yield of 6.42% (as computed above).

The last column in Exhibit 5, labeled "O/GER," shows the spread between a country's yield and the German government bond yield. For example, when the spread of the French government bond yield over the German government bond yield is computed, since both markets pay coupon interest annually, the spread is simply the difference in their conventional yields. Since the yield on the French government bond is 5.45% and the yield on a German government bond is 5.35%, the spread is 10 basis points.

D. Forward Rates and Breakeven Analysis

As explained earlier, there are various methods of evaluating relative value in international bond markets. Before these can be translated into a market allocation, the strategic outlook needs to be compared with that which is already priced into the market. This can be accomplished by either converting the economic outlook into point forecasts for bond and currency levels, or looking at the forward rates implied by current market conditions and comparing them with the economic outlook.

Bond and currency breakeven rates, those which make two investments produce identical total returns, are usually calculated versus the benchmark market over a specific time horizon. A large yield spread between two markets implies a larger "cushion" (the required spread widening to equate total returns in both markets, or the breakeven rate) the longer the investment time horizon.

Comparisons of forward interest rates can be instrumental in identifying where differences between the strategic outlook and market prices may present investment opportunities. As explained at Level I (Chapter 6), forward interest rates, which use the shape of the yield curve to calculate implied forward bond rates, allow a quick comparison of what is required in terms of yield shifts for bonds in each market to provide a return equal to the short-term risk-free rate (a zero excess return). This would correspond to a bond excess return of zero in equations (9) through (12), or $(r_i - c_i) = 0$. As explained at Level I (Chapter 6), forward interest rates represent a breakeven rate, not across markets necessarily, but within markets. The strategic bond allocation can then be derived by increasing exposure to markets where the expected return of bonds over the short-term interest rate is most positive — that is where the expected bond yield is furthest below the forward yield. Forward rate calculators are also available on systems such as Bloomberg as can been in the graph of forward rates in Exhibit 6.

The forward foreign exchange rate represents a breakeven rate between hedged and unhedged currency returns as shown above in the analysis on components of return. In terms of equations (9), (11), and (12), currency excess return is zero when the percentage change in the currency equals the forward premium or discount. As forward foreign exchange rates are determined by short-term interest rate differentials, they can be estimated from the interest rates on deposits, specifically, Eurodeposit rates as in equations (2) and (3), which can be easily obtained from market data services such as Bloomberg and Reuters.

Breakeven analysis provides another tool for estimating relative value between markets. Because the prices of benchmark bonds are influenced by coupon effects and changes in the benchmark, many international fixed income traders and portfolio managers find it easier to keep pace with changes in yield relationships than price changes in each market. A constant spread between markets when yield levels are shifting, however, may result in a variation in returns as differing maturities and coupons of benchmark bonds result in a wide spread of interest rate sensitivity across markets. For example, of the benchmark 10-year bonds listed in Exhibit 5, calculation of the duration of each issue would show that duration ranges from a low of 6.0 for Sweden to 9.0 for Japan where yields are one third that of the next lowest yielding market. (The duration for the U.S. bond was 7.3.) Thus, market duration must be taken into account in determining breakeven spread movements.

Exhibit 6: Forward Yield Curve Analysis: Germany

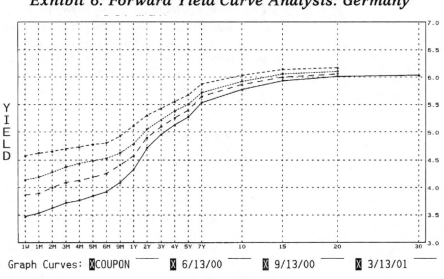

Graph Curves: ⊠COUPON   ⊠ 6/13/00   ⊠ 9/13/00   ⊠ 3/13/01

Source: Bloomberg Financial Markets

Since European Monetary Union, yield differentials within Europe have remained extremely tight. Holding Italian versus German bonds provides a running yield advantage of only 28 basis points per year. Obviously, this small amount of additional yield income can be easily wiped out by an adverse price movement between the two markets. In the mid 1990s before European Monetary Union, Italian bonds would have yielded several hundred basis points more than German bonds as the additional currency risk involved in holding Italian bonds had a substantial impact on nominal yield spreads. Even a fairly wide yield cushion, however, can also quickly evaporate.

To illustrate this and show how breakeven analysis is used, look at the spread between the U.S. and Japan in March 2000 as shown in Exhibit 5. The spread is 467 basis points, providing Japanese investors who purchased the U.S. benchmark Treasury with additional yield income of 117 basis points per quarter. This additional yield advantage can be wiped out by a widening of the spread that is substantially less than the 117 basis points of the spread itself. The widening can occur in one of the following two ways:

- yields in Japan can decrease, resulting in price appreciation of the Japanese government bond
- yields in the United States can increase, resulting in a price decline of the U.S. Treasury bond

Of course, a combination of the two can also occur. To quantify the amount of spread widening that would erase the yield advantage from investing in a higher yielding market, we need to conduct a breakeven analysis.

It is important to note that this breakeven analysis is not a total return analysis; it applies only to bond returns in local currency and ignores currency movements. This breakeven analysis is effective in comparing bond markets that share a common currency, as within the euro zone; however, currency must be taken into account when applying breakeven analysis to markets with different currencies. The additional yield advantage in the example above can be wiped out if the U.S. dollar depreciates by more than 1.17% during the quarter. Below, we illustrate how a hedged breakeven analysis can be calculated using hedged returns, or simply the forward foreign exchange premium or discount between the two currencies.

We know that the duration of the Japanese bond is 9.[29] This means that for a 100 basis point change in yield the approximate percentage price change for the Japanese bond will be 9%. For a 50 basis point change in yield, the percentage price change for the Japanese bond will change by approximately 4.5%. We can generalize this as follows:

$$\text{change in price} = 9 \times \text{change in yield}$$

If we let W denote the spread widening, we can rewrite the above equation as:

$$\text{change in price} = 9 \times W$$

We want the increase in price caused by the spread widening to be 1.17%. Therefore,

$$1.17\% = 9 \times W$$

---

[29] This is the modified duration for the issue. Since the Japanese bond and the U.S. bonds are option-free, as explained at Level I (Chapter 7), the modified duration is close to the effective duration.

Solving for W,

$$W = 1.17\%/9 = 0.130\% = 13.0 \text{ basis points}$$

Therefore, a spread widening of 13 basis points due to a decline in the yield in Japan would wipe out the additional yield from buying the U.S. Treasury issue. Hence, a change in interest rates of only 13 basis points is needed in this case to wipe out the 3-month yield advantage of 117 basis points.

We can refer to this change in spread that will eliminate the yield advantage as the **breakeven spread movement**. Note that the breakeven spread movement must (1) be related to an investment horizon and (2) utilize the higher of the two countries' modified durations. Using the highest modified duration provides the minimum spread movement that would offset the additional yield from investing in a higher yielding market. So, in our example, the 3-month breakeven spread movement due to Japanese yields is 13 basis points, meaning that it is the spread movement due to a drop in Japanese rates by 13 basis points that would eliminate the 3-month additional yield from investing in U.S. Treasury bonds. The breakeven spread movement using the 7.3 duration in the U.S. would be 16 basis points; this is a difference of only 3 basis points.

The breakeven spread movement described above completely ignores the impact on returns from currency movements. In addition, it also ignores the implied appreciation or depreciation of the currency reflected in the forward premium or discount. If we subscribe to the methodology discussed earlier in the chapter of attributing cash returns to the currency decision, and measuring bond market returns as the local return minus the cash rate, the results of the breakeven spread movement analysis on a hedged basis may be quite different. We can easily calculate the hedged breakeven spread movement by adding in the forward foreign exchange discount or premium. At the time of this breakeven analysis, 3-month interest rates were 0.25% in Japan and 6.125% in the United States. With this information we can obtain the embedded forward rate using equation (3); that is,

$$f_{\yen,\$} \approx c_{\yen} - c_{\$} = (0.25\% - 6.125\%)/4 = -1.47\%$$

The expected hedged return over the 3-month period, assuming no change in rates, is the sum of the nominal spread differential (1.17%) and the forward premium (−1.47%), or −0.30%. Thus, the breakeven spread movement on a hedged basis requires a *tightening* of 3 basis points ($-0.30\% = 9 \times W$) instead of the 13 basis points of potential widening calculated on a local currency basis. Consequently, a Japanese investor would have to expect either a spread tightening of at least 3 basis points or believe that the dollar would depreciate versus the yen by less than the embedded forward rate to make the trade attractive.

Alternatively, we could use equation (10) to calculate the expected hedged return to a yen-based investor over a 3-month period and compare it to the return on a Japanese 10-year bond over the same period. In order to do so, it is first necessary to adjust the U.S. government bond yield (which is quoted on a bond-equivalent yield basis) to an annual-pay yield basis because the Japanese yield is based on an annual basis. Earlier we showed that the conventional yield of 6.32% for the U.S. government bond as reported in Exhibit 5 is 6.42% on an annual-pay basis. Assuming no change in rates, the expected hedged return is:

$$[(r_{\$} - c_{\$}) + c_{\yen}]/4 = [(6.42\% - 6.13\%) + 0.25\%]/4 = [0.54\%]/4 = 0.14\%$$

and the expected Japanese bond return is (1.74%/4, or 0.44%). Thus, the expected return on a hedged basis is −0.30%, which matches the first answer that we calculated.

E. Security Selection

Once the bond market allocation decisions have been made and the optimal duration and yield curve profile selected for each market, this overall portfolio structure needs to be constructed through the purchase or sale of individual securities. Many international bond investors prefer to trade only benchmark issues as they offer more liquidity than other bonds of a similar maturity. This can sometimes lead to a "hump" in the yield curve as investors prefer a certain issue or maturity sector. The same phenomenon can result from a squeeze of certain issues in the repo market, or short-term demand imbalances for bonds deliverable into short bond futures positions. As mentioned earlier, few foreign markets have a developed corporate bond market; however, other instruments are available such as mortgage bonds, Eurobonds, and inflation-indexed bonds.

Taxation issues also need to be taken into account when selecting individual bonds for purchase. For example, several markets have tax systems that encourage investors to hold lower coupon bonds, hence certain bonds will tend to trade rich or cheap to the curve depending on their coupon. In markets that impose withholding taxes on coupon payments, international fixed income portfolio managers often minimize their tax liability by replacing a bond that is near its coupon date with another bond of similar maturity. Market anomalies can also arise from differing tax treatment within markets. For example, Italian Eurobonds issued before 1988 are exempt of withholding tax for Italian investors, hence they tend to trade at a lower yield than similar maturity bonds issued after 1988.

APPENDIX   The purpose of this appendix is to show how equations (9), (10), (11), and (12) in the chapter were derived.

Unhedged expected return:

To derive the unhedged expected return given by equation (9) in the chapter, we begin with equation (5) in the chapter:

unhedged expected return for country i, $R_{H,i} = r_i + e_{H,i}$

adding and subtracting c_i on the right-hand side of the equation we get:

$$R_{H,i} = r_i - c_i + c_i + e_{H,i}$$

We know that $f_{H,i} = c_H - c_i$, so $c_i = c_H - f_{H,i}$. Substituting for the second c_i in the above equation and rearranging terms we have

$$R_{H,i} = c_H + (r_i - c_i) + (e_{H,i} - f_{H,i})$$

The above equation is equation (9), which states that the unhedged expected return for country i is equal to the short-term interest rate for the home country, the excess bond return of country i, and the unhedged excess currency return of country i's currency. The excess currency return is the currency return in country i relative to the home country less the short-term interest rate differential between the home country and country i.

Hedged expected return:

The hedged expected bond return for country i, equation (6), is derived by adding a currency hedge $(-e_{H,i} + c_H - c_i)$ to the unhedged return, equation (5). By doing so we get:

hedged expected return for country i, $HR_{H,i} = r_i + e_{H,i} - e_{H,i} + c_H - c_i$

the two currency terms drop out yielding equation (6)

$$HR_{H,i} = r_i + c_H - c_i$$

To derive the expected return given by equation (10), we simply rearranged the terms in equation (6) above obtaining:

$$HR_{H,i} = c_H + (r_i - c_i)$$

The above equation is equation (10), which states that the hedged expected return for country i is equal to the short-term interest rate for the home country and the excess bond return of country i. There is no currency return component since it has been hedged out.

Cross hedged expected return:

To get the cross hedged expected return given by equation (11) we begin with equation (5) in the chapter and enter into a currency forward that creates a short position in currency i and long position in currency j $(f_{j,i} - e_{i,j})$. The currency position $e_{i,j}$ combined with the original long exposure to currency i, $e_{H,i}$, leaves a net long positioning in currency j versus the home currency, $e_{H,j}$. Thus,

cross hedged expected return for country i, $CR_{H,i} = r_i + e_{H,i} + f_{j,i} - e_{i,j}$ or, $r_i + f_{j,i} + e_{H,j}$

We know that $f_{j,i} = c_j - c_i$, so we can rewrite the above equation as:

$$CR_{H,i} = r_i + c_j - c_i + e_{H,j}$$

Rearranging terms we get:

$$CR_{H,i} = (r_i - c_i) + (c_j + e_{H,j})$$

The above is equation (7) in the chapter. We know that $f_{H,j} = c_H - c_j$ and therefore $c_j = c_H - f_{H,j}$. Substituting for c_j in the above equation and rearranging terms we get

$$CR_{H,i} = c_H + (r_i - c_i) + (e_{H,j} - f_{H,j})$$

The above equation is equation (11), which states that the cross hedged expected return for country i is equal to the short-term interest rate for the home country, the excess bond return of country i, and the currency return of country j over the home country less the short-term interest rate differential between the home country and country j.

Proxy hedged expected return:

To derive the proxy hedged expected return given by equation (12), we begin with the unhedged return, equation (5), and add a short currency position in currency j ($f_{H,j} - e_{H,j}$) to obtain the rewritten proxy hedged expected return equation given in the chapter:

$$\text{proxy hedged expected return for country } i, PR_{H,i} = r_i + e_{H,i} + f_{H,j} - e_{H,j}$$

We know that $f_{H,j} = c_H - c_j$ and therefore substituting for $f_{H,j}$ in the above equation we get:

$$PR_{H,i} = r_i + e_{H,i} + c_H - c_j - e_{H,j}$$

adding and subtracting c_i from the right hand side of the equation we get:

$$PR_{H,i} = r_i + e_{H,i} + c_H - c_j - e_{H,i} + c_i - c_i$$

Rearranging terms we get

$$PR_{H,i} = (r_i - c_i) + (c_i + e_{H,i}) + [(c_H - c_j) - e_{H,j}]$$

which is equation (8) in the chapter. Rearranging terms, this equation can be expressed as

$$PR_{H,i} = c_H + (r_i - c_i) + (e_{H,i} - e_{H,j}) - (c_j - c_i)$$

Since $f_{j,i} = c_j - c_i$ we can substitute $f_{j,i}$ for $(c_j - c_i)$ and rearrange terms to obtain equation (12) in the chapter:

$$PR_{H,i} = c_H + (r_i - c_i) + [(e_{H,i} - e_{H,j}) - f_{j,i}]$$

Equation (12) states that the proxy hedged expected return for country i is equal to the short-term interest rate for the home country, the excess bond return of country i, and the difference between the currency return of country i and the home country relative to country j and the home country, less the short-term interest rate differential between countries j and i.

The fact that equations (9), (10), (11), and (12) differ only by their last term emphasizes that the bond market decision is unrelated to the currency hedging decision.

SECTION V
KEY POINTS

❑ *Most investors are attracted to international bonds because of their historically higher returns than U.S. bonds; others are drawn because of the diversification value of international bonds in reducing overall portfolio risk.*

❑ *The investor's investment objectives (total return, diversification or risk reduction, current income, or asset/liability matching) have implications for the management of an international bond portfolio.*

❑ *The investor's investment objectives should be reflected in the investment guidelines, including return objectives, risk tolerances, benchmark selection, and an appropriate time horizon for judging performance.*

❑ *For an investor interested in the diversification benefits of international bond investing, the time horizon over which investment performance is to be measured is important.*

❑ *In selecting a benchmark for an international bond portfolio, the choice of a pure capitalization (market value) weighted index may create a benchmark that exposes the investor to a disproportionate share in some countries' markets relative to the investor's liabilities or diversification preferences.*

❑ *International bond benchmarks may be hedged, unhedged, or partially hedged depending on the investor's objectives.*

❑ *Because of currency risk, international investing requires that a portfolio manager adopt either an active or passive approach to currency management.*

❑ *Studies of currency hedging for U.S. dollar-based investors suggest that a partially hedged benchmark offers superior risk-adjusted returns as compared with either a fully hedged or unhedged benchmark.*

❑ *Historically, the returns from different exposures to currency (unhedged, partially hedged, and fully hedged) are highly variable depending on the time period chosen.*

❑ *Bond markets can be divided into four trading blocs: dollar bloc (the U.S., Canada, Australia, and New Zealand); European bloc; Japan; and, emerging markets.*

❑ *The European bloc can be further divided into the euro zone market bloc (which has a common currency) and the non-euro zone market bloc.*

❑ *The U.K. often trades on its own economic fundamentals, as well as being influenced by both the euro zone market bloc and the U.S.*

❑ *It is useful to think in terms of trading blocs because each bloc has a benchmark market that greatly influences price movements in the other markets within the bloc.*

❑ *Investment guidelines should specify limits on investments in countries outside the benchmark.*

❑ *Risk limits on duration are usually specified in investment policy statements despite the shortcomings of duration as a measure of interest rate risk across countries.*

❑ *The illiquidity of lower rated securities poses a risk for international bond portfolio managers who tend to shift funds in and out of markets frequently.*

❑ *There are a number of means by which portfolio managers can enhance returns relative to a benchmark with the major source of excess return coming from broad bond market and currency allocation decisions.*

❑ *To facilitate the market and currency selection process, a manager should employ a disciplined investment approach based upon fundamental economic factors and market indicators of value.*

❏ *International bond managers employ one or more different management styles and these styles can be divided into four general categories: experienced trader; fundamentalist; black box; and chartist.*

❏ *The seasoned trader uses experience and intuition to identify market opportunities.*

❏ *The fundamental style is based on the belief that bonds and currencies trade according to the economic cycle, and that the cycle can be forecasted; managers using this approach rely mostly upon economic analysis and forecasts in selecting bond markets and currencies.*

❏ *The black box style is used by quantitative managers who believe that computer models can identify market relationships that human beings cannot.*

❏ *The chartist style involves looking at daily, weekly, and monthly charts to try to ascertain the strength of market trends, or to identify potential turning points in markets.*

❏ *Excess returns for an international bond portfolio relative to its benchmark can be generated through a combination of five broad strategies: bond market selection; currency selection; duration management/yield curve plays; sector/credit/security selection, and; if permitted, investing in markets outside the benchmark.*

❏ *Duration management is more difficult in international bond investing as very few foreign bond markets have liquid bond issues with an original maturity greater than 10 years.*

❏ *Most foreign bond markets lack the broad range of instruments — such as stripped government securities — and a well developed market for collateralized borrowing — such as the U.S. repo market — making it difficult to manage duration on a cost effective basis.*

❏ *Because most benchmarks include only government bonds, investing in non-government bonds can also enhance returns; however, choices are more limited outside the United States because government and government-guaranteed issues account for the majority of issues.*

❏ *In a fundamental-based approach to global bond investing, the strategic decision of which bond markets and currencies to overweight typically starts with an outlook for the economic cycle and bond and currency forecasts in each of the markets to be considered for investment.*

❏ *The long-run economic cycle is closely correlated with changes in bond yields, and trends in both the economic cycle and bond yields tend to persist for a year or longer.*

❏ *Forecasting interest rates is extremely difficult and the academic literature generally holds that interest rate forecasts are unable to generate consistent risk-adjusted excess returns.*

❏ *The manager's economic outlook forms the foundation for the strategic allocation for bonds and currencies.*

❏ *The economic outlook must be compared with either consensus economic forecasts, or some measure of market value to identify attractive investment opportunities.*

❏ *The volatilities and correlations of the various bond and currency markets should be used to assess the incremental impact of any position on overall portfolio risk compared with its expected return.*

❏ *The strategic allocation decision of which markets to overweight or underweight relative to the benchmark is a complex interaction of expected returns derived from assessments of economic trends, technical and value factors, and risk factors, estimated from historical volatilities and cross-market correlations.*

❏ *The key categories of fundamental economic influences that need to be evaluated against market expectations to determine its likely impact on bond and currency prices are: cyclicals, inflation, monetary policy, fiscal policy, debt, balance of payments, and politics.*

❏ *Identification of trends in economic fundamentals can help identify attractive investment opportunities in markets.*

❏ *While the determination of relative value is highly subjective, the three more objective measures of value are: real yields, technical analysis, and market sentiment surveys.*

❏ *Sources of return for an international bond portfolio can be separated into three components: excess returns on bonds, excess returns on currencies, and the risk-free rate.*

❏ *Partitioning the sources of return into three components can assist a portfolio manager in identifying where market prices are most out of line with the strategic outlook and whether bond market exposures should be hedged or left unhedged.*

❏ *The most common vehicle used to alter exposure to exchange rates is a currency forward contract.*

❏ *Based on covered interest arbitrage, it can be shown that the spot exchange rate and the short-term interest rates in two countries will determine the forward exchange rate.*

❏ *The relationship among the spot exchange rate, the short-term interest rates in two countries, and the forward rate is called interest rate parity.*

❏ *Whether or not a manager will hedge the exposure to a given country's exchange rate using a forward exchange rate depends on (1) the manager's expectation as to the percentage return from exposure to a currency and (2) the forward discount or premium.*

❏ *If the manager expects that the percentage return from exposure to a currency is greater than the forward discount or premium, then the manager will not use a forward contract to hedge the exposure to that currency.*

❏ *If the manager expects the currency return to be less than the forward discount or premium, the manager will use a forward contract to hedge the exposure to a currency.*

❏ *Cross forward hedging replaces the currency exposure to country i with currency exposure in country j; rather than hedging with a forward contract between country i and the home currency, the manager elects to hedge with a forward contract between country j and country i.*

❏ *An alternative to hedging with a forward contract is to create a short position.*

❏ *Proxy hedging involves shorting a second currency, currency j; that is, proxy hedging keeps the currency exposure in country i, but creates a hedge by establishing a short position in country j's currency.*

❏ *A proxy hedge would normally be considered only where the currencies of country i and j are highly correlated, and the hedge costs in country j are lower than in country i.*

❏ *The expected return for country i using proxy hedging depends on the short-term interest rate in the home country plus: (1) the excess bond return (or the differential between the bond return for country i and the short-term interest rate for country i), and (2) the excess currency return (the difference between the long currency position in country i relative to the home country and the short currency position in country j relative to the home country minus the forward premium between countries i and j comprised of the short-term interest rate differential between the two countries).*

❏ *An unhedged expected return is equal to the short-term interest rate in the home country plus (1) the excess bond return (or the differential between the bond return for country i and the short-term interest rate for country i), and (2) the excess currency return (the long currency position in country i relative to the home country minus the forward premium between the home country and country i comprised of the short-term interest rate differential between the two countries).*

❏ *The short-term interest rate differential is integral to the currency hedge decision.*

❏ *The return for a strategy can be divided into three distinct components of return: the short-term interest rate for the home currency; the excess bond return of country i over the short-term interest rate of country i, and; the excess currency return (either unhedged, hedged, cross-hedged, or proxy hedged).*

❏ *The excess currency return is the currency return in excess of the forward premium (or discount) and becomes the basis for the decision of currency hedging.*

❏ *In evaluating relative value in international bond markets, it is necessary to either convert the economic outlook into point forecasts for bond and currency levels, or look at the forward rates implied by current market conditions and compare them with the economic outlook.*

❏ *Bond and currency breakeven rates are rates that make two investments produce identical total returns.*

❏ *Breakeven rates are usually calculated versus the benchmark over a specific time horizon.*

❏ *Comparisons of forward interest rates can be instrumental in identifying where differences between the strategic outlook and market prices may present investment opportunities.*

END OF CHAPTER QUESTIONS

1. Mr. Johnson is a trustee for the Wilford Corporate pension fund. At the present time the pension fund's investment guidelines do not permit investment in non-U.S. bonds. A consultant of the pension fund has suggested that the trustees consider investing 30% of the portfolio in non-U.S. bonds. The benefit, according to the consultant, is that international diversification will allow the pension fund to realize a higher expected return for a given level of risk. Moreover, the consultant noted that there are benefits from "currency plays."

Mr. Johnson asked the consultant for empirical support for benefits from international bond investing from 1985 to 1996. More specifically, he asked for an analysis of monthly returns over several time periods based on an allocation of 70% to domestic bonds and 30% to international bonds. Mr. Johnson also asked for the performance if bonds were unhedged with respect to currency exposure and hedged. The consultant provided the analysis shown below:

	1985-96	1985-88	1989-92	1993-96	1989-96
Annualized Total Return					
Unhedged Index	11.40%	15.78%	10.54%	8.16%	9.33%
Hedged Index	9.69	11.30	10.14	7.70	8.90
U.S. Aggregate Index	10.10	11.76	11.66	6.94	9.28
Standard Deviation of Returns					
Unhedged Index	4.79	5.82	4.51	3.63	4.12
Hedged Index	3.64	4.38	3.10	3.20	3.18
U.S. Aggregate Index	4.86	5.90	4.12	4.24	4.22
Sharpe Ratio					
Unhedged Index	1.13	1.54	0.87	0.43	0.91
Hedged Index	1.02	1.02	1.14	0.98	1.04
U.S. Aggregate Index	0.84	0.84	1.23	0.56	0.87

a. For the period 1985-1996, how did the performance of a portfolio of 30% international bonds compare to that of the U.S. Aggregate Index (i.e., U.S. bonds only) if the portfolio is unhedged?

b. Is the performance of an unhedged bond portfolio with 30% international bonds dependent on the time period selected?

c. If the currency risk is hedged, what does the evidence suggest about the performance of a bond portfolio with 30% international bonds compared to an all U.S. bond portfolio?

2. a. Why would an investor who is primarily concerned with diversification benefits associated with international bond investing want to place limits on the size of positions that its manager may take relative to the benchmark?

b. Why might a total-return oriented investor be far less concerned with how the portfolio composition differs from the benchmark?

3. For a client that is interested in the diversification benefits of international bond investing, why might the selection of a longer-term time horizon (such as two to three years) be preferred to a short-term time horizon (for example, one quarter) to evaluate the performance of a manager?

4. Why is the complexity associated with international bond markets more akin to the complexity associated with investing in the U.S. equity market than the U.S. bond market?

5. a. Coupon payments on U.K. government bonds are semiannual. What is the yield on an annual-pay basis for a U.K. government bond for which the conventional yield is 5%?

   b. Coupon payments on German government bonds are annual. What is the bond-equivalent yield on a semiannual-pay basis for a German government bond for which the conventional yield is 5.6%?

6. A portfolio manager is reviewing a report that shows the conventional yield on a 10-year U.S. Treasury bond (6%) and the conventional yield on a 10-year of Spanish government bond (5%). Coupon interest is paid annually on Spanish government bonds. The yield spread between the Spanish government bond and the U.S. government bond shown in the report was *not* −100 basis points. The manager does not understand why. Explain to this manager why the yield spread would not be −100 basis points. (No computation is required.)

7. Suppose the spot exchange rate between U.S. dollars and the local currency for Country A is US $2 for one unit of the local currency (LC). Assume the following interest rates in both countries:

Maturity	United States	Country A
1 month	3.0%	8.5%
3 months	3.5%	9.0%
1 year	4.0%	10.00%
5 years	4.9%	11.00%

   Assume that the borrowing and lending rate in each country is the same. A 1-year forward exchange rate contract is available between U.S. dollars and the local currency.

   a. What should the 1-year forward exchange rate be?
   b. If the 1-year forward exchange rate between U.S. dollars and the local currency of Country A is US $2.1 for one unit of the local currency, demonstrate how a U.S. portfolio manager can exploit this pricing for the forward contract?
   c. If the 1-year forward exchange rate between U.S. dollars and the local currency of Country A is US $1.7 for one unit of the local currency, demonstrate how a portfolio manager in Country A can exploit this pricing for the forward contract?

8. a. How can a portfolio manager hedge a long position exposure to a currency?
   b. How does a cross hedge differ from a proxy hedge?

9. A U.S. portfolio manager is considering whether or not to hedge its exposure to Country X's currency. Following is relevant information available to the manager, as well as the manager's expectations:

   Expected bond return in Country X = 4.0%
   Short-term interest rate in Country X = 3.2%
   Expected currency appreciation of currency X relative to U.S. $ = 5.1%
   Short-term U.S. interest rate = 4.6%

   a. What is the unhedged expected *excess currency* return?
   b. What is the unhedged expected return?
   c. What is the hedged expected return?
   d. Should the manager hedge the position?

e. Suppose that the manager is considering cross hedging with the currency of Country Y and the following information is available to the manager along with assumptions made by the manager:

Short-term interest rate in Country Y= 4.0%
Expected currency appreciation of currency Y relative to U.S. $ = 4.6%

What is the expected *excess currency* return from cross hedging using Country Y's currency?

f. What is the hedged expected return from the cross hedge?

g. Based on your answer to part f, is a cross hedge attractive relative to hedging currency X and an unhedged strategy?

h. Suppose that the manager wants to use Country Y's currency for proxy hedging. What is the expected *excess currency* return for this proxy hedge strategy?

i. What is the expected return from this proxy hedge strategy?

j. Should a proxy hedge strategy be employed?

10. A British portfolio manager is considering whether or not to hedge the portfolio's exposure to Country A's currency. Following is relevant information available to the manager, as well as the manager's expectations:

Expected bond return in Country A = 3.3%
Short-term interest rate in Country A = 2.9%
Expected currency appreciation of currency A relative to British £ = −1.2%
   (Note a negative sign means depreciation of the currency.)
Short-term British interest rate = 4.6%

a. What is the unhedged expected *excess currency* return?

b. What is the unhedged expected return?

c. What is the hedged expected return?

d. Should the manager hedge the position?

e. Suppose that the British portfolio manager is considering cross hedging with the currency of Country B and the following information is available to the manager, along with the manager's assumptions:

Short-term interest rate in Country B = 4.2%
Expected currency appreciation of currency B relative to British £ = −3.5%

What is the expected *excess currency* return from cross hedging using Country B's currency?

f. What is the hedged expected return from the cross hedge?

g. Based on your answer to part f, is a cross hedge attractive relative to hedging currency A and an unhedged strategy?

h. Suppose that the manager wants to use Country B's currency for proxy hedging. What is the expected *excess currency* return for this proxy hedge strategy?

i. What is the expected return from this proxy hedge strategy?

j. Should a proxy hedge strategy be employed?

11. Before making allocation decisions regarding country and currency based on market outlook, an international bond portfolio manager should examine what is priced into the market.

a. Where can a manager obtain information about what is priced into the market?

b. Why does information that is priced into the market provide a benchmark for comparing a manager's interest rate and currency outlook for the countries in which the manager plans to invest?

c. Why might a portfolio manager who expects that Country Y's currency will depreciate in the next year still want to increase currency exposure to that country's currency?

12. Suppose that on some date the following information is available for the 10-year government benchmark of Country M and the United States:

Country	Yield to maturity	Duration
M	3.2%	6
U.S.	7.0%	4

From the perspective of a portfolio manager in country M, there is a 3.8% annual yield advantage to invest in the United States. Suppose that the manager is interested in investing in either the benchmark government bond of his own country or the U.S. government benchmark bond and the investment horizon is three months.

a. Explain how the 380 basis point annual yield advantage from investing in the U.S. can be eliminated over the next three months?

b. What is the breakeven spread movement for the yield in Country M?

c. What is the breakeven spread movement for the yield in the United States?

d. Suppose that the 3-month rates were 2.5% in Country M and 6.5% in the U.S. What is the expected hedged return to a portfolio manager in Country M over a 3-month period assuming no change in interest rates?

e. On a hedged basis, what is the breakeven spread movement in terms of a tightening of the spread in Country M?

f. On an unhedged investment even if yields do not change in the U.S. or Country M, currency movements can eliminate the yield advantage from investing in the U.S. government bond. What is the view that the portfolio manager in Country M must have in order to benefit from the additional yield from investing in the U.S. government bond?

SOLUTIONS TO END OF CHAPTER QUESTIONS

1. a. The unhedged portfolio with 30% international bonds had both a higher return and a lower standard deviation for the 1985-1996 period than an all U.S. bond portfolio. (Accordingly, the Sharpe ratio, a measure of risk-adjusted return, was higher for the 30% international bond portfolio.)

   b. The results suggest that there are periods where the performance of an unhedged international bond portfolio with 30% international bonds may be inferior to that of a portfolio of only U.S. bonds. Specifically, for the period 1989-1992 the return was less and the standard deviation was greater for the portfolio with international bonds resulting in underperformance on a risk-adjusted basis also.

   c. The return for the entire period (1985-1996) for the international bond portfolio was less than for a U.S. bond portfolio. However, to offset that there was a reduction in risk because the standard deviation for the international bond portfolio was less than that of the U.S. bond portfolio. On a risk-adjusted basis, the Sharpe ratio indicates that the hedged international bond portfolio was superior to the U.S. bond portfolio.

   However, the results do vary depending on the period. For the periods shown in the consultant's report, the risk-adjusted return in the 1989-1992 period was higher for the U.S. bond portfolio.

2. a. The benefits of diversification via international bond investing are weakened if the manager dramatically alters exposures (i.e., positions) relative to the benchmark index. A concentration of exposures in any one market versus the benchmark may diminish the portfolio's diversification benefits.

   b. A total-return oriented investor would be concerned primarily with the performance of the portfolio and may be less concerned with how the allocation is made among the countries comprising the index. This investor's major concern is the performance relative to the benchmark.

3. A short time horizon over which investment performance is measured may encourage more short-term trading which could diminish the natural diversification benefit from international bonds as an asset class. Investors who emphasize the risk reduction benefits of diversifying by international bond investing should have a longer time horizon. This is because differences between economic cycles can be prolonged, and a longer horizon would provide enough time for a full economic cycle to play out and the diversification benefit to take effect.

4. There are two reasons for this. First, an equity manager is operating in different sectors of the market each with its own fundamental economic factors and market dynamics. Similarly, a manager operating in the global bond market must operate in the U.S. bond market plus 10 to 20 other markets, each with its own market dynamics. Second, with the exception of the market for mortgage-backed securities, changes in interest rates typically affect all sectors of the U.S. bond market in the same way; however, the magnitude of the changes may vary. Like the equity market, where it is not unusual to have some industries or market sectors move in opposite directions, international bond markets may also move in different directions depending upon economic conditions and investor risk tolerances.

5. a. The conventional yield for the U.K. government bond is the yield quoted on a bond-equivalent basis. That yield is 5% in the question. The yield on an annual-pay basis if the conventional yield is 5% is:

$$(1 + \text{yield on a bond-equivalent yield}/2)^2 - 1 = (1 + 0.05/2)^2 - 1 = 5.06\%$$

  b. The bond-equivalent yield on the German government bond given a conventional yield of 5.6% is:

$$2[(1 + \text{yield on annual-pay bond})^{0.5} - 1] = 2[(1 + 0.056)^{0.5} - 1] = 5.52\%$$

6. When there are differences in the conventions for calculating the yield in two countries, the spread between the yield on bonds in two different countries cannot be found by simply computing the difference in the conventional yields. The yield for one of the bonds must be adjusted to make it comparable to the yield on the other. In the question, the U.S. Treasury bond yield is a bond-equivalent yield based on semiannual coupon payments while the Spanish government bond yield is based on annual coupon payments. Consequently, the spread is not simply the difference between the two conventional yields of −100 basis points (5% − 6%). To compare the Spanish government bond yield to that of the U.S. government bond yield, the latter must be adjusted to the yield on an annual basis.

7. a. The forward exchange rate (equation (2) in the chapter) is

$$F_{US, A} = S_{US, A}\left(\frac{1 + c_{US}}{1 + c_A}\right)$$

where

$F_{US,A}$ = forward exchange rate between U.S. dollars and the currency of Country A

$S_{US,A}$ = spot (or cash) exchange rate between U.S. dollars and the currency of Country A

c_{US} = short-term interest rate in the United States which matches the maturity of the forward contract

c_A = short-term interest rate in Country A which matches the maturity of the forward contract

The relevant interest rate in both countries is the 1-year rate since that is the maturity of the forward contract.

In the question:

$$S_{US,A} = 2 \quad c_{US} = 4\% = 0.04 \quad c_A = 10\% = 0.10$$

Therefore,

$$F_{US, A} = 2\left(\frac{1 + 0.04}{1 + 0.10}\right) = 1.8909$$

The 1-year forward exchange rate should be 1.8909.

  b. A U.S. portfolio manager can exploit a 1-year forward exchange rate of US $2.1 for one unit of the local contract as follows: borrow in the U.S. for one year at the U.S. rate of 4% and enter into a forward contract to deliver the amount of the LC one year from now as determined by the amount that will be available at the end of one year by investing at 10% in Country A. That is, the portfolio manager will sell forward the LC of Country A, or equivalently, buy forward U.S. dollars.

For example, suppose that $100,000 is borrowed by the U.S. portfolio manager. At the spot exchange rate of US $2 for one unit of the local currency, the manager will exchange the $100,000 for LC 50,000. The LC 50,000 will then be invested at 10% in Country A for one year, so that the amount available at the end of one year is LC 55,000. So, if the portfolio manager borrows $100,000, she will agree to deliver LC 55,000 one year from now at the 1-year forward exchange rate of US $2.1 for one unit of the LC.

Here is the outcome of this strategy at the end of one year:

From investment in Country A:
LC from investment in Country A   LC 55,000

From forward contract:
U.S. $ from delivery of LC 55,000 at forward rate $115,500

Profit after loan repayment:
U.S. $ available to repay loan $115,500
Loan repayment (principal plus 4% interest) $104,000
Profit $11,500

Assuming that the counterparty to the forward contract does not default, this is a riskless arbitrage situation because a $11,500 profit is generated with no initial investment. Therefore, a 1-year forward exchange rate cannot be sustained because it permits arbitrage profits.

c. A portfolio manager in Country A can exploit this pricing of the 1-year forward contract by (1) borrowing in the local currency in Country A, (2) exchanging to U.S. dollars at the spot rate, (3) investing in the United States, and (4) selling U.S. dollars forward or equivalently by buying the local currency of Country A forward. The amount that the portfolio manager will agree to deliver forward of the U.S. dollar is the amount that can be earned in the United States on the amount borrowed.

For example, suppose that the portfolio manager in Country A borrows LC 100,000 at a 10% interest rate. The manager can exchange this amount for US $200,000 at the spot exchange rate. This amount of U.S. dollars is then invested in the United States at an interest rate of 4% and will generate US $208,000 at the end of one year. So, in terms of the forward contract, the manager will agree to deliver US $208,000 one year from now and will receive LC 122,353 (US $208,000 divided by the forward exchange rate of 1.7) upon conversion to the local currency.

The outcome of this strategy at the end of one year is:

From investment in the United States:
US $ from investment in U.S.   US $208,000

From forward contract:

LC from delivery of US $208,000 at forward rate	LC 122,353

Profit after loan repayment:

LC available to repay loan	LC 122,353
Loan repayment (principal plus 10% interest)	LC 110,000
Profit	LC 12,353

Once again, assuming that the counterparty to the forward contract does not default, this is a riskless arbitrage situation because a LC 12,353 profit is generated with no initial investment.

8. a. A manager can hedge a long position exposure to a currency by selling a forward exchange rate contract for that currency.

 b. Although cross hedging and proxy hedging sound similar, and even though they both include a third currency in the transaction, they are quite different. Cross hedging maintains foreign currency exposure, but shifts that exposure from the currency of country i in which the investment is made, to the currency of another country, say country j, using currency forwards. Proxy hedging eliminates foreign currency exposure by hedging back into the home currency, but uses a currency forward in a second currency, that of country j, to hedge back into the home currency rather than the currency of country i in which the investment is made.

9. The interest rates and expected returns are as follows:

$$r_x = 4.0\%$$
$$c_x = 3.2\%$$
$$e_{US\$,x} = 5.1\%$$
$$c_y = 4.0\%$$
$$e_{US\$,y} = 4.6\%$$
$$c_{US} = 4.6\%$$

A summary of the calculations is provided in the table below:

	Hedged	Unhedged	Cross Hedged	Proxy Hedged
Expected Returns				
Cash	$c_{US\$}$ $= 4.6\%$	$c_{US\$}$ $= 4.6\%$	$c_{US\$}$ $= 4.6\%$	$c_{US\$}$ $= 4.6\%$
Excess Bond	$(r_x - c_x)$ $= (4.0\% - 3.2\%)$ $= 0.8\%$	$(r_x - c_x)$ $= (4.0\% - 3.2\%)$ $= 0.8\%$	$(r_x - c_x)$ $= (4.0\% - 3.2\%)$ $= 0.8\%$	$(r_x - c_x)$ $= (4.0\% - 3.2\%)$ $= 0.8\%$
Excess Currency	 $= 0.0\%$	$e_{US\$,x} - (c_{US\$} - c_x)$ $= 5.1\% - (4.6\% - 3.2\%)$ $= 5.1\% - 1.4\%$ $= 3.7\%$	$e_{US\$,y} - (c_{US\$} - c_y)$ $= 4.6\% - (4.6\% - 4.0\%)$ $= 4.6\% - 0.6\%$ $= 4.0\%$	$(e_{US\$,x} - e_{US\$,y}) - (c_y - c_x)$ $= (5.1\% - 4.6\%) - (4.0\% - 3.2\%)$ $= 0.5\% - 0.8\%$ $= -0.3\%$
Total Return	$= 5.4\%$	$= 9.1\%$	$= 9.4\%$	$= 5.1\%$

The U.S. cash rate and the expected excess bond return in country i are identical for each of the strategies and equal to the expected hedged bond return. Thus we can begin with the hedged bond return and compare the excess currency returns (the third component of the equations) of the unhedged, cross hedged and proxy hedged strategies.

a. unhedged expected excess currency return = 3.7%.
b. unhedged expected return = 9.1%
c. hedged expected return = 5.4%
d. Based on the manager's expectations about the currency movement, the hedged expected return is 5.4% which is less than the 9.1% unhedged expected return. Thus, the manager will not hedge currency X.
e. Expected excess currency return from cross hedging using Country Y's currency = 4.0%
f. Expected return from the cross hedge = 9.4%
g. Since the expected return from the cross hedge of 9.4% is greater than both the unhedged expected return of 9.1% and the hedged expected return of 5.4%, based on the manager's expectations for the movement of currency X and currency Y, a cross hedge is the most attractive option.
h. Expected excess currency return for the proxy hedge strategy = −0.3%
i. Expected return for the proxy hedge strategy = 5.1%
j. Based on the expectations for the currency movement, a proxy hedge strategy is unattractive. The proxy hedge strategy offers the lowest expected return of all the strategies considered in this question.

10. The interest rates and expected returns are as follows:

$$r_A = 3.3\%$$
$$c_A = 2.9\%$$
$$e_{UK,A} = -1.2\%$$
$$c_B = 4.2\%$$
$$e_{UK,B} = -3.5\%$$
$$c_{UK} = 4.6\%$$

A summary of the calculations is provided in the table below:

Expected Returns	Hedged	Unhedged	Cross Hedged	Proxy Hedged
Cash	c_{UK} = 4.6%	c_{UK} = 4.6%	c_{UK} = 4.6%	c_{UK} = 4.6%
Excess Bond	$(r_A - c_A)$ = (3.3% − 2.9%) = 0.4%	$(r_A - c_A)$ = (3.3% − 2.9%) = 0.4%	$(r_A - c_A)$ = (3.3% − 2.9%) = 0.4%	$(r_A - c_A)$ = (3.3% − 2.9%) = 0.4%
Excess Currency	= 0.0%	$e_{UK,A} - (c_{UK} - c_A)$ = −1.2% − (4.6% − 2.9%) = −1.2% − 1.7% = −2.9%	$e_{UK,B} - (c_{UK} - c_B)$ = −3.5% − (4.6% − 4.2%) = −3.5% − 0.4% = −3.9%	$(e_{UK,A} - e_{UK,B}) - (c_B - c_A)$ = (−1.2% + 3.5%) − (4.2% − 2.9%) = 2.3% − 1.3% = 1.0%
Total Return	= 5.0%	= 2.1%	= 1.1%	= 6.0%

a. expected unhedged excess currency return = −2.9%.
b. unhedged expected return = 2.1%

c. hedged expected return = 5.0%

d. Based on the manager's expectations about the currency movement, the hedged expected return is 5.0% which is greater than the 2.1% unhedged expected return. Thus, the manager will hedge currency A.

e. Expected excess currency return from cross hedging using Country B's currency = −3.9%

f. Expected return from the cross hedge = 1.1%

g. Since the expected return from the cross hedge of 1.1% is less than both the unhedged expected return of 2.1% and the hedged expected return of 5.0%, based on the manager's expectations for the movement of currency A and currency B, a cross hedge is unattractive.

h. Expected excess currency return for the proxy hedge strategy = 1.0%

i. Expected return for the proxy hedge strategy = 6.0%

j. Based on the expectations for the currency movement, a proxy hedge strategy is attractive. This is because the expected currency appreciation of Country A versus Country B is 2.3%, which is greater than the short-term interest rate differential between Countries A and B of 1.3%. The proxy hedge offers the highest expected return of all the strategies considered in this question.

11. a. Forward rates — forward interest rates and forward exchange rates — indicate what is priced into the market. The forward rates indicate what the manager can lock in today, thus it is a *hedgeable rate*.

b. When making an allocation decision, a manager is expressing a view relative to the market or, more specifically, what the market has priced into the bonds and the currency of the country. Therefore, forward interest rates and forward exchange rates set the benchmark to determine whether or not the manager's outlook is materially different from that of the market.

c. As explained in part (b), forward exchange rates indicate what is priced into the market for the country's currency and therefore provides a benchmark. If forward exchange rates indicate that the currency will depreciate much more than the manager's outlook, and if the manager strongly believes in his or her forecast, he will want to increase exposure to the currency.

12. a. There is a 95 basis point or 0.95% three-month yield advantage by investing in the U.S. benchmark issue. This advantage can be wiped out if the U.S. dollar depreciates by more than 0.95% during the quarter or if there is a widening of the spread. The widening can occur in one of the following ways:

  • yields in country M can decrease, resulting in price appreciation of country M's government bond
  • yields in the United States can increase, resulting in a price decline of the U.S. Treasury bond

A combination of the two can occur.

b. To determine how much the yield in country M must fall in order to eliminate the 0.95% yield advantage from investing in the U.S. government bond, the following must be computed. The decline in country M's yield must be such that it generates price appreciation for country M's government benchmark issue of 0.95%. Since the duration of that bond is 6, this means that for a 100 basis point change in yield the approximate percentage price change for the country M's government bond will be 6%. In general:

change in price = 6 × change in yield

Letting W denote the spread widening, then we can rewrite the above as

change in price = 6 × W

We want the increase in price caused by the spread widening to be 0.95%. Therefore,

0.95% = 6 × W

or

W = 0.95%/6 = 0.158% = 15.8 basis points.

A decline of 15.8 basis points in country M's yield is the breakeven spread movement in country M that would wipe out the 3-month yield advantage from buying the U.S. Treasury issue.

c. The breakeven spread movement in U.S. yield is found as follows:

change in price = 4 × W

We want the decrease in price caused by the spread widening to be 0.95%. Therefore,

0.95% = 4 × W

or

W = 0.95%/4 = 0.238% = 23.8 basis points.

An increase of 23.8 basis points in the U.S. yield is the breakeven spread movement in the U.S. that would wipe out the 3-month yield advantage from buying the U.S. Treasury issue.

d. The expected hedged return is:

$[(r_\$ - c_\$) + c_M]/4 = [(7.0\% - 6.5\%) + 2.5\%]/4 = 0.75\%$

e. When compared with the return on country M's 10-year government bond over the same period (3.2%/4, or 0.80%) the expected return on a hedged basis is a negative 0.05%. Thus, a portfolio manager in country M would have to expect a nominal spread *tightening* of at least 0.8 basis points ($-0.05\% = 6 \times W$) for the trade to look attractive.

f. The manager's view must be that the dollar would either appreciate or depreciate versus country M's currency by less than the embedded forward rate. The embedded forward rate is obtained as follows:

$f_{M,\$} = c_M - c_\$ = (2.5 - 6.5\%)/4 = -1.0\%$

That is, the portfolio manager's view must be that the U.S. dollar will either appreciate or depreciate by less than 1%.

Chapter 7

CONTROLLING INTEREST RATE RISK WITH DERIVATIVES

Frank J. Fabozzi, Ph.D., CFA
Adjunct Professor of Finance
School of Management
Yale University

Shrikant Ramamurthy
Senior Vice President
Fixed-Income Research
Prudential Securities, Inc.

Mark Pitts, Ph.D.
Principal
White Oak Capital Management Corp.

LEARNING OUTCOME STATEMENTS

After reading this chapter you should be able to:

- identify the advantages of using interest rate futures rather than Treasury securities to control the interest rate risk of a portfolio.
- explain the basic principles of controlling interest rate risk.
- determine the position that must be taken in a futures contract to adjust the current dollar duration of a portfolio to that of the target dollar duration.
- calculate the number of futures contracts that must be bought or sold in order to achieve a portfolio's target duration.
- compute the dollar duration of a futures contract.
- explain why hedging is a special case of controlling interest rate risk.
- explain what a short hedge is and what a long hedge is and when each hedge is used.
- explain what a cross hedge is.
- identify the steps in the hedging process.
- identify the factors that are important for determining the appropriate hedging instrument.
- explain what basis risk is and why hedging with futures substitutes basis risk for price risk.
- explain which price or rate is locked in when a position is taken in a futures contract.
- explain what convergence refers to for a futures contract.
- calculate the number of futures contracts that must be sold in hedging a position against a rise in interest rates.
- explain how the position in a Treasury bond futures contract must be adjusted for the cheapest-to-deliver issue.
- explain why an assumption must be made between the yield spread of the bond to be hedged and the hedging instrument.
- explain what a yield beta is and how it is used to adjust the number of futures contracts in a hedge.
- identify the major sources of hedging error.
- show how the cash flows of an entity can be altered using an interest rate swap.

- calculate the cash flows of an entity that has taken a position in an interest rate swap.
- compute the dollar duration of an interest rate swap.
- explain how positions in an interest rate swap change the dollar duration of an entity.
- describe the basic hedging strategies with options.
- explain how the outcome of a protective put buying strategy differs from that of a hedge using futures contracts.
- explain the limitations of a covered call writing strategy for hedging.
- explain what a collar strategy is.
- explain how the appropriate strike price is computed when using futures options to hedge a nondeliverable bond.
- compute the number of futures options required for hedging a position.
- explain how interest rate caps and floors can be used in asset/liability management.

SECTION I
INTRODUCTION

At Level II (Chapter 7) the features and characteristics of interest rate futures and swaps were explained. In addition, at Level II (Chapter 8), the valuation of these derivative instruments were explained. In this chapter, our focus is on how derivatives can be used to control the interest rate risk of a portfolio. There are other uses for derivatives such as speculating on interest rate movements and speculating on changes in interest rate volatility. These strategies are similar to those employed in the equity market and are not covered in this book.

SECTION II
CONTROLLING
INTEREST RATE
RISK WITH
FUTURES

The price of an interest rate futures contract moves in the opposite direction from the change in interest rates: when rates rise, the futures price will fall; when rates fall, the futures price will rise. By buying a futures contract, a portfolio's exposure to a rate change is increased. That is, the portfolio's duration increases. By selling a futures contract, a portfolio's exposure to a rate change is decreased. Equivalently, this means that the portfolio's duration is reduced. Consequently, buying and selling futures can be used to alter the duration of a portfolio.

While managers can alter the duration of their portfolios with cash market instruments (buying or selling Treasury securities), using interest rate futures instead of trading long-term Treasuries themselves has the following three advantages:

Advantage 1: Transaction costs for trading futures are lower than trading in the cash market.

Advantage 2: Margin requirements are lower for futures than for Treasury securities; using futures thus permits greater leverage.

Advantage3: It is easier to sell short in the futures market than in the Treasury market.

Futures can also be used in constructing a portfolio with a longer duration than is available with cash market securities. For example, suppose that in a certain interest rate environment a pension fund manager must structure a portfolio to have a duration of 15 to accomplish a particular investment objective. Bonds with such a long duration may not be available. By buying the appropriate number and kind of interest rate futures contracts, a pension fund manager can increase the portfolio's duration to the target level of 15.

A. General
Principles of
Interest Rate Risk
Control

The general principle in controlling interest rate risk with futures is to combine the dollar exposure of the current portfolio and the dollar exposure of a futures position so that the total dollar exposure is equal to the target dollar exposure. This means that the manager must be able to accurately measure the dollar exposure of both the current portfolio and the futures contract employed to alter the exposure.

As explained at Level I (Chapter 7), there are two commonly used measures for approximating the change in the dollar value of a bond or bond portfolio to changes in interest rates: price value of a basis point (PVBP) and duration. PVBP is the dollar price change resulting from a one-basis-point change in yield. Duration is the approximate percentage change in price for a 100-basis-point change in rates. (Given the percentage price change, the dollar price change for a given change in interest rates can be computed.) There are two measures of duration: *modified* and *effective*. Effective duration is the appropriate measure that should be used for bonds with embedded options. In this chapter when we refer to duration, we mean effective duration. Moreover, since the manager is interested in dollar price exposure, it is the effective *dollar* duration that should be used. For a one basis point change in rates, PVBP is equal to the effective dollar duration for a one-basis-point change in rates.

As emphasized in earlier chapters and at Level II, to estimate the effective dollar duration, it is necessary to have a good valuation model. It is the valuation model that is used to determine what the new values for the bonds in the portfolio will be if rates change. The difference between the current values of the bonds in the portfolio and the new values estimated by the valuation model when rates are changed is the dollar price exposure. Consequently, the starting point in controlling interest rate risk is the development of a reliable valuation model. A reliable valuation model is also needed to value the derivative contracts that the manager wants to use to control interest rate exposure.

Suppose that a manager seeks a **target duration** for the portfolio based on either expectations of interest rates or client-specified exposure. Given the target duration, a target dollar duration for a small basis point change in interest rates can be obtained. For a 50 basis point change in interest rates, for example, the target dollar duration can be found by multiplying the dollar value of the portfolio by the target duration and then dividing by 200. For example, suppose that the manager of a $500 million portfolio wants a target duration of 6. This means that the manager seeks a 3% change in the value of the portfolio for a 50 basis point change in rates (assuming a parallel shift in rates of all maturities). Multiplying the target duration of 6 by $500 million and dividing by 200 gives a target dollar duration of $15 million.

The manager must then determine the dollar duration of the current portfolio. The current dollar duration for a 50 basis point change in interest rates is found by multiplying the current duration by the dollar value of the portfolio and dividing by 200. So, for our $500 million portfolio, suppose that the current duration is 4. The current dollar duration is then $10 million (4 times $500 million divided by 200).

The target dollar duration is then compared to the current dollar duration. The difference between the two dollar durations is the dollar exposure that must be provided by a position in the futures contract. If the target dollar duration exceeds the current dollar duration, a futures position must increase the dollar exposure by the difference. To increase the dollar exposure, an appropriate number of futures contracts must be purchased. If the target dollar duration is less than the current dollar duration, an appropriate number of futures contracts must be sold. That is,

> If target dollar duration − current dollar duration > 0, buy futures
> If target dollar duration − current dollar duration < 0, sell futures

Once a futures position is taken, the **portfolio's dollar duration** is equal to the sum of the **current dollar duration without futures** plus the **dollar duration of the futures position**. That is,

> portfolio's dollar duration = current dollar duration without futures
> + dollar duration of futures position

The objective is to control the portfolio's interest rate risk by establishing a futures position such that the portfolio's dollar duration is equal to the target dollar duration. Thus,

> portfolio's dollar duration = target dollar duration

Or, equivalently,

$$\text{target dollar duration} = \text{current dollar duration without futures} \\ + \text{dollar duration of futures position} \tag{1}$$

Over time, the portfolio's dollar duration will move away from the target dollar duration. The manager can alter the futures position to adjust the portfolio's dollar duration to the target dollar duration.

1. Determining the Number of Contracts

Each futures contract calls for delivery of a specified amount of the underlying instrument. When interest rates change, the value of the underlying instrument changes, and therefore the value of the futures contract changes. How much the futures dollar value will change when interest rates change must be estimated. This amount is called the **dollar duration per futures contract**. For example, suppose the futures price of an interest rate futures contract is 70 and that the underlying interest rate instrument has a par value of $100,000. Thus, the futures delivery price is $70,000 (0.70 times $100,000). Suppose that a change in interest rates of 100 basis points results in the futures price changing by about 3% per contract. Then the dollar duration per futures contract is $2,100 (0.03 times $70,000).

The dollar duration of a futures position is then the number of futures contracts multiplied by the dollar duration per futures contract. That is,

$$\text{dollar duration of futures position} \\ = \text{number of futures contracts} \times \text{dollar duration per futures contract} \tag{2}$$

How many futures contracts are needed to obtain the target dollar duration? Substituting equation (2) into equation (1), we get

$$\text{number of futures contracts} \times \text{dollar duration per futures contract} \\ = \text{target dollar duration} - \text{current dollar duration without futures} \tag{3}$$

Solving for the number of futures contracts we have:

$$\text{number of futures contracts} \\ = \frac{\text{target dollar duration} - \text{current dollar duration without futures}}{\text{dollar duration per futures contract}} \tag{4}$$

Equation (4) gives the approximate number of futures contracts that are necessary to adjust the portfolio's dollar duration to the target dollar duration. A positive number means that the futures contract must be purchased; a negative number means that the futures contract must be sold. Notice that if the target dollar duration is greater than the current dollar duration without futures, the numerator is positive and therefore futures contracts are purchased. If the target dollar duration is less than the current dollar duration without futures, the numerator is negative and therefore futures contracts are sold.

2. Dollar Duration for a Futures Position

Now we turn to how to measure the dollar duration of a bond futures position. Keep in mind what the goal is: it is to measure the sensitivity of a bond futures position to changes in rates.

The general methodology for computing the dollar duration of a futures position for a given change in interest rates is straightforward given a valuation model. The procedure is the same as for computing the dollar duration of any cash market instrument — shock (change) interest rates up and down by the same number of basis points and determine the average dollar price change.

An adjustment is needed for the Treasury bond and note futures contracts. As explained at Level II (Chapter 7), the pricing of the futures contract depends on the cheapest-to-deliver (CTD) issue.[1] The calculation of the dollar duration of a Treasury bond or note futures contract requires determining the effect a change in interest rates will have on the price of the CTD issue, which in turn affects how the futures price will change. The dollar duration of a Treasury bond and note futures contract is determined as follows:

dollar duration of futures contract

$$= \text{dollar duration of the CTD issue} \times \frac{\text{dollar duration of futures contract}}{\text{dollar duration of the CTD issue}}$$

Recall from Level II (Chapter 7), that there is a conversion factor for each issue that is acceptable for delivery for the futures contract. The conversion factor makes delivery equitable to both the buyer and seller of the futures contract. For each deliverable issue, the product of the futures price and the conversion factor is the adjusted futures price for the issue. This adjusted price is called the **converted price**. Relating this to the equation above, the second ratio is approximately equal to the conversion factor of the cheapest-to-deliver issue. Thus, we can write:

dollar duration of futures contract

$$= \text{dollar duration of the CTD issue} \times \text{conversion factor for the CTD issue}$$

conversion factor for the CTD issue

B. Hedging with Interest Rate Futures

Hedging with futures calls for taking a futures position as a temporary substitute for transactions to be made in the cash market at a later date. If cash and futures prices move together, any loss realized by the hedger from one position (whether cash or futures) will be offset by a profit on the other position. *Hedging is a special case of controlling interest rate risk. In a hedge, the manager seeks a target duration or target dollar duration of zero.*

A **short hedge** (or **sell hedge**) is used to protect against a decline in the cash price of a bond. To execute a short hedge, futures contracts are sold. By establishing a short hedge, the manager has fixed the future cash price and transferred the price risk of ownership to the buyer of the futures contract. To understand why a short hedge might be executed, suppose that a pension fund manager knows that bonds must be liquidated in 40 days to make a $5 million payment to beneficiaries. If interest rates rise during the 40-day period, more bonds will have to be liquidated at a lower price than today to realize $5 million. To guard against this possibility, the manager can sell bonds in the futures market to lock in a selling price.

A **long hedge** (or **buy hedge**) is undertaken to protect against an increase in the cash price of a bond. In a long hedge, the manager buys a futures contract to lock in a purchase price. A pension fund manager might use a long hedge when substantial cash contributions are expected and the manager is concerned that interest rates will

---

[1] The cheapest-to-deliver issue is the one issue from among all those that are deliverable to satisfy a contract that has the highest return in a cash and carry trade. This return is called the implied repo rate.

fall. Also, a money manager who knows that bonds are maturing in the near future and expects that interest rates will fall can employ a long hedge to lock in a rate for the proceeds to be reinvested.

In bond portfolio management, typically the bond or portfolio to be hedged is not identical to the bond underlying the futures contract. This type of hedging is referred to as **cross hedging**.

The hedging process can be broken down into four steps:

Step 1: Determining the appropriate hedging instrument.

Step 2: Determining the target for the hedge.

Step 3: Determining the position to be taken in the hedging instrument.

Step 4: Monitoring and evaluating the hedge.

We discuss each step below.

1. Determining the Appropriate Hedging Instrument

A primary factor in determining which futures contract will provide the best hedge is the degree of correlation between the rate on the futures contract and the interest rate that creates the underlying risk that the manager seeks to eliminate. For example, a long-term corporate bond portfolio can be better hedged with Treasury bond futures than with Treasury bill futures because long-term corporate bond rates are more highly correlated with Treasury bond futures than Treasury bill futures. Using the correct delivery month is also important. A manager trying to lock in a rate or price for September will use September futures contracts because September futures contracts will give the highest degree of correlation.

Correlation is not, however, the only consideration if the hedging program is of significant size. If, for example, a manager wants to hedge $600 million of a cash position in a distant delivery month, liquidity becomes an important consideration. In such a case, it might be necessary for the manager to spread the hedge across two or more different contracts.

2. Determining the Target for the Hedge

Having determined the correct contract and the correct delivery months, the manager should then determine what is expected from the hedge — that is, what rate will, on average, be locked in by the hedge. This is the **target rate** or **target price**. If this target rate is too high (if hedging a future sale) or too low (if hedging a future purchase), hedging may not be the right strategy for dealing with the unwanted risk. Determining what is expected (calculating the target rate or price for a hedge) is not always simple. We'll see how a manager should approach this problem for both simple and complex hedges.

a. Risk and Expected Return in a Hedge

When a manager enters into a hedge, the objective is to "lock in" a rate for the sale or purchase of a security. However, there is much disagreement about which rate or price a manager should expect to lock in when futures are used to hedge. Here are the two views:

View 1: The manager can, on average, lock in the rate at which the futures contracts are bought or sold.

View 2: The manager can, on average, lock in the current spot rate for the security (i.e., current rate in the cash market).

The truth usually lies somewhere in between these two views. However, as the following cases illustrate, each view is entirely correct in certain situations.

b. The Target for Hedges Held to Delivery

Hedges that are held until the futures delivery date provide an example of a hedge that locks in the futures rate (i.e., the first view). The complication in the case of using Treasury bond futures and Treasury note futures to hedge the value of intermediate- and long-term bonds, is that because of the delivery options the manager does not know for sure when delivery will take place or which bond will be delivered. This is because of the delivery options granted to the short.[2]

To illustrate how a Treasury bond futures contract held to the delivery date locks in the futures rate, assume for the sake of simplicity that the manager knows which Treasury bond will be delivered and that delivery will take place on the last day of the delivery month. Suppose that for delivery on the September 1999 futures contract, the conversion factor for a deliverable Treasury issue — the 11¼% of 2/15/15 — is 1.283, implying that the investor who delivers this issue would receive from the buyer 1.283 times the futures settlement price plus accrued interest. An important principle to remember is that at delivery, the spot price and the futures price times the conversion factor must converge. **Convergence** refers to the fact that at delivery there can be no discrepancy between the spot price and futures price for a given security. If convergence does not take place, arbitrageurs would buy at the lower price and sell at the higher price and earn risk-free profits. Accordingly, a manager could lock in a September 1999 sale price for this issue by selling Treasury bond futures contracts equal to 1.283 times the par value of the bonds. For example, $100 million face value of this issue would be hedged by selling $128.3 million face value of bond futures (1,283 contracts).

The sale price that the manager locks in would be 1.283 times the futures price. This is the **converted price**. Thus, if the futures price is 113 when the hedge is set, the manager locks in a sale price of 144.979 (113 times 1.283) for September 1999 delivery, regardless of where rates are in September 1999. Exhibit 1 shows the cash flows for a number of final prices for this issue and illustrates how cash flows on the futures contracts offset gains or losses relative to the target price of 144.979.

Let's look at all of the columns in Exhibit 1 and explain the computations for one of the scenarios — that is, for one actual sale price for the 11¼% of 2/15/15 Treasury issue. Consider the first actual sale price of 140. By convergence, at the delivery date the final futures price shown in Column (2) must equal the Treasury bond's actual sale price adjusted by the conversion factor. Thus to compute the final futures price in Column (2) of Exhibit 1 given the Treasury bond's actual sale price in Column (1), the following is computed:

$$\text{final futures price} = \frac{\text{Treasury bonds actual sale price}}{\text{conversion factor}}$$

---

[2] These delivery options were explained at Level II (Chapter 7).

Exhibit 1: Treasury Issue Hedge Held to Delivery

Instrument to be hedged: $100 million 11¼% Treasury Bonds of 2/15/15
Conversion factor for September 1999 = 1.283
Price of futures contract when sold = 113
Target price = (1.283 × 113) = 144.979
Par value hedged = $100,000,000
Number of futures contracts = 1,283
Futures position = Target = $144,979,000

(1)	(2)	(3)	(4)	(5)	(6)
Actual price for 11.25% T-bonds	Final futures price[1]	Market value of Treasury bonds	Value of futures position[2]	Gain or loss from futures position[2]	Effective sale price[3]
140	109.1192518	140,000,000	140,000,000	4,979,000	144,979,000
141	109.898675	141,000,000	141,000,000	3,979,000	144,979,000
142	110.6780982	142,000,000	142,000,000	2,979,000	144,979,000
143	111.4575214	143,000,000	143,000,000	1,979,000	144,979,000
144	112.2369447	144,000,000	144,000,000	979,000	144,979,000
145	113.0163679	145,000,000	145,000,000	−21,000	144,979,000
146	113.7957911	146,000,000	146,000,000	−1,021,000	144,979,000
147	114.5752143	147,000,000	147,000,000	−2,021,000	144,979,000
148	115.3546376	148,000,000	148,000,000	−3,021,000	144,979,000
149	116.1340608	149,000,000	149,000,000	−4,021,000	144,979,000
150	116.913484	150,000,000	150,000,000	−5,021,000	144,979,000
151	117.6929072	151,000,000	151,000,000	−6,021,000	144,979,000
152	118.4723305	152,000,000	152,000,000	−7,021,000	144,979,000
153	119.2517537	153,000,000	153,000,000	−8,021,000	144,979,000
154	120.0311769	154,000,000	154,000,000	−9,021,000	144,979,000
155	120.8106002	155,000,000	155,000,000	−10,021,000	144,979,000

[1] By convergence, must equal bond price divided by the conversion factor.
[2] Bond futures trade in even increments of 1/32. Accordingly, the futures prices and margin flows are only approximate.
[3] Transaction costs and the financing of margin flows are ignored.

Since the conversion factor is 1.283 for the 11¼% of 2/15/15 Treasury issue, for the first actual sale price of 140, the final futures price is

$$\text{final futures price} = \frac{140}{1.283} = 109.1193$$

Column (3) shows the market value of the Treasury bonds. This is found by dividing the actual sale price in Column (1) by 100 to obtain the actual sale price per $1 of par value and then multiplying by the $100 million par value. That is,

market value of Treasury bonds = (actual sale price/100) × $100,000,000

For the actual sale price of 140, the value in Column (3) is

market value of Treasury bonds = (140/100) × $100,000,000 = $140,000,000

Column (4) shows the value of the futures position at the delivery date. This value is computed by first dividing the futures price shown in Column (2) by 100 to obtain the futures price per $1 of par value. Then this value is multiplied by the par value per contract of $100,000 and further multiplied by the number of futures contracts. That is,

value of futures position =
    (final futures price/100) × $100,0000 × number of futures contracts

In our illustration, the number of futures contracts is 1,283. For the actual sale price of the bond at 140, the final futures price calculated earlier is 109.1193. So, the value shown in Column (4) is

$$\text{value of futures position} = (109.1193/100) \times \$100,000 \times 1,283$$
$$= \$140,000,062$$

The value shown in Column (4) is $140,000,000 because the final futures price of 109.1193 was rounded. Using more decimal places the value would be $140,000,000.

Now let's look at the gain or loss from the futures position. This value is shown in Column (5). Recall that the futures contract was shorted. The futures price at which the contracts were sold was 113. So, if the final futures price exceeds 113, this means that there is a loss on the futures position — that is, the futures contract is purchased at a price greater than for which it was sold. In contrast, if the futures price is less than 113, this means that there is a gain on the futures position — that is, the futures contract is purchased at a price less than for which it was sold. The gain or loss is determined by the following formula:

$$(113/100 - \text{final futures price}/100) \times \$100,000 \times \text{number of futures contracts}$$

In our illustration, for a final futures price of 109.1193 and 1,283 futures contracts, we have

$$(113/100 - 109.1193/100) \times \$100,000 \times 1,283 = \$4,978,938.1$$

The value shown in Column (5) is $4,979,000 because that is the more precise value using more decimal places for the final futures price than shown in Exhibit 1. The value is positive which means that there is a gain in the futures position. Note that for all the final futures prices above 113 in Exhibit 1, there is a negative value which means that there is a loss on the futures position.

Finally, Column (6) shows the effective sale price for the Treasury bond. This value is found as follows:

$$\text{effective sale price for Treasury bond} =$$
$$\text{actual sale price of Treasury bond} + \text{gain or loss on futures position}$$

which is the sum of the numbers in each of the rows of Columns (3) and (5). For the actual sale price of $140 million, the gain is $4,979,000. Therefore the effective sale price for the Treasury bond is

$$\$140,000,000 + \$4,979,000 = \$144,979,000$$

Note that this is the target price for the Treasury bond. In fact, it can be seen from Column (6) of Exhibit 1 that the effective sale price for all the actual sale prices for the Treasury bond is the target price. However, the target price is determined by the futures price, so the target price may be higher or lower than the cash (spot) market price when the hedge is set.

When we admit the possibility that bonds other than the deliverable issue used in our illustration can be delivered, and that it might be advantageous to deliver other issues, the situation becomes somewhat more involved. In this more realistic case, the manager may decide not to deliver this issue, but if she does decide to deliver it, the manager is still assured of receiving an effective sale price of approximately 144.979. If the manager does not deliver this issue, it would be because another issue can be delivered more cheaply, and thus the manager does better than the targeted price.

In summary, if a manager establishes a futures hedge that is held until delivery, the manager can be assured of receiving an effective price dictated by the futures rate (not the spot rate) on the day the hedge is set.

c. The Target for Hedges with Short Holding Periods

When a manager must lift (remove) a hedge prior to the delivery date, the effective rate that is obtained is more likely to approximate the current spot rate than the futures rate and this likelihood increases the shorter the term of the hedge. The critical difference between this hedge and the hedge held to the delivery date is that convergence will generally not take place by the termination date of the hedge.

To illustrate why a manager should expect the hedge to lock in the spot rate rather than the futures rate for very short-lived hedges, let's return to the simplified example used earlier to illustrate a hedge to the delivery date. It is assumed that this issue is the only deliverable Treasury bond for the Treasury bond futures contract. Suppose that the hedge is set three months before the delivery date and the manager plans to lift the hedge after one day. It is much more likely that the spot price of the bond will move parallel to the converted futures price (that is, the futures price times the conversion factor), than that the spot price and the converted futures price will converge by the time the hedge is lifted.

A 1-day hedge is, admittedly, an extreme example. Other than underwriters, dealers, and traders who reallocate assets very frequently, few money managers are interested in such a short horizon. The very short-term hedge does, however, illustrate a very important point: *when hedging, a manager should not expect to lock in the futures rate (or price) just because he or she is hedging with futures contracts.* The futures rate is locked in only if the hedge is held until delivery, at which point convergence must take place. If the hedge is held for only one day, the manager should expect to lock in the 1-day forward rate,[3] which will very nearly equal the spot rate. Generally hedges are held for more than one day, but not necessarily to delivery.

d. How the Basis Affects the Target Rate for a Hedge

The proper target for a hedge that is to be lifted prior to the delivery date depends on the basis. The **basis** is simply the difference between the spot (cash) price of a security and its futures price; that is:

basis = spot price − futures price

In the bond market, a problem arises when trying to make practical use of the concept of the basis. The quoted futures price does not equal the price that one receives at delivery. For the Treasury bond and note futures contracts, the actual futures price equals the quoted futures price times the appropriate conversion factor. Consequently, to be useful, the basis in the bond market should be defined using actual futures delivery prices rather than quoted futures prices. Thus, the price basis for bonds should be redefined as:

price basis = spot price − futures delivery price

---

[3] Forward rates were covered at Level I (Chapter 6) and Level II (Chapter 1).

For hedging purposes it is also frequently useful to define the basis in terms of interest rates rather than prices. The **rate basis** is defined as:

rate basis = spot rate − futures rate

where spot rate refers to the current rate on the instrument to be hedged and the futures rate is the interest rate corresponding to the futures delivery price of the deliverable instrument.

The rate basis is helpful in explaining why the two views of hedging explained earlier are expected to lock in such different rates. To see this, we first define the **target rate basis**. This is defined as the expected rate basis on the day the hedge is lifted. That is,

target rate basis
    = spot rate on date hedge is lifted − futures rate on date hedge is lifted

The target rate for the hedge is equal to

target rate for hedge = futures rate + target rate basis

Substituting for target rate basis in the above equation

target rate for hedge = futures rate
    + spot rate on date hedge is lifted − futures rate on date hedge is lifted

Consider first a hedge lifted on the delivery date. On the delivery date, the spot rate and the futures rate will be the same by convergence. Thus, the target rate basis if the hedge is expected to be removed on the delivery date is zero. Substituting zero for the target rate basis in the equation for the target rate for hedge we have the following:

target rate for hedge = futures rate

That is, if the hedge is to the delivery date, the target rate for the hedge is equal to the futures rate.

Now consider if a hedge is lifted prior to the delivery date. Let's consider the case where the hedge is removed the next day. One would not expect the basis to change very much in one day. Assume that it does not. Then,

spot rate on date hedge is lifted = spot rate when hedge was placed
futures rate on date hedge is lifted = futures rate when hedge was placed

The spot rate when the hedge was placed is simply the spot rate and the futures rate when hedge was placed is simply the futures rate. So, we can write

target rate basis = spot rate − futures rate

and substituting the right-hand side of the equation into the target rate for hedge

target rate for hedge = futures rate + (spot rate − futures rate)

or

target rate for hedge = spot rate

Thus we see that when hedging for one day (and assuming the basis does not change in that one day), the manager is locking in the spot rate (i.e., the current rate).

If projecting the basis in terms of price rather than rate is more manageable (as is often the case for intermediate- and long-term futures), it is easier to work with the target price basis instead of the target rate basis. The **target price basis** is just the projected price basis for the day the hedge is to be lifted. For a deliverable security, the target for the hedge then becomes

target price for hedge = futures delivery price + target price basis

The idea of a target price or rate basis explains why a hedge held until the delivery date locks in a price with certainty, and other hedges do not. The examples have shown that this is true. For the hedge held to delivery, there is no uncertainty surrounding the target basis; by convergence, the basis on the day the hedge is lifted is certain to be zero. For the short-lived hedge, the basis will probably approximate the current basis when the hedge is lifted, but its actual value is not known. For hedges longer than one day but ending prior to the futures delivery date, there can be considerable basis risk because the basis on the day the hedge is lifted can end up being anywhere within a wide range. Thus, the uncertainty surrounding the outcome of a hedge is directly related to the uncertainty surrounding the basis on the day the hedge is lifted (i.e., the uncertainty surrounding the target basis).

The uncertainty about the value of the basis at the time the hedge is removed is called **basis risk**. *For a given investment horizon, hedging substitutes basis risk for price risk.* Thus, one trades the uncertainty of the price of the hedged security for the uncertainty of the basis. A manager would be willing to substitute basis risk for price risk if the manager expects that basis risk is less than price risk. Consequently, when hedges do not produce the desired results, it is customary to place the blame on basis risk. However, basis risk is the real culprit only if the target for the hedge is properly defined. Basis risk should refer only to the unexpected or unpredictable part of the relationship between cash and futures prices. The fact that this relationship changes over time does not in itself imply that there is basis risk.

Basis risk, properly defined, refers only to the uncertainty associated with the target rate basis or target price basis. Accordingly, it is imperative that the target basis be properly defined if one is to correctly assess the risk and expected return in a hedge.

3. Determining the Number of Futures Contracts

The final step that must be determined before the hedge is set is the number of futures contracts needed for the hedge. This is called the **hedge ratio**. Usually the hedge ratio is expressed in terms of relative par amounts. Accordingly, a hedge ratio of 1.20 means that for every $1 million par value of securities to be hedged, one needs $1.2 million par value of futures contracts to offset the risk. *In our discussion, the values are defined so that the hedge ratio is the number of futures contracts.*

Earlier, we defined a cross hedge in the futures market as a hedge in which the security to be hedged is not deliverable on the futures contract used in the hedge. For example, a manager who wants to hedge the sale price of long-term corporate bonds might hedge with the Treasury bond futures contract, but since non-Treasury bonds cannot be delivered in satisfaction of the contract, the hedge would be considered a cross hedge. A manager might also want to hedge a rate that is of the same quality as the rate specified in one of the contracts, but that has a different maturity.

For example, it might be necessary to cross hedge a Treasury bond, note, or bill with a maturity that does not qualify for delivery on any futures contract. Thus, when the security to be hedged differs from the futures contract specification in terms of either quality or maturity, one is led to the cross hedge.

Conceptually, cross hedging is somewhat more complicated than hedging deliverable securities, because it involves two relationships. First, there is the relationship between the cheapest-to-deliver (CTD) issue and the futures contract. Second, there is the relationship between the security to be hedged and the CTD. Practical considerations may at times lead a manager to shortcut this two-step relationship and focus directly on the relationship between the security to be hedged and the futures contract, thus ignoring the CTD altogether. However, in so doing, a manager runs the risk of miscalculating the target rate and the risk in the hedge. Furthermore, if the hedge does not perform as expected, the shortcut makes it difficult to tell why the hedge did not work out as expected.

The key to minimizing risk in a cross hedge is to choose the right number of futures contracts. This depends on the relative dollar duration of the bond to be hedged and the futures position. Equation (4) indicated the number of futures contracts to achieve a particular target dollar duration. The objective in hedging is to make the target dollar duration equal to zero. Substituting zero for target dollar duration in equation (4) we obtain:

$$\text{number of futures contracts} = -\frac{\text{current dollar duration without futures}}{\text{dollar duration per futures contract}} \quad (5)$$

To calculate the dollar duration of a bond, the manager must know the precise point in time that the dollar duration is to be calculated (because price volatility generally declines as a bond matures) as well as the price or yield at which to calculate dollar duration (because higher yields generally reduce dollar duration for a given yield change). *The relevant point in the life of the bond for calculating price volatility is the point at which the hedge will be lifted. Dollar duration at any other point is essentially irrelevant because the goal is to lock in a price or rate only on that particular day. Similarly, the relevant yield at which to calculate dollar duration initially is the target yield. Consequently, the numerator of equation (5) is the dollar duration on the date the hedge is expected to be lifted.* The yield that can be used on this date in order to determine the dollar duration is the forward rate. Forward rates were discussed at Level I (Chapter 6) and Level II (Chapter 1).

Let's look at how we apply equation (5) when using the Treasury bond futures contract to hedge. The number of futures contracts will be affected by the dollar duration of the CTD issue. We can modify equation (5) as follows:

$$\text{number of futures contracts} = -\frac{\text{current dollar duration without futures}}{\text{dollar duration of the CTD issue}}$$
$$\times \frac{\text{dollar duration of the CTD issue}}{\text{dollar duration per futures contract}} \quad (6)$$

As noted earlier, the conversion ratio for the CTD issue is a good approximation of the second ratio. Thus, equation (6) can be rewritten as

$$\text{number of futures contracts} = -\frac{\text{current dollar duration without futures}}{\text{dollar duration of the CTD issue}}$$
$$\times \text{conversion factor for the CTD issue} \quad (7)$$

a. An Illustration

An example for a single bond shows why dollar duration weighting leads to the correct number of contracts to use to hedge. The hedge illustrated is a cross hedge. Suppose that on 6/24/99, a manager owned $10 million par value of a 6.25% Fannie Mae (FNMA) option-free bond maturing on 5/15/29 selling at 88.39 to yield 7.20%. The manager wants to sell September 1999 Treasury bond futures to hedge a future sale of the FNMA bond. At the time, the price of the September Treasury bond futures contract was at 113. The CTD issue was the 11.25% of 2/15/15 issue that was trading at the time at 146.19 to yield 6.50%. The conversion factor for the CTD issue was 1.283. To simplify, assume that the yield spread between the FNMA bond and the CTD issue remains at 0.70% (i.e., 70 basis points) and that the anticipated sale date is the last business day in September 1999.

The target price for hedging the CTD issue would be 144.979 (from 113 × 1.283), and the target yield would be 6.56% (the yield at a price of 144.979). Since the yield on the FNMA bond is assumed to stay at 0.70% above the yield on the CTD issue, the target yield for the FNMA bond would be 7.26%. The corresponding price for the FNMA bond for this target yield is 87.76. At these target levels, the dollar duration for a 50 basis point change in rates for the CTD issue and FNMA bond per $100 of par value is $6.255 and $5.453, respectively. As indicated earlier, all these calculations are made using a settlement date equal to the anticipated sale date, in this case the end of September 1999. The dollar duration for a 50 basis point change in rates for $10 million par value of the FNMA bond is then $545,300 ($10 million/100 times $5.453). Per $100,000 par value for the CTD issue, the dollar duration per futures contract is $6,255 ($100,000/100 times $6.255).

Thus, we know

current dollar duration without futures
   = dollar duration of the FNMA bond = $545,300

dollar duration of the CTD issue = $6,255

conversion factor for CTD issue = 1.283

Substituting these values into equation (7) we obtain

$$\text{number of futures contracts} = -\frac{\$545,300}{\$6,255} \times 1.283 = -112 \text{ contracts}$$

Consequently, to hedge the FNMA bond position, 112 Treasury bond futures contracts must be shorted.

Exhibit 2 uses scenario analysis to show the outcome of the hedge based on different prices for the FNMA bond at the delivery date of the futures contract. Let's go through each of the columns. Column (1) shows the assumed sale price for the FNMA bond and Column (2) shows the corresponding yield based on the actual sale price in Column (1). This yield is found from the price/yield relationship. Given the assumed sale price for the FNMA bond, the corresponding yield can be determined. Column (3) shows the yield for the CTD issue. This yield is computed based on the assumption regarding the yield spread of 70 basis points between the FNMA bond and the CTD issue. So, by subtracting 70 basis points from the yield for the FNMA bond in Column (2), the yield on the CTD issue (the 11.25% of 2/15/15) is obtained. Given the yield for the CTD issue in Column (3), the price per $100 of par value of the CTD issue can be computed. This CTD price is shown in Column (4).

Exhibit 2: Hedging a Nondeliverable Bond to a Delivery Date with Futures

Instrument to be hedged: $10 million FNMA 6.25% of 05/15/29
Price of FNMA as of hedge date (6/24/99) = 88.39
Conversion factor for September 1999 = 1.283
Price of futures contract when sold = 113
Target price for FNMA bonds = 87.76
Par value hedged = $10,000,000
Number of futures contracts = 112
Futures position = $12,656,000
Target market value for FNMA bonds = $8,776,000

(1) Actual sale price of FNMA bonds	(2) Yield at sale	(3) Yield of 11.25% Treasury bond	(4) Price of 11.25% Treasury bond	(5) Futures price	(6) Value of futures position	(7) Gain or loss on futures position	(8) Effective sale price
8,000,000	8.027%	7.327%	135.812	105.85510	11,855,771	800,229	8,800,229
8,100,000	7.922%	7.222%	137.024	106.79953	11,961,547	694,453	8,794,453
8,200,000	7.818%	7.118%	138.226	107.73658	12,066,497	589,503	8,789,503
8,300,000	7.717%	7.017%	139.419	108.66640	12,170,637	485,363	8,785,363
8,400,000	7.617%	6.917%	140.603	109.58913	12,273,983	382,017	8,782,017
8,500,000	7.520%	6.820%	141.778	110.50490	12,376,549	279,451	8,779,451
8,600,000	7.424%	6.724%	142.944	111.41384	12,478,350	177,650	8,777,650
8,700,000	7.330%	6.630%	144.102	112.31608	12,579,401	76,599	8,776,599
8,800,000	7.238%	6.538%	145.251	113.21175	12,679,716	(23,716)	8,776,284
8,900,000	7.148%	6.448%	146.392	114.10096	12,779,307	(123,307)	8,776,693
9,000,000	7.059%	6.359%	147.524	114.98383	12,878,188	(222,188)	8,777,812
9,100,000	6.971%	6.271%	148.649	115.86047	12,976,373	(320,373)	8,779,627
9,200,000	6.886%	6.186%	149.766	116.73101	13,073,873	(417,873)	8,782,127
9,300,000	6.801%	6.101%	150.875	117.59554	13,170,700	(514,700)	8,785,300
9,400,000	6.719%	6.019%	151.977	118.45417	13,266,868	(610,868)	8,789,132
9,500,000	6.637%	5.937%	153.071	119.30702	13,362,386	(706,386)	8,793,614

* By assumption, the yield on the cheapest-to-deliver issue is 70 basis points lower than the yield on the FNMA bond.
** By convergence, the futures price equals the price of the cheapest-to-deliver issue divided by 1.283 (the conversion factor).
*** Transaction costs and the financing of margin flows are ignored.

Now we must move from the price of the CTD issue to the futures price. As explained in the description of the columns in Exhibit 1, by dividing the price for the CTD issue shown in Column (4) by the conversion factor of the CTD issue (1.283), the futures price is obtained. This price is shown in Column (5).

The value of the futures position is found in the same way as in Exhibit 1. First the futures price per $1 of par value is computed by dividing the futures price by 100. Then this value is multiplied by $100,000 (the par value for the contract) and the number of futures contracts. That is,

value of futures position =
    (futures price/100) × $100,000 × number of futures contracts

Since the number of futures contracts sold is 112,

value of futures position = (final futures price/100) × $100,000 × 112

The values shown in Column (6) use the above formula. Using the first assumed actual sale price for the FNMA of $8 million as an example, the corresponding futures price in Column (5) is 105.8551. Therefore, the value of the futures position is

value of futures position = (105.8551/100) × $100,000 × 112 = $11,855,712

The value of $11,855,771 shown in the exhibit is the more precise value. Now let's calculate the gain or loss on the futures position shown in Column (7). This is done in the same manner as explained for Exhibit 1. Since the futures price at which the contracts are sold at the inception of the hedge is 113, the gain or loss on the futures position is found as follows:

(113/100 − final futures price/100) × $100,000 × number of futures contracts

For example, for the first scenario in Exhibit 2, the futures price is 105.8551 and 112 futures contract were sold. Therefore,

(113/100 − 105.8551/100) × $100,000 × 112 = $800,229

There is a gain from the futures position because the futures price is less than 113. Note that for all the final futures prices above 113 in Exhibit 2, there is a negative value which means that there is a loss on the futures position. For all futures prices below 113, there is a gain.

Finally, Column (8) shows the effective sale price for the FNMA bond. This value is found as follows:

effective sale price for FNMA bond =
    actual sale price of FNMA bond + gain or loss on futures position

For the actual sale price of $8 million, the gain is $800,229. Therefore the effective sale price for the FNMA bond is

$8,000,000 + $800,229 = $8,800,229

Looking at Column (8) of Exhibit 2 we see that if the simplifying assumptions hold, a futures hedge using the recommended number of futures contracts (112) very nearly locks in the target price for $10 million par value of the FNMA bonds.

b. Refining for Changing Yield Spread

Another refinement in the hedging strategy is usually necessary for hedging nondeliverable securities. (Recall from Chapter 7 (Level II) that a nondeliverable security is a bond that does not meet the specific criteria for delivery to satisfy a particular futures contract.) This refinement concerns the assumption about the relative yield spread between the CTD issue and the bond to be hedged. In the prior discussion, we assumed that the yield spread was constant over time. Yield spreads, however, are not constant over time. They vary with the maturity of the instruments in question and the level of rates, as well as with many unpredictable and nonsystematic factors.

Regression analysis allows the manager to capture the relationship between yield levels and yield spreads and use it to advantage. For hedging purposes, the variables are the yield on the bond to be hedged and the yield on the CTD issue. The regression equation takes the form:

$$\text{yield on bond to be hedged} = a + b \times \text{yield on CTD issue} + \text{error} \qquad (8)$$

The regression procedure provides an estimate of b, which is the expected relative yield change in the two bonds. This parameter b is called the **yield beta**. Our example that used constant spreads implicitly assumes that the yield beta, b, equals 1.0 and a equals 0.70 (because 0.70 is the assumed spread).

For the two issues in question, that is, the FNMA bond and the CTD issue, suppose the estimated yield beta was 1.05. Thus, yields on the FNMA issue are expected to move 5% more than yields on the Treasury issue. To calculate the number of futures contracts correctly, this fact must be taken into account; thus, the number of futures contracts derived in our earlier example is multiplied by the factor 1.05. Consequently, instead of shorting 112 Treasury bond futures contracts to hedge $10 million of the FNMA bond, the investor would short 118 (rounded up) contracts.

The formula for the number of futures contracts is revised as follows to incorporate the impact of the yield beta:

$$\text{number of futures contracts} = -\frac{\text{current dollar duration without futures}}{\text{dollar duration of the CTD issue}}$$
$$\times \text{conversion factor for the CTD issue}$$
$$\times \text{yield beta} \qquad (9)$$

where the yield beta is derived from the yield of the bond to be hedged regressed on the yield of the CTD issue [equation (8)].

The effect of a change in the CTD issue and the yield spread can be assessed before the hedge is implemented. An exhibit similar to that of Exhibit 2 can be constructed under a wide range of assumptions. For example, at different yield levels at the date the hedge is to be lifted (the second column in Exhibit 2), a different yield spread may be appropriate and a different acceptable issue will be the CTD issue. The manager can determine what this will do to the outcome of the hedge.

4. Monitoring and Evaluating the Hedge

After a target is determined and a hedge is set, there are two remaining tasks. The hedge must be monitored during its life and evaluated after it is over. Most futures hedges require very little active monitoring during their life. In fact, overactive management poses more of a threat to most hedges than does inactive management. The reason for this is that the manager usually will not receive enough new information during the life of the hedge to justify a change in the hedging strategy. For example, it is not advisable to readjust the hedge ratio every day in response to a new data point and a possible corresponding change in the estimated value of the yield beta.

There are, however, exceptions to this general rule. As rates change, dollar duration changes. Consequently, the hedge ratio may change slightly. In other cases, there may be sound economic reasons to believe that the yield beta has changed. While there are exceptions, the best approach is usually to let a hedge run its course using the original hedge ratio with only slight adjustments.

A hedge can normally be evaluated only after it has been lifted. Evaluation involves, first, an assessment of how closely the hedge locked in the target rate — that is, how much error there was in the hedge. To provide a meaningful interpretation of the error, the manager should calculate how far from the target the sale (or purchase) would have been, had there been no hedge at all. One good reason for evaluating a completed hedge is to ascertain the sources of error in the hedge in the hope that the manager will gain insights that can be used to advantage in subsequent hedges. A manager will find that there are three major sources of hedging errors:

1. The dollar duration for the hedged instrument was incorrect.
2. The projected value of the basis at the date the hedge is removed can be in error.
3. The parameters estimated from the regression (*a* and *b*) can be inaccurate.

Recall from the calculation of duration at Level I (Chapter 7) that interest rates are changed up and down by a small number of basis points and the security is revalued. The two recalculated values are used in the numerator of the duration formula. The first problem listed above recognizes that the instrument to be hedged may be a complex instrument (i.e., one with embedded options) and that the valuation model does not do a good job of valuing the security when interest rates change.

The second major source of errors in a hedge — an inaccurate projected value of the basis — is the more difficult problem. Unfortunately, there are no satisfactory simple models like the regression that can be applied to the basis. Simple models of the basis violate certain equilibrium relationships for bonds that should not be violated. On the other hand, theoretically rigorous models are very unintuitive and usually solvable only by complex numerical methods. Modeling the basis is undoubtedly one of the most important and difficult problems that managers seeking to hedge face.

SECTION III CONTROLLING INTEREST RATE RISK WITH SWAPS

As explained at Level II (Chapter 7), an interest rate swap is equivalent to a package of forward/futures contracts. Consequently, swaps can be used for controlling interest rate risk and hedging as we discussed earlier with futures.

A. Hedging Interest Rate Risk

The following illustration demonstrates how an interest rate swap can be used to hedge interest rate risk by altering the cash flow characteristics of an entity so as to better match the cash flow characteristics of assets and liabilities. In our illustration we will use two hypothetical financial institutions — a commercial bank and a life insurance company.

Suppose a bank has a portfolio consisting of 4-year commercial loans with a fixed interest rate. The principal value of the portfolio is $100 million, and the interest rate on all the loans in the portfolio is 11%. The loans are interest-only loans; interest is paid semiannually, and the principal is paid at the end of four years. That is, assuming no default on the loans, the cash flow from the loan portfolio is $5.5 million every six months for the next four years and $100 million at the end of four years. To fund its loan portfolio, assume that the bank can borrow at 6-month LIBOR for the next four years.

The risk that the bank faces is that 6-month LIBOR will be 11% or greater. To understand why, remember that the bank is earning 11% annually on its commercial loan portfolio. If 6-month LIBOR is 11% when the borrowing rate for the bank's loan resets, there will be no spread income for that 6-month period. Worse, if 6-month LIBOR rises above 11%, there will be a loss for that 6-month period; that is, the cost of funds will exceed the interest rate earned on the loan portfolio. The bank's objective is to lock in a spread over the cost of its funds.

The other party in the interest rate swap illustration is a life insurance company that has committed itself to pay an 8% rate for the next four years on a guaranteed investment contract (GIC) it has issued. The amount of the GIC is $100 million. Suppose that the life insurance company has the opportunity to invest $100 million in what it considers an attractive 4-year floating-rate instrument in a private placement transaction. The interest rate on this instrument is 6-month LIBOR plus 120 basis points. The coupon rate is set every six months.

The risk that the life insurance company faces in this instance is that 6-month LIBOR will fall so that the company will not earn enough to realize a spread over the 8% rate that it has guaranteed to the GIC policyholders. If 6-month LIBOR falls to 6.8% or less at a coupon reset date, no spread income will be generated. To understand why, suppose that 6-month LIBOR at the date the floating-rate instrument resets its coupon is 6.8%. Then the coupon rate for the next six months will be 8% (6.8% plus 120 basis points). Because the life insurance company has agreed to pay 8% on the GIC policy, there will be no spread income. Should 6-month LIBOR fall below 6.8%, there will be a loss for that 6-month period.

We can summarize the asset/liability problems of the bank and the life insurance company as follows.

Bank:
1. has lent long term and borrowed short term
2. if 6-month LIBOR rises, spread income declines

Life insurance company:
1. has lent short term and borrowed long term
2. if 6-month LIBOR falls, spread income declines

Now let's suppose the market has available a 4-year interest rate swap with a notional amount of $100 million. Suppose the swap terms available to the bank are as follows:

1. every six months the bank will pay 9.50% (annual rate)
2. every six months the bank will receive LIBOR

Suppose the swap terms available to the insurance company are as follows:

1. every six months the life insurance company will pay LIBOR
2. every six months the life insurance company will receive 9.40%

Now let's look at the position of the bank and the life insurance company after the swap. Exhibit 3 summarizes the position of each institution before and after the swap. Consider first the bank. For every 6-month period for the life of the swap, the interest rate spread will be as follows:

Annual interest rate received:		
From commercial loan portfolio	=	11.00%
From interest rate swap	=	6-month LIBOR
Total	=	11.00% + 6-month LIBOR

Annual interest rate paid:		
To borrow funds	=	6-month LIBOR
On interest rate swap	=	9.50%
Total	=	9.50% + 6-month LIBOR

Exhibit 3: Position of Bank and Life Insurance Company Before and After Swap

Position before interest rate swap:

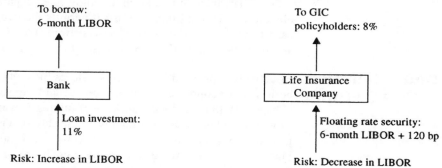

Position after interest rate swap:

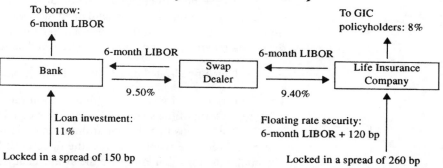

Outcome:		
To be received	=	11.0% + 6-month LIBOR
To be paid	=	9.50% + 6-month LIBOR
Spread income	=	1.50% or 150 basis points

Thus, whatever happens to 6-month LIBOR, the bank locks in a spread of 150 basis points assuming no loan defaults or early payoff of a loan.

Now let's look at the effect of the interest rate swap on the life insurance company:

Annual interest rate received:		
From floating-rate instrument	=	1.20% + 6-month LIBOR
From interest rate swap	=	9.40%
Total	=	10.60% + 6-month LIBOR

Annual interest rate paid:		
To GIC policyholders	=	8.00%
On interest rate swap	=	6-month LIBOR
Total	=	8.00% + 6-month LIBOR

Outcome:		
To be received	=	10.60% + 6-month LIBOR
To be paid	=	8.00% + 6-month LIBOR
Spread income	=	2.60% + 6-month LIBOR

Regardless of what happens to 6-month LIBOR, the life insurance company locks in a spread of 260 basis points assuming the issuer of the floating-rate instrument does not default.

The interest rate swap has allowed each party to accomplish its asset/liability objective of locking in a spread.[4] It permits the two financial institutions to alter the cash flow characteristics of its assets: from fixed to floating in the case of the bank, and from floating to fixed in the case of the life insurance company.

B. Dollar Duration of a Swap

Effectively, a position in an interest rate swap is a leveraged position. This agrees with both of our economic interpretations of an interest rate swap explained at Level II (Chapter 7). In the case of a package of futures/forward contracts, we know that futures/forwards are leveraged instruments. In the case of a package of cash instruments, it is a leveraged position involving either buying a fixed-rate bond and financing it on a floating-rate basis (i.e., fixed-rate receiver position) or buying a floating-rate bond on a fixed-rate basis (i.e., fixed-rate payer position). So, we would expect that the dollar duration of a swap is a multiple of the bond that effectively underlies the swap.

To see how to calculate the dollar duration, let's work with the second economic interpretation of a swap explained at Level II (Chapter 7) — a package of cash flows from buying and selling cash market instruments. From the perspective of the *fixed-rate receiver*, the position can be viewed as follows:

long a fixed-rate bond + short a floating-rate bond

The fixed-rate bond is a bond with a coupon rate equal to the swap rate, a maturity equal to the term of the swap, and a par value equal to the notional amount of the swap.

This means that the dollar duration of an interest rate swap from the perspective of a fixed-rate receiver is just the difference between the dollar duration of the two bond positions that comprise the swap. That is,

dollar duration of a swap for a fixed-rate receiver
  = dollar duration of a fixed-rate bond − dollar duration of a floating-rate bond

Most of the interest rate sensitivity of a swap will result from the dollar duration of the fixed-rate bond since, as explained at Level I (Chapter 7), the dollar duration of the floating-rate bond will be small. The dollar duration of a floating-rate bond is smaller the closer the swap is to its reset date. If the dollar duration of the floating-rate bond is close to zero then:

dollar duration of a swap for a fixed-rate receiver
  = dollar duration of a fixed-rate bond

Thus, adding an interest rate swap to a portfolio in which the manager pays a floating-rate and receives a fixed-rate increases the dollar duration of the portfolio by roughly the dollar duration of the underlying fixed-rate bond. This is because it effectively involves buying a fixed-rate bond on a leveraged basis.

We can use the cash market instrument economic interpretation to compute the dollar duration of a swap for the fixed-rate payer. The dollar duration is:

dollar duration of a swap for a fixed-rate payer
  = dollar duration of a floating-rate bond − dollar duration of a fixed-rate bond

---

[4] Whether the size of the spread is adequate is not an issue to us in this illustration.

Again, assuming that the dollar duration of the floater is small, we have

dollar duration of a swap for a fixed-rate payer
= −dollar duration of a fixed-rate bond

Consequently, a manager who adds a swap to a portfolio involving paying fixed and receiving floating decreases the dollar duration of the portfolio by an amount roughly equal to the dollar duration of the fixed-rate bond.
    The dollar duration of a portfolio that includes a swap is:

dollar duration of assets − dollar duration of liabilities
+ dollar duration of a swap position

    Let's look at our bank/life insurance illustration in terms of duration mismatch. The bank has a long duration for its assets (the fixed-rate loans) and a short duration for its liabilities (the short-term funds it borrows). Effectively, the position of the bank is as follows:

bank's dollar duration
= dollar duration of assets − dollar duration of liabilities > 0

The bank entered into an interest rate swap in which it pays fixed and receives floating. As just explained, the dollar duration of that swap position is negative. Thus, adding the swap position moves the bank's dollar duration position closer to zero and, therefore, reduces interest rate risk.
    For the life insurance company, the duration of the liabilities is long while the duration of the floating-rate assets is short. That is,

life insurance company's dollar duration
= dollar duration of assets − dollar duration of liabilities < 0

The life insurance company entered into an interest rate swap in which it pays floating and receives fixed. This swap position has a positive duration. By adding it to a portfolio it moves the duration closer to zero, thereby reducing interest rate risk.

SECTION IV HEDGING WITH OPTIONS

Hedging strategies using options involve taking a position in an option and a position in the underlying bond in such a way that changes in the value of one position will offset any unfavorable price (interest rate) movement in the other position. We begin with the basic hedging strategies using options. Then we illustrate these basic strategies using futures options to hedge the FNMA bond for which a futures hedge was used in Section II. Using futures options in our illustration of hedging the bond is a worthwhile exercise because it shows how complicated hedging with futures options is and the key parameters involved in the process. We also compare the outcome of hedging with futures and hedging with futures options.

A. Basic Hedging Strategies

There are three popular hedging strategies: (1) a protective put buying strategy, (2) a covered call writing strategy, and (3) a collar strategy. We discuss each strategy below.

Exhibit 4: Protective Put Buying Strategy

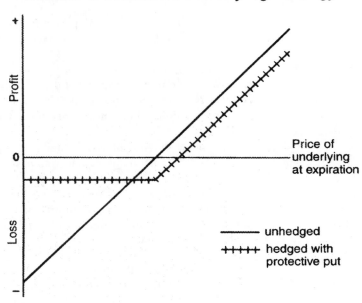

1. Protective Put Buying Strategy

Consider a manager who has a bond and wants to hedge against rising interest rates. The most obvious options hedging strategy is to buy put options on bonds. This hedging strategy is referred to as a **protective put buying strategy**. The puts are usually out-of-the-money puts and may be either puts on cash bonds or puts on interest rate futures. If interest rates rise, the puts will increase in value (holding other factors constant), offsetting some or all of the loss on the bonds in the portfolio.

This strategy is a simple combination of a long put option with a long position in a cash bond. Such a position has limited downside ask, but large upside potential. However, if rates fall, the price appreciation on the bonds in the portfolio will be diminished by the amount paid to purchase the puts. Exhibit 4 compares the protective put buying strategy to an unhedged position.

The protective put buying strategy is very often compared to purchasing insurance. Like insurance, the premium paid for the protection is nonrefundable and is paid before the coverage begins. The degree to which a portfolio is protected depends upon the strike price of the options; thus, the strike price is often compared to the deductible on an insurance policy. The lower the deductible (that is, the higher the strike price for the put), the greater the level of protection and the more the protection costs. Conversely, the higher the deductible (the lower the strike price on the put), the more the portfolio can lose in value; but the cost of the insurance is lower. Exhibit 5 compares an unhedged position with several protective put positions, each with a different strike price, or level of protection. As the exhibit shows, no one strategy dominates any other strategy, in the sense of performing better at all possible rate levels. Consequently, it is impossible to say that one strike price is necessarily the "best" strike price, or even that buying protective puts is necessarily better than doing nothing at all.

Exhibit 5: Protective Put Buying Strategy with Different Strike Prices

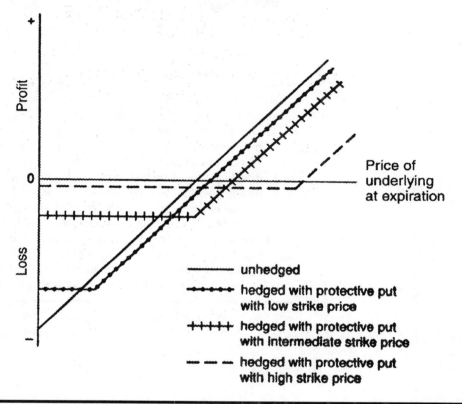

2. Covered Call Writing Strategy

Another options hedging strategy used by many portfolio managers is to sell calls against the bond portfolio. This hedging strategy is called a **covered call writing strategy**. The calls that are sold are usually out-of-the-money calls, and can be either calls on cash bonds or calls on interest rate futures. Covered call writing is just an outright long position combined with a short call position. Obviously, this strategy entails much more downside risk than buying a put to protect the value of the portfolio. In fact, many portfolio managers do not consider covered call writing a hedge.

Regardless of how it is classified, it is important to recognize that while covered call writing has substantial downside risk, it has less downside risk than an unhedged long position alone. On the downside, the difference between the long position alone and the covered call writing strategy is the premium received for the calls that are sold. This premium acts as a cushion for downward movements in prices, reducing losses when rates rise. The cost of obtaining this cushion is that the manager gives up some of the potential on the upside. When rates decline, the call options become greater liabilities for the covered call writer. These incremental liabilities decrease the gains the manager would otherwise have realized on the portfolio in a declining rate environment. Thus, the covered call writer gives up some (or all) of the upside potential of the portfolio in return for a cushion on the downside. The more upside potential that is forfeited (that is, the lower the strike price on the calls), the more cushion there is on the downside. Exhibit 6 illustrates this point by comparing an unhedged position to several covered call writing strategies, each with a different strike price. Like the protective put buying strategy, there is no "right" strike price for the covered call writer.

3. Collar Strategy

There are other hedging strategies using options frequently used by managers. For example, many managers combine the protective put buying strategy and the covered call writing strategy. By combining a long position in an out-of-the-money put and a short position in an out-of-the-money call, the manager creates a long position in a *collar*. Consequently, this hedging strategy is called a **collar strategy**. The manager who uses the collar eliminates part of the portfolio's downside risk by giving up part of its upside potential. A long position hedged with a collar is shown in Exhibit 7.

The collar in some ways resembles the protective put, in some ways resembles covered call writing, and in some ways resembles an unhedged position. The collar is like the protective put buying strategy in that it limits the possible losses on the portfolio if interest rates go up. Like the covered call writing strategy, the portfolio's upside potential is limited. Like an unhedged position, within the range defined by the strike prices the value of the portfolio varies with interest rates.

Exhibit 6: Covered Call Writing Strategy with Different Strike Prices

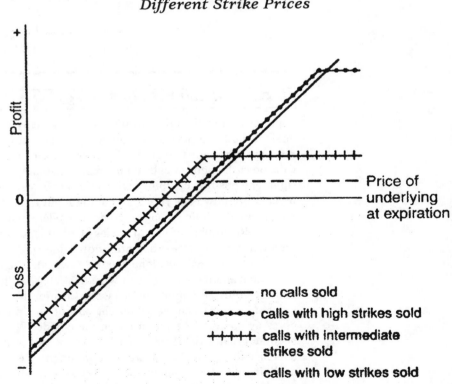

Exhibit 7: Long Position Hedged with a Collar

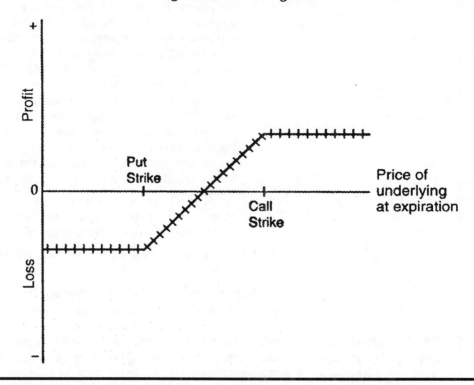

---

4. Selecting the "Best" Strategy

Comparing the two basic strategies for hedging with options, one cannot say that the protective put buying strategy or the covered call writing strategy is necessarily the better or more correct options hedge. The best strategy (and the best strike price) depends upon the manager's view of the market and risk tolerance. Purchasing a put and paying the required premium is appropriate if the manager is fundamentally bearish. If, instead, the manager is neutral to mildly bearish, it is better to receive the premium on the covered call writing strategy. If the manager prefers to take no view on the market at all, and as little risk as possible, then the futures hedge is the most appropriate. If the manager is fundamentally bullish, then no hedge at all is probably the best strategy.

B. Steps in Options Hedging   Like hedging with futures (described in Section II), there are steps that managers should consider before setting their hedges. These steps include:

> *Step 1: Determine the option contract that is the best hedging vehicle.* The best option contract to use depends upon several factors. These include option price, liquidity, and correlation with the bond(s) to be hedged. In price-inefficient markets, the option price is important because not all options will be priced in the same manner or with the same volatility assumption. Consequently, some options may be overpriced and some underpriced. Obviously, with other factors equal, it is better to use the underpriced options when buying and the overpriced options when selling.

Whenever there is a possibility that the option position may be closed out prior to expiration, liquidity is also an important consideration. If the particular option is illiquid, closing out a position may be prohibitively expensive, and the manager loses the flexibility of closing out positions early, or rolling into other positions that may become more attractive. Correlation with the underlying bond(s) to be hedged is another factor in selecting the right contract. The higher the correlation, the more precisely the final profit and loss can be defined as a function of the final level of rates. Poor correlation leads to more uncertainty.

While most of the uncertainty in an options hedge usually comes from the uncertainty of interest rates themselves, the degree of correlation between the bonds to be hedged and the instruments underlying the options contracts add to that risk. The lower the correlation, the greater the risk.

Step 2: Find the appropriate strike price. For a cross hedge, the manager will want to convert the strike price on the options that are actually bought or sold into an equivalent strike price for the actual bonds being hedged.

Step 3: Determine the number of contracts. The hedge ratio is the number of options to buy or sell.

Steps 2 and 3, determining the strike price and the number of contracts, can best be explained with examples using future options.

C. Protective Put Buying Strategy Using Futures Options

As explained above, managers who want to hedge their bond positions against a possible increase in interest rates will find that buying puts on futures is one of the easiest ways to purchase protection against rising rates. To illustrate a protective put buying strategy, we can use the same FNMA bond that we used to demonstrate how to hedge with Treasury bond futures.[5] In that example, a manager held $10 million par value of a 6.25% FNMA bond maturing 5/15/29 and used September 1999 Treasury bond futures to lock in a sale price for those bonds on the futures delivery date. Now we want to show how the manager could use futures options instead of futures to protect against rising rates.

On 6/24/99 the FNMA bond was selling for 88.39 to yield 7.20% and the CTD issue's yield was 6.50%. For simplicity, it is assumed that the yield spread between the FNMA bond and the CTD issue remains at 70 basis points.

1. Selecting the Strike Price

The manager must determine the minimum price that he wants to establish for the FNMA bonds. In our illustration we will assume that the minimum price before the cost of the put options purchased is 84.453. This is equivalent to saying that the manager wants to establish a strike price for a put option on the hedged bonds of 84.453.

---

[5] As explained at Level II (Chapter 7), futures options on Treasury bonds are more commonly used by institutional investors. The mechanics of futures options are as follows. If a put option is exercised, the option buyer receives a short position in the underlying futures contract and the option writer receives the corresponding long position. The futures price for both positions is the strike price for the put option. The exchange then marks the positions to market and the futures price for both positions is then the current futures price. If a call option is exercised, the option buyer receives a long position in the underlying futures contract and the option writer receives the corresponding short position. The futures price for both positions is the strike price for the call option. The exchange then marks the positions to market and the futures price for both positions is then the current futures price.

But, the manager is not buying a put option on the FNMA bond. He is buying a put option on a Treasury bond futures contract. Therefore, the manager must determine the strike price for a put option on a Treasury bond futures contract that is equivalent to a strike price of 84.453 for the FNMA bond.

This can be done with the help of Exhibit 8. Notice that all the boxes in the exhibit are numbered and we shall refer to these numbered boxes as we illustrate the process. We begin at Box 1 of the exhibit. The portfolio manager arbitrarily set the strike price for the FNMA bond at 84.453 for the FNMA bond. Now for the FNMA bond we must determine given its coupon rate of 6.25%, its maturity, and the price of 84.453 (the strike price desired) what this implies for the yield of this bond. The calculation is straightforward. The yield is 7.573%. That is, setting a strike price of 84.453 for the FNMA bond is equivalent to setting a strike yield (or equivalently a maximum yield) of 7.573%. Thus, 7.573% would be in Box 2.

Now let's move to Box 3 — the yield of the cheapest-to-deliver issue. To move from Box 2 to Box 3 we use the assumption that the spread between the FNMA bond and the cheapest-to-deliver issue is a constant 70 basis points. Since the strike yield for the FNMA bond is 7.573%, subtracting 70 basis points gives 6.873% as the strike yield (or maximum yield) for the cheapest-to-deliver issue.

Now we are at Box 3 and want to move to Box 4 — the price of the cheapest-to-deliver issue. Again, just as we moved from Box 1 to Box 2 using the basic price/yield relationship, we do the same in moving from Box 3 to Box 4. The cheapest-to-deliver issue was the 11.25% of 2/15/15 issue. Given the maturity and the coupon rate for the cheapest-to-deliver issue and the strike yield of 6.873%, the price can be computed. The price is 141.136. This is the value that would go in Box 4.

Now for the final value we need — the strike price for the Treasury bond futures contract. We know that for any issue that can be delivered to satisfy the Treasury bond futures contract that the converted price is found as follows:

$$\text{converted price} = \text{futures price} \times \text{conversion factor}$$

Exhibit 8: Calculating Equivalent Strike Prices and Yields for Hedging with Futures Options

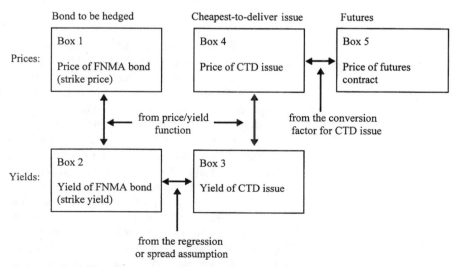

In the case of the cheapest-to-deliver issue it is:

converted price for CTD issue = futures price × conversion factor for CTD issue

The goal is to get the strike price for the futures contract. Solving the above for the futures price we get

$$\text{futures price} = \frac{\text{converted price for CTD issue}}{\text{conversion factor of CTD issue}}$$

The converted price for the CTD issue is the price in Box 4. It is 141.136 in our illustration. The conversion factor for the CTD issue is known. It is 1.283. Therefore, the strike price for the Treasury bond futures contract is

$$\text{futures price} = \frac{141.136}{1.283} = 110.0047 \text{ or } 110$$

A strike price of 110 for a put option on a Treasury bond futures contract is roughly equivalent to a put option on our FNMA bond with a strike price of 84.453.

The foregoing steps are always necessary to obtain the appropriate strike price on a put futures option. The process is not complicated. It simply involves (1) the relationship between price and yield, (2) the assumed relationship between the yield spread between the bonds to be hedged and the cheapest-to-deliver issue, and (3) the conversion factor for the cheapest-to-deliver issue. As with hedging employing futures illustrated earlier in this chapter, the success of the hedging strategy will depend on (1) whether the cheapest-to-deliver issue changes and (2) the yield spread between the bonds to be hedged and the cheapest-to-deliver issue.

2. Calculating the Number of Options Contracts

The hedge ratio is determined using the following equation similar to equation (7) since we will assume a constant yield spread between the bond to be hedged and the cheapest-to-deliver issue:

$$\text{number of options contracts} = \frac{\text{current dollar duration without options}}{\text{dollar duration of the CTD issue}}$$
$$\times \text{conversion factor for CTD issue}$$

Recall that the dollar durations are calculated as of the date that the hedge is expected to be removed using the target yield for the bond to be hedged. For the protective put buying strategy, we will assume that the hedge will be removed on the expiration date of the option (assumed to be the end of September 1999). To obtain the current dollar duration for the bond, the target yield is the strike yield for the FNMA bond of 7.573%. Computing the current dollar duration for the FNMA bond as of the end of September 1999 for a 50 basis point change in rates and for a target yield of 7.573% would produce a value of $512,320. This is different than the current dollar duration used to compute the number of futures contracts in the hedging strategy with futures. That value was $545,300 because it was based on a target yield of 7.26%.

The dollar duration for the CTD issue is based on a different target price (i.e., the minimum price) than in the hedging strategy with futures. The target price for the futures contract for the futures hedging strategy was 113. The dollar duration of the CTD issue when the target futures price was 113 was found to be $6,255. For the protective put buying strategy, since the strike price of the futures option is 110 (the target price in this strategy), it can be shown that the dollar duration for the CTD issue for a 50 basis point change in rates is $6,021.

Therefore, we know the following for a 50 basis point change in rates:

current dollar duration without options = $512,320
dollar duration for the CTD issue   = $ 6,021

Substituting these values and the conversion factor for the CTD issue of 1.283 into the formula for the number of options contracts, we find that 109 put options should be purchased:

$$\text{number of options contracts} = \frac{\$512,320}{\$6,021} \times 1.283 = 109 \text{ put options}$$

Thus, to hedge the FNMA bond position with put options on Treasury bond futures, 109 put options must be purchased.

3. Outcome of the Hedge

To create a table for the protective put hedge, we can use some of the numbers from Exhibit 2. Exhibit 9 shows the scenario analysis for the protective put buying strategy. The first five columns are the same as in Exhibit 2. For the put option hedge, Column (6) shows the value of the put option position at the expiration date. The value of the put option position at the expiration date will be equal to zero if the futures price is greater than or equal to the strike price of 110. If the futures price is below 110, then the options expire in the money and the value of the put option position is:

value of put option position =
(110/100 − futures price/100) × $100,000 × number of put options

For example, for the first scenario in Exhibit 9 of $8 million for the actual sale price of the FNMA bond, the corresponding futures price is 105.8551. The number of put options purchased is 109. Therefore,

(110/100 − 105.8551/100) × $100,000 × 109 = $451,794

The effective sale price for the FNMA bonds is then equal to

effective sale price = actual sale price + value of put option position − option cost

Let's look at the option cost. Suppose that the price of the put option with a strike price of 110 is $500 per contract. With a total of 109 options, the cost of the protection is $54,500 (109 × $500, not including financing costs and commissions). This cost is shown in Column (7) and is equivalent to 0.545 per $100 par value hedged.

The effective sale price for the FNMA bonds for each scenario is shown in the last column of Exhibit 9. This effective sale price is never less than 83.908. This equals the price of the FNMA bonds equivalent to the futures strike price of 110 (i.e., 84.453), minus the cost of the puts (that is, 0.545 per $100 par value hedged). This minimum effective price is something that can be calculated before the hedge is ever initiated. (As prices decline, the effective sale price actually exceeds the target minimum sale price of 83.908 by a small amount. This is due only to rounding and the fact that the hedge ratio is left unaltered although the relative dollar durations that go into the hedge ratio calculation change as yields change.) As prices increase, however, the effective sale price of the hedged bonds increases as well; unlike the futures hedge shown in Exhibit 2, the options hedge protects the investor if rates rise, but allows the investor to profit if rates fall.

D. Covered Call Writing Strategy with Futures Options

Unlike the protective put buying strategy, covered call writing is not entered into with the sole purpose of protecting a portfolio against rising rates. The covered call writer, believing that the market will not trade much higher or much lower than its present level, sells out-of-the-money calls against an existing bond portfolio. The sale of the calls brings in premium income that provides partial protection in case rates increase. The premium received does not, of course, provide the kind of protection that a long put position provides, but it does provide some additional income that can be used to offset declining prices. If, instead, rates fall, portfolio appreciation is limited because the short call position constitutes a liability for the seller, and this liability increases as rates decline. Consequently, there is limited upside price potential for the covered call writer. Of course, this is not so bad if prices are essentially going nowhere; the added income from the sale of call options is obtained without sacrificing any gains.

Exhibit 9: Hedging a Nondeliverable Bond to a Delivery Date with Puts on Futures

Instrument to be hedged: $10 million FNMA 6.25% of 05/15/29
Price of FNMA as of hedge date (6/24/99) = 88.39
Conversion factor = 1.283
Price of futures contract = 113
Target price per bond for FNMA bonds = 84.453
Effective minimum sale price = 83.908
Par value hedged = $10,000,000
Strike price for put = 110
Number of puts on futures = 109
Price per contract = $500.00
Cost of put position = $54,500

(1) Actual sale price of FNMA bonds	(2) Yield at sale	(3) Yield of 11.25% Treasury bond	(4) Price of 11.25% Treasury bond[1]	(5) Futures price	(6) Value of put options[2]	(7) Cost of put position	(8) Effective sale price[3]
8,000,000	8.027%	7.327%	135.812	105.85510	451,794	54,500	8,397,294
8,100,000	7.922%	7.222%	137.024	106.79953	348,851	54,500	8,394,351
8,200,000	7.818%	7.118%	138.226	107.73658	246,712	54,500	8,392,212
8,300,000	7.717%	7.017%	139.419	108.66640	145,362	54,500	8,390,862
8,400,000	7.617%	6.917%	140.603	109.58913	44,785	54,500	8,390,285
8,500,000	7.520%	6.820%	141.778	110.50490	—	54,500	8,445,500
8,600,000	7.424%	6.724%	142.944	111.41384	—	54,500	8,545,500
8,700,000	7.330%	6.630%	144.102	112.31608	—	54,500	8,645,500
8,800,000	7.238%	6.538%	145.251	113.21175	—	54,500	8,745,500
8,900,000	7.148%	6.448%	146.392	114.10096	—	54,500	8,845,500
9,000,000	7.059%	6.359%	147.524	114.98383	—	54,500	8,945,500
9,100,000	6.971%	6.271%	148.649	115.86047	—	54,500	9,045,500
9,200,000	6.886%	6.186%	149.766	116.73101	—	54,500	9,145,500
9,300,000	6.801%	6.101%	150.875	117.59554	—	54,500	9,245,500
9,400,000	6.719%	6.019%	151.977	118.45417	—	54,500	9,345,500
9,500,000	6.637%	5.937%	153.071	119.30702	—	54,500	9,445,500

[1] These numbers are approximate because futures trade in 32nds.
[2] From Maximum of [(110/100 − Futures price/100) × $100,000 × 109, 0]
[3] Does not include transaction costs or the financing of the options position.

To see how covered call writing with futures options works for the bond used in the protective put example, we construct a table much as we did before. With futures selling around 113 on the hedge initiation date, a sale of call options with a strike price of 117 might be appropriate.[6] As in the futures hedging and protective buying strategies it is assumed that the hedged bond will remain at a 70 basis point spread over the CTD issue. We also assume for simplicity that the price of each call option is $500.

Working backwards from box 5 in Exhibit 8, a strike price for the futures option of 117 would be equivalent to the following at the expiration date of the call option:

target price for CTD issue   = $117 \times 1.283 = 150.111$ (value at box 4)
target yield for CTD issue   = 6.16% (from price/yield relationship, box 3)
target yield for FNMA bond   = 6.86% (from 70 bp spread assumption, box 2)
target price for FNMA bond   = 92.3104 (from price/yield relationship, box 1)

Given the above information, the current dollar duration for the FNMA bond and the dollar duration of the CTD issue can be computed. The information above represents values as of the expiration date of the call option. It can be shown that the dollar durations based on a 50 basis point change in rates is:

current dollar duration without options = $592,031
dollar duration for the CTD issue   = $6,573

Substituting these values and the conversion factor for the CTD issue of 1.283 into the formula for the number of options contracts, we find that 116 call options should be sold:

$$\text{number of options contracts} = \frac{\$592,031}{\$6,573} \times 1.283 = 115.6 \text{ (rounded to 116)}$$

Since each call option is assumed to be $500, the proceeds received from the sale of 116 call options is $58,000. The proceeds per $100 of par value hedged is 0.580.

While the target price for the FNMA bond is 92.3104, the maximum effective sale price is determined by adjusting the target price by the proceeds received from the sale of the call options. Since the proceeds per $100 of par value hedged is 0.580, the maximum effective sale price is about 92.8904 (= 92.3104 + 0.580).

Exhibit 10 shows the outcomes of the covered call writing strategy. The first five columns of the exhibit are the same as for Exhibit 9. In Column (6), the liability resulting from the call option position is shown. The liability is zero if the futures price for the scenario is less than the strike price of 117. If the futures price for the scenario is greater than 117, the liability is calculated as follows:

(futures price/100 − 117/100) × $100,000 × number of call options

For example, consider the scenario in Exhibit 10 where the actual sale price of the FNMA bond is $9.5 million. The corresponding futures price is 119.30702. The number of call options sold is 116. Therefore,

(119.30702/100 − 117/100) × $100,000 × 116 = $267,614

That is,

effective sale price = actual sale price + proceeds from sale of the call options
− liability of call position

---

[6] Note that this is determined by the manager based on the risk-return profile he or she is willing to accept. It is not derived analytically in this illustration.

Exhibit 10: Writing Calls on Futures against a Nondeliverable Bond

Instrument to be hedged: $10 million FNMA 6.25% of 05/15/29
Price of FNMA as of hedge date (6/24/99) = 88.39
Conversion factor for September 1999 = 1.283
Price of futures contract = 113
Target price for FNMA bonds per bond = 92.3104
Effective maximum sale price = 92.8904
Par value hedged = $10,000,000
Strike price for call = 117
Number of calls on futures = 116
Price per contract = $500.00
Value of call position = $58,000

(1) Actual sale price of FNMA bonds	(2) Yield at sale	(3) Yield of 11.25% Treasury bond	(4) Price of 11.25% Treasury bond	(5) Futures price[1]	(6) Liability of call options[2]	(7) Proceeds from call position	(8) Effective sale price[3]
8,000,000	8.027%	7.327%	135.812	105.85510	—	58,000	8,058,000
8,100,000	7.922%	7.222%	137.024	106.79953	—	58,000	8,158,000
8,200,000	7.818%	7.118%	138.226	107.73658	—	58,000	8,258,000
8,300,000	7.717%	7.017%	139.419	108.66640	—	58,000	8,358,000
8,400,000	7.617%	6.917%	140.603	109.58913	—	58,000	8,458,000
8,500,000	7.520%	6.820%	141.778	110.50490	—	58,000	8,558,000
8,600,000	7.424%	6.724%	142.944	111.41384	—	58,000	8,658,000
8,700,000	7.330%	6.630%	144.102	112.31608	—	58,000	8,758,000
8,800,000	7.238%	6.538%	145.251	113.21175	—	58,000	8,858,000
8,900,000	7.148%	6.448%	146.392	114.10096	—	58,000	8,958,000
9,000,000	7.059%	6.359%	147.524	114.98383	—	58,000	9,058,000
9,100,000	6.971%	6.271%	148.649	115.86047	—	58,000	9,158,000
9,200,000	6.886%	6.186%	149.766	116.73101	—	58,000	9,258,000
9,300,000	6.801%	6.101%	150.875	117.59554	69,083	58,000	9,288,917
9,400,000	6.719%	6.019%	151.977	118.45417	168,684	58,000	9,289,316
9,500,000	6.637%	5.937%	153.071	119.30702	267,614	58,000	9,290,386

[1] These numbers are approximate because futures trade in 32nds.
[2] From Maximum of [(Futures price/100 − 117/100) × $100,000 × 116, 0]
[3] Does not include transaction costs or interest on the option premium received.

Since the proceeds from sale of the call options is $58,000, then

effective sale price = actual sale price + $58,000 − liability of call position

The last column of Exhibit 10 shows the effective sale price for each scenario.

As Exhibit 10 shows, if the hedged bond does trade at 70 basis points over the CTD issue as assumed, the maximum effective sale price for the hedged bond is, in fact, slightly over 92.8904. The discrepancies shown in the exhibit are due to rounding.

E. Comparing Alternative Strategies

In this chapter we reviewed three basic strategies for hedging a bond position: (1) hedging with futures, (2) hedging with out-of-the-money puts, and (3) covered call writing with out-of-the-money calls. Similar, but opposite, strategies exist for managers who are concerned that rates will decrease. As might be expected, there is no "best" strategy. Each strategy has its advantages and its disadvantages, and we never get something for nothing. To get anything of value, something else of value must be forfeited.

Exhibit 11: Comparison of Alternative Strategies

(1)	(2)	(3)	(4)
Actual sale price of FNMA bonds	Effective sale price with futures hedge	Effective sale price with protective puts	Effective sale price with covered calls
8,000,000	8,800,229	8,397,294	8,058,000
8,100,000	8,794,453	8,394,351	8,158,000
8,200,000	8,789,503	8,392,212	8,258,000
8,300,000	8,785,363	8,390,862	8,358,000
8,400,000	8,782,017	8,390,285	8,458,000
8,500,000	8,779,451	8,445,500	8,558,000
8,600,000	8,777,650	8,545,500	8,658,000
8,700,000	8,776,599	8,645,500	8,758,000
8,800,000	8,776,284	8,745,500	8,858,000
8,900,000	8,776,693	8,845,500	8,958,000
9,000,000	8,777,812	8,945,500	9,058,000
9,100,000	8,779,627	9,045,500	9,158,000
9,200,000	8,782,127	9,145,500	9,258,000
9,300,000	8,785,300	9,245,500	9,288,917
9,400,000	8,789,132	9,345,500	9,289,316
9,500,000	8,793,614	9,445,500	9,290,386

To make a choice among strategies, it helps to lay the alternatives side by side. Using the futures example from the previous chapter and the futures options examples from this chapter, Exhibit 11 shows the final values of the portfolio for the various hedging alternatives. It is easy to see from Exhibit 11 that if one alternative is superior to another alternative at one level of rates, it will be inferior at some other level of rates.

Consequently, we cannot conclude that one strategy is the best strategy. The manager who makes the strategy decision makes a choice among probability distributions, not usually among specific outcomes. Except for the perfect hedge, there is always some range of possible final values of the portfolio. Of course, exactly what that range is, and the probabilities associated with each possible outcome, is a matter of opinion.

F. Hedging with Options on Cash Instruments

Hedging a position with options on cash bonds is relatively straightforward. Most strategies, including the purchase of protective puts, covered call writing, and buying collars, are essentially the same whether futures options or options on physicals are used. As explained at Level II (Chapter 7), there are some mechanical differences in the way the two types of option contracts are traded, and there may be substantial differences in their liquidity. Nonetheless, the basic economics of the strategies are virtually identical.

Using options on physicals frequently relieves the manager of much of the basis risk associated with a futures options hedge. For example, a manager of Treasury bonds or notes can usually buy or sell options on the exact security held in the portfolio. Using options on futures, rather than options on Treasury bonds, is sure to introduce additional elements of uncertainty.

Given the illustration presented above, and given that the economics of options on physicals and options on futures are essentially identical, additional illustrations for options on physicals are unnecessary. The only important difference is the hedge ratio calculation and the calculation of the equivalent strike price. To derive the hedge ratio, we always resort to an expression of relative dollar durations. Thus, for options on physicals assuming a constant spread the hedge ratio is:

$$\frac{\text{current dollar duration without options}}{\text{dollar duration of underlying for option}}$$

If a relationship is estimated between the yield on the bonds to be hedged and the instrument underlying the option, the appropriate hedge ratio is:

$$\frac{\text{current dollar duration without options}}{\text{dollar duration of underlying for option}} \times \text{yield beta}$$

Unlike futures options, there is only one deliverable, so there is no conversion factor. When cross hedging with options on physicals, the procedure for finding the equivalent strike price on the bonds to be hedged is very similar. Given the strike price of the option, the strike yield is easily determined using the price/yield relationship for the instrument underlying the option. Then given the projected relationship between the yield on the instrument underlying the option and the yield on the bonds to be hedged, an equivalent strike yield is derived for the bonds to be hedged. Finally, using the yield-to-price formula for the bonds to be hedged, the equivalent strike price for the bonds to be hedged can be found.

SECTION V USING CAPS AND FLOORS

Interest rate caps can be used in liability management to create a cap for funding costs. Combining a cap and a floor creates a collar for funding costs. Floors can be used by buyers of floating-rate instruments to set a floor on the periodic interest earned. To reduce the cost of a floor, a manager can sell a cap. By doing so, the manager limits the upside on the coupon rate of a floating-rate instrument should rates rise, thereby creating a collar for the coupon rate.

To see how interest rate caps and floors can be used for asset/liability management, consider the problems faced by the commercial bank and the life insurance company we discussed in demonstrating the use of an interest rate swap in the previous chapter. Recall that the bank's objective is to lock in a spread over its cost of funds. Yet because the bank borrows short term, its cost of funds is uncertain. The bank may be able to purchase a cap, however, so that the cap rate plus the cost of purchasing the cap is less than the rate it is earning on its fixed-rate commercial loans. If short-term rates decline, the bank does not benefit from the cap, but its cost of funds declines. The cap therefore allows the bank to impose a ceiling on its cost of funds while retaining the opportunity to benefit from a decline in rates.

The bank can reduce the cost of purchasing the cap by selling a floor. In this case, the bank agrees to pay the buyer of the floor if the reference rate falls below the strike rate. The bank receives a fee for selling the floor, but it has sold off its opportunity to benefit from a decline in rates below the strike rate. By buying a cap and selling a floor, the bank has created a predetermined range for its cost of funds (i.e., a collar).

Recall the problem of the life insurance company that guarantees a 8% rate on a GIC for the next four years and is considering the purchase of an attractive floating-rate instrument in a private placement transaction. The risk that the company faces is that interest rates will fall so that it will not earn enough to realize the 8% guaranteed rate plus a spread. The life insurance company may be able to purchase a floor to set a lower bound on its investment return, yet retain the opportunity to benefit should rates increase. To reduce the cost of purchasing the floor, the life insurance company can sell an interest rate cap. By doing so, however, it gives up the opportunity of benefiting from an increase in the reference rate above the strike rate of the interest rate cap.

SECTION VI
KEY POINTS

❑ *Buying an interest rate futures contract increases a portfolio's duration, selling an interest rate futures contract decreases a portfolio's duration.*

❑ *The advantages of adjusting a portfolio's duration using futures rather than cash market instruments are that transaction costs are lower, margin requirements are lower, and selling short in the futures market is easier.*

❑ *The general principle in controlling interest rate risk with futures is to combine the dollar exposure of the current portfolio and that of a futures position so that it is equal to the target dollar exposure.*

❑ *The number of futures contracts needed to achieve the target dollar duration depends on the current dollar duration of the portfolio without futures and the dollar duration per futures contract.*

❑ *Hedging with futures calls for taking a futures position as a temporary substitute for transactions to be made in the cash market at a later date, with the expectation that any loss realized by the manager from one position (whether cash or futures) will be offset by a profit on the other position.*

❑ *Hedging is a special case of controlling interest rate risk in which the target duration or target dollar duration is zero.*

❑ *Cross hedging occurs when the bond to be hedged is not identical to the bond underlying the futures contract.*

❑ *A short or sell hedge is used to protect against a decline in the cash price of a bond; a long or buy hedge is employed to protect against an increase in the cash price of a bond.*

❑ *The steps in hedging include: (1) determining the appropriate hedging instrument; (2) determining the target for the hedge; (3) determining the position to be taken in the hedging instrument; and, monitoring and evaluating the hedge.*

❑ *The key factor to determine which futures contract will provide the best hedge is the degree of correlation between the rate on the futures contract and the interest rate that creates the underlying risk that the manager seeks to eliminate.*

❑ *The manager should determine the target rate or target price, which is what is expected from the hedge.*

❑ *The hedge ratio is the number of futures contracts needed for the hedge.*

❑ *The basis is the difference between the spot price (or rate) and the futures price (or rate).*

❑ *In general, when hedging to the delivery date of the futures contract, a manager locks in the futures rate or price.*

❑ *Hedging with Treasury bond futures and Treasury note futures is complicated by the delivery options embedded in these contracts.*

❑ *When a hedge is lifted prior to the delivery date, the effective rate (or price) that is obtained is much more likely to approximate the current spot rate than the futures rate the shorter the term of the hedge.*

❑ *The proper target for a hedge that is to be lifted prior to the delivery date depends on the basis.*

❑ *Basis risk refers only to the uncertainty associated with the target rate basis or target price basis.*

❑ *Hedging substitutes basis risk for price risk.*

❏ *Hedging non-Treasury securities with Treasury bond futures requires that the hedge ratio consider two relationships: (1) the cash price of the non-Treasury security and the cheapest-to-deliver issue and (2) the price of the cheapest-to-deliver issue and the futures price.*

❏ *In computing the hedge ratio for nondeliverable securities, the yield beta should be considered; regression analysis is used to estimate the yield beta and captures the relationship between yield levels and yield spreads.*

❏ *After a target is determined and a hedge is set, the hedge must be monitored during its life and evaluated after it is over.*

❏ *It is important to ascertain the sources of error in a hedge in order to gain insights that can be used to advantage in subsequent hedges.*

❏ *An interest rate swap can be used to hedge interest rate risk by altering the cash flow characteristics of a portfolio of assets so as to match liability cash flows.*

❏ *The dollar duration of swap follows from its economic interpretation as a leveraged position.*

❏ *For the fixed-rate receiver, the dollar duration of a swap is equal to the duration of a fixed-rate bond.*

❏ *For the fixed-rate payer, the dollar duration of a swap is equal to minus the duration of a fixed-rate bond.*

❏ *A swap in which a manager pays floating and receives fixed increases the duration of a portfolio; a swap in which a manager pays fixed and receives floating decreases the duration of a portfolio.*

❏ *Three popular hedge strategies are the protective put buying strategy, the covered call writing strategy, and the collar strategy.*

❏ *A manager can use a protective put buying strategy to hedge against rising interest rates.*

❏ *A protective put buying strategy is a simple combination of a long put option with a long position in a cash bond.*

❏ *A covered call writing strategy involves selling call options against the bond portfolio.*

❏ *A covered call writing strategy entails much more downside risk than buying a put to protect the value of the portfolio and many managers do not consider covered call writing a hedge.*

❏ *It is not possible to say that the protective put buying strategy or the covered call writing strategy is necessarily the better or more correct options hedge.*

❏ *The best strategy (and the best strike prices) depends upon the manager's view of the market.*

❏ *A collar strategy is a combination of a protective put buying strategy and a covered call writing strategy.*

❏ *A manager who implements a collar strategy eliminates part of the portfolio's downside risk by giving up part of its upside potential.*

❏ *The steps in options hedging include determining the option contract that is the best hedging vehicle, finding the appropriate strike price, and determining the number of options contracts.*

❑ *At the outset of options hedging, a minimum effective sale price can be calculated for a protective put buying strategy and a maximum effective sale price can be computed for a covered call writing strategy.*

❑ *The best options contract to use depends upon the option price, liquidity, and correlation with the bond(s) to be hedged.*

❑ *For a cross hedge, the manager will want to convert the strike price for the options that are actually bought or sold into an equivalent strike price for the actual bonds being hedged.*

❑ *When using Treasury bond futures options, the hedge ratio is based on the relative dollar duration of the current portfolio, the cheapest-to-deliver issue, and the futures contract at the option expiration date, as well as the conversion factor for the cheapest-to-deliver issue.*

❑ *While there are some mechanical differences in the way options on physicals and options on futures are traded and there may be substantial differences in their liquidity, the basic economics of the hedging strategies are virtually identical for both contracts.*

❑ *Using options on physicals frequently relieves the manager of much of the basis risk associated with an options hedge.*

❑ *An interest rate floor can be used to establish a minimum rate for a floating-rate security.*

❑ *An interest rate cap can be used to set a maximum funding cost.*

END OF CHAPTER QUESTIONS

1. Mr. Dawson is a portfolio manager who is responsible for the account of the Pizza Delivery Personnel Union (PDPU). At this time, the trustees have not authorized Mr. Dawson to take positions in Treasury bond futures contracts. At his quarterly meeting with PDPU's board of trustee, Mr. Dawson requested that the board grant him authorization to use Treasury bond futures to control interest rate risk. One of the trustees asked whether it was necessary to use Treasury bond futures contracts to control risk. The trustee noted that Mr. Dawson already had authorization by the investment guidelines to short Treasury securities and that should be sufficient to control interest rate risk combined with the opportunity to buy Treasury securities. What advantages could Mr. Dawson offer to the trustee of PDPU for using Treasury futures contracts to control risk rather than using Treasury securities to alter the portfolio's interest rate risk?

2. The trustees of the Egg Craters pension fund are discussing with their consultant, Mr. William, about establishing a new benchmark for its external bond managers. The benchmark would be based on the projected duration of the fund's liability. Currently, the investment guidelines of the fund do not permit its managers to leverage the portfolio or utilize futures.

   At the time of the meeting, the duration of the universe of Treasury coupon bonds with more than 25 years to maturity was 6. Mr. William reported that the duration of the liabilities is approximately 11. He explained that under the current investment guidelines that if a bond portfolio must be created to have a duration of 11, the trustees will have to expect that the managers will have to invest a good portion of their portfolio in longer-term zero-coupon bonds. To avoid this and still allow the managers to create a portfolio with a duration of 11, it will be necessary for the trustees to change the fund's investment guidelines to (1) permit the managers to employ leverage and/or (2) permit the managers to use futures contracts.

   The trustees asked Mr. William why it was necessary to revise the investment guidelines as he suggested. Explain to the trustees why.

3. Ms. Marcus is a portfolio manager who is responsible for a portion of the bond portfolio of UltraChip.com's pension fund. Ms. Ulman manages $200 million. The current investment guidelines specify that the duration for the portfolio can be ±1 of the benchmark. Currently, the duration for benchmark is 4 and the duration for the portfolio is 5. Ms. Marcus expects that rates will rise and wants to reduce the duration of the portfolio to the lower end of the duration range, 3. She wants to alter the duration using Treasury bond futures contracts, an instrument she is authorized to use by the pension fund's investment guidelines.

   a. Explain what position (long or short) Ms. Marcus should take in Treasury bond futures to reduce the duration from 5 to 3?

   b. Suppose that the dollar duration per Treasury bond futures contract (based on the cheapest-to-deliver issue) for a 50 basis point change in rates is $5,000. How many Treasury bond futures contracts must be bought or sold?

4. Suppose that the dollar duration for the cheapest-to-deliver issue for the Treasury bond futures contract is $6,000 per 50 basis point change in rates and the conversion factor for that issue is 0.90. What is the dollar duration for the futures contract per 50 basis point change in rates?

5. Why is hedging a special case of interest rate risk control management?

6. What factors should be considered by a portfolio manager in selecting the futures contract to employ to control the interest rate risk of a portfolio?

7. a. What is meant by the "target price" for a hedge?
   b. How is information about the target price for a hedge used by a manager in deciding whether or not to hedge?

8. Mr. Ulston is a bond portfolio manager who up until this time has not used interest rate futures in managing a portfolio. While he is familiar with interest rate futures, he has no experience in using them in portfolio management. Recently, Mr. Ulston received authorization to use interest rate futures from several clients and needed to educate himself on the use of the product.

   Mr. Ulston contacted one of his brokers about obtaining information on how to use interest rate futures to control interest rate risk. The broker suggested that Mr. Ulston contact the risk manager of the brokerage firm, Ms. Alvarez, so that she could explain how she uses interest rate futures to control the firm's interest rate risk. In his conversation with Ms. Alvarez, Mr. Ulston asked her about what he would be able to lock in by using interest rate futures. Was it the current price of the bond to be hedged or was it the futures price? Ms. Alvarez responded that when she used interest rate futures to hedge her firm's bond position overnight, she was basically locking in the current price.

   Mr. Ulston also contacted a former associate, James Granger, who managed a bond portfolio and had experience using interest rate futures. When Mr. Ulston asked Mr. Granger the same question that he asked Ms. Alvarez, he received a different answer. Mr. Granger said that typically he puts on hedges that are removed near the date that the futures contract settles and that he is locking in the futures price.

   Mr. Ulston is confused as to why he received different prices that Ms. Alvarez and Mr. Granger indicated that they were locking in by using interest rate futures. He asks you to explain what is being locked in by using interest rate futures to hedge and who was correct, Ms. Alvarez or Mr. Granger. What is your response?

9. a. In a hedging strategy, what is meant by basis risk?
   b. Explain why hedging substitutes basis risk for price risk?
   c. Explain why a manager would be willing to substitute basis risk for price risk?

10. Explain what is meant by a cross hedge?

11. What are the two important relationships to understand in cross hedging mortgage passthrough securities using Treasury note futures contracts?

12. Mr. Denton has a $20 million par value position in an investment-grade rated corporate bond. He has decided to hedge the position for one month using Treasury bond futures contracts that settles in one month. Mr. Denton's research assistant provided him with the following information:

   Information about the corporate bond:

   > coupon rate = 8%
   > years to maturity = 30

par value = $20 million
market price = 100
yield to maturity = 8%
structure = bullet bond
duration *at the settlement date* = 11.3

Information about the Treasury bond futures contract:

settlement date = 1 month
futures price = 106
cheapest-to-deliver issue:
coupon rate = 10%
years to maturity = 22
price = 133.42
yield to maturity = 7%
duration *at the settlement date* = 10.4
conversion factor = 1.16

Assumptions:

1. The yield spread between the corporate bond and the CTD issue is unchanged at its current level of 100 basis points.
2. The CTD issue will not change at the time the hedge is removed in one month.
3. Delivery will be made on the last business day of the Treasury bond futures contract settlement month.

a. What is the target price for the cheapest-to-deliver issue?
b. Based on the target price for the CTD issue found in part a, what is the target yield for the CTD issue?
c. What is the target yield for the corporate bond?
d. What is the target price for the corporate bond given the target yield found in part c?
e. What is the dollar duration per $100,000 par value of the CTD issue per 50 basis point change in rates based on the price for the CTD issue one month from now? (Remember that dollar duration calculations are based on prices at the delivery date. Assume no change in yield.)
f. What is the dollar duration per $20 million of par value of the corporate bond to be hedged per 50 basis point change in rates based on the price for the corporate bond one month from now? (Remember that dollar duration calculations are based on prices at the delivery date. Assume no change in yield.)
g. How many futures contracts should Mr. Denton short?

13. In cross hedging, what is meant by a "yield beta" and how is it used in constructing a hedge (i.e., determining the number of contracts to take a position in when hedging)?

14. A portfolio manager estimated that the duration for his $1 billion portfolio is 5.2. Suppose that the manager wants to hedge this portfolio with a Treasury bond

futures contract and that the dollar duration of the Treasury bond futures contract for a 50 basis point change in rates is $4,000. How many Treasury bond futures contracts should the manager sell?

15. Mr. Elmo is a portfolio manager who has recently begun to use interest rate futures for risk control. In his first attempt at using interest rate futures to hedge a long position in a particular bond he did in fact partially offset the loss associated with a decline in the value of that bond. However, the hedge did not perform as expected. Specifically, there was still a loss on the hedged position that was considerably greater than he anticipated. When discussing the outcome with a colleague, Ms. Rosetta, she suggested that there were three things that might have gone wrong when Mr. Elmo constructed the hedge. First, Mr. Elmo might have misestimated the price sensitivity of the futures contract and the particular bond being hedged. Second, the basis could have changed adversely. Finally, the relationship between the yield movement of the bond to be hedged and the yield on the underlying for the futures contract may have changed.

  Mr. Elmo was not quite sure what Ms. Rosetta meant and has asked you to explain the reasons Ms. Rosetta offered as to why the hedge did not work out as expected. Explain why?

16. Mr. Eddy is a portfolio manager for a finance company. The company has a portfolio of consumer loans with a par value of $500 million. Unlike typical auto loans, for the loans in the portfolio the borrowers make no periodic interest payments. Instead, the borrowers make quarterly interest payments and repay the principal at the maturity date of the loan. (That is, the loans are not amortizing loans.) All of the loans have two years to maturity and have a fixed interest rate of 12%.

  Mr. Eddy was able to fund the $500 million for the consumer loans by borrowing money at a cost of 3-month LIBOR plus 56 basis points. He recognizes that there is a mismatch between the liabilities to repay the borrowed funds and the cash flow from the consumer loans. He is considering using an interest rate swap to control this risk. The following terms are available for a 2-year interest rate swap at this time: pay fixed of 7.2% and receive LIBOR.

  a. Suppose that Mr. Eddy enter into this swap transaction with a notional amount of $500 million. What is the expected outcome of this swap for each quarter?
  b. What assumption is made about defaults and prepayments in your answer to part a?

17. Explain, in terms of equivalent cash market positions, what happens to the dollar duration of a bond portfolio if an interest rate swap is entered into in which the portfolio manager agrees to pay floating and receive fixed.

18. a. Why would a bond portfolio manager employ a protective put buying strategy?
  b. What is the trade-off in buying at-the-money puts versus out-of-the-money puts in a protective put buying strategy?

19. The investment guidelines of the Wycoff Pension Fund prohibit the fund's external bond managers from using options in any capacity. At a meeting between the trustees of the Wycoff Pension Fund, its consultant, and one of its external portfolio managers, the question of relaxing the restriction that options can be used was discussed.

One trustee agreed that its external managers should be given the opportunity to use options. However, the trustee was adamant that the manager only be able to write options on bonds in the portfolio. The trustee felt that in contrast to buying options a strategy of writing call options would not result in a loss to the fund if options expired unexercised and the fund would have wasted the option price. In the case of writing call options, the trustee argued that even if the option is exercised, the fund doesn't lose anything because it collected the option premium and, besides, it is just taking out of its portfolio a bond that it already owns.

The portfolio manager responded that he was uncomfortable with such a restrictive option strategy suggested by the trustee because it is not a true hedging strategy. Moreover, he believes that there are costs associated with the strategy suggested by the trustee.

The consultant was asked to comment on the statements made by the trustee and the portfolio manager. How should the consultant respond?

20. In an article entitled "It's Boom Time for Bond Options As Interest-Rate Hedges Bloom," published in the November 8, 1990, issue of *The Wall Street Journal*, the following appeared:

> "The threat of a large interest-rate swing in either direction is driving people to options to hedge their portfolios of long-term Treasury bonds and medium-term Treasury notes, said...."

Later in the article the following two statements appear:

> Statement 1: "If the market moves against an option purchaser, the option expires worthless, and all the investor has lost is the relatively low purchase price, or 'premium,' of the option."

> Statement 2: "Futures contracts also can be used to hedge portfolios, but they cost more, and there isn't any limit on the amount of losses they could produce before an investor bails out."

a. Explain why you agree or disagree with Statement 1.
b. Explain why you agree or disagree with Statement 2.

21. Why does the payoff of a collar strategy using options have the elements of a protective put buying strategy, a covered call writing strategy, and an unhedged position?

22. Mr. Zhao is a corporate bond portfolio manager. He is interested in hedging an issue with a maturity of 20 years and a coupon rate of 8%. The corporate issue is option free (i.e., it is a bullet bond). Mr. Zhao owns $10 million par value of this issue. The bond is trading at par value.

Mr. Zhao would like to purchase a put option on the corporate issue with a strike price of 90.80. However, because an exchange-traded option in which the corporate issue is the underlying is not available, Mr. Zhao has decided to purchase an exchange-traded put option on a Treasury bond futures contract.

The yield on the corporate issue is 8% and the yield on the cheapest-to-deliver issue for the Treasury bond futures contract is 6.75%. The cheapest-to-deliver issue has a maturity of 20 years and a coupon rate of 7.75%. Mr. Zhao expects that the spread between the corporate issue and the CTD issue will be constant at 125 basis point spread. The conversion factor for the CTD issue is 0.95.

What is the strike price for the put option on the Treasury bond futures contract that will be equivalent to a strike price on the corporate issue of 90.80?

23. Suppose that a portfolio manager owns a portfolio of bonds with a current market value of $100 million. There are no options in the current portfolio. The manager wants to purchase put options on the Treasury bond futures contract to protect against a decline in the value of the portfolio. Suppose that based upon the strike price that the manager selects for the put options, the dollar duration for a 50 basis point change in rates of the cheapest-to-deliver issue is $4,500 at the expiration date of the put option. Also assume that (1) the duration of the current portfolio is 7 at the expiration date of the put option and (2) the conversion factor for the cheapest-to-deliver issue is 0.90. How many put options should be purchased?

24. A commercial bank has a portfolio of floating-rate notes. All of the notes have as their reference rate 3-month LIBOR and they all have a cap of 9%.

a. Suppose the portfolio manager is concerned that interest rates will rise so that the cap on the floating-rate notes will be realized. Explain how the portfolio manager can use an interest rate cap agreement to protect against this.
b. Suppose the portfolio manager is concerned that interest rates will fall below the bank's funding cost of acquiring the floating-rate notes. Explain how an interest rate floor agreement can be used by a portfolio to protect against this.

SOLUTIONS TO END OF CHAPTER QUESTIONS

1. There are three advantage of using Treasury futures contracts rather than cash Treasuries to alter the interest rate risk of a portfolio. They are:

   1. Despite the highly liquid Treasury market, transaction costs for trading Treasury futures are lower than trading in the Treasury cash market.
   2. Margin requirements are lower for futures than for Treasury securities; using futures thus permits greater leverage.
   3. It is easier to sell short Treasury futures than short Treasury securities.

2. To obtain a portfolio duration of 11 in an interest rate environment where long-term Treasury bonds have a duration of 6 means that there must be bonds in the portfolio with a duration greater than 11. Zero-coupon bonds with a maturity greater than 11 years will have the desired duration. However, this can also be done by allowing leverage. As explained in Chapter 2, leverage can be used to increase the portfolio's duration. Alternatively, buying Treasury bond futures increases the dollar duration and duration of the portfolio. By buying the appropriate number of futures contracts, a manager can increase the duration of the portfolio to 11.

3. a. Ms. Marcus wants to reduce the dollar duration of the portfolio. To do so, she must sell Treasury bond futures contract. Thus, she will take a short position in the Treasury bond futures contract.

   b. To determine the number of futures contracts it is first necessary to compare the current dollar duration without futures and the target dollar duration. We can compute these values for any basis point change in rates. Suppose that 50 basis points are used. Since the current duration is 5 and the market value of the portfolio is $200 million, for a 50 basis point change in rates the current dollar duration without futures is $5 million ($200 million × 5% × 0.5). The target dollar duration for a portfolio with a target duration of 3 is $3 million. Thus,

   target dollar duration − current dollar duration without futures
   = $3 million − $5 million = −$2 million

   This means that the dollar duration of the futures position must be −$2 million in order to have a target portfolio duration of 3. We know that

   dollar duration of futures position
   = number of futures contracts × dollar duration per futures contracts

   Since we know that

   dollar duration of futures position = −$2,000,000

   and

   dollar duration per futures contracts = $5,000

   then   −$2,000,000 = number of futures contracts × $5,000

   therefore

   number of futures contracts = −400

   Ms. Marcus should short (sell) 400 futures contracts to alter the portfolio's duration to 3.

4. The dollar duration for the futures contract is

dollar duration of the CTD issue × conversion factor for the CTD issue
= $6,000 × 0.90 = $5,400

5. Interest rate risk control management involves altering the portfolio's duration to match the target duration. When hedging, the manager is setting a target duration of zero. Hence, hedging is a special case of interest rate risk control management.

6. The primary factor in determining which futures contract a manager should use to control the interest rate risk of a portfolio is the degree of correlation between the rate on the futures contract and the interest rate that creates the underlying risk that the manager seeks to eliminate. However, correlation is not the only consideration when the size of the transaction necessary to obtain the target duration is large. Liquidity of the futures contract becomes important in such situations.

7. a. The target price for a hedge is the price that on average will be locked in by the hedge.
   b. If hedging a future sale and the target price is too low, then the manager may decide not to hedge. If hedging a future purchase and the target price is too high, then the manager may decide not to hedge.

8. When hedging using interest rate futures, the outcome of the hedge depends on what happens to the basis (i.e., the difference between the spot price and the futures price). The uncertainty in the outcome of a hedge is that when he initiates the hedge, the hedger does not know what the basis will be at the time the hedge is removed, except at the settlement date of the futures contract. So, the price that will be locked in will be between the current price and the futures price. The answers given by Ms. Alvarez and Mr. Granger reflect those two extreme values. Ms. Alvarez by hedging just overnight is effectively locking in the current price, since under most circumstances, the basis will probably not change much in a day. In contrast, when Mr. Granger plans to remove the hedge at the delivery date of the futures contract, he is locking in the futures price because of convergence. So, both are correct with respect to the time period over which they plan to hedge.

9. a. Basis risk is the uncertainty about the value of the basis at the time the hedge is removed. (The basis is defined as the difference between the spot price and the futures price.) The outcome of a hedge depends on what happens to the basis at the time the hedge is removed.
   b. For a given investment horizon, hedging substitutes basis risk for price risk because the manager is exchanging the uncertainty of the price of the hedged security (i.e., price risk) at some future date for the uncertainty of how the basis will change (i.e., basis risk) at some future date when the hedge is removed.
   c. A manager will hedge because he or she believes that basis risk is less than price risk.

10. A cross hedge in the futures market occurs when the security to be hedged is not deliverable on the futures contract used in the hedge. For example, a manager who wants to hedge the sale price of a corporate bond or a mortgage-backed security might hedge with a Treasury note futures contract. Because non-Treasury bonds cannot be delivered in satisfaction of the contract, the hedge would be con-

sidered a cross hedge. Another example of cross hedging is when a manager wants to hedge a rate that is of the same quality as the rate specified in one of the available futures contracts, but that has a different maturity. For example, it is necessary to cross hedge a Treasury bond, note, or bill with a maturity that does not qualify for delivery on any futures contract. Thus, when the security to be hedged differs from the futures contract specification in terms of either quality or maturity, there is a cross hedge.

11. The two key relationships in a cross hedge of mortgage passthrough securities using Treasury note futures are:

    1. the relationship between the cheapest-to-deliver (CTD) issue for the Treasury note futures contract and the futures contract.
    2. the relationship between the mortgage passthrough securities to be hedged and the CTD issue for the Treasury note futures contract.

12. a. The target price for hedging the CTD issue would be the product of the futures price and the conversion factor for the CTD issue:

$$106 \times 1.16 = 122.96$$

b. Given the coupon rate and maturity of the issue, the yield to maturity is 7.8% if the CTD target price is 122.96.

c. Since the yield spread for the corporate bond is assumed to be constant at 100 basis points, the target yield for the corporate bond would be 8.8%.

d. The corresponding target price for the corporate bond for the target yield of 8.8% is 91.62. (This is calculated using the standard pricing formula.)

e. First the price for the CTD must be determined one month from now. Given a yield of 7.0% for the CTD issue, a coupon rate of 10%, and a remaining maturity of 21 years and 11 months, the price at the settlement date is 133.3580. (It is based on this price that the duration of 10.4 in the information set was computed.)

Given the duration for the CTD issue is 10.4 at the settlement date, the dollar duration per $100 par value for a 50 basis point change in interest rates is:

$$(10.4\%/2) \times \text{price of CTD issue at settlement date}$$

Since the price of the CTD issue at the settlement date is 133.3580,

$$(10.4\%/2) \times \$133.3580 = \$6.935$$

Per $100,000 par value of the CTD issue, the dollar duration at the settlement date is

dollar duration for the CTD issue at the settlement date
$$= (\$100,000/100) \times 6.935$$
$$= \$6,935$$

f. First the price of the corporate bond one month from now must be determined. Given a yield of 8%, a coupon rate of 8%, and a remaining maturity of 29 years and 11 months, the price one month from now is 99.9892 — which is very close to par. (The price of 99.9892 was used to calculate the duration of 11.3 in the information set.)

For the corporate bond the dollar duration per 50 basis point change in rates per $100 par value given a duration of 11.3 is

(11.3%/2) × price of corporate bond at settlement date

Since the price of the corporate bond at the settlement date is 99.9892, the dollar duration per 50 basis point change in rates per $100 par value is

(11.3%/2) × $99.9892 = $5.6533

For $20 million par value, the dollar duration per 50 basis point change in rates at the settlement date is

dollar duration for corporate bond = ($20,000,000/100) × $5.6533
= $1,130,660

g. The number of futures contract to short is

$$\frac{\text{current dollar duration without futures}}{\text{dollar duration for the CTD issue}} \times \text{conversion factor for CTD issue}$$

The current dollar duration without futures is simply the dollar duration of the corporate bond (as computed in part f), $1,130,660. The dollar duration for the CTD issue (as computed part e) is $6,945.02. Since the conversion factor for the CTD issue is 1.16, then

$$\frac{\$1,130,660}{\$6,945.02} \times 1.16 = 188.8$$

Either 188 or 189 Treasury bond futures contracts will be shorted.

13. In hedging a nondeliverable security with a Treasury futures contract, it is common in constructing the hedge ratio to assume that the yield on the nondeliverable security is equal to the yield on the cheapest-to-deliver Treasury security for the futures contract plus a spread. However, this may be an inappropriate assumption in that the relative spread may change when yields increase and decrease. The yield beta is an empirical estimate of the relative change in the spread when yields change. The estimated yield beta is then used to adjust the hedge ratio or number of futures contracts by multiplying the number of futures contracts (computed without regard to the yield beta by the yield beta).

14. The dollar duration for the portfolio for a 100 basis point change in interest rates is approximately 5.2% times $1 billion or $52 million. So, for a 50 basis point change in rates, the portfolio's market value will change by about $26 million. Since the dollar duration for the Treasury bond futures contract is $4,000 for a 50 basis point change in rates, the number of futures contracts to *short* is

$$\frac{\$26,000,000}{\$4,000} = 6,500 \text{ contracts}$$

15. To compute the hedge ratio or the number of futures contracts to implement a hedge, it is necessary to compute the dollar duration of the bond to be hedged and the dollar duration of the futures contract. If these values are not computed cor-

rectly, the hedge ratio will not be correct and while the hedge may still reduce price risk, it may not eliminate the price risk exposure Mr. Elmo thought would result from the hedge. This is the first reason suggested by Ms. Rosetta.

Evaluation of the outcome of a hedge begins with an assessment of how closely the hedge locked in the target price. But there is no evidence that Mr. Elmo computed a target price. If the hedge was removed prior to the settlement date of the futures contract, the basis could have been different from the target basis projected. This is the second reason offered by Ms. Rosetta.

Finally, in constructing a hedge an assumption is made about the relative movement in the yield on the bond to be hedged and the yield for the bond underlying the futures contract. If the relationship is assumed to be constant when yields change (i.e., a yield beta of one), but that does not actually occur, then the performance of the hedge may not be as expected. If Mr. Elmo computed a yield beta but the estimated value was wrong, then the result may not be as expected. This is the third reason offered by Ms. Rosetta.

16. a. For the swap leg of the position the finance company every quarter will have to pay interest of 7.2%/4 or 1.8%. (Note that this quick calculation ignores the exact number of days in the quarter as discussed at Level II (Chapter 8).)

Each quarter the finance company receives 3-month LIBOR/4. (Again, note that the day count for each quarter is being ignored.)

The quarterly interest payment on the funds borrowed by the finance company is (3-month LIBOR + 56 basis points)/4, or 3-month LIBOR/4 + 14 basis points.

As a result of the swap, the quarterly net payments are as follows:

Quarterly interest rate received

From consumer loan portfolio (12%/4)	= 3.00%
From interest rate swap	= 3-month LIBOR/4
Total received	= 3% + 3-month LIBOR/4

Quarterly interest rate paid

To borrow funds	= 3-month LIBOR/4 + 0.14%
On interest rate swap	= 1.80%
Total paid	= 1.94% + 3-month LIBOR/4

Quarterly Outcome

To be received	= 3.00% + 3-month LIBOR/4
To be paid	= 1.94% + 3-month LIBOR/4
Spread income	= 1.06%

Thus, whatever happens to 3-month LIBOR, the finance company locks in a spread of 106 basis points in each quarter.

b. The assumption is that there are no defaults or prepayments.

17. From the perspective of the fixed-rate receiver, the position can be viewed as follows:

long a fixed-rate bond + short a floating-rate bond

The dollar duration of an interest rate swap for a floating-rate payer (fixed-rate receiver) is:

dollar duration of a swap for a fixed-rate receiver
= dollar duration of a fixed-rate bond − dollar duration of a floating-rate bond

The fixed-rate bond is effectively a bond with a coupon rate equal to the swap rate, a par amount equal to the notional amount, and a maturity equal to the remaining number of years of the swap.

Since the dollar duration of a floating-rate bond is close to zero,

dollar duration of a swap for a fixed-rate receiver
= dollar duration of a fixed-rate bond

Thus, the dollar duration of a swap for a fixed-rate receiver is simply the dollar duration of the fixed-rate bond. This means that by adding a swap to a portfolio in which the manager pays floating (receives fixed) increases the dollar duration of the portfolio.

18. a. A protective put buying strategy is used by a manager who wants to hedge against a decline in bond prices due to an anticipated rise in interest rates.
   b. With an at-the-money put option the strike price is equal to the current market price of the underlying bond. Thus the manager locks in (before the cost of purchasing the option) the current price. With an out-of-the-money put option, the strike price is less than the current market price. Consequently, the manager locks in a price that is less than the current market price. So, the manager is locking in a higher price for the bond being hedged with the strategy by buying an at-the-money rather than an out-of-the money put option. The trade-off is that an at-the-money put option costs more (for a given expiration date) than an out-of-the money put option. As a result, while there is greater protection on the downside if rates rise and the price of the bond falls by purchasing an at-the-money put option, the upside potential is reduced by more because of the higher option price that must be paid.

19. The option strategy suggested by the trustee is a covered call writing strategy. The trustee is wrong that there are no costs. The fact that a bond for which a covered call was written is called away at the strike price of the call option does not mean that there is no cost simply because the bond is in the portfolio. The covered call writer is sacrificing the upside potential of that bond. Moreover, as the portfolio manager correctly notes, the strategy is not really providing the type of protection against a rise in interest rates that one would expect from a hedge. The only protection afforded by the covered call writing strategy is the recovery of only the loss in value equal only to the option premium received. That is, there is substantial downside risk which is only offset to the extent of the option premium received.

20. a. The statement is misleading. The fact is that a premium is lost. Institutional investors may spend a considerable amount on an option to hedge a position so the statement does not make any sense. If the cost of the option is low, this means an investor will have purchased either a put option with only a short time to expiration and/or a very low strike price. If it has a low strike price, less protection is afforded with the option.
   b. This statement is wrong and suggests a lack of understanding of the difference between the purpose of using an option and futures contract to hedge. It is true

that futures can be used, but the investor who sells futures to protect against downside risk must be willing to sacrifice the upside potential. An option strategy (specifically, a protective put buying option strategy) is one in which an investor is willing to pay a price (the option price) to set a floor on the downside but maintain upside potential. The upside potential is reduced by the amount paid for the option.

21. The collar is like the protective put buying strategy in that it limits the possible losses on the portfolio if interest rates increase. Like the covered call writing strategy, the portfolio's upside potential is limited by the cost of the option. Like an unhedged position, within the range defined by the strike prices of the put and call options, the value of the portfolio varies with interest rates.

22. The strike price that Mr. Zhao seeks for the corporate issue is 90.80. Since the issue has 20 years to maturity and a coupon rate of 8% (since the bond is trading at par and the yield to maturity is 8%), the corresponding yield to maturity is 9% (from the price/yield relationship).

    Since Mr. Zhao assumes that there is a 125 basis point spread between the corporate issue and the CTD issue, this gives a yield for the CTD issue of 7.75%. Since the coupon rate of the CTD issue is 7.75%, this means that the price for the CTD issue is par (100).

    Given the price of 100 for the CTD issue, the strike price of the futures contract is found by dividing 100 by the conversion factor of the CTD issue. The strike price computed gives the strike price for the Treasury bond futures contract that is the equivalent strike price for the option on the corporate issue of 90.80. Since the conversion factor is 0.95, the strike price for the Treasury bond futures contract is 105.2631 (=100/0.95).

23. The number of options to purchase is determined as follows:

$$\text{number of options contracts} = \frac{\text{current dollar duration without options}}{\text{dollar duration of the CTD issue}}$$
$$\times \text{conversion factor for CTD}$$

    For a 50 basis point change in rates, the market value of the portfolio will change by approximately 3.5% (one half of 7%). Since the current market value is $100 million, the current dollar duration without futures is $3.5 million. Then,

$$\text{number of options contracts} = \frac{\$3,500,000}{4,500} \times 0.9 = 700$$

24. a. The portfolio manager can purchase an interest rate cap. If interest rates do rise such that the coupon rate on the floating-rate notes becomes capped, there will be a payment to the portfolio manager by the seller of the interest rate cap agreement. The cost of this protection is the premium paid for the interest rate cap agreement.

    b. The portfolio manager can purchase an interest rate floor. If interest rates do decline below the bank's funding cost, the coupon rate on the floating-rate notes will decline but there will be a payment to the portfolio manager by the seller of the interest rate floor agreement. The cost of this protection is the premium paid for on the interest rate floor agreement.

Chapter 8

CREDIT DERIVATIVES IN BOND PORTFOLIO MANAGEMENT

Mark J. P. Anson, Ph.D., CFA, C.P.A., Esq.
Senior Principal Investment Officer
CalPERS

LEARNING OUTCOME STATEMENTS

After reading this chapter you should be able to:

- explain the different types of credit risk (default risk, downgrade risk, and spread risk) and how they may adversely impact the performance of a portfolio
- identify the reasons why a seller of credit protection may be willing to assume the credit risk of an underlying financial asset or issuer.
- explain what credit options are and how they are different from standard debt options.
- identify the types of credit options: options on an underlying asset and options on a credit spread of a referenced asset.
- explain the two types of options written on an underlying asset (binary credit option and binary credit option on a credit rating).
- calculate the payoff for an option on an underlying asset.
- explain what a credit spread option is.
- calculate the payoff of a credit spread option.
- describe the two types of credit swaps: credit default swap and total return swap.
- explain how credit swaps can be used by a portfolio manager.

SECTION I
INTRODUCTION

Credit derivatives are financial instruments that are designed to transfer the credit exposure of an underlying asset or issuer between two or more parties. They are individually negotiated financial contracts that may take the form of options, forwards, or swaps where the payoffs are linked to, or derived from, the credit characteristics of the referenced asset or issuer. Credit derivatives may also be linked to an index of credit spreads. Typically, credit derivatives are cash settled contracts. A portfolio manager can use credit derivatives to either acquire or hedge credit risk.

Many asset managers have portfolios that are very sensitive to changes in the interest rate spread between riskless and risky assets and credit derivatives are an efficient way to hedge this exposure. Conversely, other asset managers may use credit derivatives to target specific exposures as a way to enhance portfolio returns. In each case, the ability to transfer credit risk and return provides a new tool to improve portfolio performance.

In their simplest form, credit derivatives may be nothing more than the purchase of credit protection. The ability to isolate credit risk and to manage it independently of underlying bond positions is the key benefit of credit derivatives. Prior to the introduction of credit derivatives, the only way to manage credit risk was to buy and sell the underlying assets. Because of transaction costs and tax issues this was an inefficient way to hedge or gain exposure.

Credit derivatives, therefore, represent a natural extension of the financial markets to unbundle the risk and return buckets associated with a particular financial asset, such as credit risk. They offer an important method for managers to hedge their exposure to credit risk because they permit the transfer of the exposure from one party to another. Credit derivatives allow for an efficient exchange of credit exposure in return for credit protection.

We begin this chapter with a short discussion on the importance of credit risk. We then review three main types of credit derivatives: credit options, credit forwards, and credit swaps.[1] In each case, we describe their structure and then consider their practical applications.

SECTION II
WHY CREDIT RISK IS IMPORTANT

A fixed income debt instrument represents a basket of risks. There is the risk from changes in interest rates (duration and convexity risk), the risk that the issuer will refinance the debt issue (call risk) and lastly, the risk of defaults, downgrades, and widening credit spreads (credit risk). The total return from a fixed income investment such as a corporate or government bond is the compensation for assuming all of these risks. Depending upon the rating on the underlying debt instrument, the return from credit risk can be a significant part of a bond's total return.

A. Types of Credit Risk

Credit risk may affect a portfolio in three ways: default risk, credit spread risk, and downgrade risk. Each can have a detrimental impact on the value of a fixed income portfolio.

1. Default Risk

Default risk is the risk that the issuer will default on its obligations. The default rate on credit risky bonds can be quite high. For example, recent estimates of the default

---

[1] A fourth type of credit derivative is a special purpose vehicle such as a collateralized bond obligation or a collateralized loan obligation. For a complete discussion of these types of credit derivatives, see Chapter 4 in Mark Anson, *Credit Derivatives* (New Hope, PA: Frank J. Fabozzi Associates, 1999).

rates for high-yield bonds in the United States range from 3.17% to 6.25%.[2] World-wide, in 1999, a total of 106 Moody's Investor Services rated bonds defaulted on a total of $35.6 billion of long-term publicly held corporate and sovereign debt. Within the United States, 99 issuers representing $23.5 billion defaulted in 1999.[3] The greatest default rate in the United States occurred during the Great Depression in the 1930s. In 1932, the default rate for corporate bonds reached 9.2%.[4]

Credit derivatives, therefore, appeal to managers who invest in high-yield or "junk" bonds, real estate, or other credit dependent assets. The possibility of default is a significant risk for managers, and one that can be effectively hedged by shifting the credit exposure.

2. Credit Spread Risk

Credit spread risk is the risk that the interest rate spread for a risky bond over a risk-less bond will increase after the risky bond has been purchased. For instance, in the United States, U.S Treasury bonds are generally considered to be without credit risk (default free). Therefore, corporate bonds and the debt of foreign governments are typically priced at a spread to comparable U.S. Treasury bonds. Should this spread widen after purchase of the credit risky bond, the value of the bond would decline. Credit spreads can widen based on macroeconomic events in the domestic or global financial markets.

As an example, in the summer of 1998, the turmoil in the emerging markets caused by the default of the Russian government on its sovereign debt spilled over into the U.S. stock markets causing a significant decline in financial stocks.[5] The turbulence in the financial markets, both domestically and worldwide, resulted in a "flight to safety" of investment capital. In other words, investors sought safer havens of investment to avoid further losses and volatility. This flight to safety resulted in a significant increase in credit spreads of corporate and foreign government bonds compared to U.S. Treasuries.

Consider Exhibit 1. This exhibit presents the values of the monthly price value of J.P. Morgan's Emerging Market Bond Index (EMBI). EMBI is a weighted average of the returns to sovereign bonds for 15 emerging market countries from Latin America, Eastern Europe, and Asia. As Exhibit 1 demonstrates, the performance of the EMBI index was generally positive for most of 1997, with a total return of more than 18% for the first three quarters of 1997. However, this good performance soured dramatically in the month of October. October 1997 was the beginning of the "Asian Contagion," a dramatic decline in the economic development of the Southeast Asian economies that began with the devaluation of the Thai currency. From a high of about 170 points at the beginning of October, the index tumbled to 149 by the beginning of November, a decline of over 12.4%. In the space of about one month, the declining fortunes of a broad sample of emerging market sovereign wiped out most of the gains which had been earned over the 9 previous months.

---

[2] Edward Altman, "Measuring Corporate Bond Mortality and Performance," *The Journal of Finance* (June 1991), pp. 909-922; and Gabriella Petrucci, "High-Yield Review — First-Half 1997," Salomon Brothers Corporate Bond Research (August 1997).

[3] Moody's Investor Services Global Credit Research, Special Comment, "Historical Default Rates of Corporate Bond Issuers, 1920-1999," January 2000.

[4] "Historical Default Rates of Corporate Bond Issuers, 1920-1999."

[5] For instance, in the months of July and August 1998, the Dow Jones Industrial Average declined by 15% in value.

Exhibit 1: JP Morgan Emerging Markets Bond Index (EMBI)

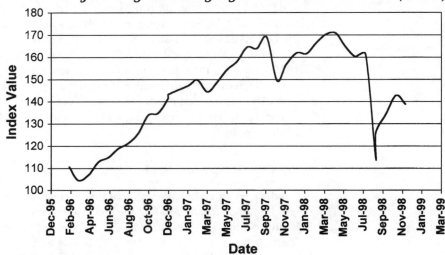

However, credit risk is not all one sided. Even though there was a rapid decline in the credit quality of emerging market sovereign debt in 1997, such a steep retreat presented opportunities for credit quality improvement. Exhibit 1 demonstrates that, from a low of about 149 points at the beginning of November 1997, the EMBI index rebounded back to a value of 172 by the end of March 1998, a gain of over 15.4%. Those investors who chose to include emerging debt in their portfolios in the first quarter of 1998 earned excellent returns. In fact the returns to EMBI for the first quarter of 1998 outperformed the S&P500 and U.S. Treasury Bonds.

Even so, this recovery was short lived. In the second quarter of 1998, emerging market debt resumed its downward slide. Furthermore, credit spreads over a comparable U.S. Treasury bond for emerging market nations widened considerably from 1997 to 1998.

For example, consider a Russian Government 10% bond due in 2007. In July 1997 when this bond was issued, its credit spread over a comparable U.S. Treasury bond was 3.50%. As of July 1998, this credit spread had increased to 9.25%, an increase of 5.75%. In fact, the change in credit spread was so large it was even greater than the yield of a 30-year U.S. Treasury bond in July 1998.

The Russian bond was sold with a coupon of 10% in July 1997. In July 1998 the credit spread was 9.25%, the Russian bond had 9 remaining annual coupon payments, and a final balloon payment of $1,000 at maturity. The rate on a 9 year U.S Treasury bond was 5.8% in July 1998. Based on this information the current value of the bond in 1998 was $759.46, a decline of $240.53, or 24% of its face value in one year's time.

Despite this decline, those investors who sold their Russian government bonds at the beginning of July 1998 and took a 24% loss counted themselves fortunate. By the end of July 1998, the Russian economy suffered a total collapse and the spread for Russian bonds over U.S. Treasury bonds increased to 53%! Russian government bonds were written down to 10 cents on the dollar, and banks, hedge funds, and other financial institutions lost billions of dollars.[6] Additionally, shockwaves

---

[6] "Financial Firms Lose $8 Billion so Far," *The Wall Street Journal* (September 3, 1998), p. A2.

reverberated throughout the emerging markets and the EMBI index declined by 27% in August 1998 (see Exhibit 1).

3. Downgrade Risk

Downgrade risk occurs when a nationally recognized statistical rating organization such Standard & Poor's, Moody's Investors Services, Duff & Phelps, or Fitch IBCA reduces its outstanding credit rating for an issuer based on an evaluation of that issuer's current earning power versus its capacity to pay its fixed income obligations as they become due.

B. Reasons for Selling Credit Protection

There are a number of reasons why a seller of credit protection may be willing to assume the credit risk of an underlying financial asset or issuer. For instance, in 1997 there were more credit rating upgrades than downgrades. Through the first half of 1997 a total $23.2 billion of corporate bonds were upgraded compared to a total of $14.7 billion that were downgraded.[7] One reason for the net credit rating upgrades was a strong stock market that encouraged public offerings of stock by credit risky companies. A large portion of these equity financings were used to reduce outstanding costly debt, resulting in improved balance sheets and credit ratings for the issuers. A second reason for the net upgrades was a strong economy that contributed to superior operating results for domestic corporations. Consequently, asset managers had ample opportunity in 1997 to target specific credit risks that benefited from a ratings upgrade.

In addition to credit upgrades, there are other events that have a positive effect on credit risky bonds. Mergers and acquisitions, for instance, are a frequent occurrence in the high yield market. Even though a credit risky issuer may have a low debt rating, it may have valuable technology worth acquiring. High yield issuers tend to be small to mid-cap companies with viable products and growing cash flows. Consequently, they make attractive takeover candidates for financially mature companies.

Lastly, with a strong economy, banks have been willing to provide term loans to high-yield companies at more attractive rates than the bond markets. Consequently, it has been advantageous for credit risky companies to redeem their high yield bonds and replace the bonds with a lower cost term loan. The resulting premium for redemption of high yield bonds is a positive credit event that enhances portfolio returns.

SECTION III CREDIT OPTIONS

Credit options are different from standard debt options because while the latter is designed to protect against market risk (i.e., interest rate risk), credit options are constructed to protect against credit risk. Thus, the purpose of credit options is to price credit risk independently of interest rate risk. Credit options may be written on an underlying asset or on a spread over a referenced riskless asset. These two types of options — one triggered by a decline in the value of an asset and one triggered by the change in the asset's spread over a comparable risk-free rate — have different payout structures.[8]

---

[7] Peter Acciavatti and Robert Manowitz, "1997 High Yield Semi-Annual Review" (New York: Chase Securities Inc., 1997), p. A-83.

[8] Note that credit options are different from options on credit risky assets. In the latter case, these options are on the outright asset, but the asset is subject to credit risk, i.e., the issuer may default on the security. Conversely, credit options recognize the possibility of default and construct the payoff on the option to be a function of the decline in asset value due to default. For a thorough analysis of options on credit risky assets, see Robert Jarrow and Stuart Turnbull, "Pricing Derivatives on Financial Assets Subject to Credit Risk," *The Journal of Finance* (March 1995), pp. 53-85.

A. Credit Options Written on an Underlying Asset

There are two types of credit options written on an underlying asset:

- binary credit option with a predetermined payout
- binary credit option based on a credit rating

1. Binary Credit Option

A **binary credit option** is the simplest form of credit protection. The option seller will pay out a fixed sum if and when a default event occurs with respect to a referenced credit (e.g., the underlying issuer is unable to pay its obligations as they become due). Therefore, a binary option represents two states of the world: default or no default. It is the clearest example of credit protection. At maturity of the option, if the referenced credit has defaulted, the option holder receives a predetermined payout. If there is no default at maturity of the option, the option buyer receives nothing and forgoes the option premium. A binary credit option could also be triggered by a ratings downgrade.

A **European binary credit option** pays out a fixed sum only at maturity and only if the referenced credit is in default. An **American binary option** can be exercised at any time during its life. Consequently, if an American binary credit option is in the money (a default event has occurred), it will be exercised immediately because delaying exercise will reduce the present value of the fixed payment.

Instead of waiting for an actual default to occur, the strike price of the option can be set to a minimum net worth of the underlying issuer below which default is probable. For instance, a credit put option can be set so that if the book value of the referenced credit (assets − liabilities) declines to a certain level say, $100 million, then the binary credit option will be in the money.

2. Binary Credit Options Based on a Credit Rating

A binary credit option can have a pay off that depends on the credit rating of the issue. These types of credit options can be embedded in an issue. We'll illustrate a binary credit option (both a put and call) based on a credit rating that is embedded in an issue below.

a. Illustration

In January 1998 bondholders forced the International Finance Corporation of Thailand (IFCT bonds) to pay back $500 million in bonds several years before their maturity. (The IFCT is a government sponsored bank.) The bond issue contained a put provision that allowed investors to put the bonds back to the issuer at face value if the sovereign credit rating of Thailand fell below investment grade.

This is an example of a bond with an embedded binary credit put option. The bonds became putable when the sovereign rating of Thailand fell to Ba1. This option was in the money and exercisable only if the credit rating of Thailand declined to below investment grade. Otherwise, it paid nothing.

Mathematically, this binary put option (on the entire bond issue) looked like this:

$$P[V(t);\$500,000,000] = \begin{cases} \$500,000,000 - V(t) \text{ if the credit rating falls} \\ \qquad\qquad\qquad \text{below investment grade} \\ \$0 \text{ if the credit rating remains investment grade} \end{cases} \quad (1)$$

where $500,000,000 is the face value of the IFCT bonds and $V(t)$ is the market value of the IFCT bonds at time t.

Exhibit 2: Binary Credit Put Option on $500 Million of IFCT Bonds

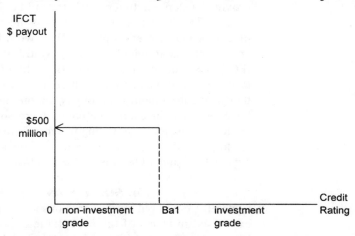

In equation (1), the conditions for the binary payout are specified (investment grade/not investment grade) but the payout to the binary put option is unknown. The option holder does not know in advance at what value the IFCT bonds will trade if the sovereign risk of Thailand declines below investment grade. Therefore, to provide adequate protection, the bondholders received a binary put option whose value was measured as the difference between the face value of the bonds of $500,000,000 and the market value of the bonds at the time Thailand's credit rating declined below investment grade. Exhibit 2 demonstrates this binary credit put option.

In addition to the binary credit put option, investors in the IFCT bonds received 50 basis points in additional coupon income per period should the bonds fall two rungs in credit rating from issue, and an additional 25 basis points per period for each additional rating downgrade until the below investment grade threshold was reached. The ability to earn higher coupons as the credit rating of Thailand deteriorated is the same as a series of binary *call* options, initially triggered by a ratings downgrade of two notches.

To see this, remember that a call option is the right to receive a payoff if the option is in the money at the time of exercise. In this case, at the time of Thailand's ratings downgrades, the bondholders had the right to *call* for additional coupon income equal to 50 basis points initially (for the first two notches of credit downgrades) and then 25 basis points thereafter.

Mathematically, the first binary credit call option can be represented as:

$$C[CR(t);ICR] = \begin{cases} \$2,500,000 \text{ if } CR(t) \text{ is two grades below ICR} \\ \$0 \text{ if } CR(t) \text{ is not two grades below ICR} \end{cases} \quad (2)$$

where $CR(t)$ is the credit rating of Thailand at time t and ICR is the initial credit rating of Thailand at the time of bond issuance. The payoff if the credit rating is two notches below the initial credit rating is:

$$0.005 \times \$500,000,000 = \$2,500,000$$

Equation (2) is different than equation (1) in that the payout to the binary credit call options is known in advance. After the first binary credit call option has been exercised and paid, each remaining binary credit call option would pay $1,250,000 with each additional ratings downgrade up to point of the exercise of the binary credit put option for the face value amount of the bonds. These series of binary credit options provided a step function payoff stream like the one presented in Exhibit 3.

The investors who purchased these IFCT bonds bought a cash instrument plus a basket of credit options. Why would the IFCT issue bonds with a basket of credit options attached, and why would investors want to purchase them? For the IFCT, the issue was one of cost. By selling a basket of binary credit options attached to its bonds, it was able to reduce its funding costs by over 100 basis points. Even though it subsequently had to pay out on the options, initially, its funding costs were lower. From an investor standpoint, the reason for purchasing the issue was credit protection. Investors were willing to accept a lower coupon payment upfront in return for credit protection against downgrades. Given the meltdown in the Asian financial markets in 1997 and 1998, it is a safe conclusion that investors made the better deal.

b. Strike Price for a Credit Put Option

Generally, credit put options are not specified in binary terms. Instead they are usually expressed in terms of the acceptable default spread of the bond in question. For instance, with respect to a high-yield bond, upon exercise of the credit option, the payoff is determined by subtracting the market price of the bond from the strike price, where the strike price is determined by taking the present value of the bond's cash flows discounted at the risk-free rate plus the strike credit spread over the remaining life of the outstanding bond.

Mathematically, the payoff is determined by the following formula:

$$P[D(t); K] = Max [0, K - D(t)] \tag{3}$$

where

$D(t)$ = the market value of the debt at the maturity of the option
K = strike price determined by:
$$C1/(1 + r + s)^{t1} + C2/(1 + r + s)^{t2} + \ldots F/(1 + r + s)^{T-t}$$

Exhibit 3: Credit Call Options on the IFCT Credit Rating

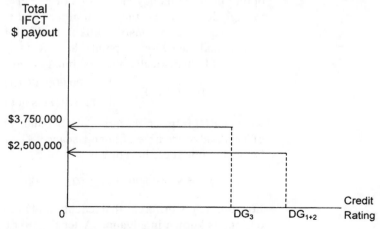

DG_{1+2} indicates the first two credit downgrades
DG_3 indicates the third downgrade

$C1$, $C2$, … are the remaining coupons to be paid on the bond at the maturity of the credit option and $t1,t2$, … are the intermediate times that the remaining coupons are paid

t = the maturity of the credit put option

$T-t$ = the time remaining until the maturity of the bond

r = the riskless rate

s = the specified (strike) credit spread over the riskless rate

F = the face or maturity value of the bond

c. Credit Put Option on a Sovereign Debt

Considering the credit risk of the emerging markets, let's take the example of a credit spread put option on the Venezuela 9.125% 2007 bonds. Although Venezuela is far from the more extreme examples of emerging market credit deterioration (compared to Russia, for instance), it does provide a good example of what an emerging market recession can do to credit spreads.

Venezuela receives significant foreign exchange revenues from the sale of oil. Venezuela is the third largest oil producing nation in OPEC; its economy is dependent upon the price of oil in world commodity markets. However, an economic slowdown throughout Asia in 1997 and 1998 coupled with an increase in global oil production led to a collapse of crude oil prices during this time period. This in turn led to shrinking oil revenues for Venezuela and a declining credit rating.

When offered at par in 1997, the spread for these bonds was 250 basis points over a comparable U.S. Treasury bond. In March 1998, a brokerage house offered to sell a European credit put option on these bonds at an exercise price to be calculated using a credit spread of 400 basis points over a comparable U.S. Treasury bond. The option's tenor was 3 months and the price was 60 basis points of the notional amount being hedged. If the credit spread on the Venezuela bonds increased above 400 basis points, the option would be in the money and the bondholder could put the bond to the broker-dealer at an exercise price determined by a credit spread of 400 basis points.

Suppose this option was purchased on April 1, 1998 with a maturity date three months later on July 1, 1998. At that time of purchase, the credit spread for these bonds was 329 basis points. Assume that the notional amount of the option was $10 million of face value Venezuela bonds, and that on July 1 the value of the Venezuela bonds would be determined by taking the present value of the 9 remaining annual coupons of $912,500 plus the present value of the final $10,000,000 balloon payment plus the current coupon due and payable of $912,500.

The strike credit spread was set on April 1 at 400 basis points but the strike price, K, of the put option was not determined until the maturity of the option on July 1 using a referenced U.S Treasury rate of 5.9%. Using the value for K in equation (3), the strike price of the credit put option was $10,464,395.

By July 1998 the credit spread for the Venezuelan bonds had increased to 467 basis points, while the U.S Treasury market had remained relatively stable. Using the same reference Treasury rate of 5.9% and a credit spread of 467 basis points, the price of the Venezuelan bonds on July 1, 1998 was $10,098,846. At maturity the credit spread put option was in the money by $365,549 ($10,464,395 − $10,098,846). The cost of the option was 60 basis points, or $60,000, so that the net profit was $305,549. This option is demonstrated in Exhibit 4.

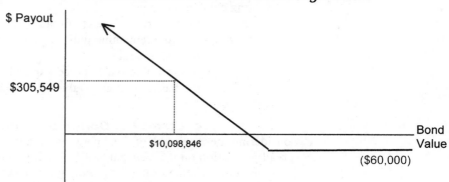

Exhibit 4: Credit Put Option on
Venezuelan 9.125% '07 Sovereign Bond

As 1997 and 1998 demonstrated, the emerging market debt market is an uncertain and volatile place. Credit spreads can change dramatically in a very short period of time. Not only did the credit spread put option provide an economic gain, it also reduced uncertainty. If there had been a dramatic collapse of Venezuela's credit quality, the put option would have provided even more insurance. As it was, the option could have provided peace of mind for an emerging markets portfolio manager as well as providing her with some additional portfolio income.

There is one problem with valuing credit options in the form of equation (3). This equation assumes constant market risk, i.e., that interest rate volatility is not essential. In other words, credit options are dependent upon the value of the firm's (or sovereign's) assets and not that of interest rates. If the option has a relatively short maturity, the simplifying assumption that interest rates are constant is not crucial to the valuation of the option, but for longer term options, the assumption that interest rates remain constant may be unrealistic.

Consider the example of the Venezuelan bonds from above. Suppose that during the life of the credit put option, the risk free rate, r, declined while the credit spread, s, increased by the exact same amount. The value of the outstanding bond would not change even though the credit risk of the bond had increased because the bond's discount rate, the value of $r + s$, had not changed. Under this scenario, the credit put option would offer little credit protection. However, empirical evidence indicates that high-yield bonds are less sensitive to interest rate changes than high-grade bonds and are more sensitive to changes in the value of the firm than high-grade bonds.[9]

d. The Value of Credit Put Options

If the credit put option is written on a corporate bond, it can be observed that the option will be a decreasing function of firm value. As the value of the firm increases, the credit rating on the outstanding debt is also expected to increase and the value of the put option decreases. In fact, the credit option becomes almost worthless when firm value is high enough because the outstanding debt becomes almost credit risk

---

[9] B. Cornell and K. Green, "The Investment Performance of Low Grade Bond Funds," *The Journal of Finance* (March 1991).

free. However, the value of a credit put option increases with the expected volatility of a firm's value for two reasons. As the volatility of the firm's assets increases, the value of outstanding bonds decrease and the value of the put option increases. Additionally, an increase in volatility has the same value enhancing impact in option pricing models as higher volatility has on the value of a put option on the firm's common stock.[10]

3. Uses of Credit Options Written on an Underlying Asset

Credit derivatives may also be used to exploit inefficiencies in the market when there is imperfect correlation between stock prices and interest rates. For instance, when interest rates and stock prices are negatively correlated, corporate debt values may be higher than when the correlation is positive. Credit spreads in the market may not correctly reflect the correlations between stocks and the term structure of interest rates. As a result, investors may hold a portfolio of corporate bonds and credit derivatives, which may cost less than equivalent riskless debt yet offer the same risk and return characteristics.

Credit options may also be used in conjunction with other derivative transactions. For instance, with respect to over-the-counter derivatives such as swaps and off-exchange options, downgrade provisions in the derivative documentation can protect a derivative buyer from credit risk. However, the buyer must be able to establish a downgrade trigger at some point before the counterparty is in the throes of financial distress. Additionally, the downgrade trigger provision terminates the transaction; a credit option hedges the credit exposure but does not automatically truncate the transaction cash flows because it is designed to provide financial security (a cash payment) rather than legal security (termination of a contract).

B. Credit Spread Options

The second type of credit option is a call option on the level of the credit spread over a referenced benchmark such as U.S. Treasury securities. If the credit spread widens, the referenced asset will decline in value, but the option will increase in value. This type of credit option is structured so that the option is in-the-money when the credit spread exceeds the specified spread level.

1. Payoff Function for a Credit Spread Call Option

The payoff is determined by taking the difference in the credit spreads multiplied by a specified notional amount and by a risk factor. In a mathematical format, the payoff at maturity of the option may be specified as:

$$C[\text{spread}(t); K] = (\text{spread} - K) \times \text{notional amount} \times \text{risk factor} \qquad (4)$$

where spread(t) is the spread for the financial asset over the risk-free rate at the maturity of the option at time t; K is the specified strike spread for the financial asset over the risk-free rate; notional amount is a contractually specified dollar amount; and the risk factor is based on the interest rate sensitivity of the unsecured debt and represents the dollar value of a 1 basis point change in the credit spread.[11]

---

[10] In practice, the pricing of credit options is quite complicated and beyond the scope of this chapter.

[11] The risk factor is determined by the standard measures of duration and convexity provided at Level I (Chapter 7).

A credit spread call option answers the issue we raised with respect to credit put options in the previous section. Recall that one problem with credit put options is that they implicitly assume that the risk-free rate, r, remains constant. However, notice that in equation (4), the risk-free rate, r, does not appear. Equation (4) is independent of the general level of interest rates. Instead, it is only dependent on the change in the credit spread. Therefore, fluctuations in the level of the risk-free rate will not affect the value of equation (4).

The risk factor is determined by the sensitivity of the underlying financial asset to changes in interest rates. This sensitivity is measured by duration and convexity as explained at Level I (Chapter 7).

To illustrate a credit spread call option, consider the BB rated, 7.75 Niagra Mohawk Power bond due in 2008. In September 1998, this bond was trading at a price of $104.77 with a yield to maturity around 7.08%. Using the formula for duration and convexity measures given at Level I (Chapter 7), the duration for this bond is 6.96 and its convexity measure is 31.241.[12]

At the time that this bond was offering a yield of 7.08%, the 10-year Treasury bond was yielding about 5.3% for a credit spread of 178 basis points. This was a very narrow spread considering Niagra Mohawk Power's BB credit rating. Perhaps the market was implying that the credit risk of Niagra Mohawk was closer to BBB than BB. Alternatively, it could be that the market overvalued the bond.

If a portfolio manager believed that the bond was overvalued she could purchase a credit spread option struck at 178 basis points. This is the same as the portfolio manager expressing a view that the price of the referenced asset is inflated at the current market spread, and she expects the credit spread to widen out to more normal levels.

Suppose that the portfolio manager believes that the credit spread for this bond will increase to 250 basis points during the course of the next year. She can purchase a $20,000,000 notional at-the-money call option on the credit spread between the debt of Niagra Mohawk Power and U.S. Treasuries. The tenor of the option is one year, the premium costs 125 basis points, and the risk factor is 6.65. At maturity of the option, the portfolio manager will receive:

(change in credit spread) × (notional amount) × (risk factor)

If the credit spread does indeed widen to 250 basis points at maturity of the option, the portfolio manager will earn:

$$(0.0072 \times \$20,000,000 \times 6.65) - \$250,000 = \$707,600$$

This payout is demonstrated in Exhibit 5.

2. Credit Spreads from a Macro and Microeconomic View

Credit spreads can be reviewed from either a macroeconomic or microeconomic analysis. Under a macroeconomic view, a slowdown in the economy can lead to a flight of capital to more secure investments such as U.S. Treasury securities, resulting in wider credit spreads across all securities. Under a microeconomic analysis, a buyer of a credit option can express the view that the credit quality of the underlying referenced issuer will decline due to poor operating performance. In either scenario, the price of the referenced asset "cheapens" relative to U.S. Treasury securities.

---

[12] Recall from Level I (Chapter 7) that there are scaling issues associated with calculating a convexity measure. Regardless of how it is computed, the same risk factor of 6.65 is obtained for a 100 basis point change in rates.

Exhibit 5: Credit Call Option
Niagra Mohawk Power Option Struck at 178 Basis Points

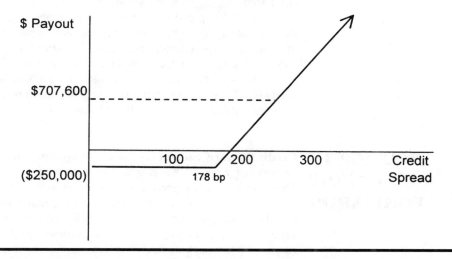

3. Credit Spread Options as an Income Enhancement Tool

Alternatively, credit spread options may be used as income enhancement tools. For instance, a portfolio manager may believe that the credit spread for Company A will not exceed 300 basis points. To monetize this view, she can sell a put option on the credit spread with the strike set at 300 basis points. Additionally, the portfolio manager can agree to physically settle the option. In effect, the portfolio manager has agreed to buy the debt of Company A at a spread to U.S. Treasuries of 300 basis points — her targeted purchase price — and she can use the premium received from the sale of the credit option to finance the purchase price should the put be exercised.

Furthermore, by selling a put option on a credit spread an investor can capitalize on a higher credit spread volatility than on a sale of the yield volatility for the same bond.[13] Higher spread volatility is the result of the less than perfect correlation between the referenced debt and the comparable Treasury bond. Therefore, an investor can receive a higher put premium by selling richer spread volatility than selling a put on the underlying debt.

4. Credit Spread Call Options are Relative Value Options

The value of a credit spread call option is not derived from the absolute price change of the underlying referenced asset, but rather from the price change of the referenced asset relative to U.S. Treasury securities. By purchasing a call option on the credit spread between the referenced asset and U.S. Treasuries, the option is in the money only if the price of the referenced asset declines more than the prices of U.S. Treasury securities (i.e., the credit spread widens).

Credit spread options are therefore, **underperformance options**. Similar to outperformance options where the payoff is contingent on the relative outperformance

---

[13] Bjorn Flesaker, Lane Hughston, Laurence Schreiber, and Lloyd Sprung, "Taking All the Credit," *Risk* (September 1994), pp. 104-108.

of one referenced asset over a second referenced asset, the payoff of a credit spread call option is contingent upon the relative underperformance of a referenced asset compared to U.S. Treasury securities.

Credit spread options are not designed to protect against market risk such as interest rate spikes where both the Treasury security and the referenced asset decline in value at the same time. Instead, credit options are another form of insurance against a credit decline in the referenced asset or issuer. This strategy can be used to protect the value of an existing portfolio position should its spread relative to U.S. Treasuries increase. However, this type of option will not protect against an absolute decline in value of the referenced asset if the value of U.S. Treasury securities also decline.

SECTION IV CREDIT FORWARDS

Credit forward contracts, like credit options, are an essential building block in the derivatives market. They may be contracted either on bond values or on credit spreads. They can be used by portfolio managers who wish to purchase credit exposure.

Consider the example of a portfolio manager who, in July 1999, wants to protect the appreciated value of her portfolio earned year-to-date. Macroeconomic events such as the "Asian Contagion" in October 1997 and the Russian debt default in August 1998 can thoroughly undermine the performance of spread products such as high-yield bonds (see Exhibit 1). Therefore, to protect the year-to-date gains earned in the investment portfolio, the manager purchases a credit forward contract custom-tailored to the economic parameters of her high-yield portfolio.

If high-yield credit spreads increase, the credit forward will increase in value while the investment portfolio will decline in value. Assume that the average credit spread for the portfolio is 300 basis points over comparable U.S. Treasury securities. Also assume that the risk factor for the overall investment portfolio is 3 years, and the value of the portfolio to be protected is $100 million.

The manager purchases a 5-month credit forward with a credit spread of 300 basis points over benchmark Treasury bonds.[14] If the credit spread of the investment portfolio increases above 300 basis points by the end of December, the portfolio manager will receive a positive payment on the credit forward contract. However, if the credit spread declines, the portfolio manager must make a payment to the credit forward seller. The exact payment amount at maturity of the credit forward is determined by the following equation:

$$[\text{credit spread at maturity} - \text{contracted credit spread}]$$
$$\times \text{risk factor} \times \text{notional amount} \qquad (5)$$

where credit spread at maturity is the observable market spread at maturity of the credit forward; the contracted credit spread is the spread established at the outset of the forward agreement; the risk factor is determined by factors of duration and convexity as discussed earlier; and the notional amount is the dollar amount of economic exposure.

Assume that, in fact, another credit crisis sends high yield spreads to 400 basis points over comparable U.S. Treasury bonds by the end of 1999. At maturity of the credit forward contract, the manager will receive a payment equal to:

$$[4\% - 3\%] \times 3 \times \$100,000,000 = \$3,000,000$$

---

[14] The credit spread embedded in the credit forward can be linked to a similar portfolio of high-yield bonds, a credit spread index (see below), or even a single bond. For the sake of our example, we make the simplifying assumption that the underlying credit spread in the forward contract matches that of the investment portfolio.

Exhibit 6: Credit Forward

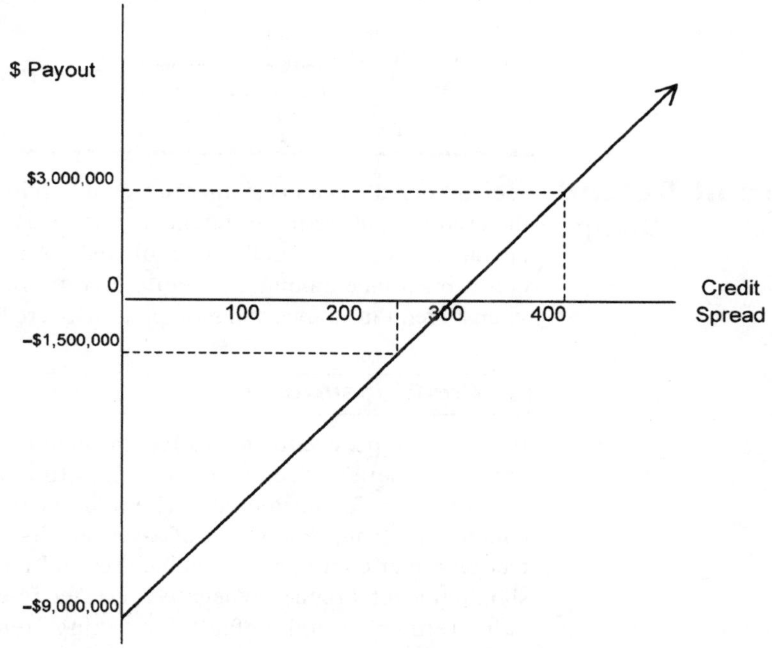

However, if the credit spread declined by 50 basis points at maturity of the credit forward, the manager would pay:

$$[2.5\% - 3\%] \times 3 \times \$100,000,000 = -\$1,500,000$$

Exhibit 6 demonstrates the payout for a credit forward.

This example of credit forwards highlights an essential difference between all forward and option contracts. The purchaser of a forward contract receives the upside appreciation of the underlying asset, but also shares in its depreciation. In the example above, the portfolio manager is required to make a payment to the credit forward seller if the credit spread on the investment portfolio narrows. In the unlikely event that the credit spread narrowed to zero, the maximum the portfolio manager would have to pay is $9,000,000. In contrast, the purchase of an option allows the investor to profit from her position but limits her downside loss to the option premium paid.

Exhibit 6 also demonstrates the symmetric payoff pattern to a forward contract. The portfolio manager shares in both the upside and the downside of the credit spread. Compare this pattern to those presented in Exhibits 4 and 5 where the payoff to a credit spread is asymmetric. In those exhibits, the manager is limited in the downside to the extent of the option premium paid.

SECTION V
CREDIT SWAPS

There are two different types of credit swaps: **credit default swaps** and **total return swaps**. Credit default swaps are used to shift credit exposure to a credit protection seller. They have a similar economic effect to credit options discussed in Section III. Total return credit swaps are a way to increase an investor's exposure to credit risk and the returns commensurate with that risk.

Exhibit 7: Credit Default Swap with a Cash Payment Upon Default

A. Credit Default Swaps

A credit default swap is similar to a credit option in that its primary purpose is to hedge the credit exposure to a referenced asset or issuer. In this sense, credit default swaps operate much like a standby letter of credit. A credit default swap is the simplest form of credit insurance among all credit derivatives. There are two types of credit default swaps: credit insurance and swapping risky credit payments for certain fixed payments.

1. Credit Insurance

In the first type, **credit insurance**, the credit protection buyer pays a fee to the credit protection seller in return for the right to receive a payment conditional upon the default of a referenced credit. The referenced credit can be a single asset, such as a commercial loan, or a basket of assets, such as a junk bond portfolio. The credit protection buyer continues to receive the total return on the referenced asset. However, should this total return be negative, i.e., the referenced basket of assets has declined in value (either through defaults, widening credit spreads, or downgrades), the total return receiver will receive a payment from the credit protection seller.

In simple terms, the credit protection buyer purchases an insurance contract. She pays an annual or quarterly premium to the credit protection seller in return for insurance against a credit event. This type of swap is presented in Exhibit 7.

The pricing of a credit default swap on a single high yield bond is reasonably straightforward. The credit protection seller uses the probability of default and the expected recovery value to determine the expected payout in the event of default. The price of the credit default swap is then equal to the discounted value of that expected payout. Pricing of credit default swaps on a basket of assets, however, remains problematic. The pricing depends not only on the credit quality of the individual assets in the baskets, but also on the default correlation among the assets in the baskets. Unfortunately, default correlations are not directly observable, and consequently, there is no satisfactory pricing model.

Mechanically, the contractual documentation for a one period credit default swap will identify the referenced asset, its initial value (V_0), the time to maturity of the swap (T), and a referenced payment rate (R). The payment R may be a single bullet payment or can be a floating-rate benchmarked to LIBOR. At maturity, if the value of the asset has declined, the credit protection buyer receives a payment of $V_0 - V_T$ from the credit protection seller and pays the referenced payment rate R. If the value of the referenced asset has increased in value, the credit protection buyer receives the value $V_T - V_0$ from the underlying asset and pays R. In this simple one period example, the credit default swap acts very much like a credit put option described in Section III. However, for multi-period transactions, there are two differences between a credit default swap and a put option.

First, the credit protection buyer can pay for the protection premium over several settlement dates, t_1 through time T instead of paying an option premium up front. Second, the credit protection buyer can receive payments $V_{t2} - V_{t1}$ at intermediate settlement dates where $t2 \leq T$ and $0 \leq t1 < t2$. Therefore, if the value of the referenced asset continues to deteriorate, the credit protection buyer may receive several payments.

2. Swapping Risky Credit Payments for Certain Fixed Payments

Alternatively, an investor can agree to swap the total return on a credit risky asset in return for periodic payments from the credit protection seller. The investor gives up the uncertain returns associated with the credit risky asset for a negotiated payment from the credit protection seller. This payment is usually in the form of LIBOR plus a spread. If the credit risky asset declines in value, the investor will be reimbursed for the decline plus she will receive a periodic payment from the seller. This type of credit default swap is presented in Exhibit 8.

Economically, a credit default swap is the same as shorting a bond. The investor gains if the bond declines in value because the dealer is obligated to reimburse the Investor for the negative total return. Conversely, if the bond increases in value, the investor must pay this amount to the dealer.

Default swaps usually contain a minimum threshold or materiality clause requiring that the decline in the referenced credit be significant and confirmed by an objective source.[15] This can be as simple as a credit downgrade by a nationally recognized statistical rating organization or a percentage decline in market value of the asset. Additionally, the payment by the credit protection seller can be set to incorporate a recovery rate on the referenced asset. This value may be determined by the market price of the defaulted asset several months after the actual default.

Large banks are the natural dealers for credit default swaps because it is consistent with their letter of credit business. On the one hand, banks may sell credit default swaps as a natural extension of their credit protection business. Alternatively, a bank may use a credit swap to hedge its exposure to a referenced credit that is a customer of the bank. In this way the bank can limit its exposure to the client without physically transferring the client's loans off its balance sheet. Therefore the bank can protect its exposure without disturbing its relationship with its client.

Additionally, banks can simultaneously be buyers and sellers of credit default swaps. A bank may buy a credit default swap on one customer's loan account and sell a credit default swap in another industry or geographic region. The bank can increase the diversification of its loan portfolio and gain exposure to other credit markets without the commitment of additional capital.

Portfolio managers can even exchange credit risks through credit default swaps. Consider Exhibit 9. This illustrates a two-way default swap where Investor 1 swaps the default risk of Bond A for the credit risk of Bond B in Investor 2's portfolio. If a credit event of one of the bonds occurs, the credit protection seller with respect to that bond will make a contingent payment to the other party.

Exhibit 8: Credit Default Swap with a Periodic Payment

---

[15] See Chapter 7 in Anson, *Credit Derivatives*, for a review of the contractual documentation associated with a credit derivative transaction.

Exhibit 9: Reciprocal Credit Default Swap

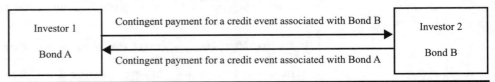

The methods used to determine the amount of the payment obligated of the credit protection seller under the swap agreement may vary greatly. For instance, a credit default swap can specify at contract date the exact amount of payment that will be made by the swap seller should the referenced credit party default. Conversely, the default swap can be structured so that the amount of the swap payment by the seller is determined after the default event. Under these circumstances, the amount payable by the swap seller is determined based upon the observed prices of similar debt obligations of the borrower in the bond market. Lastly, the swap can be documented much like a credit put option where the amount to be paid by the credit protection seller is an established strike price less the current market value of the referenced asset.

B. Total Return Credit Swap

A **total return credit swap** is different from a credit default swap in that the latter is used to hedge a credit exposure while the former is used to increase credit exposure. A total return credit swap transfers all of the economic exposure of a reference asset or a referenced basket of assets to the credit swap purchaser. A total return credit swap includes all cash flows that flow from the referenced assets as well as the capital appreciation or depreciation of those assets. In return for receiving this exposure to an underlying asset, the credit swap purchaser pays a floating rate plus any depreciation of the referenced asset to the credit swap seller.

1. How a Total Return Credit Swap Works

If the total return payer owns the underlying referenced assets, it has transferred its economic exposure to the total return receiver. Effectively then, the total return payer has a neutral position which typically will earn LIBOR plus a spread. However, the total return payer has only transferred the economic exposure to the total return receiver; it has not transferred the actual assets. The total return payer must continue to fund the underlying assets at its marginal cost of borrowing or at the opportunity cost of investing elsewhere the capital tied up by the referenced assets.

The total return payer may not initially own the referenced assets before the swap is transacted. Instead, after the swap is negotiated, the total return payer will purchase the referenced assets to hedge its obligations to pay the total return to the total return receiver. In order to purchase the referenced assets, the total return payer must borrow capital. This borrowing cost is factored into the floating rate that the total return receiver must pay to the swap seller. Exhibit 10 diagrams how a total return credit swap works.

In Exhibit 10 the dealer raises cash from the capital markets at a funding cost of straight LIBOR. The cash that flows into the dealer from the capital markets flows right out again to purchase the referenced asset. The asset provides both interest income and capital gain or loss depending on its price fluctuation. This total return is passed through in its entirety to the investor according to the terms of the swap. The investor, in turn, pays the dealer LIBOR plus a spread to fulfill its obligations under the swap.

Exhibit 10: Total Return Credit Swaps

From the dealer's perspective, all of these cash flows net out to the spread over LIBOR that the dealer receives from the investor. Therefore, the dealer's profit is the spread times the notional value of the credit swap. In return, the investor receives the total return on a desired asset without the commitment of any capital.

2. Benefits of Total Return Credit Swaps

There are several benefits in purchasing a total return credit swap as opposed to purchasing the referenced assets themselves. First, the total return receiver does not have to finance the purchase of the referenced assets itself. Instead, it pays a fee to the total return payer in return for receiving the total return on the referenced assets. Second, if the total return payer already has the asset on its balance sheet, it can reduce its risk at the same time it receives a fee. This is a prime incentive for banks and other credit intensive institutions to provide this service.

Third, the total return receiver can achieve the same economic exposure in one swap transaction that would otherwise take several cash market transactions to achieve. In this way a total return swap is much more efficient than the cash market. Furthermore, a total return credit swap can offer a diversified basket of referenced assets.

Fourth, the total return receiver can take advantage of the natural expertise of the total return payer. Large money-center banks are natural dealers in the total return credit swap market. Their core business is the credit analysis of customers and the lending of money. To the extent the total return receiver is not as experienced in credit analysis as a large money-center bank, it can rely on the bank's expertise to choose appropriate credit risks for the underlying basket of referenced assets.

Fifth, a total return swap can incorporate leverage. Leverage is the ability to achieve a greater economic exposure than capital invested. With a total return credit swap, a total return swap receiver can specify a leverage percentage to increase its exposure to a referenced basket of assets.

SECTION VI
KEY POINTS

- ❏ *Credit derivatives are financial instruments that are designed to transfer the credit exposure of an underlying asset or issuer between two or more parties.*

- ❏ *Credit derivatives may take the form of options, forwards, or swaps with the payoffs linked to, or derived from, the credit characteristics of the referenced asset or issuer.*

❑ *A portfolio manager can either acquire or hedge credit risk using credit derivatives.*

❑ *Credit risk may adversely affect a portfolio in three ways: default risk, credit spread risk, and downgrade risk.*

❑ *Default risk is the risk that the issuer will default on its obligations.*

❑ *Credit spread risk is the risk that the interest rate spread for a risky bond over a riskless bond will increase after the risky bond has been purchased.*

❑ *Downgrade risk occurs when a nationally recognized statistical rating organization reduces its outstanding credit rating for an issuer.*

❑ *Credit options are constructed to protect against credit risk, not interest rate risk.*

❑ *Credit options may be written on an underlying asset or on a spread over a referenced riskless asset.*

❑ *There are two types of credit options written on an underlying asset: binary credit option with a predetermined payout and binary credit option based on a credit rating.*

❑ *With a binary credit option the option seller pays out a fixed sum if and when a default event occurs with respect to a referenced credit (e.g., the underlying issuer is unable to pay its obligations as they become due).*

❑ *A binary credit option can have a pay off that depends on the credit rating of the issue.*

❑ *A binary credit option based on a credit rating of an issue can be embedded in an issue.*

❑ *A call option on the level of the credit spread over a referenced benchmark (such as U.S. Treasury securities) is structured so that the option is in-the-money when the credit spread exceeds the specified spread level (i.e., strike spread).*

❑ *The payoff for a call option on a spread is computed as the difference in the credit spreads multiplied by a specified notional amount and by a risk factor.*

❑ *The risk factor for an option on a spread is based on the interest rate price sensitivity of the issue and represents the dollar value of a 1 basis point change in the credit spread.*

❑ *Credit forward contracts may be contracted either on bond values or on credit spreads.*

❑ *Unlike a credit option, with a credit forward a portfolio manager shares in both the upside and the downside resulting from the credit spread change.*

❑ *There are two different types of credit swaps: credit default swaps and total return swaps.*

❑ *A credit default swap is similar to a credit option in that its primary purpose is to hedge the credit exposure to a referenced asset or issuer and is the simplest form of credit insurance among all credit derivatives.*

❑ *There are two types of credit default swaps: credit insurance and swapping risky credit payments for certain fixed payments.*

❑ *With a credit insurance type credit default swap, the credit protection buyer pays a fee to the credit protection seller in return for the right to receive a payment conditional upon the default of a referenced credit (a single asset or a basket of assets).*

❏ *The credit protection buyer in a credit insurance type credit default swap continues to receive the total return on the referenced asset unless the total return is negative, whereupon the total return receiver will receive a payment from the credit protection seller.*

❏ *An alternative for a credit insurance type of credit default swap is the investor agreeing to swap the total return on a credit risky asset for fixed periodic payments from the credit protection seller; the payoff is such that if the credit risky asset declines in value, the investor will be reimbursed for the decline plus receive a periodic payment from the seller.*

❏ *A credit default swap is the same as shorting a bond – the investor gains if the bond declines in value because the dealer is obligated to reimburse the investor for the negative total return but if the bond increases in value, the investor must pay this amount to the dealer.*

❏ *A total return credit swap is different from a credit default swap in that the credit default swap is used to hedge a credit exposure while the total return credit swap is used to increase credit exposure.*

❏ *A total return credit swap transfers all of the economic exposure of a reference asset or a referenced basket of assets to the credit swap purchaser.*

❏ *A total return credit swap includes all cash flows that flow from the referenced assets as well as the capital appreciation or depreciation of those assets; in return for receiving this exposure to an underlying asset, the credit swap purchaser pays a floating rate plus any depreciation of the referenced asset to the credit swap seller.*

❏ *The benefits of purchasing a total return credit swap rather than purchasing the referenced assets are that: (1) the total return receiver does not have to finance the purchase of the referenced assets; (2) if the total return payer already has the asset on its balance sheet, it can reduce its risk at the same time it receives a fee; (3) the total return receiver can achieve the same economic exposure in one swap transaction that would otherwise take several cash market transactions to achieve; (4) the total return receiver can take advantage of the credit analysis expertise of the total return payer; and, (5) a total return swap can incorporate leverage.*

END OF CHAPTER QUESTIONS

1. How does a credit option differ from a standard option on a bond in terms of the protection it offers the buyer of the option?

2. a. What are the two types of credit options?
   b. What determines the payoff for each of these credit options?

3. What is meant by an embedded credit option?

4. A credit put option written on an underlying bond and a credit call option written on a credit spread both protect against credit risk. What is the difference between the two options?

5. What is meant by the "risk factor" in the payoff of a credit derivative?

6. A portfolio manager purchases a binary put option on a bond of Company X. The option pays out only if the credit rating of Company X declines below investment grade. At the maturity of the option at time T, the payout to the option buyer per $1,000 bond is expressed as:

$$P[V(T); \$1,000] = \begin{cases} \$1,000 - V(T); \text{ if the credit rating is below BBB} \\ \$0; \text{ if the credit rating is BBB or higher} \end{cases}$$

   a. Suppose that at the maturity of the option, the credit rating of Company X is BBB and its bonds are worth $950 per bond. What is the payout on this binary credit put option?
   b. Suppose that at the maturity of the option, the credit rating of Company X is BB and its bonds are worth $920 per bond. What is the payout on this binary credit put option?
   c. Suppose that at the maturity of the option, the credit rating of Company X is BB+ and its bonds are worth $1,010 per bond. What is the payout on this binary credit put option?

7. Suppose the 10-year bond of Izzobaf.com was trading to yield 8.2%. The 10-year Treasury bond was yielding 6.2% at the time for a credit spread of 200 basis points.

   a. Suppose that a portfolio manager felt that the issue was overvalued and that the credit spread would be at least 300 basis points one year from now and could purchase a credit spread option with a strike spread of 200 basis points. What type of credit spread option would the portfolio manager purchase, a put or a call?
   b. Suppose the risk factor for the Izzobaf.com bond was 6. Assuming that the manager purchased the option in part a with a strike spread of 200 basis points, ignoring the cost of the option what is the payoff for this option assuming a notional amount of $10 million?
   c. Suppose that the premium paid for the credit spread option in part a is $120,000 and that the manager's expectations are realized and the credit spread in one year is 300 basis points. What is the profit from the purchase of this credit spread option?

8. On January 1, a portfolio manager purchases a 5-year bond from Company Y with a par value of $1,000. The bonds are issued at par on January 1 at a credit spread of 200 basis points over a comparable 5-year U.S. Treasury note rate of 6.5%. The first semiannual coupon payment is due on July 1.

   On January 31, the portfolio manager purchases a credit put option on the bond at a strike credit spread of 250 basis points over the 5-year U.S. Treasury note rate. The option matures on July 1 and costs the portfolio manager $10. On July 1, the credit quality of Company Y has deteriorated and its bonds now trade at a credit spread of 300 basis points over the 5-year U.S. Treasury note rate. On July 1, the yield on a 5-year U.S. Treasury note remains unchanged at 6.5%.

   a. What is the strike price for this credit put option?
   b. What is the payoff for the option by exercising on July 1?
   c. What is the profit from the purchase of this option?

9. A high-yield portfolio manager wants to protect her portfolio from macroeconomic shocks that might increase credit spreads. Her portfolio market value is $500 million, and has an average credit spread to the 5-year U.S. Treasury note of 250 basis points. The risk factor of her portfolio based on duration and convexity measures is 3.25.

   On July 1, she purchases a credit forward contract to protect against declines in the value of her total portfolio. The credit forward has a contracted credit spread of 300 basis points relative to the 5-year Treasury rate and matures on December 31.

   In November, a large U.S. company defaults on its outstanding bonds, and credit spreads increase across the credit spectrum. On December 31, the average credit spread on the manager's portfolio is 350 basis points.

   What is the payoff to the credit forward contract?

10. Explain why a credit default swap on an underlying bond is economically the same as shorting a bond?

11. In 1999, Standard & Poor's developed two credit spread indices — one for the investment-grade corporates and one for the high-yield corporates. The index for the high-yield market is called the *S&P U.S. Industrial Speculative Grade Credit Index*. Beginning in April 2000, S&P published the average credit spreads daily for both indices. Option-adjusted spread (OAS) analysis is used to determine the credit spreads. Specifically, the two indices will measure the difference between the option-adjusted yield on a selected basket of corporate bonds and comparable U.S. Treasury securities.

   Credit derivatives could be structured using these two indexes. A high-yield bond portfolio manager could use a forward or option contract to gain exposure to the S&P U.S. Industrial Speculative Grade Credit Index.

   Consider first a forward credit spread involving the Credit Index. This credit derivative is a special case of a credit swap where there is only one period where there is a payoff. For a forward credit spread, the payoff at the maturity date would be:

   [credit spread at maturity for Credit Index – forward credit spread]
   × risk factor × notional amount

   A positive value for the payoff means that the buyer of a forward credit spread contract would receive the dollar amount computed above; a negative value means that the buyer of the contract would pay the amount computed above.

Next consider a credit spread option based on the index. The payoff for a credit spread call option before deducting the cost of the option is:

[credit spread at maturity for Credit Index − strike Credit Index spread]
× risk factor × notional amount

For a credit spread put option, the payoff before deducting the cost of the option is

[strike Credit Index spread − credit spread at maturity for Credit Index]
× risk factor × notional amount

In answering the questions below, assume that the S&P U.S. Industrial Speculative Grade Credit Index existed in 1998.

a. The default by the Russian government on $40 billion in August 1998 resulted in credit spreads increasing dramatically and affected the domestic U.S. credit markets. Explain how a high-yield portfolio manager could have used a forward credit spread based on the S&P U.S. Industrial Speculative Grade Credit Index to hedge credit spread risk. Be sure to explain whether the portfolio manager would buy or sell a forward credit spread

b. Suppose that the dollar value of the portfolio that a manager wished to protect was $500 million and the risk factor for both the bond portfolio and the S&P Industrial Speculative Grade Credit Index was 2.5. Assume that on August 1, 1998 the manager purchased a 3-month forward credit spread on the Credit Index struck at a fair forward credit spread of 350 basis points. At maturity of the forward credit spread on November 1, 1998, the credit spread for high-yield bonds was according to the Credit Index about 600 basis points above comparable U.S. Treasury bonds. What would be the payoff of this forward credit spread?

c. Suppose that over the same time frame, credit spreads in the S&P index had improved by 50 basis points rather than widening as they actually did. That is, suppose that the credit spread had declined from 350 basis points to 300 basis points. What would have been the manager's obligation under the credit forward contract?

d. Suppose that instead of a forward credit spread, the manager wanted to purchase an option to protect against a widening of spreads. What type of credit spread option on the index would the manager buy, a put or call?

e. Suppose that the manager on August 1, 1998 had purchased a 3-month credit spread option of the type in the answer to part d and with a strike index spread of 350 basis points. Also assume that the cost of the option would have been $10 million. At maturity of the credit spread option on November 1, 1998, as noted in part b the credit spread for high-yield bonds was according to the Credit Index about 600 basis points above comparable U.S. Treasury bonds. What would have been the payoff after deducting the cost of the option?

f. What is the advantage and disadvantage of the credit spread option versus a forward credit spread in hedging credit risk?

g. Why did S&P use the option-adjusted spread in constructing its Credit Index rather than the nominal spread?

SOLUTIONS TO END OF CHAPTER QUESTIONS

1. A standard option on a bond protects the buyer against interest rate risk. In contrast, a credit option protects the option buyer against credit risk.

2. a. The two types of credit options are (1) an option written on an underlying asset and (2) an option on a credit spread (i.e., a credit spread option).
   b. The payoff for an option written on an underlying asset is determined by an event of default or credit rating downgrade of the underlying issuer. Or, the payoff can be structured to payoff if the net worth of an issuer falls below a specified value. For a credit spread option, the payoff is based on the change in the credit spread.

3. An embedded credit option is one which is included within a bond structure as opposed to a stand alone credit option that can be purchased. That is, when a bond is issued, the indenture includes one or more provisions that allow the bondholder to benefit from a change in the issuer's credit.

4. The payoff to a credit put option written on an underlying bond is derived from the bond's absolute price change. Conversely, a credit spread call option is a relative value option; its value is not based on the absolute price change in an underlying bond. Instead, its value is determined relative to the price change of a U.S. Treasury (or other reference) bond.

5. The risk factor is the price sensitivity of the issue to interest rates and represents the dollar value of a 1 basis point change in the credit spread at the time the credit derivative is purchased.

6. a. The value of the binary credit put option is $0 because the credit rating of Company X is not below BBB.
   b. Because the issue is rated BB, the binary credit put option expires in the money. The payoff is $80 ($1,000 − $920).
   c. While this binary credit put option has a credit rating below BBB, its price is above par. Thus, the payoff would indicate a negative value of $10. However, because the option has a negative value, the option buyer will not exercise. Therefore, the payoff from the option is zero.

7. a. Since the manager expects the credit spread to widen, the manager will benefit by purchasing a credit spread put option.
   b. The payoff for the credit spread put option is as follows:

   • if the credit spread is 200 basis points or less the payoff is zero
   • if the credit spread is greater than 200 basis points the payoff is

   $$(\text{credit spread} - 0.020) \times \$10{,}000{,}000 \times 6$$

   c. The profit for the credit spread put option is

   $$(\text{credit spread} - 0.020) \times \$10{,}000{,}000 \times 6 - \$120{,}000$$

   If the credit spread is 300 basis points (that is, 0.030), the profit is:

   $$(0.030 - 0.020) \times \$10{,}000{,}000 \times 6 - \$120{,}000 = \$480{,}000$$

8. a. The strike price (K) is the present value of the future cash flow. The discount rate for computing the present value is the 5-year Treasury rate of 6.5% plus the credit spread of 250 basis points. So, the annual discount rate is 9% and the semiannual discount rate is therefore 4.5%.

The coupon rate for the bond is 200 basis points over 6.5%, or 8.5%. The semiannual coupon payment is $42.50.

The first coupon payment of $42.50 is not discounted because it is paid on the same day when the option matures, July 1. (That is, when evaluating as of July 1, it is not a future cash flow.) Since the bond is a 5-year bond, there are 10 coupon payments. However, there are 9 remaining after July 1. The 9 future coupon payments of $42.50 per $1,000 of par value are discounted at 4.5%. It can be shown that the present value of the 9 future coupon payments is $308.92.

The present value of the maturity value of $1,000 nine periods from now when discounted at 4.5% is $672.90 (=$1,000/(1.045)^9).

Therefore the strike price is

$$K = \text{current coupon} + \text{PV of future coupons} + \text{PV of maturity value}$$

$$K = \$42.50 + \$308.92 + \$672.90 = \$1,024.32$$

b. The payout is equal to:

strike price – bond's value on July 1

The bond's value on July 1 must be determined. It is assumed in the question that on July 1 the credit spread is 300 basis points and the 5-year U.S. Treasury note rate is unchanged at 6.5%. The discount rate is 9.5% and the semiannual discount rate is 4.75%.

The semiannual coupon payment is $42.50. Again, as of July 1, the first coupon is not discounted because it is paid on the same date as when the option matures. Since the bond is initially a 5-year bond, on July 1 there are 9 remaining coupon payments of $42.50. The present value of the 9 remaining coupon payments of $42.50 when discounted at 4.75% (the semiannual discount rate on July 1) is $305.47.

The present value of the $1,000 maturity value discounted at 4.75% nine periods from now is $1,000/(1.0475)^9 = \$658.59$

The value of the bond as of July 1 is therefore equal to:

$$V(T) = \text{current coupon} + \text{PV of future coupons} + \text{PV of maturity value}$$

$$V(T) = \$42.50 + \$305.47 + 658.59 = \$1,006.56$$

The payout is

$$\$1,024.32 - \$1,006.56 = \$17.76$$

c. The profit is equal to:

strike price – bond's value – cost of the option

Since the cost of the option is $10, the profit is

$$\$1,024.32 - \$1,006.56 - \$10 = \$7.76$$

9. The payoff for the credit forward contract is:

$$\text{payoff} = [\text{credit spread at maturity of the forward} - \text{contracted credit spread}] \times \text{average risk factor} \times \text{notional amount}$$

The following is known

> credit spread at maturity of the forward (December 31) = 3.5%
> contracted credit spread = 3.0%
> average risk factor = 3.25
> notional amount = $500,000,000

Therefore,

$$\text{payoff} = [0.035 - 0.03] \times 3.25 \times \$500,000,000 = \$8,125,000$$

10. A credit default swap is a form of credit insurance. The investor agrees to surrender the appreciation in the value of the credit risky bond to a dealer in return for being reimbursed if that asset declines in value. This is the same as a short position in the bond because the short seller of the bond loses value if the bond price increases, and gains value if the bond price decreases.

11. a. For a forward credit spread, the payoff at the maturity date would be:

$$[\text{credit spread at maturity for Credit Index} - \text{forward credit spread}] \times \text{risk factor} \times \text{notional amount}$$

By buying a forward credit spread, the payoff is positive if the credit spread at maturity for the Credit Index increases above the forward credit spread. If a manager is seeking to protect against a widening of the spread, a forward credit spread should be purchased.

If the credit spread does widen, then there will be a decline in the value of the portfolio. However, this will be offset (fully or partially depending on how good the hedge is) from a payoff of the forward credit spread purchased.

b. The payoff to the forward credit spread would have been:

$$(0.06 - 0.035) \times 2.5 \times \$500 \text{ million} = \$31,250,000$$

c. If credit spreads had narrowed by 50 basis points, the portfolio manager would have *owed* at the maturity date of the forward credit spread:

$$(0.03 - 0.035) \times 2.5 \times \$500 \text{ million} = -\$6,250,000$$

Note, however, that while the portfolio manager would have owed $6.25 million on the forward credit spread, the market value of the manager's cash portfolio would have increased.

d. The payoff for a credit spread call option before deducting the cost of the option is:

$$[\text{credit spread at maturity for Credit Index} - \text{strike Credit Index}] \times \text{risk factor} \times \text{notional amount}$$

If the credit spread increases relative to the strike Credit Index, the payoff for a credit spread call option will be positive (before deducting the cost of the option). For a credit spread put option there would be no payoff if the Credit Index widens. Thus, the manager would purchase a call option on the Credit Index.

e. The payoff for the credit spread call option after deducting the cost of the option is:

$$(0.06 - 0.035) \times 2.5 \times \$500 \text{ million} - \$10 \text{ million} = \$21,250,000$$

f. With a forward credit spread, the payoff is symmetric; that is, if the spread widens the manager receives a payoff but if it narrows the manager must make a payment. The disadvantage of a credit spread call option is that if the spread widens there is a payoff but the payoff must be reduced by the cost of the option. The advantage is that if there is a narrowing of the spread, the most that the option buyer can lose is the cost of the option.

g. Option-adjusted spread is used in order to neutralize the effects of embedded optionality associated with corporate bonds. The OAS accounts for the individual bond characteristics such as sinking funds, call provisions, and other early retirement covenants.

Chapter 9

MEASURING AND EVALUATING PERFORMANCE

Frank J. Fabozzi, Ph.D., CFA
Adjunct Professor of Finance
School of Management
Yale University

The section on AIMR Performance Presentation Standards was contributed by **Jonathan J. Stokes**, Vice President, Associate General Counsel of the Association for Investment Management and Research.

LEARNING OUTCOME STATEMENTS

After reading this chapter you should be able to:

- distinguish between performance measurement and performance evaluation.
- compute a period return for a portfolio.
- interpret the various measures for computing a period return from sub-period returns (i.e., arithmetic average rate of return, time-weighted rates of return, and dollar-weighted rate of return).
- explain the effect of client contributions and withdrawals on the calculated return for a portfolio.
- explain the limitations of the arithmetic average rate of return.
- explain why the time-weighted return is superior to the dollar-weighted rate of return.
- compute the arithmetic average rate of return, time-weighted rate of return, and dollar-weighted rate of return of a portfolio.
- calculate the annualized return from the average period return.
- identify the AIMR Performance Presentation Standards requirements and recommendations.
- identify the approach for calculating returns set forth in the AIMR Performance Presentation Standards.
- explain the two types of benchmarks that have been used in evaluating bond portfolio managers (market indexes and normal portfolios).
- describe the steps involved in constructing a normal portfolio.
- compute the Treynor, Sharpe, and Jensen measures of performance.
- explain the limitations of the single-index performance evaluation measures.
- explain the objectives of return attribution analysis.

SECTION I
INTRODUCTION

In previous chapters we looked at the various active portfolio strategies. In this chapter we turn our attention to how to measure and evaluate the performance of a bond portfolio manager. **Performance measurement** involves the calculation of the return realized by a portfolio manager over some time interval. This time interval is called the **evaluation period**.

Given a performance measurement over some evaluation period, **performance evaluation** is concerned with two issues. The first is to determine whether the manager added value by outperforming the established benchmark. The second is to determine how the manager achieved the calculated return. For example, as explained in previous chapters, there are several active strategies that a manager can employ. The decomposition of the performance results used to explain how they were achieved is called **return attribution analysis**.

SECTION II
PERFORMANCE
MEASUREMENT

The starting point for evaluating a manager's performance is measuring return. Several important issues must be addressed in developing a methodology for calculating a portfolio's return. Because different methodologies are available and these methodologies can lead to quite disparate results, it is quite difficult to compare the performances of managers. Consequently, there is a great deal of confusion concerning the meaning of the data provided by managers to their clients and their prospective clients. This has led to abuses by some managers in reporting performance results that are better than actual performance. To mitigate this problem the *Committee for Performance Standards of the Association for Investment Management and Research* has established standards for calculating performance results and how to present those results.

A. Alternative Return Measures

Let's begin with the basic concept. The dollar return realized on a portfolio for any evaluation period (i.e., a year, month, or week) is equal to the sum of (1) the difference between the market value of the portfolio at the end of the evaluation period and the market value at the beginning of the evaluation period, and (2) any distributions made from the portfolio. It is important that any capital or income distributions from the portfolio to a client or beneficiary of the portfolio be included.

The rate of return, or simply return, expresses the dollar return in terms of the amount of the market value at the beginning of the evaluation period. Thus, the return can be viewed as the amount (expressed as a fraction of the initial portfolio value) that can be withdrawn at the end of the evaluation period while maintaining the initial market value of the portfolio.

In equation form, the portfolio's return can be expressed as follows:

$$R_p = \frac{V_1 - V_0 + D}{V_0} \tag{1}$$

where

R_p = the return on the portfolio
V_1 = the portfolio market value at the end of the evaluation period
V_0 = the portfolio market value at the beginning of the evaluation period
D = the cash distributions from the portfolio to the client during the evaluation period

To illustrate the calculation of a return as given by equation (1), assume the following information for an external manager for a pension plan sponsor: the portfolio's market value at the beginning and end of the evaluation period is $100 million and $112 million, respectively, and during the evaluation period $5 million is distributed to the plan sponsor from investment income. Thus:

$$V_1 = \$112,000,000$$
$$V_0 = \$100,000,000$$
$$D = \$5,000,000$$

then,

$$R_p = \frac{\$112,000,000 - \$100,000,000 + \$5,000,000}{\$100,000,000} = 0.17 = 17\%$$

1. Assumptions in Calculating the Return

There are three assumptions in measuring return as given by equation (1). First, it assumes that cash inflows into the portfolio from interest income that occur during the evaluation period but are not distributed are reinvested in the portfolio. For example, suppose that during the evaluation period $7 million is received from interest income. This amount is reflected in the market value of the portfolio at the end of the period.

The second assumption is that if there are distributions from the portfolio, they occur at the end of the evaluation period, or are held in the form of cash until the end of the evaluation period. In our example, $5 million is distributed to the plan sponsor. But when did that distribution actually occur? To understand why the timing of the distribution is important, consider two extreme cases: (1) the distribution is made at the end of the evaluation period, as assumed by equation (1), and (2) the distribution is made at the beginning of the evaluation period. In the first case, the manager had the use of the $5 million to invest for the entire evaluation period. By contrast, in the second case, the manager loses the opportunity to invest the funds until the end of the evaluation period. Consequently, the timing of the distribution will affect the return, but this is not considered in equation (1).

The third assumption is that there is no cash paid into the portfolio by the client. For example, suppose that some time during the evaluation period the plan sponsor gives an additional $8 million to the manager to invest. Consequently, the market value of the portfolio at the end of the evaluation period, $112 million in our example, would reflect the contribution of $8 million. Equation (1) does not reflect that the ending market value of the portfolio is affected by the cash paid in by the sponsor. Moreover, the timing of this cash inflow will affect the return.

Thus, while the return calculation for a portfolio using equation (1) can be determined for an evaluation period of any length of time such as one day, one month, or five years, from a practical point of view, the assumptions discussed above limit its application. The longer the evaluation period, the more likely the assumptions will be violated. For example, it is highly likely that there may be more than one distribution to the client and more than one contribution from the client if the evaluation period is five years. Thus, a return calculation made over a long period of time, if longer than a few months, would not be very reliable because of the assumption underlying the calculations that all cash payments and inflows are made and received at the end of the period.

2. Sub-Period Returns

Not only does the violation of the assumptions make it difficult to compare the returns of two managers over some evaluation period, but is also not useful for evaluating performance over different periods. For example, equation (1) will not give reliable information to compare the performance of a 1-month evaluation period and a 3-year evaluation period. To make such a comparison, the return must be expressed per unit of time, for example, per year.

The way to handle these practical issues is to calculate the return for a short unit of time such as a month or a quarter. We call the return so calculated the **sub-period return**. To get the return for the evaluation period, the sub-period returns are then averaged. So, for example, if the evaluation period is one year and 12 monthly returns are calculated, the monthly returns are the sub-period returns and they are averaged to get the 1-year return. If a 3-year return is sought and 12 quarterly returns can be calculated, quarterly returns are the sub-period returns and they are averaged to get the 3-year return. The 3-year return can then be converted into an annual return by the straightforward procedure described later.

There are three methodologies that have been used in practice to calculate the average of the sub-period returns: (1) the arithmetic average rate of return, (2) the time-weighted rate of return (also called the geometric rate of return), and (3) the dollar-weighted rate of return.

3. Arithmetic Average Rate of Return

The **arithmetic average rate of return** is an unweighted average of the sub-period returns. The general formula is:

$$R_A = \frac{R_{P1} + R_{P2} + \ldots + R_{PN}}{N}$$

where

R_A = the arithmetic average rate of return

R_{Pk} = the portfolio return for sub-period k as measured by equation (1), $k = 1, 2, \ldots, N$

N = the number of sub-periods in the evaluation period

For example, if the portfolio returns as measured by equation (1) were 12%, 25%, −15%, and −2% in months January, February, March, and April, respectively, the arithmetic average monthly return is 5%, as shown below:

$$N = 4, R_{P1} = 0.12, R_{P2} = 0.25, R_{P3} = -0.15, \text{ and } R_{P4} = -0.02$$

$$R_A = \frac{0.12 + 0.25 + (-0.15) + (-0.02)}{4} = 0.05 = 5\%$$

There is a major problem with using the arithmetic average rate of return. To see this problem, suppose the initial market value of a portfolio is $140 million and the market value at the end of each of the next two months is $280 million and $140 million, respectively, and assume that there are no distributions or cash inflows from the client for either month. Then, using equation (1), the sub-period return for the first month (R_{P1}) is 100% and the sub-period return for the second month (R_{P2}) is

−50%. The arithmetic average rate of return is then 25%. Not a bad return! But think about this number. The portfolio's initial market value was $140 million. Its market value at the end of two months is $140 million. The return over this 2-month evaluation period is zero. Yet, the arithmetic average rate of return says it is a whopping 25%.

Thus, it is improper to interpret the arithmetic average rate of return as a measure of the average return over an evaluation period. The proper interpretation is as follows: *it is the average value of the withdrawals (expressed as a fraction of the initial portfolio market value) that can be made at the end of each sub-period while keeping the initial portfolio market value intact.* In our first example above in which the average monthly return is 5%, the investor can withdraw 12% of the initial portfolio market value at the end of the first month, can withdraw 25% of the initial portfolio market value at the end of the second month, must add 15% of the initial portfolio market value at the end of the third month, and must add 2% of the initial portfolio market value at the end of the fourth month. In our second example, the average monthly return of 25% means that 100% of the initial portfolio market value ($140 million) can be withdrawn at the end of the first month and 50% must be added at the end of the second month.

4. Time-Weighted Rate of Return

The **time-weighted rate of return** measures the compounded rate of growth of the initial portfolio market value during the evaluation period, assuming that all cash distributions are reinvested in the portfolio. It is also commonly referred to as the *geometric rate of return* since it is computed using the geometric average of the portfolio sub-period returns computed from equation (1). The general formula is:

$$R_T = [(1 + R_{P1})(1 + R_{P2})...(1 + R_{PN})]^{1/N} - 1$$

where R_T is the time-weighted rate of return and R_{Pk} and N are as defined earlier.

For example, assume the portfolio returns were 12%, 25%, −15%, and −2% in January, February, March, and April, as in the first example above. Then the time-weighted rate of return is:

$$R_T = [(1 + 0.12)(1 + 0.25)(1 + (-0.15))(1 + (-0.02))]^{1/4} - 1$$
$$= [(1.12)(1.25)(0.85)(0.98)]^{1/4} - 1 = 3.92\%$$

Since the time-weighted rate of return is 3.92% per month, one dollar invested in the portfolio at the beginning of January would have grown at an average rate of 3.92% per month during the 4-month evaluation period.

The time-weighted rate of return in the second example is 0%, as expected, as shown below:

$$R_T = [(1 + 1.00)(1 + (-0.50))]^{1/2} - 1$$
$$= [(2.00)(0.50)]^{1/2} - 1 = 0\%$$

In general, the arithmetic and time-weighted average returns will give different values for the portfolio return over some evaluation period. This is because in computing the arithmetic average rate of return, the amount invested is assumed to be maintained (through additions or withdrawals) at its initial portfolio market value. The time-weighted return, on the other hand, is the return on a portfolio that varies in size because of the assumption that all proceeds are reinvested.

In general, the arithmetic average rate of return will exceed the time-weighted average rate of return. The exception is in the special situation where all the sub-period returns are the same, in which case the averages are identical. The magnitude of the difference between the two averages is smaller the less the variation in the sub-period returns over the evaluation period. For example, suppose that the evaluation period is four months and that the four monthly returns are as follows:

$$R_{P1} = 0.04, R_{P2} = 0.06, R_{P3} = 0.02, \text{ and } R_{P4} = -0.02,$$

The average arithmetic rate of return is 2.5% and the time-weighted average rate of return is 2.46%. Not much of a difference. In our earlier example in which we calculated an average rate of return of 25% but a time-weighted rate of return of 0%. The large discrepancy is due to the substantial variation in the two monthly returns.

5. Dollar-Weighted Rate of Return

The **dollar-weighted rate of return** is computed by finding the interest rate that will make the present value of the cash flows from all the sub-periods in the evaluation period plus the terminal market value of the portfolio equal to the initial market value of the portfolio. The cash flow for each sub-period reflects the difference between the cash inflows due to contributions made by the client to the portfolio and the cash outflows reflecting distributions to the client. Notice that it is not necessary to know the market value of the portfolio for each sub-period to determine the dollar-weighted rate of return.

The dollar-weighted rate of return is simply an internal rate of return calculation; hence, it is also called the **internal rate of return**. The general formula for the dollar-weighted rate of return is:

$$V_0 = \frac{C_1}{(1 + R_D)^1} + \frac{C_2}{(1 + R_D)^2} + \dots + \frac{C_N + V_N}{(1 + R_D)^n}$$

where

R_D = the dollar-weighted rate of return
V_0 = the initial market value of the portfolio
V_N = the terminal market value of the portfolio
C_k = the cash flow for the portfolio (cash inflows minus cash outflows) for sub-period k, $k = 1, 2,..., N$

For example, consider a portfolio with a market value of $100 million at the beginning of July, capital withdrawals of $1 million at the end of July and August, no cash inflows from the client in any month, and a market value at the end of September of $129,635,124. Then $V_0 = \$100,000,000$, $N = 3$, $C_1 = C_2 = -\$1,000,000$, and $V_3 = \$129,635,124$. R_D is the interest rate that satisfies the following equation:

$$\$100,000,000 = \frac{-\$1,000,000}{(1 + R_D)^1} + \frac{-\$1,000,000}{(1 + R_D)^2} + \frac{\$129,635,124}{(1 + R_D)^3}$$

It can be verified that the interest rate that satisfies the above expression is 8.4%. This, then, is the dollar-weighted rate of return.

The dollar-weighted rate of return and the time-weighted rate of return will produce the same result if no withdrawals or contributions occur over the evaluation period. The problem with the dollar-weighted rate of return is that it is affected by factors that are beyond the control of the manager. Specifically, any contributions made by the client or withdrawals that the client requires will affect the calculated return. This makes it difficult to compare the performance of two managers.

To see this, suppose that a pension plan sponsor engaged two managers, A and B, with $10 million allocated to A and $200 million to B. Suppose that both managers have identical portfolios (that is, the two portfolios have the same securities and are held in the same portion). For the following two months, the monthly return is 20% for month 1 and 50% for month 2. Assuming no cash contributions or withdrawals by the plan sponsor, the dollar-weighted rate of return would be identical. The portfolio value at the end of month 2 for the portfolio managed by A would be $18 million ($10 million $\times$ 1.2 $\times$ 1.5). Since C_0 = $10,000,000, C_1 = $0, and C_2 = $18,000,000, the dollar-weighted rate of return would then be computed as follows:

$$\$10,000,000 = \frac{\$0}{(1 + R_D)^1} + \frac{\$18,000,000}{(1 + R_D)^2}$$

Solving for R_D we get 34.2%.

For the portfolio managed by B, the portfolio value at the end of two months would be $360 million ($200 million $\times$ 1.2 $\times$ 1.5). The values used in computing the dollar-weighted rate of return would be C_0 = $200,000,000, C_1 = $0, C_2 = $360,000,000. The dollar-weighted rate of return is approximately 34.2%, the same as for manager A.

Now let's assume that the plan sponsor withdrew $3 million at the end of month 1 from manager A. The portfolio value at the end of month 1 would be equal to $10 million increased by the 20% return in month 1, reduced by the $3 million withdrawn by the plan sponsor. That is, at the end of month 1 the portfolio value will be $9 million. Since the amount invested in month 2 is $9 million and the return in month 2 is 50%, then the portfolio value at the end of month 2 is $13.5 million. Then C_0 = $10,000,000, C_1 = −$3,000,000, and C_2 = $13,500,000. The dollar-weighted rate of return is about 2.15%. Quite a difference in performance from the 34.2% even though the manager did nothing more than return $3 million to the plan sponsor!

Suppose that the plan sponsor made a contribution of $15 million to manager B at the end of month 1. Then the portfolio value at the end of month 2 will equal the $15 million increased by the 20% return plus the $15 million contribution by the plan sponsor. Thus, at the end of month 1, the portfolio value is $255 million. Reinvesting this amount in month 2 and earning the 50% return gives a portfolio value at the end of month 2 of $382,500,000. The following values are then used in the dollar-weighted rate of return calculation: C_0 = $200,000,000, C_1 = $15,000,000, C_2 = $382,500,000. The dollar-weighted rate of return is about 42.1% – an improvement in return from the case where no funds are contributed by the plan sponsor.

Despite this limitation, the dollar-weighted rate of return does provide information. It indicates information about the growth of the fund which a client will find useful. This growth, however, may not be attributable to the performance of the manager because of contributions and withdrawals.

6. Annualizing Returns

The evaluation period may be less than or greater than one year. Typically, return measures are reported as an average annual return. This requires the annualization of the sub-period returns. The sub-period returns are typically calculated for a period of less than one year for the reasons described earlier. The sub-period returns are then annualized using the following formula:

$$\text{Annual return} = (1 + \text{Average period return})^{\text{Number of periods in year}} - 1$$

So, for example, suppose the evaluation period is three years and a monthly period return is calculated. Suppose further that the average monthly return is 2%. Then the annual return would be:

$$\text{Annual return} = (1.02)^{12} - 1 = 26.8\%$$

Suppose instead that the period used to calculate returns is quarterly and the average quarterly return is 3%. Then the annual return is:

$$\text{Annual return} = (1.03)^{4} - 1 = 12.6\%$$

B. AIMR Performance Presentation Standards

Just as there are subtle issues in calculating investment return over a particular evaluation period, there are numerous possible ways to present performance results to clients and potential clients.[1] Traditionally, those seeking to hire an investment manager had to sort through very different presentations in which the performance information shown could have resulted from several practices that hindered comparability and accuracy of the results. These practices included:

- the use of returns of "representative" accounts as a proxy for firm performance
- excluding returns of accounts that have left due to poor performance from total performance
- showing model or simulated results
- using historical performance of predecessor firm
- selecting only certain time periods when presenting information to clients

Without guidelines for managers to follow in presenting performance results, clients and potential clients had difficulty receiving accurate performance presentations with which they could make meaningful comparisons.

1. Developing a Performance Presentation Standard

To address this problem, the Association for Investment Management and Research developed the AIMR Performance Presentation Standards (AIMR-PPS). The standards are based on the fundamental principles of fair representation and full disclosure. The goal of AIMR in developing the AIMR-PPS Standards was to establish a common, accepted set of guidelines for the calculation and presentation of investment firms' performance results.

The AIMR-PPS Standards were first introduced in the September/October 1987 issue of *Financial Analysts Journal*. Since that time, AIMR has reviewed and revised the AIMR-PPS Standards extensively based on industry comment and recommendations to ensure that the Standards remain current. Over the years, AIMR has supplemented the Standards to provide guidance on specific issues such as real estate, bank trust issues, venture and private placements, and wrap fee portfolios.

Since their effective date of January 1, 1993, the AIMR-PPS Standards have received overwhelming acceptance from the North American investment community. However, AIMR recognized the need for one set of standards that is accepted worldwide to further the goals of accuracy and comparability of investment results on a glo-

---

[1] This section was contributed by Jonathan J. Stokes, Vice President, Associate General Counsel of the Association for Investment Management and Research.

bal basis. As a result, in February 1999, AIMR established the Global Investment Performance Standards (GIPS) as the worldwide standard for calculating and presenting investment performance. The GIPS Standards are based on the same principles of fair representation and full disclosure and are fundamentally the same as the AIMR-PPS Standards. Over time, AIMR blended the GIPS and AIMR-PPS Standards such that the GIPS Standards now make up the core of the AIMR-PPS Standards. At this point the AIMR-PPS Standards can be considered the North American version of GIPS.

2. Structure of the GIPS/AIMR-PPS Standards

The GIPS standards are divided into five main sections reflecting the basic elements involved in presenting performance:

1. *Input Data:* The Standards dictate certain requirements regarding the information used to calculate and present performance history.
2. *Calculation Methodology:* The Standards mandate the use of a certain calculation methodology to ensure comparability of performance.
3. *Composite Construction:* A composite is an aggregation of a number of accounts into a single group based on similar investment style or strategy. Creating meaningful composites is critical to the fair presentation, consistency, and comparability of investment results over time and among firms.
4. *Disclosures:* The Standards mandate that firms disclose certain information about the performance history in its presentations to clients.
5. *Presentation and Reporting:* Once a firm has gathered the input data, constructed the composites, made the calculations and formulated its disclosures, the Standards dictate certain presentation procedures to ensure comparability of presentations among firms.

3. Highlights of the Standards

Each of these sections includes requirements and recommended provisions. For a firm to claim that complies with the Standards, the firm must satisfy all of the required elements listed in the standards. Firms are strongly encouraged to adopt and implement the recommendations to ensure that they fully adhere to the spirit and intent of the Standards.

a. Requirements

The requirements are:

- Portfolio valuations must be based on market values (not cost basis or book values).

- Accrual accounting must be used for fixed income securities and all other assets that accrue interest income.

- Time-weighted rates of return that adjust for cash flows must be used. Periodic returns must be geometrically linked. Time-weighted rates of return that adjust for daily-weighted cash flows must be used for periods beginning January 1, 2005. Actual valuations at the time of external cash flows will likely be required for periods beginning January 1, 2010.

- Returns from cash and cash equivalents held in portfolios must be included in total return calculations.

- All actual, fee-paying, discretionary portfolios must be included in at least one composite. Firm composites must be defined according to similar investment objectives and/or strategies.

- Terminated portfolios must be included in the historical record of the appropriate composites up to the last full measurement period that the portfolio was under management. .

- Composites must include only assets under management and may not link simulated or model portfolios with actual performance.

- Firms must disclose whether performance results are calculated gross or net of investment management fees and other fees paid by the clients to the firm or to the firm's affiliates

- Firms must present either 5 years (GIPS) or 10 years (AIMR-PPS) of annual returns for all years.

- Firms must disclose the number of portfolios and amount of assets in the composite, and the percentage of the firm's total assets represented by the composite at the end of each period.

- Firms must show a measure of the dispersion of individual component portfolio returns around the aggregate composite return.

- The total return for the benchmark (or benchmarks) that reflects the investment strategy or mandate represented by the composite must be presented for the same periods for which the composite return is presented. If no benchmark is presented, the presentation must explain why no benchmark is disclosed.

b. Recommendations

The recommendations are:

- Separate composites should be created to reflect different levels of allowed asset exposure.

- Unless the use of hedging is negligible, portfolios that allow the use of hedging should be included in different composites from those that do not.

- Firms should disclose the portfolio valuation sources and methods used by the firm.

- Firms should disclose the calculation method used by the firm.

- When gross-of-fee performance is presented, the firm should provide the firm's fee schedule(s) appropriate to the presentation.

- Firms should disclose any significant events within the firm (such as ownership or personnel changes) that would help a prospective client interpret the performance record.

- Relevant risk measures such as volatility, tracking error, beta, modified duration, etc., should be presented along with total return for both benchmarks and composites.

SECTION III PERFORMANCE EVALUATION

In the previous section, we concentrated on performance measurement and the AIMR performance reporting standards. But a performance measure does not answer two questions: (1) how did the manager perform after adjusting for the risk associated with the strategy employed? and (2) how did the manager achieve the reported return?

⸴ The answer to these two questions is critical in assessing how well or how poorly the manager performed relative to some benchmark.

A. Requirements for a Bond Performance and Attribution Analysis Process

Any bond performance and attribution analysis process should satisfy three basic requirements. First, the process should be accurate. For example, as we will explain, there are several ways of measuring portfolio return. The return should recognize the timing of each cash flow, resulting in a much more accurate measure of the actual portfolio performance.

Second, the process should be informative. It should be capable of evaluating the managerial skills that go into bond portfolio management. To be informative, the process must effectively address the key management skills, and explain how these can be expressed in terms of realized performance. For example, the process should be able to identify the degree to which the performance was attributed to changes in the level of interest rates, changes in the shape of the yield curve, changes in spreads, and individual security selection. There should be recognition of the effect of transaction costs on performance.

The third requirement is that the process be simple. Whatever the output of the process, it should be understood by the manager and client, or others who may be concerned with the performance of the portfolio.

While the first requirement is that the process provide accurate information, this does not mean that attribution analysis needs to be accurate to the *n-th* decimal place. Rather, it should be able to give the client an accurate picture of the major areas and order of magnitude of outperformance or underperformance. A client engages a manager based on claims of the manager as to the strategies that will be pursued. Information about whether a manager is doing what he claims is critical in the decision to retain or discharge the manager.

B. Benchmark Portfolios

To evaluate the performance of a manager, a client must specify a benchmark against which the manager will be measured. There are two types of benchmarks that have been used in evaluating bond portfolio managers: (1) market indexes published by dealer firms and vendors and (2) normal portfolios. We discussed the various types of bond market indexes in Chapter 1.

A **normal portfolio** is a customized benchmark that includes "a set of securities that contains all of the securities from which a manager normally chooses, weighted as the manager would weight them in a portfolio."[2] Thus, a normal portfolio is a specialized index. It is argued that normal portfolios are more appropriate benchmarks than market indexes because they control for investment management style thereby representing a passive portfolio against which a manager can be evaluated.

The construction of a normal portfolio for a particular manager is no simple task. The principle is to construct a portfolio that, given the historical portfolios held by the manager, will reflect that manager's style in terms of assets and the weighting of those assets. The construction of a normal portfolio for a manager requires (1) defining

---

[2] Jon A. Christopherson, "Normal Portfolios: Construction of Customized Benchmarks," Chapter 6 in Frank J. Fabozzi (ed.), *Active Equity Portfolio Management* (New Hope, PA: Frank J. Fabozzi Associates, 1998), p. 92.

the universe of bonds to be included in the normal portfolio and (2) determining how these securities should be weighted (i.e., equally weighted or capitalization weighted).

Defining the set of securities to be included in the normal portfolio begins with discussions between the client and the manager to determine the manager's investment style. Based on these discussions, the universe of all publicly traded bonds is reduced to a subset that includes those securities that the manager considers eligible given his or her investment style.

Given these securities, the next question is how they should be weighted in the normal portfolio. The two choices are equal weighting or capitalization weighting of each security. Various methodologies can be used to determine the weights. These methodologies typically involve a statistical analysis of the historical holdings of a manager and the risk exposure contained in those holdings.

Plan sponsors work with pension consultants to develop normal portfolios for a manager. The consultants use vendor systems that have been developed for performing the needed statistical analysis and the necessary optimization program to create a portfolio exhibiting similar factor positions to replicate the "normal" position of a manager. A plan sponsor must recognize that there is a cost to developing and updating the normal portfolio.

There are some who advocate that the responsibility of developing normal portfolios should be left to the manager. However, many clients are reluctant to let their managers control the construction of normal portfolios because they believe that the managers will produce easily beaten, or "slow rabbit," benchmarks.

C. Single-Index Performance Evaluation Measures

In the 1960s, several single-index measures were used to evaluate the relative performance of money managers. These measures of performance evaluation did not specify how or why a money manager may have outperformed or underperformed a benchmark. The three measures are the **Treynor**,[3] the **Sharpe**,[4] and the **Jensen**.[5] All three measures assume that there is a linear relationship between the portfolio's return and the return on some broad-based market index.

In the early studies of investment managers, these measures were used to evaluate the performance of the managers of mutual funds. However, they are of very limited use in the evaluation of money managers today because of the development of the performance attribution models discussed in the next section.

---

1. Treynor Measure

The **Treynor measure** is a measure of the excess return per unit of risk. The excess return is defined as the difference between the portfolio's return and the risk-free rate of return over the same evaluation period. The risk measure used is the relative systematic risk as measured by the portfolio's beta. Treynor argues that this is the appropriate risk measure since in a well-diversified portfolio the unsystematic risk is close to zero.

In equation form, the Treynor measure is:

$$\frac{\text{Portfolio return} - \text{Risk-free rate}}{\text{Portfolio's beta}}$$

---

[3] Jack Treynor, "How to Rate Management of Investment Funds," *Harvard Business Review* (January-February 1965), pp. 63-75.
[4] William F. Sharpe, "Mutual Fund Performance," *Journal of Business* (January 1966), pp. 119-138.
[5] Michael C. Jensen, "The Performance of Mutual Funds in the Period 1945-1964," *Journal of Finance* (May 1968), pp. 389-416.

2. Sharpe Measure

As with the Treynor measure, the **Sharpe measure** is a reward/risk ratio. The numerator is the same as in the Treynor measure. The risk of the portfolio is measured by the standard deviation of the portfolio. The Sharpe measure is thus:

$$\frac{\text{Portfolio return} - \text{Risk-free rate}}{\text{Standard deviation of portfolio}}$$

Thus the Sharpe measure is a measure of the excess return relative to the total variability of the portfolio. The Sharpe and Treynor measures will give identical rankings if the portfolios evaluated are well diversified. If they are poorly diversified, the rankings could be quite different.

3. Jensen Measure

The **Jensen measure** uses the capital asset pricing model (CAPM) to determine whether the money manager outperformed the market index. The empirical analogue of the CAPM is

$$E(R_P) - R_F = \beta_P[E(R_M) - R_F] + e$$

where

$$
\begin{aligned}
E(R_P) &= \text{the expected return on the portfolio} \\
R_F &= \text{the risk-free rate} \\
\beta_P &= \text{the beta of the portfolio} \\
E(R_M) &= \text{the expected return on the market} \\
e &= \text{the random error term}
\end{aligned}
$$

In words:

Excess return = Beta × [Excess return on market index] + Random error term

If the excess return produced by the manager does not exceed the excess return described by this formula the manager has added nothing. After all, the historical beta of the portfolio represents an expectation of information-free performance; a random portfolio should perform this well. Jensen, then, added a factor to represent the portfolio's performance that diverges from its beta. This alpha is a measure of the manager's performance. Using time-series data for the return on the portfolio and the market index, the following equation can be estimated by regression analysis:

$$R_{Pt} - R_{Ft} = \alpha_P + \beta_P[(R_{Mt}) - R_{Ft}] + e_{Pt}$$

The intercept term alpha, α_P, in the above equation is the unique return realized by the money manager. That is:

Excess return = Unique return + Beta × Excess return on market index
+ Random error term

The Jensen measure is the alpha or unique return that is estimated from the above regression. If the alpha is not statistically different from zero, there is no unique return. A statistically significant alpha that is positive means that the money manager outperformed the market index; a negative value means that the money manager underperformed the market index.

As with the Treynor measure, the Jensen measure assumes that the portfolio is fully diversified so that the only risk remaining in the portfolio is systematic risk.

D. Return Attribution Analysis

The single-index performance evaluation measures do not answer the question of how the manager achieved a return. The reason why a client must have the answer to this question is that a manager may tell a client that he or she plans to pursue an active strategy. The client would then expect that any superior return accomplished is a result of such a strategy. But how can the client be certain?

For example, suppose a manager solicits funds from a client by claiming he can achieve superior performance by selecting underpriced bonds. Suppose also that this manager does generate a superior return compared to the Lehman Aggregate Bond Index. The client should not be satisfied with this performance until the return realized by the manager is decomposed into the various components that generated the return. A client may find that the superior performance is due to the manager's timing of the market (i.e., revising the duration in anticipation of interest rate movements) rather than due to selecting underpriced bonds. In such an instance, the manager may have outperformed the index (even after adjusting for risk), but not by following the strategy that the manager told the client that he intended to pursue.

Return attribution analysis seeks to identify the active management decisions that contributed to the performance of a portfolio and give a quantitative assessment of the contribution of these decisions. In Chapter 2 we discussed the factors that have been observed to drive bond returns. Active strategies include interest rate expectations strategies, yield curve expectations strategies, yield spread strategies, and individual security selection strategies. The performance of a portfolio can be decomposed in terms of these strategies.

In the equity area, the BARRA model for equity attribution analysis — PER-FAN factor model — is the most popular model used. In the bond area, several commercial vendors have developed models for return attribution analysis. The analysis is performed relative to a benchmark (i.e., a bond index). These models have been used by pension consultants to evaluate the performance of money managers. We will illustrate attribution models using the models of two vendors.

1. Application of Attribution Analysis to a Domestic Corporate Portfolio

Our first illustration will use the system developed by Global Advanced Technology (G.A.T.) which was acquired by BARRA. The illustration is provided by Frank Jones and Leonard Peltzman.[6] This commercially available model decomposes a portfolio's total return into the following factors: (1) static return, (2) interest sensitive returns, (3) spread change returns, and (4) trading return. The difference between the total return and the sum of the four factors is called the **residual (error)**. Each of the return factors can be further decomposed as described below.

The **static return** is the portion of a portfolio's total return that is attributable to "rolling down the yield curve."[7] This return calculates how much is earned assuming a static (meaning zero volatility) world defined as one in which the yield curve evolves to its implied forward curve. In turn, the static return can further be decomposed into two components: (1) **risk-free return** and (2) **accrual of OAS return**. The

---

[6] Frank J. Jones and Leonard J. Peltzman, "Fixed Income Attribution Analysis," Chapter 28 in Frank J. Fabozzi (ed.), *Managing Fixed Income Portfolios* (New Hope, PA: Frank J. Fabozzi Associates).
[7] The various spread measures were explained at Level I (Chapter 6).

risk-free return is based on the assumption that the portfolio consists of only Treasury strips. The risk-free return is then calculated based on the rolling down of the yield curve. The accrual of OAS return is also calculated from rolling down the yield curve. However, it is based on investment spread products.

The **interest sensitive return** is that portion of a portfolio's return attributable to changes in the level, slope, and shape of the entire yield curve. In turn, this return is decomposed into two components: (1) effective duration return and (2) convexity return. As explained at Level I (Chapter 7), key rate durations can be used to measure the sensitivity of a portfolio to changes in the shape of the yield curve. The **effective duration return** is the sum of returns attributable to each key rate duration. The **convexity return** is the return due to a change in the portfolio's duration over the evaluation period.

The **spread change return** is the portion of a portfolio's return that is due to changes in both (1) bond sector spreads and (2) individual security richness/cheapness. The portion of the spread return attributable to changes in the sector's OAS is called the **delta OAS return** and the spread return due to a widening or tightening of a specific issue's spread is called the **delta rich/cheap return**.

The portion of a portfolio's total return that is attributable to changes in the composition of the portfolio is called the **trading return**. This return allows for the identification of a manager's value added by changing the composition of the portfolio as opposed to a simple buy-and-hold strategy.

In the illustration, an attribution analysis is performed on a portfolio of corporate securities. We will refer to this portfolio as Portfolio A. The evaluation period is the month of September 1996, a month when the yield curve shifted downward. The shift was almost a parallel shift. The effective duration for Portfolio A was 7.09. The benchmark index is the Merrill Lynch Corporate Index. The effective duration for the index is 5.76. Thus, Portfolio A had a larger duration than the index (7.09 versus 5.76).

Exhibit 1 presents the results of the attribution analysis for the portfolio and by sector. Exhibit 2 provides a summary of the analysis. The return on Portfolio A was 2.187% while that on the index was 1.954%. Thus, Portfolio A outperformed the index by 23 bps during September.

Because the yield curve shifted downward in an almost parallel fashion, Portfolio A would be expected to outperform the index because of the portfolio's larger duration. This is captured in the interest sensitive return. Exhibit 1 indicates that holding all other factors constant, the outperformance would have been 37.9 basis points. The reason why Portfolio A did not outperform by that much was due to the spread change return which was −18.5 basis points. The static return and the trading return were minimal.

The second column in Exhibit 1 provides information about the sector views that the manager took (i.e., underweighting or overweighting). The third column shows how the allocation paid off for each sector.

2. Application of Attribution Analysis to an International Bond Portfolio

Our second illustration is an application of attribution analysis to an international bond portfolio. The Gifford Fong Associates attribution model is used. The illustration is provided by Gifford Fong, Daihyun Yoo, and Zandra M. Zelaya.[8] First a brief description of the attribution model.

---

[8] Gifford Fong, Daihyun Yoo, and Zandra M. Zelaya, "Global Performance Attribution," Chapter 12 in Frank J. Fabozzi (ed.), *Perspectives on International Fixed Income Investing* (New Hope, PA: Frank J. Fabozzi Associates).

Exhibit 1: Performance Attribution Example

Portfolio A: $3.0 billion corporate bond portfolio with an effective duration of 7.09
Merrill Corporate Index: Benchmark index with a duration of 5.76

	% of Portfolio	Total Return	Static Return	Interest Sensitive Return	Spread Change Return	Trading Return	Residual
Portfolio Totals							
Portfolio A	100.000	2.187	0.453	1.813	−0.087	−0.003	0.011
Merrill Corporate	100.000	1.954	0.452	1.433	0.098	0.000	−0.029
Difference	0.000	0.233	0.001	0.379	−0.185	−0.003	0.040
Sector Analysis*							
Agencies							
Portfolio A	0.000	0.000	0.000	0.000	0.000	0.000	0.000
Merrill Corporate	12.044	2.083	0.476	1.918	−0.118	0.000	−0.193
Difference	−12.044	−2.083	−0.476	−1.918	0.118	0.000	0.193
Industrials							
Portfolio A	31.480	2.325	0.459	1.924	−0.026	−0.059	0.027
Merrill Corporate	26.769	2.121	0.460	1.606	0.108	0.000	−0.053
Difference	4.711	0.204	−0.001	0.318	−0.134	−0.059	0.080
Financials							
Portfolio A	15.580	2.023	0.439	1.560	0.077	−0.057	0.004
Merrill Corporate	37.363	1.707	0.444	1.210	0.060	0.000	−0.008
Difference	−21.783	0.316	−0.006	0.350	0.017	−0.057	0.012
Utilities							
Portfolio A	15.900	0.310	0.528	−0.090	0.540	0.042	−0.711
Merrill Corporate	7.385	2.167	0.469	1.564	0.185	0.000	−0.051
Difference	8.515	−1.857	0.060	−1.654	0.356	0.042	−0.660
Telephones							
Portfolio A	17.080	2.439	0.439	1.843	0.027	0.144	−0.014
Merrill Corporate	4.440	2.331	0.447	1.723	0.201	0.000	−0.040
Difference	12.640	0.108	−0.008	0.120	−0.174	0.144	0.026
Oil							
Portfolio A	4.940	0.562	0.467	2.035	−1.939	0.000	0.000
Merrill Corporate	1.670	2.123	0.462	1.513	0.194	0.000	−0.047
Difference	3.270	−1.561	0.004	0.522	−2.133	0.000	0.047
Internationals							
Portfolio A	14.180	2.264	0.443	1.891	−0.079	0.021	−0.011
Merrill Corporate	10.022	2.118	0.446	1.597	0.095	0.000	−0.021
Difference	4.158	0.147	−0.004	0.294	−0.174	0.021	0.010
Miscellaneous							
Portfolio A	0.000	0.000	0.000	0.000	0.000	0.000	0.000
Merrill Corporate	0.308	0.796	0.416	0.384	−0.025	0.000	0.021
Difference	−0.308	−0.796	−0.416	−0.384	0.025	0.000	−0.021

* In the sector analyses, we are comparing the constituents of Portfolio A that fall into a particular sector to the constituents of the benchmark that fall into the same sector. For example, the industrials from Portfolio A are being evaluated against the industrials from the Merrill Corporate Index.

Source: G.A.T. Integrative Bond System

Exhibit 2: Summary of Return Attribution Analysis

Risk Factor	Portfolio A Returns (bps)	Merrill Corporate Index Returns (bps)	Difference	% of Total Return Difference
Static Return	45.3	45.2	0.1	0.4%
Interest Sensitive Return	181.3	143.3	37.9	162.7%
Spread Change Return	−8.7	9.8	−18.5	−79.4%
Trading Return	−0.3	0.0	−0.3	−1.3%
Residual	1.1	−2.9	4.0	17.2%
Total	218.7	195.4	23.3	100.0%

Exhibit 3: Hypothetical Portfolio and Transactions

CUSIP	Bond Description	Initial/Last Date	Beg/End Par Value ($000)	Beg/End Price ($)	Capital Gain/Loss
539830AF	Lockheed Martin	5/31/94	2,000	98.00	1.41
		6/30/94	1,500	98.75	
887315BB	Time Warner	5/31/94	1,000	105.5	0.06
		6/30/94	1,000	105.00	
912810CC	U.S. Treasury Bond	5/31/94	1,000	106.62	0.63
		6/30/94	1,000	106.62	
912810DS	U.S. Treasury Bond	5/31/94	1,500	131.77	1.72
		6/30/94	2,000	133.21	
912827WW	U.S. Treasury Note	5/31/94	2,500	108.34	0.66
		6/30/94	2,500	108.34	
912827ZX	U.S. Treasury Note	5/31/94	1,000	104.18	0.86
		6/30/94	1,500	104.46	
913994CE	United Kingdom	5/31/94	500	102.21	0.71
	Treasury Government	6/30/94	500	102.21	
913994CJ	United Kingdom	5/31/94	1,000	102.71	0.70
	Treasury Government	6/30/94	1,000	102.71	
9139959D	United Kingdom	5/31/94	1,000	104.87	0.70
	Treasury Government	6/30/94	1,000	104.87	
984994CT	Japanese Government Bond	5/31/94	5,000	105.81	2.68
		6/30/94	5,000	102.42	
984994CX	Japanese Government Bond	5/31/94	5,000	103.62	0.37
		6/30/94	5,000	100.46	
984994SY	Japanese Government Bond	5/31/94	5,000	108.17	6.27
		6/30/94	5,000	108.17	
JYM50000	Japanese Currency Futures	5/31/94	−25,000	98.54	
		6/30/94	−25,000	104.72	

The model decomposes the return into local returns and foreign exchange returns. For the **local return**, there is a further decomposition into a return attributable to changes in the interest rate environments of the countries included in the portfolio. This return is beyond the manager's control. The second part of the local return is the return attributable to the decisions made by the manager. These decisions include the selection of the exposure to interest rates and credits, and the selection of individual securities. The **foreign exchange return** is also divided into a component that is beyond the control of the manager and a component of currency risk that is controlled by the manager.

The further breakdown of the return components is described using the hypothetical portfolio and transactions shown in Exhibit 3. The portfolio has U.S., U.K., and Japanese government bonds and two U.S. corporate bonds. There is also a position in Japanese currency futures. The evaluation period is May 31, 1994 to June 30, 1994. The benchmark index is Salomon World Government Bond Index.

Over the evaluation period, the total return for the hypothetical portfolio was almost 200 basis points. For the index the total return was 143 basis points. Exhibit 4 reports the results of the attribution analysis for the portfolio and identifies the reasons why the hypothetical portfolio outperformed the index.

The analysis is divided into four sections. Section I shows the "Interest Rate Effect." This return over the evaluation period is not controllable by the manager; that is, it is the result of the external internal rate environment. Effectively, it the cost of being in the bond market. As can be seen, there are two components of the interest rate effect: expected and unexpected. The expected return is the effect of rolling down the spot rate curve. The unexpected interest rate effect is the return attributable to the actual change in rates.

Exhibit 4: Results of the
Performance Attribution Analysis Evaluation

	Evaluation Period Return (%)	Market Index Evaluation Period Return (%)
I. Interest rate effect		
1. Expected	0.363	0.373
2. Unexpected	0.359	−1.092
Subtotal	0.722	−0.719
II. Interest rate management effect		
3. Duration	−0.368	0
4. Convexity	−0.006	0
5. Yield curve shape change	0.019	0
Subtotal (options adjusted)	−0.355	0
III. Other management effects		
6. Sector/Quality	1.287	0
7. Bond selectivity	−0.773	0
8. Transaction costs	0	0
Subtotal	0.514	0
IV. Trading activity return	0.359	0
V. Currency return		
9. Foreign exchange	0.864	2.145
10. Currency hedging	−0.105	0
Subtotal	0.759	2.145
VI. Total Return (sum of I, II, III, IV, and, V)	1.999	1.426

Sections II and III show the factors controllable by the manager in generating the local return. The "Interest Rate Management Effect" (Section II), shows the default-free return for the portfolio due to the duration, convexity, and yield curve shape exposure of the portfolio. From the results reported it can be determined whether or not the manager was successful in anticipating changes in interest rates and the shape of the yield curve. For this evaluation period, the manager was not successful with respect to interest rate management.

The "Other Management Effects" are controllable returns attributable to sector/quality, bond selectivity, and transaction costs (i.e., hypothetical effect of transactions on the portfolio). The manager was clearly successful in selecting the sector and quality. The return attributable to the sector/quality decision was 129 basis points — the major reason for the outperformance of this portfolio relative to the index.

The currency return can be attributable to changes beyond the control of the manager and the ability of the manager to control the exposure. This analysis is shown in Section V. The change in portfolio value from exchange rate changes before hedging is the first component shown. The effect of currency hedging is the second component of return shown. For our hypothetical portfolio, the Japanese currency futures reduced the return by 10.5 basis points.

The same analysis can be performed for each bond in the portfolio. This is shown in Exhibit 5.

Exhibit 5: Decomposition of Return of Individual Securities

CUSIP	Bond Description	Initial/ Last Date	Beg/End Par Value ($000)	Market Expected Rate of Change	Int. Rate Effect: Duration/ Convexity/Yield Curve	Sector Effect Sector/Selectivity	Currency Exchange Return (%)	Local Currency Return (%)	Base Currency Return (%)
539830AF	Lockheed Martin	5/31/94 6/30/94	2,000 1,500	0.352 -0.535	-0.979 -0.185 0.003	1.546 1.213	0	1.415	1.415
887315BB	Time Warner	5/31/94 6/30/94	1,000 1,000	0.352 -0.535	-1.201 -0.245 0.010	1.10 0.583	0	0.066	0.066
912810CC	U.S. Treasury Bond	5/31/94 6/30/94	1,000 1,000	0.352 -0.535	-0.372 0.003 -0.011	0.00 1.19	0	0.636	0.636
912810DS	U.S. Treasury Bond	5/31/94 6/30/94	1,500 2,000	0.352 -0.535	-0.744 -0.105 -0.008	0.00 2.761	0	1.722	1.722
912827WW	U.S. Treasury Note	5/31/94 6/30/94	2,500 2,500	0.352 -0.535	0.176 0.42 -0.043	0.00 0.674	0	0.666	0.666
912827ZX	U.S. Treasury Note	5/31/94 6/30/94	1,000 1,500	0.352 -0.535	-0.054 0.028 -0.053	0.00 1.129	0	0.868	0.868
913994CE	United Kingdom Treasury Government	5/31/94 6/30/94	500 500	0.397 2.450	-0.139 0.201 0.387	0.00 -2.583	2.814	0.713	3.547
913994CJ	United Kingdom Treasury Government	5/31/94 6/30/94	1,000 1,000	0.397 2.450	-0.181 0.371 -0.098	0.00 -2.232	2.814	0.7070	3.540
9139959D	United Kingdom Treasury Government	5/31/94 6/30/94	1,000 1,000	0.397 2.450	0.002 -0.090 0.189	0.00 -2.196	2.814	0.752	3.587
984994CT	Japanese Government Bond	5/31/94 6/30/94	10,000 10,000	0.176 3.870	-0.935 0.034 0.068	0.00 -6.027	6.093	-2.814	3.107
984994CX	Japanese Government Bond	5/31/94 6/30/94	10,000 10,000	0.176 3.870	-0.968 0.034 0.068	0.00 -6.027	6.093	-2.814	3.107
984994SY	Japanese Government Bond	5/31/94 6/30/94	20,000 20,000	0.176 3.870	0.375 -0.039 -0.199	0.00 -3.809	6.093	0.373	6.489
JYM50000	Japanese Currency Futures	5/31/94 6/30/94	50,000 50,000	0.00 0.00	0.000 0.000 0.000	0.00 0.00	0.00	0.00	6.272

SECTION IV
KEY POINTS

❑ *Performance measurement involves the calculation of the return realized by a manager over some evaluation period.*

❑ *Performance evaluation is concerned with determining whether the manager added value by outperforming the established benchmark and how the manager achieved the calculated return.*

❑ *The rate of return expresses the dollar return in terms of the amount of the initial investment (i.e, the initial market value of the portfolio).*

❑ *There are three methodologies that have been used in practice to calculate the average of the sub-period returns: (1) the arithmetic average rate of return, (2) the time-weighted (or geometric) rate of return, and (3) the dollar-weighted rate of return.*

❑ *The arithmetic average rate of return is the average value of the withdrawals (expressed as a fraction of the initial portfolio market value) that can be made at the end of each period while keeping the initial portfolio market value intact.*

❑ *The time-weighted rate of return measures the compounded rate of growth of the initial portfolio over the evaluation period, assuming that all cash distributions are reinvested in the portfolio.*

❑ *In general, the arithmetic average rate of return will exceed the time-weighted average rate of return with the magnitude of the difference between the two averages being smaller the less the variation in the sub-period returns over the evaluation period.*

❑ *The dollar-weighted rate of return is computed by finding the interest rate that will make the present value of the cash flows from all the sub-periods in the evaluation period plus the terminal market value of the portfolio equal to the initial market value of the portfolio.*

❑ *The dollar-weighted rate of return is an internal rate of return calculation and will produce the same result as the time-weighted rate of return if no withdrawals or contributions occur over the evaluation period and all cash inflows are reinvested.*

❑ *Because the dollar-weighted rate of return is affected by factors that are beyond the control of the manager (i.e., any contributions made by the client or withdrawals that the client requires), it is difficult to compare the performance of managers.*

❑ *The Association of Investment Management and Research has adopted standards for the presentation and disclosure of performance results.*

❑ *The Committee for Performance Presentation Standards of the AIMR recognizes that in practice there is no single ideal set of performance presentation standards that are applicable to all users.*

❑ *Any bond performance and return attribution analysis process should be accurate, informative, and simple.*

❑ *An attribution analysis should be understood by the manager and client, or others who may be concerned with the performance of the portfolio.*

❑ *Performance evaluation requires the establishment of a benchmark portfolio.*

❑ *There are two types of benchmark portfolios commonly used: bond market indexes and normal portfolios.*

❏ *A normal portfolio is a customized benchmark that includes a set of securities that contains the universe of securities that a manager normally selects from and weighted as the manager would weight them in a portfolio.*

❏ *Advocates claim that normal portfolios are more appropriate benchmarks than market indexes because they control for investment management style, thereby representing a passive portfolio against which a manager can be evaluated.*

❏ *There are three single-index measures that have been used to evaluate the relative performance of managers: Treynor measure, Sharpe measure, and Jensen measure.*

❏ *The single-index measures of performance evaluation do not specify how or why a manager may have outperformed or underperformed a benchmark.*

❏ *Bond attribution analysis seeks to identify the active management decisions that contributed to the performance of a portfolio and give a quantitative assessment of the contribution of these decisions.*

❏ *Return attribution models are available from commercial vendors.*

END OF CHAPTER QUESTIONS

1. What is the difference between performance measurement and performance evaluation?

2. The trustees for the Tool Shop Corporation's pension fund are reviewing a report provided by two its of its external bond managers, Reliable Associates and Alpha Group, for the first four quarters of the year. The monthly returns are provided below:

Month	Reliable Associates	Alpha Group
1	8%	24%
2	12%	9%
3	20%	25%
4	−11%	−22%

   a. What is the arithmetic average monthly rate of return for the two managers?
   b. What is the time-weighted average monthly rate of return for the two managers?
   c. Why does the arithmetic average monthly rate of return diverge more from the time-weighted monthly rate of return for Alpha Group than for Reliable Associates?

3. Lewis and Davis Associates is a money management firm specializing in fixed income securities. One of its clients is a municipal pension fund. The fund gave Lewis and Davis Associates $100 million to manage. The market value for the portfolio for the five months after receiving the funds was as follows:

End of month	Market value (in millions)
1	$108
2	$115
3	$121
4	$111
5	$101

   There were no distributions made to the municipality or additional funds given to the management company during the period.

   a. Calculate the rate of return for each month.
   b. Lewis and Davis Associates reported to the municipality that over the five-month period the average monthly rate of return was 49 basis points (0.49%). How was that value obtained?
   c. Is the average monthly rate of return of 49 basis points indicative of the performance of Lewis and Davis Associates for this client? If not, what would be a more appropriate measure?
   d. Suppose that the results are available for month 6 and that the market value of the portfolio is 100. What would Lewis and Davis Associates report for the return using the same methodology it employed to compute the 49 basis points for the first five months? Without performing any calculations, what return should be reported?

4. FixedIncomeSecurities.net is a fixed income management firm that manages the funds of pension plan sponsors. For one of its clients it manages $100 million. The cash flow for this particular client's portfolio for the past three months was $10 million contribution from the client, $4 million withdrawal by the client, and $4 million contribution from the client. The market value of the portfolio at the end of three months was $104 million.

   a. What is the dollar-weighted rate of return for this client's portfolio over the 3-month period?

b. What is the problem with using the dollar-weighted rate of return as a measure of performance?

5. a. If the average monthly return for a portfolio is 1.16%, what is the annualized return?

b. If the average quarterly return for a portfolio is 1.38%, what is the annualized return?

6. The Image Group is a bond management firm that was has been in operation for 10 years. The firm has 60 discretionary, fee paying accounts with an aggregate amount under management of $2 billion. In preparing a report for a client that it is prospecting for funds The Image Group has done the following:

(i) presented the return for the past three years for five representative portfolios

(ii) calculated the arithmetic average annual return over the past three years where the return sub-period was measured each year.

(iii) disclosed what the return would have been for the past 10 years based on simulated returns for the 10 years using the strategy it currently employs in managing funds for clients since it is more representative than prior strategies that it used.

Based on the above, explain whether the Image Group is in compliance with the AIMR-PPS Standards.

7. In a panel discussion of the Committee for Performance Presentations of AIMR (published in *Performance Presentation Standards: Setting the Standards, Interpreting the Numbers* (Charlottesville, VA: AIMR, 1989), p. 21), John Sherrerd, a member of the committee, stated:

It is important to keep in mind that the objective of these performance statistics is to measure the capabilities of the manager, not the cash flows. It is not an attempt to measure how many dollars the client has earned over a period of time. If the performance of the manager is being measured, those results should not be influenced by whether the client is taking money out and spending it, the way most endowments might, or leaving it in, as many corporations do.

a. Why is the dollar-weighted rate of return affected by contributions and withdrawals by the client?

b. What rate of return methodology does the AIMR standards require?

8. Why is it difficult to calculate daily returns for fixed-income portfolios?

9. What are the difficulties of constructing a normal portfolio?

10. A trustee of a pension fund discussed with the fund's consultant various ways to evaluate the performance of its external managers. The trustee indicated that he had heard of various measures such as the Sharpe measure, Jensen measure, and Treynor measure. The trustee asked the consultant which of these measures would be the best one to use to identify the reasons why a manager was able to achieve inferior or superior performance relative to a benchmark index. How should the consultant respond?

11. The following is a statement from John H. Watts, Chairman of Fischer Francis Trees & Watts ("A Fixed-Income Manager's Perspective," in *Performance Reporting for Investment Managers: Applying the AIMR Performance Presentation Standards* (Charlottesville, VA: AIMR, 1991), p. 57):

> Results are often analyzed, for either comparison or evaluation purposes, over an arbitrary specified number of years. The period we see most often used is five years. Particularly for fixed-income portfolios, an arbitrarily chosen period can lead to an unintended, if not perverse, conclusion. For example, if a five-year reporting period happens to fall within a bull market, a manager that has a long-term bond bias will look strong, and vice versa.

a. Why is this statement true for fixed-income portfolios if comparisons are based on actual returns?

b. How does performance attribution analysis reduce the risk of distorting performance results for a fixed-income portfolio.

12. The trustees of the Order.com pension fund are reviewing the annual performance of its three external bond managers (Rollins Group, M&M Company, and Beta Associates) with its consultant. The benchmark for all three external managers is the Lehman Brothers U.S. Aggregate Index. The consultant provided a two-page summary of the performance of the managers. On the first page, the following was reported for the 1-year return:

External manager			
Rollins Group	M&M Company	Beta Associates	Index
8.025%	7.806%	7.661%	7.000%

The second page was a return attribution analysis of each external manager relative to the index for the 1-year evaluation period. The values reported are in percent and are all relative to the benchmark index.

	Rollins Group	M&M Company	Beta Associates
I. Interest rate effect			
1. Expected	0.033	0.036	0.034
2. Unexpected	0.061	0.066	0.059
Subtotal	0.094	0.102	0.093
II. Interest rate management effect			
3. Duration	0.954	0.124	0
4. Convexity	−0.045	0.022	0
5. Yield curve shape change	0.148	0.101	0
Subtotal	1.057	0.247	0
III. Other management effects			
6. Sector/quality	−0.225	0.518	0.125
7. Bond selectivity	−0.286	−0.113	0.443
Subtotal	−0.511	0.405	0.568
IV. Trading activity return	0.385	0.052	0
V. Total return over index (sum I, II, III, and IV)	1.025	0.806	0.661

The trustee also reviewed the promotional material that was provided by each management firm in which its investment strategies were described. The consultant summarized the investment strategies (and the management fee) as follows:

Rollins Group: This management firm states that it can identify undervalued issues and bond sectors that will enhance returns relative to the benchmark index. The firm states that it seeks to be close to neutral with respect to the interest rate exposure relative to the benchmark index. (Management fee: 50 basis points)

M&M Company: This management firm states that it can enhance return through active management of the interest rate exposure of the portfolio relative to the benchmark index. Management seeks to be neutral with respect to bond sectors and quality. However, it does believe that it can identify individual issues that are mispriced using its analytical models. (Management fee: 45 basis points)

Beta Associates: This management firm follows a strategy of being neutral with respect to the interest rate risk exposure relative to the benchmark index. Management believes it can add value relative to the benchmark index through credit analysis and selecting issues that are likely to be upgraded. (Management fee: 30 basis points)

a. After evaluating the documents provided by the consultant, Trustee A stated that he believes that the Rollins Group clearly outperformed the benchmark index and the other two external managers. He believes this is the case because the Rollins Group had the largest return over the benchmark index even after adjusting for its higher management fees relative to the other external managers. Moreover, he did not understand why it was necessary to review the reasons for the outperformance. How should the consultant respond to Trustee A?
b. How would the consultant assess the performance of the three external manager and what should the consultant suggest the trustees discuss with each manager?

SOLUTIONS TO END OF CHAPTER QUESTIONS

1. Performance measurement involve the computation of the rate of return of a manager over some evaluation period. Performance evaluation involves identifying the reasons for any outperformance or underperformance of a manager relative to a benchmark index over the evaluation period.

2. a. The arithmetic average monthly rate of return for the two external managers is:

Reliable Associates: $(8\% + 12\% + 20\% - 11\%)/4 = 7.25\%$
Alpha Group: $(24\% + 9\% + 25\% - 22\%)/4 = 9\%$

b. The time-weighted average monthly rate of return for the two external managers is:

Reliable Associates: $[(1.08)(1.12)(1.20)(0.89)]^{1/4} - 1 = 0.0661 = 6.61\%$
Alpha Group: $[(1.24)(1.09)(1.25)(0.78)]^{1/4} - 1 = 0.0714 = 7.14\%$

c. The greater the dispersion of the monthly returns, the greater will be the difference between the arithmetic average monthly return and the time-weighted average monthly return. Since the dispersion of the monthly return for the Alpha Group (which varies from −22% to 25%) is greater than for Reliable Associates (which only varies from −11% to +20%), Alpha Group's arithmetic average monthly return diverges by more from its time-weighted average monthly return by more (9% versus 7.14%) than for Reliable Associates (7.25% versus 6.61%).

3. a. The monthly rate of return is found as follows:

$$\frac{\text{End of month market value} - \$100,000,000}{\text{Market value at end of previous month}} - 1$$

The initial market value is $100 million.

End of month	Market value (in millions)	Monthly rate of return
1	$108	8.00%
2	$115	6.48%
3	$121	5.22%
4	$111	−8.26%
5	$101	−9.01%

b. The 49 basis point return reported is simply the arithmetic average monthly return:

$(8.00\% + 6.48\% + 5.22\% \text{-}8.26\% - 9.01\%)/5 = 0.49\% = 49$ bp

c. The correct measure is the time-weighted average monthly return, found as follows:

$[(1.0800)(1.0648)(1.0522)(0.9174)(0.9099)]^{1/5} - 1 = 0.0020 = 20$ bp

Thus, Lewis and Davis Associates overstated the 5-month performance by using the arithmetic average monthly return of 49 basis points.

d. To obtain the 49 basis points average monthly return, Lewis and Davis Associates computed an arithmetic average monthly return. For month 6, since the market value at the end of the month is $100 million and the market value at the beginning of the month is $101 million, the return for month 6 is -0.99%. The arithmetic average monthly return is then:

$(8.00\% + 6.48\% + 5.22\% - 8.26\% - 9.01\% - 0.99\%)/6 = 0.24\% = 24$ bp

It is obvious that the return for the period is zero — the initial amount invested was \$100 million and six months later the market value of the portfolio is unchanged at \$100 million.

4. a. The dollar-weighted rate of return is simply the internal rate of return. It is computed by solving the following equation for R:

$$\$100,000,000 = \frac{\$10,000,000}{(1+R)^1} + \frac{-\$4,000,000}{(1+R)^2} + \frac{(\$4,000,000 + \$104,000,000)}{(1+R)^3}$$

Solving for R we would get 4.70%. Thus, the dollar-weighted rate of return is 4.70%.

b. Because management had no control over the contribution or withdrawal of funds by the client, the resulting return is distorted. A return should reflect a manager's skills and not be impacted by factors beyond the manager's control.

5. a. The annualized return is computed as follows:

$$(1 + \text{average monthly return})^{12} - 1 = (1.0116)^{12} - 1 = 14.84\%$$

b. The annualized return is computed as follows:

$$(1 + \text{average quarterly return})^4 - 1 = (1.0138)^4 - 1 = 5.64\%$$

6. For the following reasons, Image Group is not in compliance:

(i) Image Group must present the return for the entire 10-year period for all accounts, not just selected (or representative) portfolios.

(ii) In addition to failing to provide 10 years of performance, the Image Group fails to use the correct method for computing the return. The average annual return should not be presented. Rather it should be the time-weighted rate of return (and possibly the dollar-weighted rate of return depending on the amount of the contributions and withdrawals during the periods for the accounts).

(iii) Simulated return performance is not acceptable even if it is more reflective of management's current portfolio strategy.

7. a. The dollar weighted rate of return is computed is an internal rate of return calculation based on the cash flow for each subperiod in the evaluation period plus the market value at the end of the evaluation period. The cash flow for each subperiod will be affected by any contributions made by the client or distribution requested by the client. In turn, this impacts the performance of the manager even though the manager has no control over contributions and withdrawals.

b. Time-weighted rates of return that adjust for cash flows are required. (There are other requirements for periods beginning January 1, 2005 and January 1, 2010.)

8. While mutual funds compute returns daily, it is costly for other institutional investors of fixed-income portfolios to do so because of possible illiquid securities with possible unreliable price information.

9. The main idea of a normal portfolio is to construct a portfolio that, given the historical portfolios in which a manager invests, will reflect that manager's style in

terms of assets and the weighting of those assets. This is not a simple task for the client. If a client allows its managers to develop the normal portfolio themselves, the managers would have incentives to provide easily beaten benchmarks (called "slow rabbits"). If the client constructs the normal portfolio, the client has to either define the universe of fixed-income securities to be included in the normal portfolio or determine how those securities should be weighted.

10. The consultant should tell the trustee that while the three measures — Sharpe, Jensen, and Treynor — can be used to measure relative performance, none of these measures can be used to explain the reasons why there was superior or inferior performance.

11. a. For fixed-income portfolios, actual returns are attributed to those elements beyond the managers control, such as interest rate environment and duration policy constraints imposed by a client, and those that the management process contributes to, such as interest rate management, sector/quality allocations, and individual bond selection.

 b. Performance attribution analysis reduces the risk of distorting performance results for a fixed-income portfolio by decomposing the realized return into those elements beyond the manager's control and those that the management process contributes to and identifies active management decisions that contributed to the performance of the portfolio.

12. a. The consultant should remind Trustee A that the firm engages managers based on the likelihood that the manager will outperform the index for the reasons the manager it alleges it can outperform. Consequently, the performance must be evaluated relative to the skills that the manager claimed will produce the outperformance. Just looking at the difference of the manager's return relative to the benchmark index is not adequate to assess the skills the manager put forth in seeking to obtain money to manage from the pension fund. The return attribution analysis provides that information.

 b. All the managers outperformed relative to the benchmark index after adjusting for the management fee they charge. While the Rollins Group had the largest return over the benchmark index, 102.5 basis points, the reason for the outperformance was inconsistent with what the trustees were lead to believe would produce the outperformance. Rollins Group stated that it could identify undervalued issues and sectors. Yet, the return attribution analysis indicates that it underperformed the benchmark index by 51 basis points in selecting sectors and individual issues. This negative performance was offset by structuring the portfolio to have a different interest rate exposure than the benchmark index, which lead to 106 basis points outperformance. Yet, the trustee were told that management would remain neutral relative to the benchmark index.

 Consequently, the trustees should be concerned with the performance of the Rollins Group despite its better "raw" performance relative to the other external managers. The trustees should meet with the Rollins Group to determine if there has been a change in the investment management style.

 The M&M Company added 24 basis points using one of the strategies it indicated it would use — adjusting the portfolio to have a different interest rate risk exposure than the benchmark index. However, this management firm claimed that by using analytical models it could identify undervalued issues.

Yet, with respect to the selection of individual issues, there was underperformance relative to the benchmark index of 11 basis points. The major portion of the return was due to sector/quality exposure that was different from the benchmark index; however, M&M had stated that their strategy was to remain neutral to the benchmark with respect to sector and quality. The trustees should discuss with M&M Company whether or not there has been a change in investment style.

While Beta Associates had the lowest return relative to the benchmark index, it still outperformed the benchmark index after accounting for the management fee. Clearly, this management firm outperformed for the reasons that it said it would. The major reason for the outperformance was the selection of individual issues (44 basis points). In accomplishing this, the interest rate risk exposure was neutral to the benchmark index, just as management stated it would seek to do.

Index